Cambodia's Second Kingdom

Cornell University

Astrid Norén-Nilsson

Cambodia's Second Kingdom:

Nation, Imagination, and Democracy

SOUTHEAST ASIA PROGRAM PUBLICATIONS
Southeast Asia Program
Cornell University
Ithaca, New York
2016

Cornell Southeast Asia Program Publications
640 Stewart Avenue, Ithaca, NY 14850-3857

Studies on Southeast Asia Series No. 68

Printed in the United States of America

ISBN HC: 9780877277989
ISBN PB: 9780877277682
E-ISBN: 9780877272281

Cover: designed by Kat Dalton

Cover image: "Monks walk in front of the Royal Palace early in the evening," by Sothy Eng, Ph.D

To Francis Sisaridh

TABLE OF CONTENTS

Acknowledgments   ix

Foreword by David Chandler   xi

Preface   xvii

Biographical Notes   xxi
    Hun Sen, Norodom Ranariddh, Sam Rainsy, Kem Sokha

CHAPTER ONE

Cambodia's Second Kingdom: Starting Points   1
    Cambodia as an Unfinished Imagined Community
    Setting and Context
    Politicized Identities and the Post-PPA Nation
    Legitimacy-building
    Cambodian Nationalism in Perspective—Historical Givens
    The Building Blocks of Cambodian Political Discourse
    Outline of the Book
    Notes on Sources
    Note on Translation and Transcription

CHAPTER TWO

Of Hun Sen: The Sdech Kân Narrative   39
    The "Original" Narrative
    Changing Ideas of Kingship
    Performing Sdech Kân
    (Re)birth of a Modern Saga
    Establishing Origins
    The Retrieval of Democracy
    National Reconciliation
    Statuemania
    Film, Overlap, and Invulnerability
    Modeling Just Leadership

CHAPTER THREE

Royalists: Between Embodiment and Doctrine   65
    Unity in Diversity?
    Embodied Politics: Constitutional Monarchy and Political Royalism
    Royalist Democracy
    Doctrine vs. Embodiment
    From Political Royalism to Royal Irrelevancy

CHAPTER FOUR

Democrats: Democracy and the Post-PPA Nation   117
    The CPP's "People's Democracy"
    Democratic Opposition Starting Points
    Identifying the People's Will
    The Limits of Electoral Democracy
    Determining a Political Identity
    Nation, Religion, King: Transforming Post-resistance Identities
    Democracy as a Core of Cambodian Political Discourse

CHAPTER FIVE

Reassessing Political Contestation in the Kingdom of Cambodia   163
    Legitimacy, Discourses of Democracy, and Cambodia's Democratization
    Continuity and Change
    Ideology, Identities, and Representation of the Nation
    Public Appeal
    Implications in Southeast Asian Perspective

Epilogue   181

Bibliography   195

Index   221

ACKNOWLEDGMENTS

My greatest debt of gratitude lies with the interviewees, who are the heart of this research. In particular, I am profoundly grateful to the politicians who, to a large extent, define contemporary Cambodian politics for agreeing to be interviewed for this project: Samdech Hun Sen, Samdech Krom Preah Norodom Ranariddh, His Excellency Sam Rainsy, and His Excellency Kem Sokha.

This project has been hugely gratifying, not only on an intellectual but also a human level. As I set out to map public discourses, but also—more elusively—politicians' perceptions, intimate thoughts, and dearly held beliefs, over eighty people agreed to be interviewed, and many more integrated me into their social circles and life. I am hugely indebted to all, both those who are quoted in this book, as well as the many more who do not figure but who nonetheless played a crucial part in helping to shape the arguments here presented. They each added valuable pieces to this analysis and enriched my thinking, and I shall forever treasure the friendships that followed from many of these encounters. They are all in my thoughts as I complete this book. For their support during my years in Cambodia, I would additionally like to mention Heng Hamkheng, Khuon Sethisak, Mony Chenda and family, Than Sothea, Sam Sareth, Sem Chhinita and family, and Hong Rakin and family, and a special thought goes to Samdech Sisowath Pongneary.

This book would probably not have seen the light of day if David Chandler had not asked to read the manuscript—which started out as my PhD thesis—and encouraged me to submit it for publication. His enthusiasm has enlivened the completion of this book. David Chandler, Henri Locard, Martin Rathie, Frédéric Bourdier, and Deth Sok Udom read the entire manuscript, which was much improved by their insightful comments, as well as those of Kheang Un, Ashley Thompson, and the late Ian Harris, who read sections thereof. Steve Heder made several initial introductions and helped clarify my thinking at the outset of the research. Over the years, my work has benefited from discussions with colleagues and friends who, in addition to those mentioned above, include (but are by no means limited to) Phoak Kung, Hart Nadav Feuer, Sarah Milne, John Marston, James Gerrand, Sothy Eng, Daniel Bultmann, Benny Widyono, Ian Baird, Stéphanie Giry, and Adeline Seah.

This book emerges from my PhD thesis at the University of Cambridge's department of Politics and International Studies (POLIS), which was supervised by Tomas Larsson. His Socratic maieutic midwifery lies behind each stage of this text's production, and in the process, he injected theoretical rigor. The Gates Cambridge Trust funded this research (2008–13), and the Gates Scholars' community gave me some of my closest friends. My on-and-off home during these years, King's College, will always remain my home in some sense. At Cambridge, the friendships, and more, of Hassan Akram, Fabio Bolzonaro, Liz Dzeng, Puli Fuwongcharoen, Lu Gram, Bérénice Guyot-Réchard, Humera Iqbal, Francesco Messineo, Lindsay Scorgie-Porter, Murat Şiviloğlu, Sandy To, Sam Zhiguang Yin, Kiki Yu, and Timor

Sharan have been particularly important to me. I must also mention my SOAS (University of London) friend, Thanos Petouris, and my constant companion in life, Marta Östborn.

A fellowship (2013–15) at the Royal Netherlands Institute of Southeast Asian and Caribbean Studies (KITLV), Leiden, the Netherlands, allowed me to complete this book. I am hugely grateful to my publisher, Cornell University's Southeast Asia Program Publications, in particular its managing editor, Sarah Grossman, whose speedy and secure advice, and lively support for this project, has made the final stages of work delightful.

I would like to thank my mother, Åsa Norén, for dedicating her life to giving her daughters opportunities in life; my sister, Ingrid Norén-Nilsson, for always being by my side, and, following a childhood instruction, never letting go of my hand; my father, Bo G. Nilsson, and family, for our unforgettable travels and adventures; and my parents-in-law, Sisowath Ayravady and Ngo Pin, for the warmth and love with which they have welcomed me into their family. The book was written in loving memory of my grandmother Thyra Norén, who belonged to the very earliest generation of female academics in Sweden and was a president of the Swedish Association of University Women (KAF).

My husband, Amrun, has infused the completion of this work—and my life in general—with joy. Our discussions on Cambodian affairs are a perpetual source of excitement, which have brought me many insights. His support for my work translated into a readiness to move our family to the Netherlands so that I could finish this book. Our life together has itself grown out of this project. Little did I know, when first setting up an interview with his mother, that it would take me on a long and winding road to meet my future husband. As I put the last hand to this book, our son, Francis Sisaridh, has turned one year old. This book is dedicated to him.

FOREWORD

It's an honor and a pleasure for me to introduce Astrid Norén-Nilsson's deft, clear-eyed, and persuasive study of contemporary Cambodian politics. Her novel approach is to examine the kingdom's political landscape via the ways in which competing political actors and the political groups they represent imagine the Cambodian nation. She also demonstrates how these actors, whom she has interviewed at length, legitimize themselves by privileging different segments of Cambodia's troubled past.

I admired *Cambodia's Second Kingdom* as a dissertation, but when I started to write this foreword I asked Ms. Norén-Nilsson to explain when and why she chose to focus the book as she did. She replied:

> This book came about because of unbridled curiosity. It is the outcome of a genuine desire to understand the ideas and worldviews that circulate among Cambodian politicians today. The political reality in contemporary Cambodia is one of money politics, corruption, opportunism, and greed. But this is a familiar story attracting much worthy academic attention and it has been skillfully—and repeatedly—written down, and risks precluding a range of worthwhile research directions. The picture is bound to be incomplete, if we do not address the human beings who make up this system.

Instead of passing judgment on the Cambodian scene, in other words (although her sympathies with the hard-pressed Cambodian people are always very clear), Ms. Norén-Nilsson has courageously tried to comprehend and explicate that scene from the inside, largely in terms that political actors use themselves in a process that she calls "elite nationalist imaginings."

The contemporary actors, factions, and parties dealt with in this book are all embedded in the past. In what follows, I'll try to position them inside a historical context, working backwards from the Paris Peace Accords of 1991.

In Paris, as potential signatories of the accords convened to resolve the Cambodian "problem," four Cambodian political groups competed for attention. These included the Cambodian Peoples Party (CPP) that was governing the State of Cambodia (SOC) at the time and had done so under various names since 1979. Three other groups were arrayed militarily against it, operating from refugee camps in Thailand and from "liberated" enclaves inside Cambodia. These were a royalist faction known by its French acronym FUNCINPEC (United National Front for an Independent, Neutral, Peaceful, and Cooperative Cambodia), the non-royal Buddhist Liberal Democratic Party (BLDP), and a hardline Communist faction, Democratic Kampuchea (DK), known colloquially as the Khmer Rouge.

Starved of local and international support, the DK faction dissolved in 1998, but the other three factions have survived in slightly different forms. The CPP remains in power in what is now the Kingdom of Cambodia. FUNCINPEC, although weakened, still offers a royalist interpretation of the nation while opposition parties, calling for radical reform, are lineal descendants of the BLDP.

In 1991, the four factions had a history of despising one another. They had each governed Cambodia on their own at one stage. En route to holding or regaining power they offered their followers contrasting pedigrees, differing visions of the nation, and unique interpretations of the past. Ms. Norén-Nilsson examines these pedigrees, visions, and interpretations in detail in her absorbing book.

FUNCINPEC was founded in 1981, but drew its inspiration from the so-called Sihanouk era, which ran from 1955 to 1970. Norodom Sihanouk (1922–2012), a charismatic and controversial figure, was crowned King of Cambodia by the French in 1941. He abdicated the throne in 1955, soon after Cambodia gained its independence, because he wanted to become a full-time politician. He named his unambitious father, Norodom Suramarit, in his place. As prime minister, Sihanouk went on to shape and dominate Cambodian life. In 1960, when his father died, Sihanouk refused to name a successor and became chief of state. He was removed from office in a bloodless coup in 1970 and spent most of the next twenty years in exile.

In the 1980s and 1990s, FUNCINPEC never claimed that its intention was to return Sihanouk to the kind of power that he had enjoyed before 1970. Nonetheless, the prince's survival, combined with widespread nostalgia for the peaceful prosperous times that he embodied, gave FUNCINPEC an ideological head start in 1991 over the other contenders.

The BLDP, founded at the same time as FUNCINPEC, traced its pedigree to the anti-Sihanouk grouping that took shape in the late 1960s among Cambodia's small elite, and especially inside the National Assembly. Anti-Sihanouk feeling became widespread as the Vietnam War intensified and as Sihanouk seemed to many to be losing his grip. In March 1970, after the prince was overthrown, a pro-American regime, soon to be called the Khmer Republic (1970–75) came to power.

The *coupistes* hoped that a republican style of government would deliver commonsensical policies and that an alliance with the United States would keep Cambodia out of the Vietnam War. That they were tragically wrong on both counts did not mean that survivors of the Khmer Republic in 1991, choosing to follow the BLDP, had any enthusiasm for the Sihanouk era. Indeed, antipathy toward both Sihanouk and Vietnam were what held the quarrelsome leaders of the BLDP together.

Starting in about 1966, two antagonistic factions sprang up inside the small, concealed, and powerless Communist Party of Kampuchea (CPK). Hoping to come to power at some stage, the party secretary, Pol Pot (1925–98), and some of his colleagues were inspired by Maoist China and North Korea and wanted to dissociate Cambodia from communist Vietnam. Others in the party hoped to continue to accept Vietnamese patronage and advice, as the CPK and its predecessor parties had done ever since the First Indochina War (1946–54).

After the 1970 coup, the Khmer Rouge entered an uneasy alliance with North Vietnam in order to defeat the Khmer Republic and ostensibly to return Prince Sihanouk to power. Over the next two years, North Vietnamese forces, in the course of severely weakening those of the Khmer Republic, provided the Khmer Rouge with arms, training and logistical support. By the end of 1972, the Khmer Rouge had become an effective fighting force. The Khmer Republic's army, plagued by corruption, heavy casualties, and poor leadership, mounted no further offensives and three-quarters of Cambodian territory was in Khmer Rouge hands.

In 1973, North Vietnam withdrew its forces from Cambodia as part of a far-reaching cease-fire agreement with the United States that affected all of Indo-China. Pol Pot and his colleagues interpreted the Vietnamese action as a betrayal. They began to purge anyone whom they suspected of sympathy with Vietnam. The purges intensified after the Khmer Rouge came to power in 1975. Over the next three years, tens of thousands of suspects, especially in the eastern part of the country, were hunted down and put to death. Thousands of others sought refuge in Vietnam. One of the refugees was a DK regimental commander named Hun Sen (1952–), who became prime minister of Cambodia in 1985. He has dominated Cambodian politics ever since.

In January 1979, a Vietnamese invasion ousted the CPK, and in one of history's perennial somersaults, the invaders placed a handful of pro-Vietnamese Cambodians, including Hun Sen, in command of the newly established Peoples Republic of Kampuchea (PRK). Over the next ten years, at least 100,000 Vietnamese troops, sustaining heavy casualties, prevented the Khmer Rouge from regaining power. When these troops withdrew in 1989, the PRK changed its name to the State of Cambodia (SOC), instituted some popular reforms, and abandoned Marxism–Leninism as its governing ideology. The moves had little effect on Cambodian politics. Opposition to the CPP remained out of the question, and everyone in the ruling party—hundreds of whose members, like Hun Sen, were former Khmer Rouge—remained in place.

In Paris two years later, the foreign sponsors of the accords were anxious to remove Cambodia from the Cold War that they had inflicted on the country. They urged the four factions to disarm, to disregard the past and to compete in United Nations-sponsored national elections. Those foreign negotiators sidestepped the importance of past events—especially the brutality of the defunct DK regime—and overlooked the fact that Cambodian politics had always been a brutally contested zero-sum game. Throughout Cambodian history, winners have been expected to take all and losers have been expected to collapse, change sides, or disappear. The four factions were now being asked to abandon the game and to become friends, for a while at least.

It's worth recalling that when three of the factions identified in Paris had governed Cambodia—the anti-Sihanoukists as the Khmer Republic, the Khmer Rouge as DK, and the pro-Vietnamese faction of the Khmer Rouge as the PRK/SOC—their leaders, on coming to power, took pains to condemn their predecessors to death. It's not surprising in this context that the people charged with drafting a definitive Khmer-language text of the accords had great difficulty in finding a Cambodian word that translated as "consensus."

The United Nations Transitional Authority in Cambodia (UNTAC, 1991–93), set in motion by the accords, was the UN's most expensive operation to date. It was heavily criticized at the time. With hindsight, I think it was a partial success. To its credit, UNTAC freed up Cambodian print media, sponsored multi-party national elections (boycotted by the DK faction), prioritized human rights, allowed Sihanouk to be re-crowned as a constitutional monarch, and repatriated over 300,000 Cambodians from refugee camps in Thailand. UNTAC also opened up Cambodia to extensive foreign assistance and investment.

Unfortunately, UNTAC failed to disarm the Khmer Rouge and failed to disarm and disempower the CPP, which remained in day-to-day control of the country throughout the UNTAC period. After FUNCINPEC won the UNTAC-sponsored elections in 1993, the CPP refused to accept the results and insisted on co-governing with the royalist party in an acrimonious, ill-fitting coalition. Soon afterwards, UNTAC ended its mandate and its participants went home.

Over the next two decades—the period dealt with in what follows—outside powers, international institutions, and over two hundred NGOs donated years of their time and tens of billions of dollars to Cambodia. The country's infrastructure slowly improved, tourism boomed, the civil war came to an end, foreign investment increased and a thriving industrial sector dominated by foreign-owned garment factories was established in the outskirts of Phnom Penh.

Alongside these positive developments, and claiming credit for them, the CPP remained firmly in power. Hun Sen, relishing the name "strong man," brushed aside efforts by outsiders and opposition parties to open up and improve Cambodian governance. In 1997, a brutal CPP-led *coup de force* tightened the CPP's grip and eliminated FUNCINPEC as a political force.

By then, many donors, advisors and analysts had become impatient, pointing to the CPP's stranglehold on politics, as well as to Cambodia's corrosive patronage arrangements, widening inequity, culture of impunity, and endemic corruption. To a large extent, these conditions characterize the Cambodian scene today.

Some encouraging signs came to the surface in 2013–14, after national elections in which the CPP unexpectedly suffered some bruising losses. Ms. Norén-Nilsson discusses these developments in a perceptive epilogue. On balance, however, the political landscape of Cambodia in 2015 is almost as bleak as ever.

It's against this distressing historical background that *Cambodia's Second Kingdom* seeks explanations for the ideologies behind competing factions in Cambodian politics today.

In her years of engagement with Cambodia, Ms. Norén-Nilsson has absorbed many harsh readings and assessments of Cambodian politics without losing her affection and respect for the Cambodian people. As she gained fluency in spoken and written Khmer, she also gained the confidence and good will of dozens of talkative sources, including the most prominent Cambodian politicians—Hun Sen, Prince Norodom Ranariddh, and Sam Rainsy—who spoke with her at length. To my knowledge, no other scholars of Cambodian politics have assembled their findings in this innovative and rewarding fashion.

Nonetheless, formulating the orientation of the book caused her some methodological problems for a time. As she has written:

> Though my intellectual ambition was clear in my mind, in pursuing the topic I had to steer through serious problems of vocabulary and concepts. The first challenge was to identify the categories of analysis: "ideology" did not take me very far, nor did "nationalism"... I came to realize that the most fruitful perspective was that of political imaginations revolving around the nation, but that these had to be approached in a broad, historically informed sense—capable of identifying national imaginations where they might otherwise not be detected, and of deciphering them by situating them in their histories of meaning.

In this passage Ms. Norén-Nilsson describes the direction, rewards, and complexity of her book *from the inside*. In a similar fashion, the book examines Cambodian politics by working outward from informants and from what is on the minds of these men and women. In doing so, Ms. Norén-Nilsson has come up with a fresh, clear-headed interpretation of Cambodian politics that might surprise some "experts" but would be recognizable to Cambodian practitioners.

Most of Ms. Norén-Nilsson's informants seem to have been unaware of the large, complex, and often moralistic literature in foreign languages that has sprung up over the years about the Cambodian political scene. Similarly, the authors of these studies, with a few notable exceptions, don't seem to have spent much time listening to the people whose actions and policies they often overconfidently describe.

This pathbreaking, enjoyable book remains faithful to Ms. Norén-Nilsson's research agenda, and is also notable for its scholarly reach and sophistication. In the course of writing it, Ms. Norén-Nilsson has responded directly or indirectly to a wide range of materials in English, French, and Khmer that deal with Cambodia's history and politics. She has also read and commented on theoretical materials concerned with nationalism, political imaginings and political thought. She pays sustained attention, for example, to *Imagined Communities*, the iconic work by Benedict Anderson,[1] and challenges Anderson's occasionally Olympian findings when they fail to fit with her own.

Cambodia's Second Kingdom is an impressive and pleasing scholarly work that opens up new vistas for anyone interested in the ways that Cambodia works or fails to work. It may also be of interest to people concerned with the imaginings that we call on to explain or criticize our own nation, or justify our political stance.

Finally, because this volume is so accessibly written, I found it a joy to read.

David Chandler

Melbourne, Australia

---

[1] Benedict Anderson, *Imagined Communities: Reflections on the Origin and Spread of Nationalism* (London and New York: Verso, 1983).

PREFACE

How do different Cambodian political projects interpret the political identity of the nation? How do competing national imaginings play out in contemporary Cambodian politics? In today's Cambodia, marked by power politics, widespread corruption, and opportunism, these questions seem a little off the mark. Scholarly silence on these issues suggests a tacit shared understanding that they are dwarfed, or made outright irrelevant, by the crudeness of the political game. Yet, in ignoring them, our understanding of contemporary political practice is fragmentary and incomplete. This book seeks to show the ways in which, in resurrecting Cambodia from the ashes and the void left by civil war, the idea of the nation has been intrinsically bound up with political competition and outcomes. It outlines how national imaginings have been entwined with competition for electoral victory within the reinstated multi-party democratic framework. By extension, this book suggests ways in which attention to national imaginings can be useful for understanding political developments in a post-conflict setting.

In 1991, more than two decades of Cambodian civil war came to a close when four contending factions signed the Paris Peace Agreements (PPA).[1] Out of these four factions, the political parties that would come to dominate Cambodian politics in the resulting multi-party democratic system emerged. The last phase of the prolonged civil war had split Cambodia into what can be thought of as two contending nations: one under the control of the Phnom Penh-based government of the People's Republic of Kampuchea (PRK, 1979–89), and one—itself internally fractured—under the control of the tripartite coalition resistance government, the Coalition Government of Democratic Kampuchea (CGDK).[2] These were divided geopolitically, in that each enjoyed the backing of contending Cold War power blocs; physically, by a border of landmines; as well as in their imaginations, maintaining (sets of) disparate historiographies and future visions with both sides claiming to represent the genuine Khmer nation. On the brink of a new era in which the keywords were peace, national reconciliation, and multi-party democracy, the imperative of "Khmer unity" emerged as paramount, whilst, with no secure conceptualization of the Cambodian nation, the outlines and character of the national community were unclear.[3]

---

[1] The "Agreements on a Comprehensive Political Settlement of the Cambodia Conflict" were signed in Paris on October 23, 1991, at the final meeting of the Paris Conference on Cambodia.

[2] The coalition comprised the Party of Democratic Kampuchea (Khmer Rouge), the anti-communist Kampuchean People's National Liberation Front, and the royalist Front Uni National pour un Cambodge Indépendant, Neutre, Pacifique et Coopératif (FUNCINPEC, National United Front for an Independent, Neutral, Peaceful, and Cooperative Cambodia).

[3] Caroline Hughes, "Reconstructing Legitimate Political Authority through Elections?" in *Beyond Democracy in Cambodia: Political Reconstruction in a Post-Conflict Society*, ed. Joakim Öjendal and Mona Lilja (Copenhagen: NIAS Press, 2009), 47–48.

Two decades on, two contending nations again stand pitted against each other. In the national elections of 2013, the vote emerged almost equal between the long-ruling Cambodian People's Party (CPP) and the united, self-identified democratic opposition, the Cambodia National Rescue Party (CNRP). Representing sharply different visions and interpretations of Cambodia, these two parties have split the electorate in two. Baffled observers, who in this polarized duel see a first credible challenge to the CPP's seemingly monolithic hold on power, search for ways of approaching current goings-on. To make sense of these, we need to look beyond the idea of a post-conflict nation, and instead turn to examine what disparate histories are being created and what contrasting visions for the future are expressed. Although these questions are of key importance, their significance from a political perspective has yet to be adequately explored. Political science scholarship has produced a solid corpus of analyses of how power politics has played out in post-PPA Cambodia. We now have the beginnings of an understanding of the workings of formal and informal institutions in relation to political party competition. Yet, a systematic analysis of how political competition is, and has been, anchored in more fundamental debates over the character of the national community has been missing.

This is a book that unearths these debates, charting them and their workings from optimism in the wake of the PPA through to the stirring present. It explores the ways in which political party actors in the multi-party democratic system in the Kingdom of Cambodia (KOC, 1993–), the state instituted following the PPA, have advanced different articulations of the nation. It proposes that, to make the new democratic politics mean something in post-PPA Cambodia, all political party actors turned to the nation as the most important part of the answer. Following the agreements, which were intended to unite the competing nations, the imperative of nation-building loomed larger than ever. Yet the main political parties continued to advance radically different imaginings of the national community.

In this sense, they continued to advance competing nations, whilst each laid claims that their version, alone, represented the true Cambodia. Referring to the political dimensions of art, Ashley Thompson has suggested that there is a crisis of representation in today's Cambodia, where the wartime destruction of art raises the question of what form the modern nation will take.[4] This book brings to light a crisis over the representation of the contemporary Cambodian nation that has similarly permeated political party competition, albeit in a manner largely hidden from outside observers.

The 1991 PPA and the resulting 1993 multi-party elections constituted but the latest turning point in Cambodian modern history, marked by discontinuity. Cambodia has gone through six successive post-independence regimes since 1953, each of which attempted to realize widely different political systems. With the reintroduction of a multi-party democratic system, the factions-turned-parties redefined their political projects to compete within the new framework. They did so by rearticulating, brushing up, and patching up ideas of the political contents of the nation, and their own role in representing, embodying, or defending it. This entailed renegotiating the character and contours of the nation and its people, and the role

---

[4] Ashley Thompson, "Angkor Revisited: The State of Statuary," in *What's the Use of Art: Asian Visual and Material Culture in Context*, ed. Jan Mrázek and Morgan Pitelka (Honolulu: University of Hawai'i Press, 2008), 202–3.

and mandate of national political leadership. Principal notions of the new political setting, such as democracy, royalism, and populism, were articulated as part of the same process. Among these notions, that of democracy was key, since, within the nominally democratic framework, it provided a language in which all imaginings were partly phrased.

Now that a profound divide has once again surfaced, this book seeks to reorient our understanding of political competition in today's Cambodia by proposing that competing national imaginings have formed a powerful underlying dynamic structuring it. The main political party actors in the KOC all vocally advanced different claims to represent the nation. They did so in ways that encompassed the symbolic and discursive contestation of the political contents of the nation. They sought to forge links between themselves and the nation, advancing claims that they were uniquely poised to realize the nation's aspirations. These competing bids for representation of the nation are central to understanding the trajectories of different political party actors, and for the making of key political notions in post-PPA Cambodia, and therefore are inseparable from larger contemporary political developments. Finally, political legitimacy in the KOC was no exception to the string of successive Cambodian post-independence regimes, which all firmly tied legitimacy to representation of the political community of the nation. This book traces the crucial, critical, surprising, extraordinary, curious, ill-fated, thwarted, futile, and, occasionally, dull ways in which different bids for legitimacy are ultimately tied to different ideas of the nation.

BIOGRAPHICAL NOTES

HUN SEN

Hun Sen was born Hun Bunall in 1952 (in Peam Kohsna village, Steung Trang district, Kompong Cham province) to farmer parents. He was sent at the age of thirteen to continue schooling in Phnom Penh at Indradevi high school, boarding at Neaga Vorn pagoda as a pagoda boy. Although he desired to be a teacher when he grew up, Cambodia's political developments would get in the way. He joined the maquis and, as a Khmer Rouge soldier, known first as Hun Samrach and then as Hun Sen, he quickly rose in ranks. Wounded in battle, he lost his left eye one day before the April 17, 1975, fall of Phnom Penh. In January 1976, he was married to Bun Rany, a nurse, in a Khmer Rouge-organized ceremony alongside twelve other couples. (Hun Sen and Bun Rany would have six children.) He escaped to Vietnam in 1977, only to return to Cambodia after Vietnamese troops, aided by the Kampuchean United Front for National Salvation, of which he was a founding member, overthrew the Khmer Rouge-regime on January 7, 1979. At the age of twenty-seven, he became foreign minister for the resulting People's Republic of Kampuchea (PRK), and in 1985, at the age of thirty-three, the world's youngest premier. After the multi-party elections of 1993, he was made second prime minister for the Cambodian People's Party and, since 1998, he has held the position of prime minister. Currently the longest-serving premier in Asia, he has announced his intention to remain in power until age seventy-four.

NORODOM RANARIDDH

Born in 1944 to Norodom Sihanouk and Phat Kanhol, a royal ballet dancer, Ranariddh left for France in 1958 to attend school in Marseille. He studied public law at the University of Provence, eventually obtaining a PhD degree, in 1974. That was after spending a brief interlude in Cambodia, to which he had returned just before the establishment of the Khmer Republic (which imprisoned him for six months). He built a career as an academic: he was a research fellow at the French National Centre for Scientific Research (CNRS) and became an associate professor at the University of Provence. In 1983, Ranariddh left to join the royalist resistance movement Front Uni National pour un Cambodge Indépendant, Neutre, Pacifique et Coopératif (FUNCINPEC, National United Front for an Independent, Neutral, Peaceful, and Cooperative Cambodia). He became commander-in-chief of its army, the Armée Nationale Sihanoukiste (ANS) in 1986, FUNCINPEC secretary general in 1989, and FUNCINPEC president in 1992. After the 1993 elections, in which FUNCINPEC emerged victorious, a power-sharing formula was put in place that made Ranariddh first prime minister. In July 1997, he was violently overthrown by second prime minister Hun Sen, a defeat from which Ranariddh never recovered. Under Ranariddh, FUNCINPEC became a government coalition partner to the CPP in 1998 and 2003. In 2006 he was ousted from the FUNCINPEC presidency, and spent the following decade making occasional political comebacks as leader of minor royalist parties, including the eponymous Norodom Ranariddh Party (NRP). He was reinstalled as the FUNCINPEC president in 2015, reportedly at the suggestion of Hun Sen.

SAM RAINSY

The son of prominent politician Sam Sary and In Em, Sam Rainsy (literally "ray of light") was born in 1949 and named after la Ville Lumière—the city of Paris. His childhood was marked by his father's falling out with Sihanouk, an event that led Sary to flee Cambodia in 1959 to join the Khmer Serei. (Sary died in 1962, and it is likely that he was assassinated.) In 1965, Sihanouk exiled the remainder of Sary's family, and Rainsy grew up in Paris. Here he courted his wife-to-be, Tioulong Saumura, daughter of Sihanouk loyalist Nhiek Tioulong, and they married in 1971. He earned degrees in political science and economics, and a master of business administration at INSEAD's (Institut européen d'administration des affaires) Paris campus, and he and Saumura successfully pursued careers in finance. Rainsy joined the newly formed FUNCINPEC in 1981, and, upon returning to Cambodia in 1992, was made minister of finance in the 1993 government. While in office he railed against corruption, and was expelled after seventeen months. He founded the Khmer Nation Party in 1995, which changed its name to the Sam Rainsy Party in 1998. In 1997, during a political rally led by Rainsy, a grenade attack killed at least sixteen of his supporters. Twice he has gone into self-imposed exile in France to avoid prison, and returned by royal pardon (once over a charge of defamation, 2005–06, and another time for charges of racial incitement and destruction of property, 2009–13—charges that he claims were all politically motivated). When the SRP merged with the Human Rights Party into the Cambodia National Rescue Party (CNRP) in 2012, Rainsy assumed the party presidency. Returning to Phnom Penh in July 2013, just nine days before national elections in which the CNRP's strong showing was the best electoral performance by any party of Rainsy's, he was greeted by huge crowds of supporters.

KEM SOKHA

Born in Takeo province in 1953, Kem Sokha studied law at Phnom Penh's Royal University of Law and Economics, and left for Prague in 1981, where he earned a master of science degree in biochemistry. Returning to Cambodia in 1986, he applied his studies to the distillery sector. He became secretary general of the Buddhist Liberal Democratic Party (BLDP, 1992–95), secretary general of the Son Sann Party (1995–98), and deputy secretary general of FUNCINPEC (1999–2002). In parallel, he made a name for himself as a human rights activist. In 1991, he created the human rights NGO Human Rights Vigilance of Cambodia. In 2002, he left FUNCINPEC, which he criticized for its lack of independence vis-à-vis the government, and set up the Cambodian Center for Human Rights (CCHR), a nationwide network that organized commune-level public forums and human rights training. He was briefly imprisoned in 2005 on defamation charges after a Human Rights Day celebration, but released upon pressure from the international community. In 2007, he left the CCHR to set up the Human Rights Party (HRP), which won three out of 123 contested seats in the 2008 elections. Over the next mandate period, the HRP saw a surge in popularity, and made a strong showing in the 2012 commune elections. In July 2012, the SRP and HRP merged into the CNRP ahead of the 2013 elections, and Kem Sokha became the party's deputy president.

CHAPTER ONE

CAMBODIA'S SECOND KINGDOM: STARTING POINTS

Nationalism, in different guises, runs like a red thread through modern Cambodian history. In a country that has served as the testing ground for a string of sharply contrasting political systems, this amounts to a rare, striking continuity. The nationalism of various historical agents can be understood as their minimum common denominator. In today's Cambodia, even at a casual glance, references to the nation, *cheat*, abound. Visual imagery, first and foremost that which depicts the iconic temple of Angkor Wat, reproduces the idea of national belonging with incessant insistence. The most casual conversation quickly drifts to deliberate ideas of national identity with different degrees of passion. Expressions of nationalism appear everywhere you turn, but there is no agreed-upon understanding of how to make sense of it in the Cambodian context.

CAMBODIA AS AN UNFINISHED IMAGINED COMMUNITY

To account for the omnipresent idea of "nation" in Cambodia, it makes sense to turn to one of the most influential books on nationalism of our times. Conceptualizing the nation as an "imagined community," Benedict Anderson rewrote the research agenda for the study of nationalism. In *Imagined Communities,* he traced the origins of national consciousness to the modern industrial age of Western European Enlightenment, when economic change sparked the rise of scientific discoveries, rapid communication, capitalism, and print-as-commodity.[1] Print capitalism helped create and disseminate national languages across territories previously lacking a shared identity. It also spread the idea of "homogeneous, empty time" by creating a sense of the simultaneous activities of different persons within the same imagined community, bestowing a sense of shared "calendrical" time.[2] In this way, economic factors helped spread universal, "horizontal-secular" notions of national space and time, which enabled diverse groups of people to relate to each other as parts of a national community.[3] The resulting nation was an imagined community, "because the members of even the smallest nation will never know most of their fellow members, meet them, or even hear them, yet in minds of each lives the image of their communion."[4] Anderson emphasized the role of creative imagery, invented traditions and symbols of tradition in the construction of modern nations.

---

[1] Benedict Anderson, *Imagined Communities: Reflections on the Origin and Spread of Nationalism* (London: Verso, 1991), 36.

[2] Ibid., 22–36.

[3] Ibid., 37–46.

[4] Ibid., 6.

Imagined Communities opened up a range of research directions that will be pursued in this book. First, Anderson demonstrated that the nation is a historical invention rather than a natural, pre-existing entity. All nations, according to Anderson, are imagined artifacts that bestow feelings of identity. Because all nations are imagined, it is the particular way in which they are imagined that becomes the key research question, rather than their objective "genuineness."[5] Second, economic, social, and political conditions that enable people to conceive of themselves as part of an imagined community are the backdrop to "imagination." Thus, national imaginations are firmly rooted in a structural and material context. Third, Anderson's argument suggests that the nation is real and imagined at the same time. This is because, once established, the imagined community institutes a new sense of self, space, and time, thereby changing the parameters of action and making nationalism a real institutional and political agent.[6]

The fact that nationalism is now an institutional and political agent, however, limits its homogenizing aspect, and the case of Cambodia alerts us to this. Nationalism is not merely a historical phenomenon that gave rise to imagined communities around the world. Nations also represent a spatial, political, and historical category of political and social life. Applying Anderson's framework to contemporary nations necessitates taking into account the different contexts and characteristics of long-established nations, in the sense that they have long been imagined as communities of equals based on "a deep horizontal comradeship."[7] Enduring contemporary nations can be said to exist in a dialectical relationship between their particular histories and the practice of imagination.[8] Around the world, these "imagined communities" can be thought of as "unfinished" in the sense that national membership is often contested and the communities' boundaries are thus subject to negotiation.[9] Many countries, conceived of as horizontal communities, are crosscut by categories of exclusion, often along ethno-racial lines. Theorizing contemporary nationalisms thus entails considering nations as entities with particular histories that are subject to continuous reimagination. While rival political projects often claim to represent one and the same nation, they reimagine not only the contours but also the characteristics of the nation in widely different ways—producing rival "nationalisms" to compete electorally.

Cambodia is best thought of as an "unfinished imagined community," both in terms of its boundaries and its characteristics. While Cambodia is a long-established nation, in the sense that a successive string of political projects undertaken since the colonial era have thought of it as a community of equals based on a deep horizontal comradeship, the contours and characteristics of this imagined community have been articulated in sharply distinct ways. In contemporary Cambodia, membership in the national community and related questions of citizenship remain contested, particularly with reference to ethnic Vietnamese, Chinese, and Thai minorities,

---

[5] Ibid.

[6] Andreas Roepstorff and Nils Bubandt, "General Introduction: The Critique of Culture and the Plurality of Nature," in *Imagining Nature: Practices of Cosmology and Identity*, ed. Andreas Roepstorff, Nils Bubandt, and Kalevi Kull (Aarhus: Aarhus University Press, 2003), 16.

[7] Anderson, *Imagined Communities*, 7.

[8] Roepstorff and Bubandt, "General Introduction," in Roepstorff et al., *Imagining Nature*, 16.

[9] José Itzigsohn and Matthias vom Hau, "Unfinished Imagined Communities: States, Social Movements, and Nationalism in Latin America," *Theory and Society* 35, no. 2 (2006): 193.

while the communal and national identities of ethnic Lao and of indigenous upland minorities and the Muslim Cham—generally viewed as bona fide Khmers—are subject to continuous negotiation.[10] Competing reimaginations of the nation's characteristics are negotiated through political party contestation.

The Cambodian case, then, defies the Andersonian assumption of nationalism as an unproblematic agent of homogenization. Postcolonial theory has challenged the homogenous nature of "nation" by asking the question, "whose imagined community?"[11] It proposes difference in the articulation of nationalisms, by indicating historically and culturally specific dynamics in the postcolonial world. Anderson's notion of calendrical time has also been criticized for obfuscating important processes of recollecting and retracing the past. Rather, the nation may be thought to move in salvational time, "the time in which the past can be recovered and redeemed."[12] The recovery of the past is vital to any national project, as processes of rereading the past are important preconditions for imagining alternative futures. This suggests that national imaginings, while aspiring to create notions of homogeneity, make up contentious imaginings promoting difference. To approach these contentious imaginings necessitates an extension of Anderson's original concept of imagined communities, shifting from passive to active procedural imagining.[13] Communities should be considered "not as homogenous entities or fictions, but as arenas of struggle, negotiation, and creation."[14] Tanabe suggests that Anderson's imagined community of bounded, homogeneous, empty time and space is only half of the story. The imagined community, Tanabe asserts, still "remains rather an ideal, or a *model for* a modern nation itself with an autonomous, sovereign form of political rationality, without addressing other moments of *imagining* where perpetual movements of the marginal integration of individuals and groups

---

[10] See, for example: Penny Edwards, "Imagining the Other in Cambodian Nationalist Discourse before and during the UNTAC Period," in *Propaganda, Politics, and Violence in Cambodia: Democratic Transition under United Nations Peace-keeping*, ed. Stephen Heder and Judy Ledgerwood (Armonk: M. E. Sharpe, 1996), 50–72; Alexander Hinton, "Khmerness and the Thai 'Other': Violence, Discourse, and Symbolism in the 2003 Anti-Thai Riots in Cambodia," *Journal of Southeast Asian Studies* 37, no. 3 (2006): 445–68; Jan Ovesen and Ing-Britt Trankell, "Foreigners and Honorary Khmers—Ethnic Minorities in Cambodia," in *Civilizing the Margins: Southeast Asian Government Policies for the Development of Minorities*, ed. Christopher R. Duncan (Ithaca: Cornell University Press, 2004), 241–69; Stefan Ehrentraut, "Perpetually Temporary: Citizenship and Ethnic Vietnamese in Cambodia," *Ethnic and Racial Studies* 34, no. 5 (2011): 779–98; and Claire F. Escoffier, "Les Lao au Cambodge: Une Cohabitation Harmonieuse?" in *Ethnic Groups in Cambodia*, ed. Hean Sokhom (Phnom Penh: Center for Advanced Study, 2009).

[11] Partha Chatterjee has challenged Anderson's conception of nationalism as composed of a set of basic tenets appropriated from Europe by the postcolonial world. Chatterjee argues that, while anticolonial nationalist movements shared the same discursive field as the colonialists, they insisted on a form of inner sovereignty and claimed their own "essential" cultural identity. See Partha Chatterjee, *The Nation and Its Fragments: Colonial and Postcolonial Histories* (Princeton: Princeton University Press, 1993), 220.

[12] Cairns Craig, "Benedict Anderson's Fictional Communities," in *The Influence of Benedict Anderson*, ed. Alistair McCleery and Benjamin A. Brabon (Edinburgh: Merchiston Publishing, 2007), 38–39.

[13] Roepstorff and Bubandt, "General Introduction," 16.

[14] Shigeharu Tanabe, "Introduction: Imagined and Imagining Communities," in *Imagining Communities in Thailand: Ethnographic Approaches*, ed. Shigeharu Tanabe (Chiang Mai: Mekong Press, 2008), 1.

emerge."[15] This realization has been readily translated into an interest in marginalized positions and strategies of response and resistance among so-called "othered" populations.[16]

In Cambodia, successive brands of nationalism have acted successfully as Andersonian agents of homogenization, in the sense that the string of political projects since Cambodia's independence in 1953 have united around the Cambodian nation as a common identity. This has entailed a homogenization of time and space insofar as all political projects purport to represent a Cambodian nation, with a roughly similar temporal and spatial frame. Yet, at the same time, national imaginings have been contentious, such that, while not uprooting the Cambodian nation as the ultimate object of allegiance, they have shown the limits of nationalism as an agent of homogenization. This is certainly the case at the "margins" of the nation, where ethnic minority communal identities are negotiated, as a small body of literature suggests.[17] Though it has escaped serious attention, contentious imaginings also play out at the center stage of the national political scene, where actors tied to different political parties launch competing visions of the political identity of the nation. Nations as imagined communities—understood as collectives with intersubjectively shared understandings of their common identity—are, all over the world, made up of groups with different ideas about appropriate political institutions and practices. In Cambodia, however, contestation goes beyond that to the very fundamentals of how the nation should be conceived, the implications for political representation and practice, and which political project, in turn, shares in Cambodian identity. In this sense, political contestation can be understood to center on the advancement of competing imagined communities.

In contemporary Cambodia, all political actors claim to represent the same, Cambodian nation, advancing competing imaginings that correspond to Anderson's definition of the nation as an "imagined political community that is imagined as both inherently limited and sovereign."[18] Yet, in doing so, each of these actors claims to exclusively represent the *true* Cambodian nation. By the same token, political adversaries are portrayed as false representatives of the Cambodian nation—not sharing in Cambodian identity and threatening its very survival. In this sense, rivals who compete to represent the nation put forward different concepts of the true imagined community, while characterizing alternative conceptualizations of the nation as non-Cambodian. This perspective certainly challenges the homogenizing aspect of nationalism. Rather than a shared imagined community,

---

[15] Ibid., 5.

[16] Compare to how Homi Bhabha invites us to consider nations as "narrative constructions," where contending national constituencies negotiate "nationness" and minority discourse speaks "between times and places." See Homi Bhabha, "Dissemination: Time, Narrative, and the Margins of the Modern Nation," in *Nation and Narration*, ed. Homi Bhabha (London: Routledge, 1990), 308–9.

[17] On the making of the Cambodian nation at its margins, see also: Frédéric Bourdier, *The Mountain of Precious Stones: Ratanakiri, Cambodia* (Phnom Penh: Center for Khmer Studies, 2006); Peter Hammer, ed., *Living on the Margins: Minorities and Borderlines in Cambodia and Southeast Asia* (Phnom Penh: Center for Khmer Studies, 2009); and Mathieu Guérin, Andrew Hardy, Nguyen Van Chinh, and Stan-Tan Boon Hwee, *Des Montagnards aux Minorities Ethniques: Quelle Intégration Nationale pour les Habitants des Hautes Terres du Viêt Nam et du Cambodge?* (Paris: L'Harmattan; Bangkok: IRASEC, 2003).

[18] Anderson, *Imagined Communities*, 7.

there are competing ones, each denying the shared nationality of rival points of view. This reframes Chatterjee's question, "whose imagined community?," by refocusing attention to the role of alternative elite imaginations. These are arenas of struggle, negotiation, and Tanabian-brand creation. In these arenas, the nation moves forward in "salvational" time, as the past is constantly reimagined in order to negotiate alternative futures.

This book sets out to consider contemporary political contestation in Cambodia through the prism of these competing, unfinished, imagined communities. They are *competing* imagined communities insofar as they are elite imaginings, each striving to become hegemonic in order to cement a particular understanding of the true characteristics and contours of the nation. They are *unfinished* insofar as they are continuously subject to practices of reimagination of their particular histories. Though they are imagined, they are also, in some sense, real. Just as, once established, the imagined community changed the parameters of action and made nationalism a real political agent by introducing a new sense of self, space, and time, these rival imagined communities have informed political action, and thereby become real political agents. National imaginings have been influenced and shaped by political, social, and economic conditions, and, in turn, prescribed and refuted forms of political action: people either believed in these ideas, worldviews, and related policies, or purported to do so, and took political action informed by them. This study of national imaginings is therefore at once a study of the imagined and the real. Anderson's "imagined community" referred to the emergence of a homogenous vision in society, shared in equal part by all its members, who were thereby tied together in horizontal notions of equality. Today, while such a notion of a Cambodian nation as an overarching identity prevails, a prominent dynamic is how political elites equate this nation exclusively with their own political projects, while denying or questioning the shared nationality of their political adversaries. Electoral victory within the multiparty democratic framework is their main objective. What follows is a study of these elite alleged, supposed, and desired versions of the Khmer nation.

SETTING AND CONTEXT

On 23 October 1991, the signing of the Paris Peace Agreements (PPA) ended civil war between the State of Cambodia (SOC) and the tripartite Coalition Government of Democratic Kampuchea (CGDK); the last phase of more than two decades of conflict in Cambodia. The People's Republic of Kampuchea (PRK, 1979–89; renamed the SOC in 1989) had been a single-party state under the Kampuchean People's Revolutionary Party (KPRP; renamed the Cambodian People's Party, CPP, in 1991) and controlled the bulk of Cambodian territory. The tripartite coalition government—formed in 1982 between the Party of Democratic Kampuchea (the so-called Khmer Rouge), the anti-communist Kampuchean People's National Liberation Front (KPNLF), and the royalist Front Uni National pour un Cambodge Indépendant, Neutre, Pacifique et Coopératif (FUNCINPEC)—had been based on the Thai–Cambodian border, controlling a strip of territory along the border as well as enclaves scattered across the heartland. The CGDK also represented Cambodia at the UN from 1982 through 1990, where the flag of the Khmer Rouge-regime of Democratic Kampuchea (1975–79), which the CGDK maintained, was flown until that year. Following the PPA, Cambodia became subject to the largest peace-building mission in UN history to date, known as the United Nations Transitional

Authority in Cambodia (UNTAC, 1991–93). This ended PRK-era isolation, a period when the PRK found itself on the Soviet–Vietnamese side of the Cold War divide, while the tripartite government in turn was backed by China, the US, and ASEAN. International intervention through a variety of international actors has since been continuously implicated in outlining the contours of the domestic polity itself, and domestic strategies of state- and party-building.[19]

One month after the signing of the PPA, deposed former monarch Norodom Sihanouk (1922–2012) returned to Cambodia to head a Supreme National Council to oversee the transition to a multiparty democratic system proposed by the agreements. The wide-reaching changes that followed the PPA have often been summed up as a triple transition: from war to peace, from a socialist People's Republic to multiparty democracy, and from a planned economy to a free market economy.[20] In May 1993, general elections formally introduced multiparty democracy. While maintaining bitter enmity, the different political factions emerging from civil war now became electoral rivals competing through political parties. The exception was the Khmer Rouge, which boycotted the 1993 elections and rejected its results.[21] Although royalist party FUNCINPEC won a narrow victory, with 45 percent of the vote, the CPP, finishing second with 38 percent of the vote, refused to cede control. As a result, a quadripartite coalition government was formed between FUNCINPEC, the CPP, and two smaller parties of limited importance: the Buddhist Liberal Democratic Party (BLDP) coming out of the KPNLF, and MOULINAKA (Mouvement pour la Libération Nationale du Kampuchea; Movement for the National Liberation of Kampuchea). The fifty–fifty power-sharing formula between FUNCINPEC and the CPP that was put in place introduced two prime ministers, two deputy prime ministers, and equal representation in all ministries.[22] The same year, a new constitution was adopted that set out liberal democracy and pluralism as the political principles of the nation. A constitutional monarchy was reinstated and the SOC changed its name to the Kingdom of Cambodia (KOC), often referred to as the Second Kingdom—to distinguish it from the first kingdom, which had been abolished by the Khmer Republic in 1970.[23] Sihanouk reascended the throne, and the national motto "nation, religion, king" was reinstated. A few years into the coalition government, the events of July 5–6, 1997, permanently altered the political landscape in favor of the CPP. Then Second Prime Minister Hun Sen (of the CPP) violently ousted First Prime Minister Norodom Ranariddh (of FUNCINPEC), crushed the royalist resistance, and seized power. This cemented CPP's strong grip over Cambodia's

---

[19] Caroline Hughes, *The Political Economy of Cambodia's Transition, 1991–2001* (Richmond: Curzon, 2002), 85.

[20] Ibid., 1.

[21] They subsequently established the Provisional Government of National Union and National Salvation of Cambodia (PGNUNSC) in 1994, which was dissolved in 1998 when the movement disintegrated.

[22] David Roberts, "Democratization, Elite Transition, and Violence in Cambodia, 1991–1999," *Critical Asian Studies* 34, no. 4 (2002): 523–25.

[23] The first kingdom refers to the first post-independence state under Norodom Sihanouk, which was also known as the Kingdom of Cambodia, *Preah Reach Anachakr Kampuchea* (1953–70). The Cambodian monarchy traces its roots to the Angkorean kings and the foundation of the Khmer Empire in the year 802. The absolute monarchy was replaced by a constitutional monarchy in 1947. In 1970, the monarchy was abolished by the Khmer Republic.

political scene, cutting short what some had read as an incipient transition to a genuine democracy. The next few years were marked by the steady decay of FUNCINPEC, as it entered into successive coalition governments as CPP's junior partner in 1998, 2003, and 2008. (In 2013, FUNCINPEC failed, for the first time, to win any seats in parliament.) Meanwhile, the BLDP was split by infighting and dissolved in 1997. In its place, the main party to represent an anti-Vietnamese, anti-communist alternative was the Khmer Nation Party (KNP), founded in 1995 by Sam Rainsy. The party was known after 1998 as the Sam Rainsy Party (SRP). In 2007, the SRP was joined by the Human Rights Party (HRP) to form an opposition to the CPP. In 2012, the SRP and HRP joined forces as the Cambodia National Rescue Party (CNRP), and came in a close second to the CPP in the 2013 national elections—the opposition's strongest performance to date.

In this political framework, liberal democracy nominally provides the format and language of political contests, while the constitutional monarchy delineates the political space. However, the CPP's overwhelming dominance of Cambodian political realities compromises, if not contradicts, both. Second Kingdom Cambodia can be characterized as an electoral democracy, where elections are the main arena of political competition, yet have their own limitations.[24] Steve Heder, writing in 2012, calls it an "electoral system with many un-free and un-fair aspects," which he suggests—together with the CPP's monopoly of force, control of the courts, performance legitimacy, and patronage resources, as well as Hun Sen's benefactions to society—electorally marginalize the opposition.[25] Steven Levitsky and Lucan Way refer to the contemporary Cambodian regime as "competitive authoritarianism," which they define as "civilian regimes in which formal democratic institutions exist and are widely viewed as the primary means of gaining power, but in which incumbents' abuse of the state places them at a significant advantage vis-à-vis their opponents."[26] These regimes are "competitive in that opposition parties use

---

[24] Markus Karbaum argues that, since 1993, "Hun Sen has consolidated an autocratic regime in which elections are the only way political competition plays out, and even that competition is limited." Citing evidence from Southeast Asia, Dan Slater suggests that competitive national elections amid robust mass mobilization act as a spur for enhancing state infrastructural power through the creation of parties that mobilize mass publics, energizing state registration of marginal populations and compelling central state authorities to expand their coercive monopoly into areas previously controlled by local strongmen or militias. All three mechanisms can arguably be identified in Cambodia. See: Markus Karbaum, "Cambodia's Façade Democracy and European Assistance," *Journal of Current Southeast Asian Affairs* 30, no. 4 (2011): 111–43; and Dan Slater, "Can Leviathan be Democratic? Competitive Elections, Robust Mass Politics, and State Infrastructural Power," *Studies in Comparative International Development* 43, no. 3–4 (2008): 252–72.

[25] Steve Heder, "Cambodia: Capitalist Transformation by neither Liberal Democracy nor Dictatorship," in *Southeast Asian Affairs* 2012, ed. Daljit Singhand Pushpa Thambipillai (Singapore: ISEAS, 2012), 113.

[26] Steven Levitsky and Lucan A. Way, *Competitive Authoritarianism: Hybrid Regimes after the Cold War* (New York: Cambridge University Press, 2010), 5. This is a useful concept because, as noted by the authors, other subtypes of authoritarianism, referring to non-democracies with multiparty elections, such as electoral authoritarianism (Andreas Schedler, ed., *Electoral Authoritarianism: The Dynamics of Unfree Competition* [Boulder and London: L. Rienner Publishers, 2006]) or semi-authoritarianism (see: Thomas Carothers, "Struggling with Semi-Authoritarians," in *Democracy Assistance: International Cooperation for Democratization*, ed. Peter Burnell [London: Frank Cass, 2000], 210–25; Marina Ottaway, *Democracy Challenged: The Rise of Semi-authoritarianism* [Washington: Carnegie Endowment for International Peace, 2003]), refer to both competitive and noncompetitive authoritarian regimes, while "competitiveness

democratic institutions to contest seriously for power, but they are not democratic because the playing field is heavily skewed in favor of incumbents," through measures such as electoral manipulation, unfair media access, abuse of state resources, and varying degrees of harassment and state power.[27] In the 1990s, as the internationally sponsored peace-building project turned into a democracy-building one, the international community was increasingly "othered" by the incumbent CPP and claimed as an ally by the opposition.[28] Meanwhile, the CPP has made it clear that retention of the constitutional monarchy depends on its readiness to accommodate the ruling interest, and has repeatedly threatened to abolish the monarchy at times when the monarchy seemed unwilling to comply with that condition. The current system of governance is best understood as neo-patrimonial: a hybrid of informal patrimonial power based on patron-client relations mixed with formal legal-bureaucratic power. The state is structured by patron-client networks (*khsae*), and political power stems from the ability to fulfill the material aspirations of clients. Power is centralized in political figures and central ministries exercising control over resources, and has been maintained by the distribution of material gifts and physical infrastructure.[29]

What political systems are domestic political actors trying to realize in this context, so rife with contradiction and conflict? The Second Kingdom defies easy categorization, despite the apparent simplicity of overall dynamics that have concentrated power in the CPP, and in the hands of Prime Minister Hun Sen. Scholarship from a political perspective has predominantly focused on *power* in contemporary politics. Other scholars have examined the changing political economy bound up with this elusive transition, where state and social structures have undergone fundamental changes, yet, ultimately, have served to strengthen the power of the same elite. The rhetoric of the dominant CPP has, to observers, appeared as little more than a thinly veiled disguise of the power grab by that same elite.[30] Opposition royalist and democratic projects have been understood primarily

---

is a substantively important regime characteristic that affects the behavior and expectations of political actors" (Levitsky and Way, *Competitive Authoritarianism*, 16). Moreover, Levitsky and Way classify Cambodia's trajectory from 1990 to 2008 under "stable authoritarianism," in which "authoritarian incumbents or their chosen successors remained in power for at least three presidential/parliamentary terms following the establishment of competitive authoritarian rule" (Levitsky and Way, *Competitive Authoritarianism*, 22, 328–38).

[27] Levitsky and Way, *Competitive Authoritarianism*, 5.

[28] Compare to: Frederick Z. Brown and David G. Timberman, eds., *Cambodia and the International Community: The Quest for Peace, Development, and Democracy* (New York: Asia Society; Singapore: Institute of Southeast Asian Studies, 1998); Caroline Hughes, "International Intervention and the People's Will: The Demoralization of Democracy in Cambodia," *Critical Asian Studies* 34, no. 4 (2002): 539–62; and Pierre P. Lizée, *Peace, Power, and Resistance in Cambodia: Global Governance and the Failure of International Conflict Resolution* (Basingstoke: Macmillan, 1999).

[29] Kimchoeun Pak, "A Dominant Party in a Weak State: How the Ruling Party in Cambodia Has Managed to Stay Dominant" (PhD dissertation, Australian National University, 2011), 85–156; Kheang Un, "Patronage Politics and Hybrid Democracy: Political Change in Cambodia, 1993–2003," *Asian Perspective* 29, no. 2 (2005): 203–30; and Kimchoeun Pak et al., "Accountability and Neo-Patrimonialism in Cambodia: A Critical Literature Review," (Phnom Penh: Cambodia Development Resource Institute, 2007): 43–47.

[30] See, for example, Steve Heder, "Political Theatre in the 2003 Cambodian Elections: State, Democracy, and Conciliation in Historical Perspective," in *Staging Politics: Power and*

to expound a reactive rhetoric to the context set out by CPP maneuverings, and dismissed as representing shallow populism.[31] The apparent hollowness of political rhetoric that this has been taken to indicate has eclipsed interest in closer study of contemporary political discourse. Meanwhile, "ideology" has been shown to be an eroded, meaningless concept, by extension rendering the question of political imaginations superfluous, or, at best, peripheral.[32]

This book seeks to turn this debate on its head by tracing how political party actors engaged in a discursive contest over the outline and character of the nation and its political content, which, in turn, bore on ideas of national leadership and political representation. This contest was not disconnected rhetoric, but intrinsically bound up with post-PPA political competition. It took place in a wide variety of formats: public speech, political writing, scholarship, and art. It selectively assembled components from available discursive material from earlier, post-independence regimes and contemporary global contexts, which provided resources as well as constraints to addressing immediate political exigencies. These claims to representation and their internal cohesion were, in turn, bound up with the appeal and trajectories of different political party actors. As such, they were entwined with larger political developments.

POLITICIZED IDENTITIES AND THE POST-PPA NATION

The 1993 advent of a multiparty democratic system changed the format and language of adversarial politics, which now centered on winning elections. Political actors became electoral contenders competing through political party vehicles inside a nominally liberal democratic framework. In their manifestos and campaign materials, political parties launched lists of "principles" they purported to represent. These commonly included democracy, human rights, and social justice. Yet these principles often overlapped among parties and seemed void of meaning—to the point that they served to obfuscate, rather than clarify, policy differences for voters.[33] This scenario baffled some observers, who expected that candidates would have phrased their viewpoints and programs in the language of ideology. Joakim Öjendal and Mona Lilja note that "the idea that the existence of competing party ideologies is one of the cornerstones of liberal democracy does not seem to have taken root in Cambodian society."[34] In an oft-quoted Asia Foundation survey from 2003, only 28 percent of respondents considered political parties' policies, views, and ideology as motives for voting, while, in terms of policy differences among the parties, 44 percent of respondents said they did not know if there were differences,

---

Performance in Asia and Africa, ed. Julia C. Strauss and Donal B. Cruise O'Brien (Richmond: I. B. Tauris, 2007), 159.

[31] Caroline Hughes, "Transforming Oppositions in Cambodia," *Global Society* 15, no. 3 (2001): 301–3.

[32] Margaret Slocomb, "The Nature and Role of Ideology in the Modern Cambodian State," *Journal of Southeast Asian Studies* 37, no. 3 (2006): 375–95.

[33] Un, "Patronage Politics and Hybrid Democracy," 222.

[34] Mona Lilja and Joakim Öjendal, "The Never-Ending Hunt for Political Legitimacy in a Post-Conflict Context," in *Beyond Democracy in Cambodia: Political Reconstruction in a Post-Conflict Society*, ed. Joakim Öjendal and Mona Lilja (Copenhagen: NIAS Press, 2009), 303.

11 percent said there were no differences, and 16 percent said there were differences, but were unable to specify them.[35]

If not evident in the policies and principles set out in their campaign materials, electoral competitors in the new multiparty system did retain important differences based on the perpetuation and exacerbation of identity-based conflict. This is consistent with a larger trend, observed in a range of democratizing contexts in the wake of the Cold War, whereby emerging political parties functioned as outgrowths of intra-elite contestation. Democratic transition in these contexts was therefore conducive to continued domination of the political process by elites who mobilized along the lines of politicized identity. Multiparty elections, as a consequence, served to exacerbate conflicts of identity rather than ameliorate conflicts of interest. Caroline Hughes has identified how, in Cambodia, political parties favored a "politics of charismatic leadership and mobilization around politicized identities, rather than a politics of representation" and the articulation of competitive policy platforms or policy agendas.[36] Hughes locates this in the continued attachment to civil war strategies and identities of the 1980s, which the parties refused to change to a political conflict over pragmatic issues and grassroots concerns. The emergence of a multiparty environment did not transform the civil war conflict over fundamentals into a political conflict over issues, whereby each party acknowledged the others as legitimate political forces. Cambodian political parties, she argues, sought to gain advantage over one another by means of two main strategies: the attempted manipulation of democratic processes and institutions, and the rhetorical portrayal of opponents as a threat to the survival of the Cambodian nation, rather than mere illegitimate participants in politics.[37]

Such identity-based conflict between political parties was, I argue, located in the advancing of competing imaginings of the Cambodian nation, with each party presenting itself (or its party leader) as the nation's genuine representative. Responding to a crisis of national representation, the full range of political party actors offered different solutions to the Cambodian public which entailed the forging of exclusive links between themselves and the nation. These competing articulations of the Cambodian nation formed a powerful underlying dynamic for structuring political contestation in the multiparty system. The two strategies suggested by Hughes were ultimately rooted in larger narratives of the Cambodian nation. In a way, the main political party actors advanced contending nations.

An elementary form of identity-based conflict has been over the definition of who is a Khmer *tout court*—and therefore recognized as a Khmer political actor in the first place. Many exiles returning to Cambodia following the PPA to fill the ranks of the royalist and democratic parties (and to a lesser extent the CPP) held dual citizenship. They were accused by some who had remained during the sufferings of Democratic Kampuchea and the PRK-era civil war of having abandoned the nation, and thus dual citizenship came to carry a stigma. During the first mandate period of the KOC, the CPP called for government officials to renounce their second

---

[35] See: Asia Foundation, *Democracy in Cambodia—2003: A Survey of the Cambodian Electorate* (Phnom Penh: Cambodia, 2003); Lilja and Öjendal, "The Never-Ending Hunt," 303; and Un, "Patronage Politics and Hybrid Democracy," 222.

[36] Caroline Hughes, "Parties, Protest, and Pluralism in Cambodia," *Democratization* 9, no. 3 (2002): 167.

[37] Ibid., 167–68.

citizenships—aiming, in particular, at FUNCINPEC's leader, Norodom Ranariddh, who was both a Cambodian and French citizen. In response, those targeted emphasized patriotism over nationality, and argued that their status enabled them to speak "the truth" about Cambodia.[38] In March 2014, a government spokesman, referring to a plan under consideration, said those holding dual citizenship might be banned from running for the office of prime minister—now obviously targeting Sam Rainsy, who over the preceding months repeatedly had called for Hun Sen to step down. In December, Hun Sen alluded to the possibility of applying such a ban to the National Assembly and the executive branch.[39] At that time, new National Election Committee (NEC) rules had rekindled the perennial debate. In July 2014, a year-long political deadlock between the CPP and the CNRP was ended by an agreement centered on reforming the NEC, which was to be bipartisan but with a neutral ninth member to hold the tie-breaking vote. After Pung Chhiv Kek, president of the human rights group LICADHO (La Ligue Cambodgienne pour la Promotion et la Défense des Droits de l'Homme; Cambodian League for the Promotion and Defense of Human Rights), was offered the position, the CPP demanded that NEC members not hold foreign passports (a condition finalized in new election laws in March 2015)—making the offer contingent on Kek renouncing her French and Canadian citizenships. Kek rejected the offer. For politicians, dual citizenships have been a mixed blessing, offering access to a safe haven in times of political turmoil, while the possibility that they might withdraw at the last minute reduces the credibility and weight of their political struggle in the eyes of the public.

If the debate over dual nationalities is the most obvious manifestation of the contest to define the nation's true representative, this contest stretches further and runs deeper. Competing articulations of Cambodia permeate the political field. Political actors have invested significant effort in communicating their different versions to the electorate. Although their references to "principles" might appear hollow, political actors convey vital information to the electorate about the different political systems they envisage, which is manifested and anchored in their identities. This has sometimes taken place by means of party programs and manifestos, but—perhaps more importantly—also occurs outside and beyond these. Hughes notes that the behavior and rhetoric of political parties often communicated messages that contradicted official campaign material, writing that "the mismatch between the letter of campaign materials and the behavior and rhetoric of political parties was so wide as to render political manifestos irrelevant to the election campaign, reflecting the subordination of policy debates to intra-elite struggles focused on identities that linger from the civil war years."[40] This book traces and interprets the messages communicated, explicitly and implicitly, through a variety of channels, including public discourse, political writings, and even artistic production. Rather than promoting identities simply inherited from the civil war years, however, these messages reflected changing political imaginings. They were attempts to imbue

---

[38] Kathryn Poethig, "Sitting between Two Chairs: Cambodia's Dual Citizenship Debate," in *Expressions of Cambodia: The Politics of Tradition, Identity, and Change*, ed. Leakthina Chan-Pech Ollier and Tim Winter (London: Routledge, 2006), 73–85.

[39] See: Mech Dara and Alex Willemyns, "Dual Citizens May Be Banned from Prime Minister Role," *The Cambodia Daily*, March 11, 2014; Hul Reaksmey, "Hun Sen Suggests Expanding Dual-Citizen Ban beyond NEC," *The Cambodia Daily*, December 17, 2014.

[40] Hughes, "Parties, Protest, and Pluralism in Cambodia," 170.

morphing political identities with meaning to accommodate the changing social and political context following the end of the Cold War.

These identities, I suggest, focused precisely on a politics of representation. This was certainly not a politics of representation in the sense that Hughes refers to above in terms of "inserting pragmatic grassroots concerns into elite political agendas."[41] Rather, these were elite bids to represent the nation through equating a particular political identity with exclusive representation of the nation's aspirations. This distinction explains the otherwise mind-boggling discrepancy between the failure of political actors to represent actual grassroots concerns on the one hand, and their insistent claims to representation on the other. This paradox was clearly observed in the royalist FUNCINPEC party. While FUNCINPEC did very little "to establish a clear relationship of representation with its rural campaigners and supporters," at the same time, "the party portrayed itself as possessed of a right to rule by virtue of its status as the embodiment of the natural aspirations of 'traditional' Cambodians for a monarchical system," claims that were made by attempting to mobilize voters around a party identity of "royalism."[42] The belief of the political elite in their own exclusive ability to represent the nation confirmed an elite attitude to politics observed to be based on the "co-optation of the broader population into elite-determined political trajectories," rather than a turning of political parties into organs to represent grassroots-level social forces.[43] Yet, at the same time, it was also a testament to how central claims to representation of the nation, as defined by the elite, remained in the exercise of politics. Meanwhile, the power of the political elite to define the Cambodian political trajectory makes the dynamics of its purported representation of the nation all the more important for the analysis of contemporary political developments.

This book traces the transformation of these political identities, bound up with different national imaginings of Cambodia's Second Kingdom, following the changing context after the end of civil war. Cambodian political discourse distinguishes between the CPP, royalist parties, and democratic parties—and this is also how political actors self-define. The primary divide between these three main political identities in Second Kingdom electoral politics lies in different conceptions of how to relate to the nation. The CPP, to fill the vacuum after abandoning a half-hearted socialist identity, turned to a brand of populism that equated the party with the people, and that claimed legitimate national leadership for Prime Minister Hun Sen through renegotiating historical ideas of kingship. Royalists claimed to represent the nation through different strategies of embodiment. Democrats purported to represent a victimized nation, using local grievances as microcosms of the ailing nation. Articulating these political identities in relation to the nation meant staking out the boundaries of what it meant to be a populist, a royalist, and a democrat, in a process of co-constitution between such political identities and the nation. This, in turn, went hand in hand with the making of the contested categories of democracy, legitimate leadership, and the mandate of the reinstated monarchy.

Identities inherited from the civil war era metamorphosed. Hughes specifies the "politicized identities" lingering from the civil war years as "an association of FUNCINPEC and the SRP with instability, anarchy, and the genocide of the '*Khmer*

---

[41] Ibid., 166–67.

[42] Hughes, *The Political Economy of Cambodia's Transition*, 118–19.

[43] Ibid., 126.

Rouge' on the part of the CPP, and the casting of the CPP as traitors and 'Vietnamese puppets' on the part of FUNCINPEC and the SRP."[44] While these continued to be propagated in the two decades following the PPA, they have also been accompanied by the emergence of novel, and more elaborate, political imaginings and meanings. The CPP has changed from a civil war era socialist identity to a post-socialist identity entailing a complex mix of legitimizations, merging historical ideas of kingship with contemporary ideas of social mobility and meritocracy. The end of the Cold War-induced coalition between democrats and royalists also resulted in the transformation of resistance identities, with a renewed emphasis on separate royalist and democratic identities. A democratic identity was defined and claimed in a very different way by the democrats and by the royalists, and also in a third way by the CPP. For all three, democracy was rooted in national imaginings. The "reshaping of pro-democratic party identities" was thus more complex than previously suggested, involving more actors and more tension both between and within the royalists and the democrats. Hughes describes FUNCINPEC as having two core identities: one resistance/democratic opposition identity, and one royalist identity focused on celebrating the Sangkum legacy.[45] The following discussion traces a tension between these two identities, concluding that they did not coexist easily. In particular, FUNCINPEC's reinvention of royalist identity as Sangkum legacy was increasingly used to justify closer cooperation with the CPP, and precluded the possibility of serious cooperation between FUNCINPEC and the SRP. The hollowness of royalism as a political project permeated FUNCINPEC, which, weakened by Ranariddh's corrupt behavior, and the negligence of party activists at the base, broke down. This exemplifies how these identities were inseparable from larger political developments in the KOC.

Transforming party identities were fragmented by a range of tensions, contradictions, and conflicts. Some were internal to the political projects themselves. For the CPP and Hun Sen, tension centered on the mandate and nature of legitimate leadership in a post-socialist context, while building on their revolutionary legitimacy of the recent past. For royalists, their central dilemma was how to reconcile the constitutional monarchy with political royalism. Democrats, in turn, struggled to represent the will of a people that they imagined to be clouded by false consciousness. Additionally, these identities were destabilized by external challenges. The collapse of boundaries between political identity categories, and the rearticulation and hijacking of these, were bound up with wider political contestation. The CPP and Prime Minister Hun Sen were challenged in their national leadership roles by the opposition's denunciation of them as national traitors, making out their national leadership as symptomatic of a nation turned upside down. The crisis of defining "royalism" left room for the CPP to claim the royalist identity. While a democratic identity was primarily claimed by the self-identified democratic opposition, they were challenged by rival claims to democratic identity by the CPP and royalists.

These identities were employed to promote parties in political, including electoral, competition. Studying them therefore helps illuminate the trajectories of different political parties. They were, however, not necessarily articulated strictly along party lines. For example, one set of political parties appealed to a royalist

---

[44] Hughes, "Parties, Protest and Pluralism in Cambodia," 171.

[45] Hughes, "Transforming Oppositions in Cambodia," 307.

identity, which transcended that of the individual party. Moreover, royalist identity also entailed references to the institution of the monarchy. The unit of identity was susceptible to being claimed and hijacked by actors from rival political parties because these identities transcended a strict party political division.

Moreover, many identities were individual in nature. This testifies to the continuously personalized character of leadership in the Second Kingdom, with individual "strongmen" trumping political parties as mobilizers of opinion.[46] Indeed, contemporary claims to legitimate power are often made by reference to would-be archetypes that fuse different aspects of power in an individual identity. Heder identifies three "claims of qualification to rule" in post-independence Cambodia, namely *sdech*, "king" or "prince," confined to the royal family; *neak cheh-doeng*, a person with higher education; and *neak tâ-sou*, a person who has taken part in armed struggle.[47] Taking on such models of legitimacy enabled actors to negotiate the meanings they evoked, reconfiguring them in their favor. Since these "personal legitimizations" were also employed to further the political party that individual political actors were associated with, a tension between them and those of the political party developed that permeates the contemporary political landscape. I illustrate this in the second chapter with a narrative promoted by Hun Sen, which was a personal attempt at legitimization reflecting his ambition to personalize power—while certainly also carrying a claim to legitimacy on the part of the CPP. In the third chapter, I explore the difficulty of transferring the legitimacy tied to the person of Sihanouk to his son, Norodom Ranariddh, and to the FUNCINPEC party. The dwindling credibility of political royalists' claims to legitimate power, I suggest, reflects how royal power is converted from something incarnate, and thus personal, to belonging to the institution of the monarchy.

LEGITIMACY-BUILDING

The different versions of the nation advanced by party political actors were intrinsically linked to a search for political legitimacy. Thoroughgoing political change in Southeast Asia in the wake of the Cold War has made the question of legitimacy paramount in the region. Yet political scientists have been relatively reluctant to use the concept of legitimacy when analyzing regional political developments, reflecting problems of definition and measurement. In the most influential piece of work in recent years on political legitimacy in Southeast Asia, Muthiah Alagappa rightly outlines a picture of the contestation of legitimacy as defining much of Southeast Asia, including Cambodia, in the post-colonial period.[48] He suggests that the key elements of legitimacy are shared norms and values, conformity with established rules for acquiring power, proper and effective use of power, and consent of the governed.[49] According to Alagappa, countries with weak,

---

[46] Caroline Hughes, "Dare to Say, Dare to Do: The Strongman in Business in 1990s Cambodia," *Asian Perspective* 24, no. 2 (2000): 121.

[47] Steve Heder, "Cambodia's Democratic Transition to Neoauthoritarianism," *Current History* 94 (December 1995): 425–29.

[48] Muthiah Alagappa, "Introduction," in *Political Legitimacy in Southeast Asia: The Quest for Moral Authority*, ed. Muthiah Alagappa (Stanford: Stanford University Press, 1995), 3.

[49] Muthiah Alagappa, "The Anatomy of Legitimacy," in Alagappa, *Political Legitimacy in Southeast Asia*, 15.

contested political systems and a low level of institutionalization do not generally emphasize procedural elements to confer legitimacy. Instead, the emphasis in political legitimation shifts to normative elements, concerned with "prescribed goals or values for society on the basis of which the incumbent power holders seek to construct a normative framework," and performance elements, concerned "less with the use of power within the law and more with its effective use for promotion of the collective welfare." In addition, authority may also be claimed "on the basis of charisma, a politically defining moment, and international support."[50]

Cambodia conforms to this pattern. CPP legitimation is heavily performance based, and the party routinely refers to its achievements at providing domestic infrastructure—roads, hospitals, and schools. This bestows an aura of certainty, stability, and predictability on the CPP. Although the CPP emphasizes elections in its bid to legitimacy, which appear to be procedural elements, this emphasis is also anchored in a performance-based claim, as elections are intended to demonstrate the CPP's capacity to organize them.[51] The CPP has also framed its electioneering practices of gift-giving by alluding to shared cultural symbols of the meritorious benefactor, situating their electioneering practices in larger political imaginings that are heavily normative.[52] Political contestation continues to center on a reinvented civil war-era conflict over fundamentals, which now manifests as a conflict over the implementation of procedures. The opposition contests the way the CPP applies the PPA and the 1993 Constitution, including holding elections, thereby crippling the appeal of procedural elements in bestowing legitimacy.[53] Cambodia's main politicians all have some crowd appeal, or at least aspire to it, cultivating their varying styles: Hun Sen is fearsome in his power, Norodom Ranariddh is silky, Sam Rainsy shrill, and Kem Sokha raucous. For the CPP, the January 7, 1979, overthrow of the Khmer Rouge regime by Vietnamese troops accompanied by the Kampuchean United Front for National Salvation (the nucleus of the PRK regime) is the defining national moment—Cambodia's "second birthday." Royalists and democrats, by contrast, look back to the October 23, 1991, signing of the PPA, which ended civil war and hailed in a new era of multiparty democracy. FUNCINPEC, SRP, HRP, and now CNRP have continuously portrayed themselves as "the favored allies of Western governments" to harness domestic confidence and support.[54] The CPP under Hun Sen, meanwhile, although it maintains reasonably good relations with the United States, has cemented a strong relationship with Vietnam and, increasingly, with China.[55]

Just how efficient these contemporary bids for political legitimacy are is debatable. As the basic ingredients for procedural democratic legitimacy have been in place since 1993, this bestows the CPP with a degree of external (international) legitimacy, while there is no scholarly consensus on whether it has also conferred

[50] Muthiah Alagappa, "The Bases of Legitimacy," in Alagappa, *Political Legitimacy in Southeast Asia*, 31.

[51] Caroline Hughes, "Reconstructing Legitimate Political Authority through Elections?" in *Beyond Democracy in Cambodia*, ed. Öjendal and Lilja, 51–54.

[52] Caroline Hughes, "The Politics of Gifts: Generosity and Menace in Contemporary Cambodia," *Journal of Southeast Asian Studies* 31 (3): 469–89.

[53] Hughes, "Parties, Protest, and Pluralism in Cambodia," 167–68.

[54] Hughes, "International Intervention and the People's Will," 552.

[55] Heder, "Cambodia: Capitalist Transformation," 105–8.

internal (domestic) legitimacy. Though the holding of elections has come to be viewed by international policymakers as a hallmark of internal legitimacy, the Cambodian opposition strategies of continuously challenging subsequent elections suggest that the reality is more complex. Some charge that the CPP-led government's use of political violence, its widespread corruption, and its exploitation of natural resources have led to an internal legitimacy crisis.[56] Perhaps as a response to such a crisis, the CPP has engaged in a number of efforts to build internal legitimacy. In a recent volume, a number of authors explore the CPP's efforts to build legitimacy from the perspective of the construction and reconstruction of social and political institutions. Kheang Un finds that embedded corruption, nepotism, patronage politics, and government interference engender a negative popular perception toward government institutions, particularly the judiciary. Yet, he argues, the ruling party uses the judiciary, through showcases of ad hoc judicial reform, to legitimize their actions.[57] Laura McGrew finds that bringing the Khmer Rouge to internationally recognized, high profile trials has constituted one state strategy for winning internal and external legitimacy.[58] Kim Sedara and Joakim Öjendal argue that decentralization and local elections have introduced a new rationale for local government, whereby local government leaders increasingly gain acceptance as legitimate authorities.[59] Sophal Ear, who conceptualizes political legitimacy to include the rule of law, working institutions, and popular consent, and operationalizes it by examining development outcomes, concludes that there has been a significant boost of external legitimacy due to the use of aid post-UNTAC, although it is "debatable" how much internal legitimacy this aid successfully achieved.[60] John Marston, discussing NGO movements linked to Buddhism, dissident monks, and two religious figures as challengers to state legitimacy, finds an ambiguous relationship between religion and social legitimacy.[61] In sum, the extent of the incumbent regime's internal legitimacy is unclear, while there are indications that it actively seeks legitimacy—both internal and external—through a range of strategies.

Following Barker, Alagappa defines political legitimacy as "the belief in the rightfulness of a state, in its authority to issue commands, so that the commands are obeyed not simply out of fear or self-interest, but because they are believed to have moral authority, because subjects believe that they ought to obey."[62] He argues that the objects of legitimation are usually three associated institutions of the state, namely: the nation state, concerned with expressing political identity; the regime, or

---

[56] Kim Sedara, "From Peace Keeping to Peace Building: Cambodia Post-Conflict Democratization" (Political Studies Association, 2007), 7–8.

[57] Kheang Un, "The Judicial System and Democratization in Post-Conflict Cambodia," in Öjendal and Lilja, *Beyond Democracy in Cambodia*, 90–95.

[58] Laura McGrew, "Re-establishing Legitimacy through the Extraordinary Chambers in the Courts of Cambodia," in Öjendal and Lilja, *Beyond Democracy in Cambodia*, 250–96.

[59] Kim Sedara, and Joakim Öjendal, "Decentralization as a Strategy for State Reconstruction in Cambodia," in Öjendal and Lilja, *Beyond Democracy in Cambodia*, 115, 122.

[60] Sophal Ear, "The Political Economy of Aid and Regime Legitimacy in Cambodia," in Öjendal and Lilja, *Beyond Democracy in Cambodia*, 173.

[61] John Marston, "Cambodian Religion since 1989," in Öjendal and Lilja, *Beyond Democracy in Cambodia*, 225.

[62] Alagappa, "Introduction," in Alagappa, *Political Legitimacy in Southeast Asia*, 2; following Rodney S. Barker, *Political Legitimacy and the State* (Oxford: Clarendon, 1990), 11.

type of government; and the government, which actually controls state power.[63] According to Alagappa, the legitimation of the nation state rests on shared identity; regime legitimation on shared norms and values; and government legitimation on conformity with established rules and performance.[64] Nonetheless, attempts to legitimize successive Cambodian regimes and governments consistently refer back to the shared identity on which the legitimation of the nation state is based. In this context, it may be instructive to consider the nation itself as an object of legitimacy, which as the larger frame of reference suggested by Anderson offers a new, overarching framework for linking fraternity, power, and time.[65] If the nation is a framework that defines, in turn, regime legitimation and government legitimation, the impetus to define national imaginings is all the more pronounced. The Cambodian post-independence regimes successively attempted to base their legitimacy on representing the political community of the nation. Since the 1946 emergence of the first Cambodian political party, the Democratic Party, Hughes finds the bottom line of bids for internal legitimacy to be conceptions of community. From the Sangkum Reastr Niyum onwards (1955–), successive regimes' attempts to promote their own legitimacy have been heavily based on claims to defend a *national imagining* of the community. In creating this sense of nationhood, imaginings have been paramount, as national identity has generally lacked administrative shape and has only been manifest in "hazy visions" of "Khmerness."[66] These claims have continuously been contested by rival political projects.[67] Power holders and the political opposition alike have made claims to legitimacy by purporting to represent the nation, confirming that modern nationalisms do not exclusively belong to rulers.[68]

In contemporary Cambodia, bids for internal legitimacy, hitherto neglected by scholars, continue to center on claims to represent the nation—claims transplanted from the past into the arena of multiparty liberal democracy. The mixed procedural and performance-based bids for legitimacy as those outlined above are ultimately traceable to such claims to represent the nation. Rather than a battle of political ideologies or policy platforms, contemporary political contests can be understood as a battle over *representation of the nation*, which in turn is tied to wide power dynamics and structures. The contemporary period can be understood, in this sense, as an era of identity politics, integrally bound up with the machinations of the politics of power. These imaginings provide a necessary lens to qualify Cambodian party political contestation.

---

[63] Alagappa, "The Anatomy of Legitimacy," in Alagappa, *Political Legitimacy in Southeast Asia*, 26.

[64] Ibid., 30.

[65] Anderson situates the origin of nationalism in the decline of a divinely ordained dynastic realm, its legitimacy eroded by enlightenment and revolution, which called for a new foundation of legitimacy, in time provided by the nation. See Anderson, *Imagined Communities*, 12–22.

[66] Hughes, "Reconstructing Legitimate Political Authority through Elections?" 34–40.

[67] Peter Gyallay-Pap, "Reconstructing the Cambodian Polity: Buddhism, Kingship, and the Quest for Legitimacy," in *Buddhism, Power, and Political Order*, ed. Ian Harris (Abingdon; New York: Routledge, 2007), 72.

[68] Lynn White, *Legitimacy: Ambiguities of Political Success or Failure in East and Southeast Asia* (Singapore: World Scientific, 2005), 16.

Serious attention to the importance of national imaginings for legitimizing domestic political action leads us to reassess the role of democratic legitimizations in contemporary Cambodia. Understanding Cambodia's social, cultural, historical, and institutional contexts to be unreceptive to Western-style democracy, current scholarship is rife with arguments that democracy, consequently, does not form a basis for legitimate leadership in any straightforward way.[69] The body of scholarship examining contemporary democratic practice and discourse has predominantly sought to explain the causes for the failure of liberal democracy to consolidate in the Cambodian context, and to classify the system that has now emerged.[70] These accounts generally share an understanding that Cambodian political actors pay lip service to the notion of "democracy" to please the international audience, while, in practice, exhibiting distinctly undemocratic, illiberal tendencies. The incumbent CPP is typically understood to have made a rhetorical commitment to liberal democracy to placate the international community, while, in practice, deviating from democratic principles at will.[71] The SRP (now part of CNRP) and FUNCINPEC, meanwhile, have been understood to employ an identity of democratic opposition for an international audience, in contradistinction to a nationalist resistance identity they flaunt at home.[72] Democratic legitimizations in contemporary Cambodia are thus predominantly understood as external in nature, oriented toward an international audience. Exasperation with how parts of the democratic package have been established and others not has led Öjendal and Lilja to suggest that contemporary Cambodia finds itself "beyond democracy," in the sense that "democracy and democratization have been exhausted as concepts that can be used with any precision to analyze political change and social development in Cambodia."[73]

This book reframes this dilemma, arguing that notions of democracy, contrary to most analyses, have been central to the domestic legitimizing discourses of the

[69] Compare to Kim,"From Peace Keeping to Peace Building"; Un, "Patronage Politics and Hybrid Democracy"; Hughes, "The Politics of Gifts"; Ozay Mehmet, "Development in a War-Torn Society: What Next in Cambodia?" *Third World Quarterly* 18, no. 4 (1997): 673–86; Peter Blunt and Mark Turner, "Decentralisation, Democracy, and Development in a Post-Conflict Society: Commune Councils in Cambodia," *Public Administration and Development* 25, no. 1 (2005): 75–87; and Ronald Bruce St. John, "Democracy in Cambodia—One Decade, US$5 Billion Later: What Went Wrong?" *Contemporary Southeast Asia: A Journal of International and Strategic Affairs* 27, no. 3 (2005): 406–28.

[70] See, for example, Brown and Timberman, ed., *Cambodia and the International Community*; Karbaum, "Cambodia's Façade Democracy and European Assistance"; Aurel Croissant, "The Perils and Promises of Democratization through United Nations Transitional Authority—Lessons from Cambodia and East Timor," *Democratization* 15, no. 3 (2008), 649–68; Sorpong Peou, *Intervention and Change in Cambodia: Towards Democracy* (New York: St Martin's Press, 2000); David W. Roberts, *Political Transition in Cambodia 1991–99: Power, Elitism, and Democracy* (Richmond: Curzon, 2001); John Sanderson and Michael Maley, "Elections and Liberal Democracy in Cambodia," *Australian Journal of International Affairs* 52, no. 3 (1998): 241–53; Simon Springer, *Cambodia's Neo-Liberal Order: Violence, Authoritarianism, and the Contestation of Public Space* (Abingdon and New York: Routledge, 2010); Kheang Un, "State, Society, and Democratic Consolidation: The Case of Cambodia," *Pacific Affairs* 79, no. 2 (2006): 225–45; and Un, "Patronage Politics and Hybrid Democracy."

[71] See also Heder, "Political Theatre in the 2003 Cambodian Elections," 161–62.

[72] Hughes, "Transforming Oppositions in Cambodia," 311–12.

[73] Joakim Öjendal and Mona Lilja, "Beyond Democracy in Cambodia: Political Reconstruction in a Post-Conflict Society?" in *Beyond Democracy in Cambodia*, ed. Öjendal and Lilja, 2.

full range of contending political party actors. While not defined along liberal democratic lines, democracy has provided the language to connect domestic political imaginings to ideas about the nation. This no doubt reflects how the process of imbuing politics with meaning has meant imbuing democracy with meaning, given that the present era in Cambodia is nominally democratic. The nation has been a central part of how this is to be achieved. National and democratic imaginings have thus evolved in tandem. In this analysis, I take my lead from a body of literature that has shown how a variety of interpretations of the essence of democracy are bound up with the histories and contexts of each society, providing resources as well as constraints to political models and "reform trajectories."[74] Rather than measuring local realities against predefined concepts of democracy, this literature maps out national democratic imaginings to gain a fine-grained understanding of domestic realities, and assesses these within the context of legitimacy and political change. This framework constitutes a formidable tool for illuminating shades and dimensions of the current process of democratization, as called for by Öjendal and Lilja.[75] Applied to contemporary Cambodia, it exposes how political party actors advanced different visions of the organization of the polity and popular representation framed in the language of distinctly national forms of democracy and presented those as such to the domestic population. References to democracy were not merely the externally motivated charade that the current literature would have us believe. On the contrary, a hegemonic and relevant definition of what democracy means in the particular context of Cambodian politics has been discursively contested in post-PPA Cambodia.

Can these discourses be characterized as localized demands for democratization? Multiparty democracy was reinstituted in Cambodia in the early 1990s as part of a global drive for democratization, often referred to as the "Third Wave."[76] In its wake, Öjendal and Lilja write that the old is being affected by liberal democratic discourse and local variations are emerging. They charge that "the outcome is unlikely to match the high ideals of the newborn democracy that guided the UNTAC intervention and subsequent reconstruction support. Instead, we see something else emerging. It is as yet unclear exactly what this is, but it is certainly more open-ended and less linear than what is typically anticipated in the reconstruction discourse."[77] The discourses I trace in this book are part of that "something else emerging." They took place in a larger historical context of globalization, entailing the spread of liberal democratic discourse, and, inevitably, responded to and interacted with associated changes induced in national governance

---

[74] This suggests that each society has democracy "sui generis." Acknowledging this, a body of work has set out to map society-specific discourses of democracy. In Southeast Asia, see: Benedict Anderson, *Language and Power: Exploring Political Cultures in Indonesia* (Ithaca: Cornell University Press, 1988); and Michael Kelly Connors, *Democracy and National Identity in Thailand* (London: RoutledgeCurzon, 2003). In Asia, see John Kane, Haig Patapan, and Benjamin Wong, eds., *Dissident Democrats: The Challenge of Democratic Leadership in Asia* (New York; Basingstoke: Palgrave Macmillan, 2008). And in post-communist societies, see John S. Dryzek and Leslie Holmes, ed., *Post-Communist Democratization: Political Discourses across Thirteen Countries* (Cambridge: Cambridge University Press, 2002).

[75] Öjendal and Lilja, "Beyond Democracy in Cambodia," in Öjendal and Lilja, *Beyond Democracy in Cambodia*, 2.

[76] Ibid., 5.

[77] Ibid.

practices.[78] It is striking, however, that they are not most aptly characterized as localized liberal democratic discourse. In some ways, concerns pertaining to the liberal democratic agenda influenced these domestic discourses, or at least found resonance in them. This is most evident in the self-identification by democrats and some royalists with a liberal democratic identity. Yet, contestation over the meaning of democracy revolved primarily around notions of leadership and political organization, in ways that reassessed embodied, hereditary, and elected leadership—questions deeply embedded in the Cambodian historical and political context. Political party discourses were engaged in debates that, while not self-contained, went beyond the parameters of a global liberal democratic discourse.

While this points to the importance of a close study of Cambodian historical and cultural realities, it does not support the widespread tendency within current scholarship to write off contemporary conceptions and realities of Cambodian democracy in terms of general notions of Cambodian "political culture." Cambodian elites have been understood to build on historically inherited absolutist notions of power, so that contemporary political culture—hierarchical, absolutist, and patronage-oriented—is seen to be evolving within the framework of such a "traditional" concept of power.[79] The tired dichotomy of modern and traditional legitimations on which these accounts build is called into question by the vivid evidence given below of how so-called "traditional" notions and concepts are marked by contradictions and paradoxes, and subject to competing reinventions by contemporary actors. This calls for a much more precise, historicized account of national and democratic imaginations, suggesting that contemporary bids for legitimacy are better understood in the specific historical context of the entanglement of notions of democracy and national identity since independence.

From this perspective it is possible to assess how these discourses of the nation as the endpoint of political action, and democracy as its means, engaged with historical Cambodian models of leadership, and to understand the moral and religious conceptualizations attached to them. The institution of the monarchy provides a case in point. Legitimacy is being reconfigured through changing conceptualizations of historical kingship across mainland Southeast Asia. Employing national vocabularies and analytical tools derived from specific cultural and religious contexts, the regional literature has charted an apparent post-Cold War "retraditionalization," whereby ideas of kingship have resurfaced. In Thailand, the veneration of reigning king Bhumibol Aduljadej has been mirrored by a cult around king Chulalongkorn (r. 1868–1910), allowing middle class ideas of Thai modernity to be negotiated through a concept of modern Buddhist kingship.[80] The revolutionary parties of former Indochina, meanwhile, suffer from the fading significance of their armed struggle, and of the selfless sacrifice that early

---

[78] Joakim Öjendal, "Democratization Amidst Globalization in Southeast Asia: Empirical Findings and Theoretical Reflections," in *Southeast Asian Responses to Globalization—Restructuring Governance and Deepening Democracy*, ed. Francis Kok Wah-Loh and Joakim Öjendal (Copenhagen: NIAS Press, 2005), 345.

[79] See: Mehmet, "Development in a War-torn Society," 676; Kim, "From Peace Keeping to Peace Building," 4; St. John, "Democracy in Cambodia," 415; and Martin Gainsborough, "Elites vs. Reform in Laos, Cambodia, and Vietnam," *Journal of Democracy* 23, no. 2 (2012), 34–46.

[80] Irene Stengs, *Worshipping the Great Moderniser: King Chulalongkorn, Patron Saint of the Thai Middle Class* (Singapore: NUS Press, 2009).

generations of party leaders then displayed. In Laos, a communist People's Republic attempting to transform its public face, the ruling Lao People's Revolutionary Party (LPRP), has increasingly tried to boost its credibility by reference to resurging ideas of kingship.[81] It promotes historical warrior kings as martial leaders, national "ancestors," and patriots. In post-*đổi mới* Vietnam, where ideas of kingship are derived from a Sino-Vietnamese rather than a Theravada Buddhist tradition, the Communist Party of Vietnam (CPV) has begun to explore ancestor worship as a foundation for nationalism. Kate Jellema describes how the Đô Temple in northern Vietnam, devoted to the eight kings of the Lý Dynasty (1010–1225), enjoys increasing attention from party and state leaders who "remember the debt" all Vietnamese owe to the Lý kings. She reads it as a shift sparked by a post-Cold War legitimacy crisis, from the state's previous defensive martial ideology to a "kinetic nationalism" able to coalesce disparate people around the goal of national development.[82] Also in Cambodia, as this book will show, political legitimation has been renegotiated in important ways around culturally embedded ideas of kingship. Charting the reconfiguration of the relationships among the nation, kingship, and ideas of Buddhism is essential for unmasking contemporary bids for political legitimation.[83] Although it shares family similarities with its neighbors, the Cambodian case is unique in the region, in the sense that this renegotiation has taken place within the framework of a reinstated constitutional monarchy. Moreover, in Cambodia, unlike the one-party states of Laos and Vietnam, different meanings of kingship and legitimate leadership have become an essential part of party political contestation in the multiparty democratic system.

The nationalist discourses here explored as projects for establishing legitimate power can also be understood as projects through which the moral order in the KOC has been negotiated, producing the national space as a moral geography. In line with how the spatial organization of Southeast Asian polities emerged intertwined with the moral order, the creation of the nation state necessitated new conceptualizations of the moral community.[84] In today's Cambodia, earlier notions of power and moral

---

[81] See: Grant Evans, *The Politics of Ritual and Remembrance: Laos Since 1975* (Chiang Mai: Silkworm Books, 1998); Grant Evans, "Revolution and Royal Style: Problems of Post-Socialist Legitimacy in Laos," in *Elite Cultures—Anthropological Perspectives*, ed. Chris Shore and Stephen Nugent (London: Routledge, 2002), 189–206; and Volker Grabowsky and Oliver Tappe, "Important Kings of Laos: Translation and Analysis of a Lao Cartoon Pamphlet," *The Journal of Lao Studies* 2, no. 1 (2011), 1–44.

[82] Kate Jellema, "Returning Home: Ancestor Veneration and the Nationalism of Đổi Mới Vietnam," in *Modernity and Re-enchantment: Religion in Post-Revolutionary Vietnam*, ed. Philip Taylor (Singapore: ISEAS, 2007), 57–89.

[83] Gyallay-Pap has outlined the modern Cambodian conception of political order as an allotropy formed by conjoining the Western concept of the nation with indigenous notions of Buddhist kingship and the *sangha* to create a civic religion of loyalty to the Cambodian state. Rather than to the *state*, this book makes the case that loyalty to the *nation* is the central idea around which notions of kingship and Buddhism are modeled. See Gyallay-Pap, "Reconstructing the Cambodian Polity," in Harris, *Buddhism, Power, and Political Order*, 72, 75–76.

[84] In the classical Southeast Asian states, the spatial organization of the state linked religion and geography, allowing them to co-determine each other. See, for example: Robert von Heine-Geldern, *Conceptions of State and Kingship in Southeast Asia* (Ithaca: Cornell University Southeast Asia Program, 1956); Stanley Jeyaraya Tambiah, *World Conqueror and World Renouncer: A Study of Buddhism and Polity in Thailand against a Historical Background* (Cambridge: Cambridge University Press, 1976); George Condominas, "A Few Remarks about Thai

order were overturned by large-scale upheavals over the two decades preceding the PPA, provoking much scholarly interest in the ongoing reshaping of moral worlds those upheavals necessitated. The bulk of this scholarship explores the remaking of the "moral geology" of contemporary Cambodia from the perspective of the revival of Cambodian Buddhism, often from a grassroots, rural perspective.[85] While these studies, to varying extents, place religious revival in its political context, there are fewer studies that take elite bids to reconfigure the contemporary moral order as the direct object of study.[86] This book aims to correct this bias, by demonstrating how the political elite vocally engaged in attempts to reshape and define Cambodian moral geography. Cambodian politicians, through articulating their national visions, were crucial bidders taking part in the remaking of Cambodian moral worlds.

Partly as a consequence of its inherent moral dimension, legitimacy is an intrinsically ambiguous and contested concept that can only ever be partially

---

Political Systems," in *Natural Symbols in South East Asia*, ed. G. B. Milner (London: School of Oriental and African Studies, 1978), 105–12; and Tony Day, *Fluid Iron: State Formation in Southeast Asia* (Honolulu: University of Hawai'i Press, 2002). The emergence of national thinking entailed a consequential restructuring of the moral nature of social and individual identities. See: Anne R. Hansen, "Khmer Identity and Theravada Buddhism," in *History, Buddhism, and New Religious Movements in Cambodia*, ed. John Marston and Elizabeth Guthrie (Honolulu: University of Hawai'i Press, 2004), 40–62; Anne R. Hansen, *How to Behave: Buddhism and Modernity in Colonial Cambodia, 1860–1930* (Honolulu: University of Hawai'i Press, 2007); and Penny Edwards, "Making a Religion of the Nation and its Language: The French Protectorate (1863–1954) and the Dhammakay," in Marston and Guthrie, *History, Buddhism, and New Religious Movements in Cambodia*.

[85] This literature includes ethnographies of contemporary religion (Elizabeth Guthrie, "Khmer Buddhism, Female Asceticism, and Salvation," in Marston and Guthrie, *History, Buddhism, and New Religious Movements in Cambodia*, 133–49); contemporary millenarian movements and their nationalist overtones (John Marston, "Clay into Stone: A Modern-day Tapas," in Marston and Guthrie, *History, Buddhism, and New Religious Movements in Cambodia*, 170–92); the reconstruction of village Buddhism (see: Judy Ledgerwood, "Buddhist Practice in Rural Kandal Province, 1960 and 2003—An Essay in Honor of May M. Ebihara," in *People of Virtue: Reconfiguring Religion, Power, and Moral Order in Cambodia*, ed. Alexandra Kent and David Chandler [Copenhagen: NIAS Press, 2008], 147–68; and Kobayashi Satoru, "Reconstructing Buddhist Temple Buildings: An Analysis of Village Buddhism after the Era of Turmoil," in Kent and David Chandler, *People of Virtue*, 169–94); wider perceptions of moral order at the village level (Eve Zucker, "The Absence of Elders: Chaos and Moral Order in the Aftermath of the Khmer Rouge," in Kent and David Chandler, *People of Virtue*, 195–212); rural efforts to recreate moral order through reestablishing pagodas and consecrating pagoda boundaries and the increasing politicization of the local, Buddhist world (Alexandra Kent, "Purchasing Power and Pagodas: The Sīma Monastic Boundary and Consumer Politics in Cambodia," *Journal of Southeast Asian Studies* 38, no. 2 [2007], 335–54); monks' political involvement (Heng Sreang, "The Scope and Limitations of Political Participation by Buddhist Monks," in Kent and David Chandler, *People of Virtue*, 241–56); and the politicization of the *sangha* (Ian Harris, "Buddhist Sangha Groupings in Cambodia," *Buddhist Studies Review* 18, no. 1 [2001], 73–106.)

[86] Important exceptions are: Judy Ledgerwood, "Ritual in 1990 Cambodian Political Theatre," in *At the Edge of the Forest: Essays on Cambodia, History, and Narrative in Honor of David Chandler*, ed. Anne R. Hansen and Judy Ledgerwood (Ithaca: Cornell University Southeast Asia Program, 2008), 195–220, who analyzes the 1990 water festival as an attempt by the CPP to reassert a particular social and political order; Penny Edwards, "The Moral Geology of the Present: Structuring Morality, Menace, and Merit," in Kent and Chandler, *People of Virtue*, 213–37, who explores government strategies to redefine morality through policing social ethics; and Hughes, "The Politics of Gifts," who explores the moral economy of gift-giving by political actors.

possessed.[87] This is all the more pronounced in Cambodia, given the nature of historical and contemporary Cambodian concepts of power, which merge legitimacy with moral considerations. Historically, in Cambodian imaginations, moral, spiritual and political powers were fused, following Buddhist notions of merit and karmic law. The interplay between merit, wealth, and power was, and still is, reflected in language.[88] The word denoting political power, *omnach*, carries connotations of these different sources or indicators of power, such as *barami* (spiritual, charismatic power), *bon* (merit), and *mean* (wealth).[89] Other Khmer words for "power," such as *atthipol* (influence), imply different shades of moral and religious authority. Such concepts of legitimate leadership contain their own ambiguities and paradoxes. For example, the structural incompatibility between worldly leadership and Buddhist values represents an age-old standoff in Buddhist thinking on kingship, a tension also present in popular understandings of kingship.[90] Discussing the nineteenth century Cambodian polity, which underwent large-scale upheavals in a manner not dissimilar from recent history, David Chandler suggests that, in the eyes of the population, the relationship between wealth, power, and merit was considered problematic, as high rank followed from meritorious, yet unverifiable, behavior in another life. There were gaps in the narrative underpinning social order between "what ought to happen in the world, what often happens, and the 'normal.'"[91] Following Chandler's exploration of the dichotomy between the orderly and the disorderly as the realms of *srok* (human settlements) and *prei* (the forests), these notions have become the loci of a debate on an indigenous moral geography.[92] Penny Edwards, following Chandler's hint about the highly ambiguous nature of the *prei*, suggests this to be a "complex dialectical terrain" rather than a "bipolar moral geography [...] where notions of civilized or wild contract, expand, and shape-shift in relation or reaction to violations of moral or societal norms."[93] This suggests that the possession of *selothor* (moral power) was never unequivocal or undisputed. The ambiguous nature of moral power is further intensified by the blurring of intimacy and hierarchy in the Cambodian context, whereby "the closer and more intimate a relationship [...] the more absolute the relationship of authority."[94] Manifested in a

---

[87] White, *Legitimacy*, 3.

[88] The Khmer term for "merit," *bon*, appears in compounds such as *bon-omnach* ("power," "authority") and *bon-sak* ("rank"). See Penny Edwards, *Cambodge: The Cultivation of a Nation, 1860–1945* (Honolulu: University of Hawai'i Press, 2007), 69.

[89] Trudy Jacobsen, *Lost Goddesses: The Denial of Female Power in Cambodian History* (Copenhagen: NIAS Press, 2008), 6.

[90] Compare to Ian Harris, "The Monk and the King: Khieu Chum and Regime Change in Cambodia," *Udaya* 9 (2008), 81–112.

[91] David P. Chandler, "Songs at the Edge of the Forest: Perceptions of Order in Three Cambodian Texts," in Hansen and Ledgerwood, *At the Edge of the Forest*, 45. Compare to "Gaps in the World: Violence, Harm, and Suffering in Khmer Ethical Narratives," in Hansen and Ledgerwood, *At the Edge of the Forest*, 47.

[92] Edwards, "Between a Song and a *Prei*," in Hansen and Ledgerwood, *At the Edge of the Forest*, 143.

[93] Ibid., 143, 152.

[94] Erik Davis, "Imaginary Conversations with Mothers about Death," in Hansen and Ledgerwood, *At the Edge of the Forest*, 226. Davis writes that mothers and patrons "both are capable either of properly supporting those who serve them—their "children"—or of behaving cruelly and thoughtlessly toward them in ways that break all bounds of human morality" (p. 231).

close association between notions of patronage and motherhood, it permeates the patron–client relations that characterize Cambodian social and political life. Framed in terms of kinship and invested with apparent intimacy, relations of authority can only with difficulty be assessed in terms of the legitimacy they carry for the involved parties. Such ambiguities are arguably present in the important role of physical power or strength, *kâmleang*, as an ingredient of contemporary political power.[95] Linking the threat of violence with a promise of protection, it radicalizes the intimacy/hierarchy nexus, and thereby problematizes attempts to appraise the legitimacy of power-holders in the eyes of the general public. There are therefore fundamental difficulties in measuring legitimacy, while it cannot be thought to be possessed in any total sense.

Tracing how moral claims to power were reinvented in the Second Kingdom, this book explores how different political actors attempted to use such ambiguities in their own favor, making their particular interpretation of the moral right to rule hegemonic. Manipulating these ambiguities for political gain has been an integral feature of political contestation. Yet also, precisely because of the contested nature of moral legitimacy, their ability to make their interpretation gain large-scale social acceptance is more problematically assessed. While political actors' efforts to redraw the moral geography of the nation will be outlined, in the end, whether these bids are seen to be invested with moral legitimacy has no straightforward answer.

CAMBODIAN NATIONALISM IN PERSPECTIVE—HISTORICAL GIVENS

The vocabulary of nationhood was brought to Cambodia by French observers during the French protectorate (1863–1953). According to Edwards, the concept of "nation," based on the French understanding of it, only reached Cambodian elite consciousness in the first decades of the twentieth century. It was translated into the vernacular as *cheat*, a term derived from the Pali word *jāti*, meaning "birth." The nineteenth century usage of *cheat* was as a "moral and cosmological term that literally had to do with one's birth," and, at the turn of the last century, "encompassed a multiplicity of concepts, including ethnic identity and social status."[96] Through the first decades of the twentieth century, secular literati and the *sangha* (Buddhist monkhood) used *cheat* to denote both race and nation, in line with how French discourse at the time used "race" and "nation" interchangeably.[97] This usage was firmly established by the 1930s. Around this time, Edwards identifies a "shift in focus from royal ancestry to national genealogy," and to ethnicity as the main locus of identity. Race and nation competed with and sometimes defeated royalty as the "primary object of loyalty."[98] This was paralleled by a shift in the meaning of *sasana*, which was broadened from its turn of the century meaning of "religion," to "encompass notions of race and ethnicity."[99] The formula "nation, religion, king" (*cheat, sasana, mohaksatr*), which, copying the Thai motto, first appeared in Khmer usage in the 1930s, established these three notions as the central notions of the polity, while arranging them in seeming equilibrium. Among

---

[95] Hughes, "Dare to Say, Dare to Do," 137.

[96] Edwards, *Cambodge*, 13.

[97] Ibid., 13, 15.

[98] Ibid., 15.

[99] Ibid.

these, the nation came to define political legitimacy-seeking from then onward. Any ensuing nationalist project, including all post-independence regimes, needed to articulate its relation to kingship and the *sangha* either in support or opposition.[100]

Cambodia achieved national independence in 1953; since then, six regimes have followed each other, establishing Cambodian modern history as one characterized by discontinuity. Sharing little else in common, the string of post-independence political projects, advocating vastly different political systems, all claimed to represent particular national imaginings. Anthony Barnett writes about the idea that the very identity of the nation is under threat, that "there can be few countries where the theme has been accorded such weight."[101] The close intertwining of ideology and nationalist thought throughout Cambodian modern history has time after time made a separation of the two difficult. National imaginings were important animators of all competing political projects and their self-professed ideologies. They were said to motivate Sihanouk's Buddhist Socialism, underpinning his *Sangkum Reastr Niyum* (People's Socialist Community), 1955–1970,[102] and Lon Nol's Mon-Khmerism, guiding the Khmer Republic, 1970–1975,[103] as well as their opponents. The political thinking of the Khmer Rouge, climaxing in the regime of Democratic Kampuchea, 1975–1979, conflated the party with the nation and the nation with the "base people."[104] The regime's goal was the assimilation of all nationalities into a classless Kampuchean people, while the revolutionary analysis of the association of class stratification with ethnic groups led to the disproportionate suffering of certain ethnic minorities.[105] After the demise of Democratic Kampuchea, the Khmer Rouge movement rerouted to an "end of socialism," and increasingly portrayed nationalism, defined as the mobilization and victory of the base people, as the underlying rationale of the revolution.[106] All these successive projects also put forth different ideas of how Theravada Buddhism and kingship related to the nation.[107]

---

[100] Gyallay-Pap, "Reconstructing the Cambodian Polity," 72.

[101] Anthony Barnett, "Cambodia Will Never Disappear," *New Left Review* 180 (1990), 101.

[102] During the late 1950s and 1960s, Sihanouk developed Buddhist Socialism in a series of writings published in journals, such as *Sangkum, Kambuja,* and *Réalitées Cambodgiennes.* See, for example, "Notre Socialisme Buddhique," *Kambuja,* November 15, 1965. Compare: Ian Harris, *Cambodian Buddhism: History and Practice* (Honolulu: University of Hawai'i Press, 2005), 147; David P. Chandler, *The Tragedy of Cambodian History: Politics, War, and Revolution Since 1945* (New Haven and London: Yale University Press, 1991), 87; and Milton Osborne, *Sihanouk: Prince of Light, Prince of Darkness* (Honolulu: University of Hawai'i Press, 1994), 135.

[103] See: Lon Nol, *Le Neo-Khmerisme* (Phnom Penh: [publisher unknown], 1974); and Justin Corfield, *Khmers Stand Up! A History of the Cambodian Government 1970–1975* (Clayton: Center for Southeast Asian Studies, Monash University, 1994).

[104] John Marston, "Democratic Kampuchea and the Idea of Modernity," in *Cambodia Emerges from the Past: Eight Essays,* ed. Judy Ledgerwood (DeKalb: Center for Southeast Asian Studies, Northern Illinois University, 2002), 38–59.

[105] Steve Heder, "Racism, Marxism, Labeling, and Genocide in Ben Kiernan's *The Pol Pot Regime,*" *South East Asia Research* 5, no. 2 (1997): 109, 112, 146.

[106] D. W. Ashley, *Pol Pot, Peasants, and Peace: Continuity and Change in Khmer Rouge Political Thinking, 1985–1991* (Bangkok: Indochinese Refugee Information Center, Institute of Asian Studies, Chulalongkorn University, 1992), 23.

[107] See: Ian Harris, *Cambodian Buddhism;* and Ian Harris, *Buddhism Under Pol Pot* (Phnom Penh: Documentation Center of Cambodia, 2007).

Contemporary appeals to nationalism relate back in important ways to dynamics from the period of the People's Republic of Kampuchea (1979–89). The PRK claimed legitimacy primarily through appeals to an intense sense of national threat via continual reminders that the regime constituted the only bulwark against the "return of the Khmer Rouge." Although most Cambodians initially welcomed the invasion, there was soon suspicion of what came to be seen in terms of additional years of socialism, and, by many, Vietnamese annexation. In particular, Cambodians resented the K5 project, in which the PRK state mobilized Cambodian civilians to lay mines along the Thai border, and the conscription of a Cambodian army to prepare for the Vietnamese troop withdrawal.[108] Margaret Slocomb concludes that:

Despite all of its achievements, the PRK was not genuinely popular. At the same time, despite the overwhelming presence of Vietnamese troops and advisers, neither was it unpopular [...] The majority of people remained indifferent to efforts which attempted to engage them in revolutionary restructuring, and evaded when they could the new state's best efforts to co-opt them into schemes for the construction and defense of the country.[109]

Hughes, on the other hand, argues that the open links of the PRK to Vietnam, internal displacement, and the splitting of Cambodia into two contending nations, were so grave as to cause an internal legitimacy crisis.[110] Plausibly, there were geographical variations in the degree of PRK legitimacy. Certainly the PRK era left a lasting imprint in terms of the sense of urgency it bestowed on conceptualizing the nation in the Second Kingdom. The question of how the "nation" was to be imagined emerged "significantly problematized." The outlines and character of the national community were unclear, manifest in an "obsessive questioning within Cambodian political discourse of the ethnic origins of individuals, and exact location of borders," reflecting "difficulties in creating any secure imagining of the Cambodian nation" or definition of the people.[111] Yet, the imperative of Khmer unity was felt more powerfully than ever before.

This state of affairs formed the backdrop to Cambodia's Second Kingdom. In line with earlier patterns, national imaginings animated and fed into a wide range of political projects. Yet, how these consistently informed party politics remains obscure. By consequence, contemporary nationalism is typically treated with near-exclusive focus on the anti-Vietnamese discourse of the political opposition, read as a simplistic strategy of populist mobilization. Several existing studies of contemporary nationalist discourses examine their role in particular events or over more limited time periods, including the UNTAC period,[112] the persecution of Vietnamese communities immediately thereafter,[113] the 2003 anti-Thai riots,[114] and

---

[108] Evan Gottesman, *Cambodia after the Khmer Rouge: Inside the Politics of Nation Building* (New Haven and London: Yale University Press, 2003), 223–37.

[109] Margaret Slocomb, *The People's Republic of Kampuchea, 1979–1989: The Revolution after Pol Pot* (Chiang Mai: Silkworm Books, 2003), 262.

[110] Hughes, "Reconstructing Legitimate Political Authority through Elections?" 47.

[111] Ibid., 47–48.

[112] Edwards, "Imagining the Other in Cambodian Nationalist Discourse," 50–72.

[113] Jay Jordens, "Persecution of Cambodia's Ethnic Vietnamese Communities during and since the UNTAC Period," in Heder and Ledgerwood, *Propaganda, Politics, and Violence in Cambodia*, 134–58.

[114] Hinton, "Khmerness and the Thai 'Other,'" 445-68.

the 1997 dual citizenship debate.[115] Additionally, aspects of competing constructions of the nation by contemporary political parties have been explored by Hughes in a series of articles. Understood in the context of a wider resurgence of populism in Southeast Asia, she has given the nationalist discourse of the political opposition particular attention,[116] and, to a lesser extent, considers the incumbent CPP's discourse.[117]

This book aspires to nothing less than the *bouleversement* of the existing state of studies by showing systematically how all political parties advanced competing constructions of the nation. Tracing out patterns and tensions among and within competing imaginings, it paints a picture of the larger debates that thereby emerged between the political parties. Venturing into this uncharted territory, this book exposes little known dimensions of political contestation taking place in a partly different language than that theorized by previous scholarship, as ideas of the nation and its representation were negotiated through notions of embodiment, genealogy, and elected leadership.

THE BUILDING BLOCKS OF CAMBODIAN POLITICAL DISCOURSE

The Cambodian case shows vividly that nationalism is not an ideology *per se*. What else accounts for the starkly contrasting ideological beliefs attached to competing, self-styled nationalist projects? Modern Cambodia, therefore, illustrates Benedict Anderson's ideas of nationalism particularly well, in contradistinction to other conceptualizations, which treat the nation as a political ideology,[118] a primordial category,[119] or a political principle that follows from industrialization,[120] or that emphasize the ethnic origins of modern nationalisms.[121] Anderson charges that nationalism as a category is closer to the phenomena of kinship and religion than to political doctrines such as liberalism and fascism.[122] He writes that part of the difficulty of theorizing nationalism is the tendency to "hypostasize the existence of Nationalism-with-a-big-N (rather as one might Age-with a-capital-A) and then to

---

[115] Poethig, "Sitting between Two Chairs," 73-85.

[116] See: Caroline Hughes, "Khmer Land, Khmer Soul: Sam Rainsy, Populism, and the Problem of Seeing Cambodia," *Southeast Asia Research* 9, no. 1 (2001), 45–71; Caroline Hughes, "Mystics and Militants: Democratic Reform in Cambodia," *International Politics* 38, no. 1 (2001): 47–64; Hughes "International Intervention and the People's Will"; and Hughes, "Parties, Protest and Pluralism in Cambodia."

[117] See: Hughes, "Reconstructing Legitimate Political Authority through Elections?"; and Hughes, "The Politics of Gifts."

[118] Compare to Michael Freeden, "Is Nationalism a Distinct Ideology?" *Political Studies* 46, no. 4 (2002): 748–65; and Alan Finlayson, "Ideology, Discourse, and Nationalism," *Journal of Political Ideologies* 3, no. 1 (1998): 99–118.

[119] Clifford Geertz, *The Interpretation of Cultures: Selected Essays* (New York: Basic Books, 1973); and Pierre van den Berghe, *The Ethnic Phenomenon* (New York: Elsevier, 1979).

[120] Ernest Gellner, *Nations and Nationalism* (Oxford: Blackwell, 1983).

[121] Compare to: John A. Armstrong, *Nations before Nationalism* (Chapel Hill: University of North Carolina Press, 1982); Walker Connor, *Ethno-nationalism: The Quest for Understanding* (Princeton: Princeton University Press, 1994); John Hutchinson, *The Dynamics of Cultural Nationalism* (London: Allen & Unwin, 1987); and Anthony D. Smith, *The Ethnic Origins of Nations* (Oxford: Oxford University Press, 1986).

[122] Anderson, *Imagined Communities*, 5.

classify 'it' as *an* ideology."[123] The "imagined community" is a tacitly shared cultural script, rather than an ideology. Yet, at the same time, as nationalism came to replace earlier hierarchical orderings of society, ideologies became essential for reinventing the political order so that modern nations came to be built on philosophical bases. While not reducible to an ideology *per se*, nationalism nevertheless requires an ideological basis to exist.

The intertwining of nationalist thought and ideology is a recurring theme in modern Cambodia, where successive political projects have attempted to realize widely different political systems by pairing their national imaginings with more or less genuinely held ideological beliefs. This reflects how the introduction of modern nationalist imaginings was accompanied by the spread of universal political ideologies as standardized building blocks of modern political discourse. Anderson writes that the "planetary spread of nationalism" was accompanied by the spread of a "profoundly standardized conception of politics."[124] This shift necessitated its own discursive bases, which, as a rule, were created through the translation of key concepts of an emerging universal political discourse into vernaculars. The very notion of "politics" conceptualized as a separate domain, together with concepts such as "ideology" that this novel domain entailed, were coined as neologisms not long after the birth of Cambodian nationalism, in line with a pattern common to many Asian and African societies. The emergence of modern Khmer political discourse went hand in hand with imagining it as pertaining to the realm of *politics*, as a distinct domain of the *nation*.[125]

Yet, ever since the emergence of national thinking, the very notion of ideology has been a contested category in Cambodia, which has been understood and employed differently by Cambodian political actors relative to their Western counterparts. Contemporary politicians also employ other categories to articulate political imaginations, such as ideas of embodiment, enmeshed in historical ideas of representation, which have persisted and been reinvented by political actors. This book unveils a contemporary contest over the very categories used to define political vision and national representation, positing the doctrinal against the incarnate. This challenges Anderson's insistence on the homogenizing force of modern political discourse in a universal language of ideology. By examining these ambiguities, this book offers a reinterpretation of Cambodian political thought and the notion of "ideology" in the contemporary setting.

Part of the difficulty in discussing political imaginings in the contemporary Cambodian context relates to the inadequacy of employing "political ideology" in an unproblematized manner. This, in turn, is indicative of the more fundamental problem of applying "ideology" as an axis of analysis, anchored in historical ambiguities derived from the fact that "ideology" is an imported concept. In neighboring Thailand, Michelle Tan finds that the term "ideology" has "never found

---

[123] Ibid.

[124] Benedict Anderson, *The Spectre of Comparisons: Nationalism, Southeast Asia, and the World* (London: Verso, 1998), 29.

[125] For Anderson, two provisions enabled the imagination of "politics" as a distinctly demarcated domain of life. First, "social practices and institutions need[ed] to be set up which could not be cloaked in earlier vocabularies pertaining to cosmologically and religiously sustained kingship." Second, the world had to "be understood as one," so that "politics" was something taking place everywhere at the same time, albeit in the context of different social and political systems. Ibid., 32.

equivalents in Thai across its various incarnations."[126] She explores the word *udomkān* as a problematic translation of political "ideology" and finds that, rather than the domestication of the foreign term "ideology," there has been an ideology of *udomkān* as a parallel, Thai intellectual construct. [127] Thailand, arguably, is marked by the absence of ideology. This differs sharply from the Cambodian case, which could be said to have an excess of ideology. Yet Tan's warning against cross-country comparisons of "coding political factions along universal standards of coherence, contrast, or temporal stability" is also pertinent to the Cambodian context.[128] In Cambodia, as in Thailand, political standpoints since the spread of Western political discourse have had to be coded into the language of ideological belief, while not always corresponding to Western mainstream understanding of the notion in terms of coherence, contrast, or stability over time. In Khmer, the standard translation of "ideology" is *monokom vichea*, from Sanskrit and Pali (Sanskrit, *mono*: "idea," "mind"; Pali, *kom* (*gama*): "associated"; Sanskrit, *vichea*: "knowledge").[129] Similar meanings are regularly transmitted through the suffix *-niyum* (Sanskrit: "to tend to"), translated as "-ism"; *litthi*, "beliefs"; and *tossânah*, "vision" or "viewpoint." The suffix *-niyum* was first used in this fashion by early nationalists to produce concepts for political self-identification that could readily be translated as "-isms," and thereby readily identified as more or less coherent ideologies. Edwards discusses a 1938 editorial in the journal *Nagaravatta*, linked to early Buddhist nationalism, that explains the journal's name by reference to *khmer-niyum*, "Khmerism."[130] Under the 1950 Cultural Commission, *-niyum*, by then already established, was officially defined as "-ism" (French, *-isme*).[131] The rendering of "ideology" in Khmer has been closely tied to different political projects, cast in the particular terms appropriate to the interpretation advanced by different actors. Cambodian communists from the Khmer Issarak era onward used the alternative translation of *sate-aram*, in what

---

[126] Michelle Tan, "Passing over in Silences: Ideology, Ideals, and Ideas in Thai Translation," *Journal of Southeast Asian Studies* 43, no. 1 (2012): 32.

[127] Ibid.

[128] Ibid.

[129] Keng Vannsak proposed that "ideology" be translated as *mono nimman vichya* (from Sanskrit, *mono*/"idea," *nimman* /"formation," *vichea*/"knowledge"). See Keng Vannsak, *Principes de Creation des Mots Nouveaux* (Phnom Penh: Faculté des Lettres, 1964), 336. However, that suggestion has not been popularly used or known. In Thai, apart from *udom kar*, two other terms, very similar to Khmer counterparts, are used for ideology: *mono keti vichya* and *lathi kwam chheu*. Khmer *outdom kote* shares a similar etymology to Thai *udomkān*, but has largely maintained the meaning of "ideal" or "idealism," rather than the conflation between idea and ideal that Tan identifies in the Thai context. Compare to: Sar Sartun, *Vappathor neung Areythor Khmer* [*Khmer Culture and Civilization*] ([Publisher unknown.], 1970); Hun Kim Sea, "Picharana Deumbei Yol pi Takkavichea [A Synthesis of Logic]," *Kampuja Suriya*, 1967; and Ministry of Education, *Sâttheanukrom khemara yeanokâm* [*Fundamental Khmer Dictionary*] ([city, publisher unknown], 1973).

[130] Pach Choeun coined what Penny Edwards refers to as the "ideology" of *khmer niyum*, a notion that was later taken up by Lon Nol during the Khmer Republic. See: Penny Edwards, *Cambodge*, 218; and compare to Lon, *Le Neo-Khmerisme*.

[131] Judith J. Jacob, "The Deliberate Use of Foreign Vocabulary by the Khmer: Changing Fashions, Methods, and Sources," in *Cambodian Linguistics, Literature and History: Collected Articles*, ed. Judith J. Jacob and David A. Smyth (London: School of Oriental and African Studies, 1993), 159.

seems to be a fairly direct translation of the Vietnamese *tư tưởng*, literally, "thought."[132]

Studying the nature and role of ideology in the post-independence Cambodian state, Slocomb has named the contemporary era "post-ideological." She contrasts "30 years of ideology" between 1955 and 1984 with a contemporary abandonment of ideology by the Cambodian state, marked by Hun Sen's 1985 accession to the post of prime minister.[133] Yet this obscures ambiguities in the concept of "ideology" in the Cambodian context, both before and after the sharp divide that she draws. The discrepancy between the Western idea of ideology and the way that indigenous actors have conceptualized their political projects, while using some of this language, was manifest from the outset. One illuminating example is Sihanouk's ambivalent response. Sihanouk argued that post-independence Cambodia needed a political and social ideology for the purpose of nation-building, and portrayed the creation of the Sangkum Reastr Niyum as the response to this need.[134] Yet at the same time, Sihanouk was deeply distrustful of the French concept of *idéologie* and was even said to "hate ideologies like The Plague."[135] In an article entitled "Le Sihanoukisme," published in Sihanouk's Sangkum Reastr Niyum-era mouthpiece *Sangkum*, Tep Chhieu Kheng describes Sihanouk's viewpoint as follows:

> To define the political line of Samdech Euv,[136] the neologism "Sihanoukism" has been forged. Is it a doctrine? A new philosophy? Or a new ideology? In fact, Sihanouk had no part in the formation of the new term. Wary of the establishment mindset, he deliberately avoided words ending in "ism" that express a general trend, a profession of faith which is a little too categorical. But the new term has been introduced. It is good to try to analyze it. If not a doctrine or a philosophy, nor an ideology, what is it? "Sihanoukism" is an attempt, but a successful attempt, to grasp reality, to capture the fact from life in its authenticity and dynamism. It is also a way of being, a sort of way of life, a *savoire-faire* for the Khmer people and for all placed in the same situation. When we speak of "Sihanoukism" it is almost always evoked in political terms. But it is not valid in this area only. Some other areas (social or religious) have for their part their field of application.[137]

This illustrates the conflict inherent to Sihanouk's embrace of the "-ism" that had been coined, and simultaneous continued attachment to the idea that he embodied the nation, at a breaking point when the language of ideology had become hegemonic in world politics.

Contemporary politicians generally avoid the language of "political ideology" in the Western sense of a grand, totalizing corpus of principles. In political discourse, *monokum vichea* is virtually absent. There are, however, other notions that political

---

[132] Steve Heder, personal communication, February 26, 2012.

[133] Slocomb, "The Nature and Role of Ideology in the Modern Cambodian State," 388.

[134] Norodom Sihanouk, "Notre Sangkum," *Le Monde*, October 8, 1963; and Slocomb, "The Nature and Role of Ideology in the Modern Cambodian State," 378.

[135] Tep Chhieu Kheng, "Le 'Sihanoukisme,'" *Sangkum* 41 (1968) (author's translation from French).

[136] An epithet for Sihanouk.

[137] Tep, "Le 'Sihanoukisme,'" 8.

actors employ to explicate their political thinking (*kumnit noyobay*) that do not imply a totalizing ideology in the Western sense, reflecting the particular problems such a construct poses in the contemporary Cambodian context. The incumbent CPP has refrained from substituting its former communist identity with adherence to any other grand ideology. Yet Hun Sen has outlined his political thinking by reference to his political vision, *tossânah noyobay*. CNRP leaders, meanwhile, state that their agenda does not correspond to any one ideology, either socialist or liberal, while incorporating aspects of both; this reflects a fundamental pragmatism that defies any such categorization.[138]

The frustration of framing contemporary political thinking as "ideology" is most clearly manifest in royalist debates. "Royalism," *reachniyum*, forms one category of political self-identification. The closest to a mutually agreed understanding of what this concept means is the corollary notion of "Sihanoukism," *Sihanoukniyum*. Yet Sihanoukism, ever since the creation of the term, has related to ideas that the person of Sihanouk has a unique mandate. Contemporary contestation of royalist discourse has come to center precisely on whether Sihanoukism is to be understood as an ideology in the Western sense, detached from Sihanouk, or if it remains linked to Sihanouk himself and, by extension, the royal family. This testifies to how constructs with the suffix *-niyum* cannot be translated into "ideology" in the Western sense without further qualifications. Pointing to how these questions remain unresolved in the present day, it perhaps also indicates that a Western-style interpretation of what an "ideology" necessarily must be has gained increasing legitimacy, much to the detriment of royalists as a political force.

Although the notion of "political ideology" thus remains an ambiguous concept, modern political actors have selectively employed Western-derived political concepts in their discourse, while also embracing, to different extents, Western-derived ideologies.[139] The process of incorporating foreign-derived political notions into the Cambodian context can be understood following Anderson and Thongchai Winichakul. Rejecting notions of "imitation and derivative discourses," Anderson charges that Western concepts were "read about and modeled from," resulting in a hybridized political discourse. The resultant neologisms and the original Western concepts clearly did not mean exactly the same thing, but still "stood in for [one] another."[140] In his writing on the "transculturation" of politically charged Western concepts in Siam during the period of colonialism in the region, Winichakul similarly suggests that European ideas and practices were appropriated, localized, and hybridized in the Siamese setting.[141] Winichakul makes the point that "the success of the transliterated term indicates that there are needs in the Thai context

---

[138] Compare to author's interview with Tioulong Saumura.

[139] Sihanouk's Buddhist Socialism and the Khmer Rouge can be considered two extremes in this regard, both in terms of the degree of adaptation of the Western concepts and the sincerity with which they promoted them. Sihanouk's Buddhist Socialism, created as an indigenous Cambodian doctrine that entailed some Western-derived notions, such as "socialism," essentially upheld the status quo. The Khmer Rouge turned Cambodian society upside down in its quest, however misguided, to faithfully implement their Marxist–Leninist models.

[140] Anderson, *The Spectre of Comparisons*, 34.

[141] Thongchai Winichakul, "The Quest for 'Siwilai': A Geographical Discourse of Civilizational Thinking in the Late Nineteenth and Early Twentieth-Century Siam," *Journal of Asian Studies* 59, no. 3 (2000), 529.

for such a concept, but that there is no adequate substitute for it."[142] That is, the survival of the concept indicates that it responds to something that some actors in society wish to express, yet the transliterated form retains a trace of the foreignness of the concept, and there is never complete overlap between the neologism and the original foreign concept.

In Cambodia, contesting the emerging modern political concepts was, from the outset, part of a wider political contestation to articulate the political contents of the young nation. French officials and Francophone Khmer under King Sisowath (r. 1904–27) together formulated concepts of a Cambodian "nation," "soul," and "race." While French remained the language of incipient nationalism, the vernacularization of Khmer was envisaged as an integral part of the nation-building project.[143] In 1927, the first Khmer-language newspaper, *Kambuja Suriya*, was produced by the Royal Library, followed by the emergence, in the 1930s, of the first quasi-political newspapers, magazines, and novels in Khmer, including the "flagship publication" of the early nationalist movement, *Nagaravatta*, in 1936.[144] This confirmed Anderson's emphasis on the importance of print media in the vernacular for the early stages of nationalism.[145] *Nagaravatta*'s contributors advocated the use of the Khmer language to spread *Khmer-niyum*, and called for Khmer to be used as the official language and language of education. Neologisms were coined based on the translation of French terms into Khmer, often by Buddhist scholars proficient in French, Sanskrit, Pali, and Khmer—and many such neologisms turned out to be what Heder has called "Pali–Sanskrit jawbreakers," unintelligible to virtually everyone.[146] In the period leading up to independence, linguistic divisions accompanied political and geographic divisions, producing three "political dialects" with parallel vocabularies. Most aristocratic youth in Phnom Penh favored continued Francophonia, whereas some democrat nationalists wished to raise the standard of elite-level Khmer.[147] A second political dialect was developed by the anticolonial and anti-royalist Khmer Issarak movement, which created a communist Khmer language by translating basic Soviet and Maoist terms into Khmer, often using Pali or Sanskrit, and throwing in some Thai-isms influenced by Thai Marxism.[148] Current Khmer concepts of democracy (*pracheathipatey*), communism (*litthi kommuynis*), feudalism (*sâkdephoum niyum*), and revolution (*padevott*) closely follow the respective

---

[142] Ibid., 530.

[143] Steve Heder, "Cambodia," in *Language and National Identity in Asia*, ed. Andrew Simpson (Oxford: Oxford University Press, 2007), 294.

[144] Harris, *Cambodian Buddhism*, 137–38; and Edwards, *Cambodge*, 188.

[145] Edwards *Cambodge*, 188; and Anderson, *Imagined Communities*, 37–46.

[146] Heder, "Cambodia," 296.

[147] Ibid.

[148] Ibid., 297–98. In neighboring Thailand, the translation of key political and ideological words was similarly a highly contested issue, where, from the 1920s to the mid-1940s, the invention of official Thai neologisms discriminated against, retranslated, or "pretranslated" radical discourse. Thai Prince Wan invented a range of political coinages, some very similar to Khmer counterparts, including *sangkhom* ("society"), *nayobai* ("policy"), *rabob* ("system"), *patiwat* ("revolution"), *wiwat* ("evolution"), *kammachip* ("proletariat"), *kradumphi* ("bourgeoisie"), *mualchon* ("masses"), *sangkhomniyom* ("socialism"), *ongkan* ("organization"), *sahaphap* ("union"), *watthanatham* ("culture"), and *wiphak* ("critique"). See Kasian Tejapira, "Commodifying Marxism: The Formation of Modern Thai Radical Culture, 1927–1958" (PhD dissertation, Cornell University, 1992 [Ann Arbor: University Microfilms, 1994]), 198.

Thai translations.[149] They prioritized colloquial Khmer over Vietnamese words, avoided polysyllabic Pali–Sanskritisms, and did away with social hierarchy markers. This communist language, Heder writes, was accessible to peasants and was rapidly popularized. A third competing political dialect was developed by the republican-leaning "Populo Movement" (*pracheachalana*), largely purged of royalisms, yet maintaining other social hierarchy markers and elite neologisms while adding its own distinct political terminology. In this way, parallel concepts were expressed through different words, according to political geography. For example, "the people" were referred to by the Franco-aristocratic elite as the *precheareastr*, "the subjects"; by the communist Issarak as the *pracheachon*, the simplest formulation for "people"; and by the republicans as *pracheapol roath*, or "popular citizens." Reference to either of the three indicated which warring political side one was on, for peasants and elite alike.[150] Tellingly, today these three terms are still employed to different extents by different factions, so that royalists will typically use the notion *precheareastr*, the CPP *pracheachon*, and democrats *pracheapol roath*.

In this context, the state set out to create and define a new "Khmer" vocabulary of more than three thousand terms as the language of independence, regarded as Khmer, but deliberately using foreign vocabulary.[151] A cultural commission produced what was known as "cultural words" (*peak voppothor*), published by the ministry of education in the 1950 dictionary *Sâttheanukrom phearom khmer*, as well as in *Kambuja Suriya*. French words in need of translation were compiled, and the commission then took either a French loan word and "matched" it to the relevant French word, or created a new word using Sanskrit and Pali. The degrees of overlap between the neologisms and existing Khmer and French words varied and worked in different directions. In some cases, the new words were intended to cover only some meanings of the French word being translated, while in other cases they were intended to translate the full array of meanings.[152] The collection included political terms with an "aura of newness" in the Khmer context,[153] such as "independence," which the cultural commission wanted to coin as *issarapheap* ("powerfulness," "condition of overlordship"), but was more popularly translated as *aekareach* ("single kingdom," "one power"), still in use today. The notion of *setthi* was introduced as "rights."[154] An old Khmer word, *omnach*, which had referred to "power" in an abstract sense, also took on the secondary meanings of the French equivalent, *pouvoir*, so that it came to include the meaning of a "powerful state." New

---

[149] Compare to how Thai scholars have explored the problematic translations of *prachatipatai* ("democracy") (Connors, *Democracy and National Identity in Thailand* and Tejapira, "Commodifying Marxism," 198), *khommiunit* ("communist") (Tejapira, "Commodifying Marxism," 197), *sakdina/saktina* ("feudalism") (Craig J. Reynolds, *Thai Radical Discourse: The Real Face of Thai Feudalism Today* [Ithaca: Cornell University Southeast Asia Program Publications, 1987] and Craig J. Reynolds, *Seditious Histories: Contesting Thai and Southeast Asian Pasts* [Seattle: University of Washington Press, 2006]), and *patiwat* ("revolution") (Thak Chaloemtiarana, *Thailand: The Politics of Despotic Paternalism* [Ithaca: Cornell University Southeast Asia Program Publications, rev. ed., 2007], 167, 214, and Tejapira, "Commodifying Marxism," 197).

[150] Heder, "Cambodia," 297–98.

[151] Jacob, "The Deliberate Use of Foreign Vocabulary by the Khmer," 157.

[152] Ibid., 158.

[153] Ibid., 157.

[154] Ibid., 159.

vocabulary also confirmed the previous coinage of the "nation" as *cheat*, as well as concepts for making a Marxist-style class analysis, including "worker" (*kâmmokâr*), "farmer" (*kâsekâr*), and "imperialist" (*châkrâpotte*). This new vocabulary was implemented in newspapers from the 1950s onward.[155] During the Sangkum Reastr Niyum, prompted by urban graduates' translation of their political ideas into Khmer, Sihanouk resumed efforts toward standardized Khmerization of political language.[156] These began in 1967 with a National Committee of Khmerization, which published a glossary providing new or standardized Khmer translations for French terms. Sihanouk also supported his political strategy on the spread of a particular Sihanoukist lingo, disseminated through village speeches, leaflets, and radio, breaking with the previous confinement of the royal word to the palace. The Sihanoukist phraseology set out to strengthen ties between the people and its leadership through a range of linguistic and discursive devices.[157] The successive regimes of the Khmer Republic, Democratic Kampuchea, and the People's Republic of Kampuchea all created their particular vocabulary.[158]

Just as the discursive contestation of political concepts formed an integral part of the debate over the nature of the Khmer nation ever since the emergence of the idea of *cheat*, so in the post-PPA era it continues to be central to contemporary reimaginations of it. This book uncovers how an important part of contemporary political contestation takes place through political actors manipulating and rearticulating concepts long central to modern political discourse—such as democracy, socialism, royalism, class struggle, and freedom rights—and mobilizing them so as to support different claims to represent the nation. There is also an ongoing process of new coinages, often derived from liberal democratic discourse, which sometimes entail a productive hybridization.[159] References to these concepts should not be evaluated as part of coherent or stable universal "ideologies," but more fruitfully in terms of their context of articulation, their particular histories of meaning, and, in particular, how they link back to the nation.[160]

---

[155] Ibid.

[156] Heder, "Cambodia," 299–300.

[157] See Nasir Abdoul-Carime, "Réflexion sur le Régime Sihanoukien: La Monopolisation du Verbe par le Pouvoir Royal," *Péninsule* 31, no. 2 (1995): 77–97. Abdoul-Carime identifies the "abrupt humanization of political authority," a passionate, theatrical, and warm language, and the fusion of interests between Sihanouk and the people as some of the innovations of Sihanoukist phraseology.

[158] Heder, "Cambodia," 302.

[159] One example is the notion of "good governance," which entered the region with the financial crisis of 1997–98. In late 1999, it was translated into Khmer as *kar krop krong l'or*, but was later substituted for *aphibal kech* (*aphi* "high," *bal* "upholder," *kech* "affairs," "duty"), which, first heard in a 2002 Hun Sen speech, has remained the standard translation ever since. (Touch Bora, personal communication, February 26, 2012.) Another example is the concept of human rights, *setthi monus*, introduced with the PPA. Judy Ledgerwood and Kheang Un find that this concept was not "grafted onto" an existing political discourse, but, rather, a hybrid was created as local human rights organizations employed Buddhist ideas of morality when translating it. See Judy Ledgerwood and Kheang Un, "Global Concepts and Local Meaning: Human Rights and Buddhism in Cambodia," *Journal of Human Rights* 2, no. 4 (2003), 531–49.

[160] Often, insufficient attention is paid to these concepts' histories of meaning. For example, the seemingly novel language of "freedom rights" precedes the post-1991 inflow of global vocabulary discussed by Ledgerwood and Un (see "Global Concepts and Local Meaning"). Jacob quotes the comedy *Sombok ot me pa* ("A nest without the parents"), by Hang Thon Hak,

OUTLINE OF THE BOOK

This book maps out the national imaginings advanced in Cambodia since 1993 by political actors with an institutional base in Cambodia's main political parties competing electorally in the KOC multiparty democratic system. It examines these as three contending sets of post-PPA political actors: the CPP, royalist parties, and democratic parties. This categorization follows Cambodian political discourse and corresponds to how political actors self-define. A fourth major political force in Second Kingdom Cambodia, the Khmer Rouge, is not included. This is because the Khmer Rouge did not compete electorally in the KOC. While the Khmer Rouge were signatories of the PPA, their concerns that a neutral political environment had not been ensured led them to boycott the 1993 elections and reject its results.[161] In 1994, the Khmer Rouge movement was declared illegal.[162] In response, the Khmer Rouge set up the Provisional Government of National Union and National Salvation of Cambodia (PGNUNSC), an unrecognized government in opposition to the KOC. The Khmer Rouge thereafter engaged in ongoing guerrilla warfare until the movement's disintegration in 1998.

The second chapter of this book examines a narrative promoted by Prime Minister Hun Sen of the CPP. It is argued that the narrative testifies to the increasing personalization of political and symbolic power to the prime minister. At the same time, as the prime minister of subsequent CPP-led governments and vice president of the CPP, Hun Sen's renegotiation of his political identity bears on CPP legitimacy. Chapter 3 turns to examine royalist imaginings of the nation. It includes actors associated with political parties that claimed a royalist identity, including FUNCINPEC, Norodom Ranariddh Party (NRP), and the Sangkum Jatiniyum Front Party (SJFP). Chapter 4 examines the national imaginings of actors associated with self-identified democratic parties, with roots in a political faction associated with an anti-Vietnamese, anti-Communist identity. This includes the Sam Rainsy Party (SRP), the Buddhist Liberal Democratic Party (BLDP), the Son Sann Party, the Human Rights Party (HRP), and the Cambodia National Rescue Party (CNRP).

Each chapter employs a slightly different focus. The second chapter deals with the politics of memory, the political use of art, and how historical myths and legends are used in creating, renegotiating, and disseminating national imaginings. The following chapter charts the difficulty in transposing historical ideas of the nation's political representation associated with the monarchy to a party political vehicle. It offers a case study of the process of transferring a pre-party political language and grammar of national representation to the party political framework with an associated language of ideology and doctrine. The next chapter more specifically reassesses domestic debates about democratization. While all chapters

---

in which one of the young characters speaks the sentence, "Give me the right (*setthi*) to have the freedom (*seripheap*) to fulfill my duty (*kâroneykâch*) with justice (*yuttethor*), boldness, and heroism (*viropheap*)." While Jacob does not provide the year in which the play was written, each of these words, including the notions of rights and of freedom, were typical of the New Vocabulary created by the cultural commission in the 1950s. See Jacob, "The Deliberate Use of Foreign Vocabulary by the Khmer," 163.

161 Roberts, *Political Transition in Cambodia 1991–99*, 93–103.

162 David P. Chandler, *Brother Number One: A Political Biography of Pol Pot* (Oxford: Westview Press, 1999), 179.

outline and discuss the intersection of domestic Cambodian national and democratic imaginings, this chapter offers a focused examination of this nexus. Beyond the confined discussions pertaining to the individual chapters, a larger debate emerges across the chapters. From different angles, these discussions are concerned with the contours and characteristics of the nation and how the nation is to be represented by the political leadership, entailing questions of the nature of democracy, constructions of the people, elected versus inherited leadership, embodiment, and, ultimately, continuity and change in such conceptualizations. In the concluding chapter, I pull these strands together to reassess political contestation in the Kingdom of Cambodia.

NOTES ON SOURCES

This book is the outcome of a long and winding process of political ethnography, solidified by and made sense of through historical interpretation that draws on a large amount of archival sources. I carried out ethnographic research between 2009 and 2011, which was complemented by another prolonged stay in Cambodia in 2013–2014. During this time, I immersed myself in the circles of national-level politicians, gaining access to the leadership and members of all main political parties. Deep immersion in the thrilling, sometimes mind-blowingly frivolous, and most often stern, no-nonsense world of the political center—the proverbial eye of the storm—allowed me to develop an understanding of the worldview of various political actors. This was complemented by around eight semi-structured, discursive interviews with key politicians.

These central players involved in shaping the contemporary Cambodian political landscape were interviewed in person, sometimes on two or more occasions. Interviews were carried out in three languages: Khmer, English, and French. Official translators, who provided Khmer–English translation, often accompanied high-level government officials. Some interviewees, who had been schooled in the French language, preferred to be interviewed in French. These were elite interviews in both senses of the concept: referring to the socio-economic position of the respondent, and to the manner in which the interviewer treats the interviewee—as an expert on the topic at hand. The interviewees included political party leaders, members of parliament, and government officials. Rather than having to answer within the bounds set by predefined assumptions, interviewees were allowed to define the problems to be addressed. These elite interviews were a *sine qua non* for the purposes of this book. They provided an unparalleled insight into the mindset of political actors, their theoretical position, perceptions, beliefs, values, and attitudes.[163] Semi-structured interviews with open-ended questions allowed the interviewees to define the parameters of the discussion, to organize answers within their own frameworks, and to articulate their own worldviews without predetermined response categories. They also allowed me to probe into the reasoning, background, and assumptions underlying the answers.[164] In addition, these elite interviews unveiled some of the informal considerations that lie behind political practice.[165] They therefore shed light

---

[163] Compare to: Joel D. Aberbach and Bert A. Rockman, "Conducting and Coding Elite Interviews," *PS: Political Science and Politics* 35, no. 4 (2002), 673; and David Richards, "Elite Interviewing: Approaches and Pitfalls," *Politics* 16, no. 3 (1996), 199–200.

[164] Compare to Aberbach and Rockman, "Conducting and Coding Elite Interviews," 674.

[165] Compare to Richards, "Elite Interviewing," 200.

on elements of recent political action that are not clear from other sources. Finally, these first-hand testimonies provided information not recorded elsewhere, compensating for scarce and limited documentary evidence.[166]

Elite interviews face special hurdles, of which none perhaps looms as large as problems of access, which easily cause severe bias.[167] I was fortunate to enjoy the enormous privilege of being granted interviews with the leaders of all main political parties, including: Prime Minister Hun Sen (CPP); Prince Norodom Ranariddh, long-term leader of FUNCINPEC and, at the time, president of the Norodom Ranariddh Party (NRP); Keo Puth Reasmey, then president of FUNCINPEC; and Sam Rainsy and Kem Sokha, then presidents of SRP and HRP, respectively, now both leaders of the CNRP. One of the main values of this book, I believe, lies in the unique array of information assembled from these and other key contemporary politicians. The reliability of the interviewee, particularly how the interviewee presents his or her own viewpoint in a favorable way, and, ultimately, controls the information passed on, is another typical hurdle.[168] This problem is less of a concern for research that traces the interviewees' points of view. In fact, since this is a study of meaning-making, the subjective nature of the information suitably addressed its objectives.[169]

In addition, I have ransacked archives, including the National Archives of Cambodia, the holdings of the Cambodian Senate Library and the Hun Sen library at the Royal University of Phnom Penh (RUPP), documents passed on from the archives of the various political parties, and the personal archives of politicians themselves. The political writings of politicians, including published books by Hun Sen and Norodom Ranariddh, which, to my knowledge, have not been consulted in other academic analyses, proved to be an unexploited-by-others treasure. Another interesting source was the autobiographies and memoirs many politicians have taken to writing. I have also referred to Cambodian media, extensively reviewing newspaper articles, as well as reports, statements, studies, and pamphlets published by political parties, the government, and non-governmental organizations. Perhaps most unexpectedly, contemporary statues provided another, quietly arresting, source. I have also engaged in close reading of Cambodian historical sources, including chronicle texts. These primary sources were then studied against the backdrop of relevant, larger secondary literature, to enable a historically informed interpretation of contemporary dynamics. These written sources were also used to cross-check interview data in order to support the findings, situate these in context, and guard against self-serving accounts.[170]

---

[166] Ibid.; and Philip H. J. Davies, "Spies as Informants: Triangulation and the Interpretation of Elite Interview Data in the Study of the Intelligence and Security Services," *Politics* 21, no. 1 (2001), 74.

[167] Richards, "Elite Interviewing," 201.

[168] Ibid.

[169] Compare to Jeffrey M. Berry, "Validity and Reliability Issues in Elite Interviewing," *PS: Political Science and Politics* 35, no. 4 (2002): 680.

[170] Compare to Oisín Tansey, "Process Tracing and Elite Interviewing: A Case for Non-probability Sampling," *PS: Political Science and Politics* 40, no. 4 (2007), 766; and Davies, "Spies as Informants," 73.

NOTE ON TRANSLATION AND TRANSCRIPTION

Throughout this book I base transcriptions on the Franco–Khmer transcription system, which was set forward by Franklin E. Huffman in 1983, building on an earlier transcription system employed by the French in the colonial period. The main advantage of the system is that it closely follows Khmer pronunciation.[171] Whereas the Franco–Khmer transcription system, as originally devised, included many diacritics to distinguish between different vowel sounds, academic works of recent years have tended to drop many of these. Transcriptions in this book follow the Franco–Khmer transcription system as reproduced by Heder and Ledgerwood.[172] This chart retains only one of the original diacritics (â).

All translations from Khmer and French language sources, unless otherwise stated, are my own.

---

[171] Marston and Guthrie, eds., *History, Buddhism, and New Religious Movements in Cambodia*, ix; and see pages ix–x for a discussion of the comparative advantages of the Franco–Khmer transcription system versus the Pou system (Saveros Lewitz, "Note sur la Translittération du Cambodgien," *Bulletin de l'École Française d'Extrême-Orient* 55 [1969], 163–69).

[172] Heder and Ledgerwood, *Propaganda, Politics, and Violence in Cambodia*, xvii.

CHAPTER TWO

OF HUN SEN:
THE SDECH KÂN NARRATIVE

At the helm of the Cambodian nation since 1985, Hun Sen has made an impression on it that is unsurpassed by any of his contemporaries. As the country transitioned from a one-party socialist republic, he continuously dominated the new multiparty democratic system as premier. Yet Hun Sen claims to represent the nation not only on the basis of being its elected prime minister. One of Hun Sen's most elaborate attempts to link his own destiny to that of the nation has been to invoke the name of Sdech Kân, a controversial historical figure who rose to occupy the throne after killing a supposedly unjust king. Through this story, Hun Sen uproots the idea of kingship itself—accommodating his claim to personally embody the nation.

On July 5–6, 1997, Cambodia's first prime minister, Prince Norodom Ranariddh, was overthrown by Second Prime Minister Hun Sen, ending their co-premiership and the coalition government, installed in 1993, of the royalist party (FUNCINPEC) and the Cambodian People's Party. A few years later, a striking new narrative started spreading in Cambodia. This centered on the idea that the life of Prime Minister Hun Sen was intimately connected with that of sixteenth-century King Sdech Kân, a man of the people who rose through his own prowess to topple the reigning king, Srey Sokonthor Bât. Although this was always suggested implicitly, the idea conveyed was that the prime minister was the reincarnation of the legendary king.

Beginning with the 1993 reinstatement of the monarchy and a multiparty system, a rickety relationship had developed between the royalists and the CPP. With the reinstated monarchy, "nation, religion, king" (cheat, sasana, mohaksatr) became the national motto of the new, second Kingdom of Cambodia. These three notions and their historical precursors stand at the center of historical Cambodian imaginations of power and moral order.[1] The Sdech Kân narrative can be understood as Prime Minister Hun Sen's bid to remold the relationship between the nation, religion, and the monarchy in his favor, using a potent cultural legend that invokes a deeply ingrained tension between inherited and non-inherited leadership within Khmer Buddhist kingship. The narrative is in this way central to reworking the boundaries of power in the second kingdom, between the monarchy and the royalist faction on one hand, and the CPP and, primarily, Hun Sen, on the other.

For all its particularity, the narrative of Sdech Kân has wider Southeast Asian resonances. In Burma, Thailand, and Laos, for example, historical kings have been used to bolster political legitimacy, at the same time as the idea of reincarnation has

---

[1] Heng Monychenda, "In Search of the Dhammika Ruler," in Kent and Chandler, *People of Virtue*, 310.

spread.[2] As examples of "performative politics," each of these interacts with the fabric of political, historiographical, and moral imaginations of their polities in different ways. The alleged reincarnation of Sdech Kân carries meanings and consequences that are particular to the contemporary Cambodian context. Hun Sen's claim to incarnation attempts to remodel the "ideal" configuration of political power in contemporary Cambodia so as to ensure that he emerges uniquely placed to represent the nation.

Linking Hun Sen to the Sdech Kân narrative accords Hun Sen an exclusive role in standing in for the nation. Naturally, as the prime minister of successive CPP-led governments, Hun Sen's legitimacy-seeking strategies necessarily affect the standing of the CPP. Yet, this narrative carries claims on behalf of Hun Sen, rather than of the CPP as a party. It is therefore complicit in the personalization of symbolic and political power to Hun Sen, and can be understood in the context of Hun Sen's consolidation of power not only vis-à-vis rival political parties, but also within the CPP. Prior to reinstating the constitutional monarchy, the then State of Cambodia leaders tried to assert their legitimacy as rulers of Cambodia by seizing control of the right to define the concepts "nation," "religion," and "king" to their own advantage. The triumvirate of Hun Sen, Heng Samrin, and Chea Sim acted as kings ceremonially and politically.[3] In offering a further redefinition of kingship, the Sdech Kân narrative makes new claims that go beyond those of the SOC period. By engaging with historical ideas of kingship, the Sdech Kân narrative posits Hun Sen as the legitimate national leader.[4] Hun Sen's performance of Sdech Kân inserts him into a series of associations implied by Khmer Buddhist ideas of the king having multiple substitute bodies, ideas that continue to hold sway. By standing in for kingship, Hun Sen stands in for the nation itself.

---

[2] In Burma, Than Schwe was rumored to believe himself to be the reincarnation of a Burmese monarch, and styled himself this way. See "Burma: The End of an Era or a Dynasty's Beginning?" *Irrawaddy*, January 26, 2011. In Laos, the socialist state uses the legacy of ancient Lao kingdoms for self-legitimization, incorporating pre-colonial kings into an "official national hero pantheon." See Grabowsky and Tappe, "Important Kings of Laos." In Thailand, Irene Stengs (*Worshipping the Great Moderniser*) finds that the cult of King Chulalongkorn, peaking in the 1990s, exalted expectations on King Bhumibol, so that images of and veneration for Bhumibol gradually came to replace that of Chulalongkorn, thus testifying to the interconnectedness of the two as ideal personifications of "modern Buddhist kingship." General Sonthi, leader of the 2006 coup, had in his turn been identified by a "political" astrologer as the reincarnation of a general under King Taksin who had saved the nation after Ayutthaya's fall in 1767, therefore being destined to save the Thai nation yet again. See Pasuk Phongpaichit and Chris Baker, "The Spirits, the Stars, and Thai Politics," lecture presented at the Siam Society, Bangkok, Thailand, December 2, 2008.

[3] Ledgerwood, "Ritual in 1990 Cambodian Political Theatre," 213, 216–20.

[4] Steve Heder identifies three "claims of qualification to rule" in postcolonial Cambodia: being *sdech* ("king" or "prince"), a title associated with the royal family; *neak cheh doeng*, a person with much education; and *neak tâsou*, a person who has taken part in armed struggle. Hun Sen routinely portrays himself as a military figure, *neak tâsou*. His claims to being a *neak cheh doeng* are epitomized by his election into the Royal Academy of Cambodia (RAC) on April 28, 2010. Performing Sdech Kân can be seen as his ultimate claim to being *sdech*. See Heder, "Cambodia's Democratic Transition to Neoauthoritarianism," 425–29.

THE "ORIGINAL" NARRATIVE

Sdech Kân, also known by his royal name Preah Srey Chettha, is known in Khmer history as the commoner who became the leader of a popular uprising toppling King Srey Sokonthor Bât (r. 1504–12). Though several written versions of the story exist, Adhémard Leclère narrates the story of Sdech Kân as follows.[5] Kân belonged to the temple-servant class. When his sister was offered to Srey Sokonthor Bât as a concubine, Kân came to live in the royal palace where he soon built up a certain standing. One night in 1508, Srey Sokonthor Bât had a nightmare in which he saw an ominous *neak* (dragon) drive him out of the palace and wreak havoc on the kingdom. Gathering the members of the royal family and court dignitaries, who offered him candles and flower garlands, the king then had a vision of two dragons hovering around either side of Kân's head. Immediately thereafter, he received news of ominous signs from all parts of the kingdom. Perturbed, King Srey Sokonthor Bât gathered his fortune-tellers, who foresaw that he would be toppled by a man born in the year of the dragon, a man who would reign in the direction of the east. Given that Kân was indeed born in the year of the dragon, the king schemed to have Kân killed in what was to seem like a fishing accident. The king's ignoble plot failed, however, as Kân was warned of the danger by his sister, who had overheard the king's conversation. Escaping the king's trap, Kân fled eastward to build up an army. Marching against Srey Sokonthor Bât in 1512, Kân defeated the king, who was struck down by one of Kân's aides. Thereafter, Kân ruled benevolently over Cambodia, bringing order and prosperity. He introduced the first currency in the kingdom, the *sleung*, with the image of a dragon imprinted on it. However, in 1516, a few years into his reign, a civil war broke out, which ended in 1525 with Sdech Kân being killed by the soldiers of King Chânt Reachea. The story allows plenty of space for interpretation as to whether Kân was a traitor or a just warrior rising against an unjust king. Historians have dwelt on the Sdech Kân story because it reflects on what Michel Tranet calls the "psycho-sociological reality" of Cambodian history, while aspiring to historical truth-value.[6]

CHANGING IDEAS OF KINGSHIP

In establishing himself as *the* national leader with a tight grip over most aspects of the polity, Hun Sen can be thought to have (after a hiatus) replaced Sihanouk—the other defining presence at the helm of post-independence Cambodia. Similarities between Hun Sen's and Sihanouk's leadership styles—a mixture of the

---

[5] Adhémard Leclère, *Histoire du Cambodge Depuis le 1ᵉʳ Siècle de Notre Ère, d'Après les Inscriptions Lapidaires: Les Annales Chinoises et Annamites et les Documents Européens des Six Derniers Siècles* (Paris: Paul Guethner, 1914): 235–78. The account given in Adhémard Leclère, "Le Sdech Kân," *Bulletin de la Société des Études Indochinoises (BSEI)* 59 (1910): 17–55, is largely identical, but omits King Srey Sokonthor Bât's dream. Leclère does not provide a reference for the text on which he based his account. But, see Eng Soth, *Aekâsar Mohaboros Khmer* [*Documents on the great Khmer heroes*] (Paris: Association Culturelle Pierres d'Angkor, [1969] 1985), vol. 8–19, which largely mirrors Leclère's account as retold above, while providing a lengthier account of events. Leclère's 1910 article was reprinted in Michel Tranet, *Le Sdach Kan* (Phnom Penh: Atelier d'Impression Khmère, 2002). Khin Sok, ed. and trans., *Chroniques Royales du Cambodge—De Bañā Yāt à la Prise de Laṅvaek: de 1417 a 1595* (Paris: École Française d'Extrême-Orient, 1988), discusses Sdech Kân's reign, but does not retell the legend recounted above, for which Khin instead references Leclère's 1910 account (p. 258).

[6] Tranet, *Le Sdach Kan*, preface.

mercurial, the benign, and the heavy-handed—are thoroughgoing. Hun Sen has been a leader in the footsteps of Sihanouk, leading some to conclude that he sought legitimacy by setting out to impersonate Sihanouk. [7] Yet the performance of this narrative was something more than "staging Sihanouk."[8] The invocation of the name of Sdech Kân was a *mise-en-scène* of the idea of kingship itself.

Sdech Kân is known in Khmer historiography as the quintessential *neak mean bon* (man of merit). He is a famous and controversial figure who, after killing a supposedly unjust king, ascended the throne himself. By invoking him, the narrative engages with ideas of kingship itself.[9] These ideas are enmeshed in historical Cambodian Buddhist conceptualizations of authority and moral order, linking power to karmic laws of rebirth based on merit accrued in previous existences. Since the establishment of Theravada Buddhism as the dominant religion in the country, kingship has been bound up with the notion of *neak mean bon*.[10] The *neak mean bon* is associated with revolutionary activities, and typically refers to a man who rises to power through his own prowess. His right to rule is a consequence of the accumulation of good deeds in previous lives. When recognized, his merit bestows him with the legitimacy to take the fate of the country in his hands or to ascend the throne.[11] The *neak mean bon* is a potent cultural concept alive in Cambodian collective memory.[12]

Cambodian kingship was traditionally associated with extraordinary virtue, leading the country to prosperity.[13] The organic link between the moral behavior of the king and the welfare of the kingdom was conceptualized as a structure that, as in theories of kingship in many other parts of the world, presumed the unity of the physical, mortal body of the king, and his mystical body, the "body politic."[14] In Khmer Buddhist kingship, Ashley Thompson identifies the royal body as "one in a series of substitute bodies, including the Buddha and the stūpa, each being an image

[7] See, for example, Roberts, *Political Transition in Cambodia 1991–99*, 115–16.

[8] This phrase is taken from Ashley Thompson's talk "Staging Sihanouk," delivered at SOAS, University of London, November 2, 2010, on the Khmer-language production of Hélène Cixous's 1985 play, *The Terrible but Unfinished Story of Norodom Sihanouk, King of Cambodia* (Lincoln & London: University of Nebraska Press, 1994).

[9] Heder, "Political Theatre in the 2003 Cambodian Elections," 162, suggests that Hun Sen has "occasionally attempted to present himself as a *neak mean boun*," and quotes a 1993 UNTAC report. The reinvention of Sdech Kân is the first more or less coherent narrative to frame such claims.

[10] Harris, *Cambodian Buddhism*, 50. For a discussion of the historical Sdech Kân as a *neak mean bon*, see Khing Hoc Dy, "Neak Mean Boun, 'Être de Mérites' dans la culture et la littérature du Cambodge," *Péninsule* 56 (2008): 79–85. See also Ashley Thompson, "The Future of Cambodia's Past: A Messianic Middle-Period Cambodian Royal Cult," in Marston and Guthrie, *History, Buddhism, and New Religious Movements in Cambodia*, 13–39, on the *neak mean bon* during Cambodia's Middle Period (i.e., after the fall of Angkor and before the French protectorate, c. 1450–1863).

[11] Khing, "Neak Mean Boun," 71.

[12] Ibid.

[13] Ashley Thompson, "The Suffering of Kings: Substitute Bodies, Healing, and Justice in Cambodia," in Marston and Guthrie, *History, Buddhism, and New Religious Movements in Cambodia*, 91–112.

[14] See Ernst H. Kantorowicz, *The King's Two Bodies: A Study in Mediaeval Political Theology* (Princeton: Princeton University Press, 1957), a classical study of the king's two bodies as a political theology of early–modern Western monarchies.

of Mount Meru, which substitute one for the other in substituting for the kingdom or the universe governed by the *dharma*."[15] The "king as a substitute body" meant in the Khmer Buddhist context that Khmer royalty had multiple substitute bodies, and that the king was "both transcendent or universal *and* uniquely particular."[16] The conception of just leadership/kingship in Cambodia is epitomized by the *Preah Bat Thommik* (Dharmic King or Just Ruler), a concept with messianic overtones, also present in the popular mind.[17] This Just Ruler is thought to uphold what is known in Theravadin terms as the *dasavidha-rājadhamma*, the "tenfold virtues of the righteous king," and to enjoy invulnerability.[18] In a "traditional" conceptualization of the ideal configuration of political power, the *Preah Bat Thommik* was envisioned as a charioteer, supporting himself on the two wheels of state affairs (*anachakr*, the pillar of *Cheat*) and Buddhism (*Putthichakr*, the pillar of *Sasana*) to lead the people forward.[19]

The *neak mean bon* and the *Preah Bat Thommik* overlap conceptually.[20] The well-known nineteenth-century prophecy *Putth Tumneay* (Predictions of the Buddha) foretells the appearance of the *Preah Bat Thommik* as a *neak mean bon* who will come to pacify Cambodia after a period of violent upheavals.[21] These upheavals have turned the world upside down: traditional values undergo a complete reversal, Buddhism is destroyed, and the ignorant gain power. The *Preah Bat Thommik* restores religion and maintains peace until the end of the 5000 years of the law of the historical Buddha, after which the world will be saved by the future Buddha, *Preah Serei Ary Metrey*. Now largely associated in the Cambodian popular mind with the Khmer Rouge period, the era of calamities described in *Putth Tumneay* has been seen by many political opponents, including the royalist faction, to apply to the ascension of the incumbent regime to power.[22] They point to the communist origins of the CPP and the modest backgrounds of the party's leaders. The recurring messianic search to find the *Preah*

---

[15] Thompson, "The Suffering of Kings," in Marston and Guthrie, *History, Buddhism, and New Religious Movements in Cambodia*, 92.

[16] Ibid., 91.

[17] Heng, "In Search of the Dhammika Ruler," in Kent and Chandler, *People of Virtue*, 310.

[18] Ibid., 313. The "tenfold virtues of a righteous king" (*dasavidha-rājadhamma*) are *dāna* (charity), *sīla* (morality), *pariccāga* (self-sacrifice), *ājjava* (honesty), *maddava* (kindness), *tapa* (self-control), *akkoda* (non-anger), *avihimsa* (non-violence), *khanti* (tolerance), and *avirodhana* (conformity to the law). Ibid., 317–18.

[19] Ibid., 310.

[20] Khing, "Neak Mean Boun," 106, suggests a complete overlap between the *Preah Bat Thommik* and *neak mean bon* through the conceptual link "dhammik = bodhisatta = neak mean boun." According to Olivier de Bernon, "Le Buddh Daṃnāy: Note sur un Texte Apocalyptique Khmer," *Bulletin de l'École Française d'Extrême-Orient* (*BEFEO*) 81 (1994), 91, the word "dhammik" [thommik], part of the Cambodian royal title, designates in *Putth Tumneay* not only a just monarch, but also the warriors who submit only reluctantly to the sovereign Bodhisattva.

[21] See: Khing, "Neak Mean Boun," 103–106; and de Bernon, "Le Buddh Daṃnāy," 91.

[22] On the association of the upheavals described in *Putth Tumneay* with the Khmer Rouge, see: Carol Mortland, "Khmer Buddhists in the United States: Ultimate Questions," in *Cambodian Culture Since 1975: Homeland and Exile*, ed. May Ebihara, Carol Anne Mortland, and Judy Ledgerwood (Ithaca: Cornell University Press, 1994), 82; Frank Smith, *Interpretive Accounts of the Khmer Rouge Years: Personal Experience in Cambodian Peasant World View* (Madison: Center for Southeast Asian Studies, University of Wisconsin, 1989), 18–23; and Ledgerwood, "Ritual in 1990 Cambodian Political Theatre," 216.

Bat Thommik persists in the second kingdom.[23] Royalists have nurtured the idea that the reinstated king Norodom Sihanouk was this just leader, as the father of peace and national reconciliation.[24]

The reinvention of the Sdech Kân narrative can be understood as a counter-narrative to a reading of *Putth Tumneay* that casts Sihanouk, and the royalist faction with him, as the rightful leaders of the nation. Immediately before the restoration of the monarchy, when expectations of the imminent coming of the *Preah Bat Thommik* ran high, Hun Sen, Chea Sim, and Heng Samrin, the SOC leaders, tried to distance themselves from the infidels mentioned in the *Putth Tumneay* by sponsoring Buddhist ritual activity.[25] Later on, after the July 1997 events, Hun Sen made reference to the short and violent war lasting only as long as it takes "to fry a shrimp," which, according to *Putth Tumneay,* hails in a new era of prosperity—thereby seemingly casting himself as the *Preah Bat Thommik.*[26] In 2003, Hun Sen seemed to suggest an association between himself and King Jayavarman VII, the quintessential *Preah Bat Thommik,* using the language of reincarnation.[27] Hun Sen's subsequent revival of Sdech Kân represents the emergence of a full-fledged counter-narrative to a royalist reading of the *Putth Tumneay,* with the prime minister casting himself as a savior figure, while omitting the other two members of the CPP top troika.

This counter-narrative engages with an age-old tension between inherited and non-inherited leadership, deeply ingrained in Buddhist thinking on kingship and in the Khmer political and cultural context. The productive tension between inherited and non-inherited leadership is entailed in the terms *sdech,* generally translated as "king" or "prince," and *samdech,* which historically meant prince, but is now an honorific also accorded by the king to non-royals, including the CPP's leaders. These titles historically covered a semantic range within and outside of actual "kingship," an ambiguity persisting into the present day. The Old Khmer origin of the word *sdech* is derived from the root verb *tac,* "to detach, to separate, to be superior," and was used to designate people of the ruling class, not only the king.[28] Using this preexisting tension, the Sdech Kân narrative employs the *neak mean bon* imagery to glorify and exalt nonhereditary leadership. It thus engages with questions debated by a rapidly changing monarchy that is internally divided over whether a constitutional monarchy can be reconciled with political royalism. Following his reinstatement as king, Sihanouk continuously sought a political role for himself, often ending up closer to the CPP than to FUNCINPEC. Sihanouk's 2004 abdication in favor of his son Sihamoni, who has shown no interest in assuming a political role,

---

[23] See Heng, "In Search of the Dhammika Ruler," in Kent and Chandler, *People of Virtue,* 313.

[24] Some Cambodians consider Sihanouk as the *Preah Bat Thommik* or as a *Bodhisattva,* which would make him a *neak mean bon.* See: de Bernon, "Le Buddh Daṃnāy," 93; and Khing, "Neak Mean Boun,"106.

[25] Ledgerwood, "Ritual in 1990 Cambodian Political Theatre," 216.

[26] Olivier de Bernon, "La Prédiction du Bouddha," *Aséanie* 1 (1998), 43–66.

[27] Hun Sen released a press statement denying that he was a reincarnation of Jayavarman VII; this was prompted, he stated, by how many people believed this to be the case. Ledgerwood, "Ritual in 1990 Cambodian Political Theatre," 219.

[28] See: Saveros Pou, "Dieux et Rois dans la Pensée Khmère Ancienne," *Journal Asiatique* 286, no. 2 (1998): 656. Saveros Pou, *Dictionnaire Vieux Khmer-Français-Anglais* (Paris: CEDORECK, 1992), 508, defines the Old Khmer meaning as "To be aloof, above all. The supreme one. Sacred beings, espec. Princes. (Of these) To be, stand, move."

has given Cambodia a constitutional monarch along Western lines. Meanwhile, Sihamoni's half-brother Ranariddh, as the leader of FUNCINPEC until 2006, maneuvered his way through coalition governments with the CPP that compromised his political independence, as well as his royal stature. The Sdech Kân narrative is primarily understood to justify the July 1997 events and Ranariddh's political downfall. More broadly, it undermines the legitimacy of a national leadership role for royal family members, and particularly the idea of Sihanouk as the father of national reconciliation. By revealing a telling absence of rival rumors concerning the actual occupant of the throne, Sihamoni, it highlights the actual throne's hollowness.

Although the "traditional" ideal configuration of power as the trinity of nation, Buddhism, and kingship persists in Cambodia today, contestation over the relationships among the three has colored Cambodian politics ever since independence. Ian Harris charges that the idea that the king is indispensable to the flourishing of Theravada Buddhism may be a kind of caricature of Khmer Buddhism. Anticolonial Buddhist nationalism was non-monarchist and sometimes anti-monarchist, and several people at its heart later rose to prominence in the Khmer Republic. Their thinking was informed by larger debates within Buddhist thinking on kingship.[29] The Sdech Kân narrative can be understood as the latest response to a long-standing legitimacy crisis of the trinity—in important ways the narrative forms a continuity with the response of Sihanouk. Sihanouk's Sangkum Reastr Niyum (People's Socialist Community, 1955–70) and its Buddhist socialism, launched as a social and political foundation for building independent Cambodia, was said by Sihanouk to build precisely on the "traditional" base of the monarchy and Buddhism as "irreplaceable factors of unity."[30] Sihanouk claimed direct descent from Jayavarman VII, the model *Preah Bat Thommik*, and likened his Sangkum Reastr Niyum to the Angkorean era.[31] Yet at the same time, Sihanouk referred to the popular legend of King Trâsâk Ph'aem, a *neak mean bon*, to justify his 1955 abdication in favor of his father, Suramarit, and his new role as chairman of the Sangkum Reastr Niyum. According to legend, Trâsâk Ph'aem was a gardener of the Samre minority, renowned for his skill in growing sweet cucumbers. Acting on the orders of the king to kill any intruder, the gardener one night killed a trespasser who then turned out to be the king himself. In recognition of the gardener's obedience, the gardener was made king and started a new dynasty of popular origin. Harris notes that "by drawing on the legend, Sihanouk was able to replace the idea of rule by traditional quasi-divine right with a slightly more democratic and popular notion of exclusive political power."[32] This was reflected in how around the same time

---

[29] These included Son Ngoc Thanh, Pang Khat, and Bunchhan Mul. An interesting case is monk Khieu Chum, an Umbrella demonstration veteran and, later, Lon Nol speechwriter. Harris has found ample examples of how Khieu refutes the institution of the monarchy on Buddhist grounds. For example, Khieu argues that submitting to the ten duties of the King, the *dasabiddha rājadhamma*, leads to renouncement of kingship—exemplifying how a Buddhist reading can unsettle kingship. Harris identifies both Theravada canonical sources and Cambodian *chbaps*, post-canonical sources, which justify insurrection as a consequence of misrule; see Harris, "The Monk and the King," 82–88.

[30] Norodom Sihanouk, "Pour Mieux Comprendre le Cambodge Actuel," *Le Sangkum: Revue politique illustrée* 1 (1965): 14.

[31] Edwards, *Cambodge*, 250.

[32] Harris, *Cambodian Buddhism*, 146.

Sihanouk started to be called by the newly invented kinship-term *Samdech Euv*, often translated as "Monsignor Papa," rather than by Sanskrit and Pali terms hitherto associated with high status.[33] Ever so slightly, the idea of kingship shifted toward a more democratic ideal, by referring to the *neak mean bon* imagery.

In the Second Kingdom, genealogical lines are again central to the royals' claims to legitimacy. Meanwhile, in contemporary society, historical imaginations of overlapping substitute bodies, whereby the king embodies the people and the state, persist. Alexandra Kent tells the story of how two middle-aged Cambodian women set out to recover the king's body through spirit performances in order to, ultimately, reconstitute Cambodia.[34] Just as these women use their bodies to channel that of the king, as the substitute in turn for the body social and the body politic, the Sdech Kân performance can be understood as a mirror response by the prime minister to reorient Cambodia—through replacing the ailing monarchy. Through becoming the substitute body of Sdech Kân, the prime minister plunges himself into a series of associations, ultimately representing what in the modern context is imagined as the nation. The discourse surrounding Hun Sen's reincarnation of Sdech Kân can be understood as a bid to articulate and cement an interpretation of legitimate leadership to define the present era and to negotiate future political developments; a concern that goes beyond that of convincingly, in any straightforward sense, aspiring to be a *neak mean bon* or *Preah Bat Thommik*.

PERFORMING SDECH KÂN

By (re)incarnating or performing Sdech Kân, Prime Minister Hun Sen has tapped into the sphere of emotion, drama, and performance, testifying to what an important part such performance plays in contemporary Cambodian politics. Julia Strauss and Donal Cruise O'Brien identify three distinct modes of performative politics as the politics of "affect, emotion, and drama": state rituals (primarily staged ceremonies); theatrical performance by politicians and activists, such as elections and street protests; and individual or micro-performances, including speeches or events intended to engage people's emotions and rally support.[35] The performances of the Sdech Kân narrative predominantly belong to the third type. The prime minister makes individual performances in the form of his long, elaborate speeches. There are also individual and micro-performances by different members of the political elite and their clientelistic networks, *khsae*. Performing the Sdech Kân narrative exalts the importance of Hun Sen's bureaucratic, military, and economic networks, which make up what Steve Heder has referred to as an "involuted façade state."[36] It has tied together government officials with artists and academics who have been mobilized in a process of enlisting intellectuals into the prime minister's

---

[33] Sihanouk was granted the title of *dhammik mahārāj* [thommik mohareach] (great righteous king) in the 1947 Constitution, but renounced it by abdicating. He occasionally referred to himself as king-monk (Ibid., 144). In contrast, legend has it that after Trâsâk Ph'aem ascended the throne, the title *Preah Bat Thommik* was added to Trâsâk Ph'aem's royal title, underlining the overlap between the *neak mean bon* and the *Preah Bat Thommik*. See de Bernon, "Le Buddh Daṃnãy," 91.

[34] Alexandra Kent, "The Recovery of the King," in Kent and Chandler, *People of Virtue*, 109–27.

[35] Julia C. Strauss and Donal B. Cruise O'Brien, "Introduction," in Strauss and O'Brien, *Staging Politics*, 2–3.

[36] Heder, "Political Theatre in the 2003 Cambodian Elections," 162.

network. In a way, the narrative has become an inverted "façade" by providing a platform for these individuals to come to the surface of public space, reinforcing existing power structures and integrating a new set of people into them. Their performances include the erection of statues of Sdech Kân across the country, a book about Sdech Kân, and the work of a research team to locate Sdech Kân's capital. The narrative has also been disseminated nationwide through the media.

These public spectacles contain their own internal logic, aspirations, and expressions. In contrast to Cambodian elections, which could be said to (sometimes schizophrenically) interact with both an international and domestic audience, the performances discussed here are aimed exclusively at a domestic audience. As a realm "thoroughly saturated with symbols, as the script for the performance either implicitly or explicitly calls upon tropes, symbols, and metaphors presumed to be well understood by those audiences," performative politics alludes to and draws meaning from a sphere of shared understandings.[37] It thus naturally intersects with the politically embedded contestation of social memories. Sdech Kân was already a controversial figure in Cambodian collective memory prior to being co-opted by Hun Sen, with interpretations of his rule ranging from a republican one making him out to be a false revolutionary, to a royalist one casting him as a simple usurper of the throne.[38] The most recent reinvention by Hun Sen thus picks up and uses tropes and symbols fresh in the collective memory. The performance can paradoxically be understood as a particularly "sincere" medium by which Hun Sen communicates with the citizenry. Through it, Hun Sen sends important messages which are not part of explicit official pronouncements.

(RE)BIRTH OF A MODERN SAGA

From the early 2000s onwards, Hun Sen started referring to Sdech Kân in speeches. The similarities between the two were given particular attention. They were both born in the year of the *neak* (dragon). Just as Sdech Kân came from the class of temple-servants, Hun Sen famously spent part of his youth as a pagoda boy. The implicit similarity was the idea of a commoner rising through his own revolutionary prowess to govern the polity by toppling an unjust king.

This narrative emerged in the context of Hun Sen's restructuring of relations between himself and the royal family to the detriment of the latter, and particularly in relation to his ultimate outmaneuvering of Prince Ranariddh. Ranariddh was ousted as co-prime minister in July 1997. The Sdech Kân narrative appeared in a period when Ranariddh was struggling to reinsert himself into national politics. He was appointed president of the National Assembly (NA) in 1998, and again in 2003. Yet by 2006, the political significance to which Ranariddh aspired would be pulled out of his reach. As his conflict with Hun Sen increased, Ranariddh resigned from the NA presidency in March, a few months before being removed as FUNCINPEC party president in October.

On February 26, 2006—shortly before Ranariddh's resignation—Hun Sen went with his wife, Bun Rany, to visit the site that had been identified as Sdech Kân's

---

[37] Strauss and Cruise O'Brien, "Introduction," in Strauss and O'Brien, *Staging Politics*, 3.

[38] Saing Hell, *Neak Padevott Klaeng Klay* [The False Revolutionary] (Phnom Penh: Ed. Ariyathor, 1972); and Tauch Chhoung, *Sdech Kân Chrek Reach* [Sdech Kân the Usurper] (Paris: Ed. Association des Écrivains Khmers à l'Étranger, 1995).

former capital, Srolop Prey Nokor, in Kompong Cham province. Here, Hun Sen gave a speech, providing the fullest account to date of his perspective on Sdech Kân. The prime minister started off by declaring that a religious ceremony had been conducted to ask permission from former king Sdech Kân's spirit for a restoration effort aimed at developing Srolop Prey Nokor into a tourism site. He then spoke at length about how the development of Srolop was to take place. An irrigation system was to be constructed, bringing water to the 213-hectare inner area of the former city or palace, as well as almost 2,000 hectares in the vicinity (about five thousand acres, almost eight square miles). More than five hundred meters of the seven-meter-high city wall were to be rebuilt. Water reservoirs around the palace were to be restored. Canals were to be dug, ranging from 2,750 to 4,000 meters long. Four water gates were to be put in. Two other canals were to be restored, together with a number of water-flow control mechanisms. By addressing the area's overall water needs, the development would benefit local residents as well as the tourist site. As Hun Sen concluded, "I think we have a long-term involvement here."[39]

Hun Sen went on to narrate his version of the Sdech Kân story:

> After the Ponhea Yat reign, Cambodia was ruled as a Kingdom that was divided into three separate areas [...] The war later broke out. It is interesting to study its cause for the sake of preventing mistakes in the present. King Preah Srey Sokonthor Bât had a concubine whose brother was named Kân. One day, the King dreamed of a fire-breathing dragon and fortune tellers spread rumors of instability believed to originate from Kân, since everyone was unhappy about him being promoted from the status of an outcast. A plot to kill Kân was hatched, but Kân was saved by a secret letter from his sister and fled to gather forces, which later fought and defeated the forces of King Srey Sokonthor Bât. He became king himself and was named Preah Srey Chettha. [...] Sdech Kân or Preah Srey Chettha did wonderful work in what should be termed a democratic revolution, because he liberated all outcasts under his area of control. Because of this, he became the strongest commander and King in his own right.[40]

Hun Sen continued the speech by addressing a deal struck between the CPP and opposition Sam Rainsy Party for a constitutional amendment that would require a simple majority rather than a two-thirds majority to pass laws in the National Assembly; such a deal would make FUNCINPEC a redundant coalition partner for the CPP. Hun Sen referred to his recent audience with Sihamoni to address rumors that this would lead to the monarchy's downfall. He had informed the king that the constitutional amendment was aimed merely at avoiding a political deadlock, not at abolishing the monarchy. He further stated that the CPP should be called the monarchy's supporter, "if not the monarchist," and that anyone wishing to abolish the monarchy had to first "get me [Hun Sen] out."[41] In his speech, the prime minister explicitly addressed the recent moves affecting the royalist party by

---

[39] Hun Sen, "Visit of Samdech Hun Sen and Bun Rany to the Former Royal City of Sanlob Prey Nokor in Kompong Cham," *Cambodia New Vision* 97, February 28, 2006, 1–2.

[40] Ibid, 2. This account of the Sdech Kân story as typically referred to by Hun Sen evidently picks the parts of the legend that serve to deliver his message, while omitting other parts, such as how Sdech Kân was ultimately killed and replaced by another monarch.

[41] Ibid.

claiming to be the defender of the monarchy. He also gave a much longer account, retelling the historical legend of Sdech Kân defeating the king, and he delivered it all at the site of Sdech Kân's capital. If read as a statement on the present situation, this latter part seemed to contradict the more explicit assertions.

Shortly after the speech, on March 2, two developments sealed FUNCINPEC's fate as a political party. Crucially, the National Assembly amended the constitution, enabling it to pass bills with a simple majority, and ending CPP's reliance on cooperation from FUNCINPEC. Second, Hun Sen removed FUNCINPEC Co-minister of Defense Nhek Bunchhay and Co-minister of Interior Norodom Sirivudh. This brought an end to the quota system of partisan ministerial appointments that had been in place since 1993. Seeing his presidency of the National Assembly seriously weakened, Ranariddh resigned on March 3, confidently counting on being asked to return—which did not happen. One month later, Hun Sen delivered another forceful speech reiterating the Sdech Kân story. This time, he drew explicit parallels between present and past actors, stating that "we should not be afraid to get exposed to history as some people should," and that "we should not be afraid of the *truth* recorded by history," as, presumably, others should.[42] He noted the historical events as proof that "all are born equal," and that "it was not true at all that some people are born to be respected people and others not," a message not lost on the royal family.[43]

ESTABLISHING ORIGINS

Hun Sen's message, however, was not directed exclusively at the royal family. This was to be a truly national attempt at renegotiating the "ideal political configuration," the dissemination of which, crucially, was built on academic work on the historical Kân commissioned by the prime minister. On this occasion, Hun Sen also announced his support for research by then vice-president of the Royal Academy of Cambodia (RAC), historian Ros Chantraboth, on Sdech Kân. Having spent the previous thirty years in France, Chantraboth returned to Cambodia in 2000 and helped set up the Royal Academy reestablished the previous year.[44] He immediately set about the task of identifying the location of Sdech Kân's second capital, recorded by historical sources as Srolop Doun Tipichety Prey Nokor. The location of this capital was shrouded in the mist of history. Leclère had situated Prey Nokor about twenty-two kilometers east of Prey Veng on a high plateau, and most historians referred to this location.[45] However, since Chantraboth argued that, according to Khmer historical sources, the capital was situated in Tboung Khmum

---

[42] Hun Sen, "Inaugurating Buddhist temple in Serei Suosdei Pagoda," *CNV*, 99, April 27, 2006.

[43] Author's interviews with senior royal family members suggest that they generally perceive of Hun Sen's references to Sdech Kân as a pledge to take revenge on the monarchy, by means of invoking their wrongdoings against Sdech Kân.

[44] The RAC, the nation's highest academic body, falls directly under the Office of the Council of Ministers and its Minister DPM Sok An, Hun Sen's close associate. In April 2010, Hun Sen and Sok An were appointed as full members of the RAC, and in April 2011 Hun Sen was appointed its honorary president.

[45] Leclère, *Histoire du Cambodge*, 235, cited in Ros Chantraboth, *Preah Sdech Kân* (Phnom Penh: Bânnakear Angkor, 2007), 223.

province, Tboung Khmum district, his research team conducted their search there.[46] Finding a square brick wall at the nearby site of the pre-Angkorean temples Banteay Prey Nokor, the team concluded that this matched the description of Sdech Kân's capital in Khmer sources.[47]

Touristic development of the area started in 2006, at the height of the conflict with Ranariddh. The pagoda known variously as Wat Angkor Knong, Wat Prasat, or Wat Khmau, which stands in the center, was renovated. The pagoda consists of a newer *vihear* (central shrine hall), raised on the site of an older one; behind it, there are two smaller, pre-Angkorean *prasat* (brahmanical temples). In November 2009, following the repairs, Wat Angkor Knong was formally inaugurated in a ceremony presided over by the premier.[48] Hun Sen announced that the government had invested a staggering sum in the area, much of which was spent on improving and building road and water systems, turning the area into one of "agro-tourism."[49] He also called on domestic and foreign investors to invest in the site as one with important tourism potential.

Although at first the site was slow to attract any tourists, the regular television broadcasts that advertise it as a place of leisure and historical discovery appear to have had some success. Today, the site is known as Hluang Preah Sdech Kan Cultural Historical Site. It receives a steady stream of visitors, including some on trips organized by schools and educational institutes in Phnom Penh. Every November 30, a Hluang Preah Sdech Kan boat race is celebrated here, with participants from across Cambodia.

---

[46] The Khmer sources listed by Ros, *Preah Sdech Kân*, 224, include the records of the Thiounn committee, the history of Teuk Virl pagoda in Saang district, Kandal, and Eng Soth's *Mohaboros Khmer*. An August 2011 search for the sources listed in Ros's bibliography proved unsuccessful apart from one entry. The *Preah Reach Pongsavada Mohaksatr Khmer* could not be found in the Buddhist Institute's library as listed; it was contrary to what was listed by Ros in a different entry from *Preah Reach Pongsavada Krong Kampuchea Tepatey* which was not authored by Veang Thiounn as listed by Ros, and which was found in the EFEO rather than in the Buddhist Institute library (per Ros) and contained nothing on Kân. The only entry authored by Veang Thiounn was the *Pongsavada Brotes Khmer* from 1931, which contained nothing on Kân. Neither was the *Preah Reach Pongsavada Nokor Khmer* to be found, nor the *Pongsavada Wat Kaok Kak sastra slek rith joh nr 1403*. Of the sources listed by Ros, I could only locate one, Eng Soth's *Mohaboros Khmer*. This would suggest that the *Mohaboros Khmer* was the only source used, unless Ros had access to the listed sources in ways other than through the libraries noted. Eng's *Mohaboros Khmer*, 162, indicates that Prey Nokor was built at the far end of Tboung Khmum province, at the border to Ba Phnom province (roughly equivalent to modern-day Prey Veng). Apart from this source, I found mentions of Kân in *Pongsavada Nei Brotes Kampuchea*, published by the Ministry of Education in 1952; as well Long Siem's *Provathasastra Sangkep Nei Brotes Kampuchea*, both of which can be found at the EFEO library in Wat Onalom, Phnom Penh. The *Pongsavada Nei Brotes Kampuchea*, p. 65, gives the same location for Srolop as the *Mohaboros Khmer*, whereas *Provathasastra Sangkep Nei Brotes Kampuchea*, p. 149, simply states that the capital was located in Tboung Khmum province. Thus, it seems correct that Khmer sources give Tboung Khmum province as the capital's location, although locating the exact spot is made difficult by the uncertainty surrounding Ros's sources.

[47] Ros, *Preah Sdech Kân*, 225.

[48] Hun Sen, "New Achievements—Hluong Preah Sdej Kan City," *CNV* 141, November 30, 2009.

[49] Hun Sen (Ibid.) placed the figure at an implausible 11,638 bn riels (US$2,909 billion), perhaps a mistake of the speech transcriber.

The value of locating Sdech Kân's capital is readily apparent. It has enabled the development of a national tourism site, which has helped to further popularize and disseminate the narrative. Yet the location of Srolop carries a further significance. Locating Srolop in Tboung Khmum provided another parallel between the trajectories of Sdech Kân and Hun Sen. What are now Kompong Cham and Tboung Khmum provinces was long Kompong Cham province—it was only in 2013 that the province was split in two—and key events in Hun Sen's biography are tied to this area. Hun Sen was born in Steung Trang district, Kompong Cham, in 1952. He claims to have joined the maquis in Kompong Cham's Memot district in 1970, and later married Bun Rany in Tboung Khmum district, then Kompong Cham, now Tboung Khmum province.

Chronicling his life as a *neak tâsou*, a person who has taken part in armed struggle, Hun Sen's narration of a series of events taking place in this area, are well-known to a popular audience. Hun Sen has explicitly related this personal history of revolutionary struggle in the area to the story of Sdech Kân. In his speech delivered at his first visit to Srolop Prey Nokor, in early 2006, Hun Sen started out by recalling that he and his wife had a memorable history there.[50] He recalled how they had reunited in the area after two months of separation, citing widely known songs about the fate of a woman separated from her husband, and compared his story to that of Sdech Kân, finding it no less pitiful.[51] This was arguably intended to ensure that the well-known story of Hun Sen's revolutionary activities throughout the 1970s—and how these contributed to the toppling of the Khmer Rouge regime—would henceforth invoke the image of Sdech Kân. In a speech delivered in Memot in 2007, Hun Sen outlined his relation to the area as follows:

> […] everyone knows that I started my political life in Memot from April 4, 1970, as I decided to join the Maquis in response to the appeal made by Samdech Preah Norodom Sihanouk […] At another juncture, on June 20, 1977, I left the district of Memot to lead the struggle movement for national liberation against Pol Pot's genocidal regime, which later achieved victory on January 7, 1979. However, another event that shocked me the most happened right before this building […] My first son died on November 10, 1976. My other son, who is also here today, was born not far from this place. January 5, 2007, is, indeed, our thirty-first wedding anniversary. We got married in the commune of Chrab, Tboung Khmum District, with twelve other pairs […] My star had been full of dangers, not just simple hardships and comforts.[52]

Hun Sen described his distress when, in 1976, his pregnant wife, Bun Rany, was sent to work at the site of Srolop Prey Nokor. He took her to nearby Memot to give birth, but during the night she delivered the baby while he was away on a mission.

---

[50] Hun Sen, "Visit of Samdech Hun Sen and Bun Rany to the former Royal City."

[51] These episodes from Hun Sen's and Bun Rany's life during the time of revolutionary struggle have been made famous through songs such as *Tukkh srey bdey proat* ("The sorrow of a woman separated from her husband"), authored by the PM himself. It is included in Chhay Yiheang, ed., *Samdech Hun Sen: Tossânah Noyobay Aphirok Selobah Aphivoddh Sangkom neung Chomrieng 115 Bot* [*Samdech Hun Sen: Political Thought, Arts Conservation, Social Development and 115 Songs*], (Phnom Penh: Im Savoan, 2005).

[52] Hun Sen, "Opening Junior High School Bun Rany—Hun Sen Memot," *CNV* 108, January 5, 2007.

Upon returning the next morning, he found his first-born dead. Hun Sen asked for a proper burial, but was denied even this. He remarked, "I was accused of being a traitor for a long time, but I knew that it was not my time yet. I could have taken revenge because I had a pistol with loaded chamber already in hand. I did not do it." Instead, Hun Sen left Memot on June 20, 1977, for Vietnam. From there, he built up his army and power base, culminating in his revenge—the (in reality, Vietnamese-led) toppling of Democratic Kampuchea on January 7, 1979.

In this *neak tâsou* narrative, well-known to the public, Hun Sen's revolutionary activities recall those of Sdech Kân. Indeed, Hun Sen has suggested that the soul of Sdech Kân may have been there to help him during the time spent in Srolop Prey Nokor, although he did not know at the time that this was Sdech Kân's capital.[53] Like Sdech Kân, when accused of treachery and struck by misfortune, Hun Sen "kills his anger" and escapes eastward, to Vietnam, where he builds up an army that eventually returns to topple the regime.[54] The Sdech Kân story resonates with the earlier narrative surrounding Hun Sen, an association encouraged by the prime minister, and draws strength from this.[55] In turn, this analogy bestows on Hun Sen's personal revolutionary history the range of meanings attached to that of the historical king.

THE RETRIEVAL OF DEMOCRACY

It fell on Cambodian academia to judge the nature of Kân's rule. To qualify the meaning of the overlap between the bodies of Kân and the prime minister, it had to be conclusively determined whether Kân was a traitor, or, indeed, a just warrior who rose up against an unrighteous king. Beyond establishing this, an academic rereading of the history of Kân would also be used for outlining Hun Sen's broader political vision.

Hun Sen commissioned Ros Chantraboth to write a book about the historical king. Published in Khmer as *Preah Sdech Kân* in October 2006, and funded by the prime minister and first lady, Bun Rany, it had the stated purpose of identifying a political doctrine and ruling strategy in Khmer history for how to best govern,

---

[53] Hun Sen, "New Achievements."

[54] Although Hun Sen now claims to have joined the maquis in 1970 in response to Sihanouk's call to arms, during the PRK he claimed to have joined the resistance in 1967, long before the anti-Sihanouk coup of 1970. For the former, see, for example, Chhay Yiheang, ed., *Samdech Akka Moha Sena Padei Techo Hun Sen: Neayok Rothmontrey Brosaut Chenh pi Trokaul Kâsekâr* [Samdech Akka Moha Sena Padei Techo Hun Sen: Prime minister born to a farmer's family], (Phnom Penh: Ponleu Pech, 2007), 32. On his claims during the PRK, see Ben Kiernan, *How Pol Pot Came to Power: A History of Communism in Kampuchea, 1930–1975* (London: Verso, 1985), 254.

[55] The consequence of aligning the *neak tâsou* narrative with that of Sdech Kân, is, evidently, how this shifts the enemy from the monarchy to the Khmer Rouge; and further serves to conceptually link the monarchy to the Khmer Rouge. This could also be read to indict Sihanouk, whose call to arms Hun Sen now claims to have motivated him to join the revolution that would go so frightfully wrong that he had to overturn it; emphasizing Sihanouk's role in enabling the horrors of Democratic Kampuchea.

develop, and rebuild the nation.[56] Five thousand copies of the book were distributed to libraries and schools around Cambodia.[57]

Chantraboth identified three major regime changes in Khmer history that occurred when a commoner dared to stand up to dismantle a royalist regime. These were the rise to power of, in turn, Trâsâk Ph'aem in the thirteenth century, Sdech Kân in the sixteenth century, and, lastly, Lon Nol, through the 1970 coup that overthrew Sihanouk as head of state.[58] These extraordinary events, Chantraboth stated, begged the question of why so many people had come together to overthrow the king. During times of conflict between a commoner and the king, Chantraboth found that the commoner was typically likened to Sdech Kân, as a traitor and usurper.[59] Setting out to contextualize Sdech Kân's rise to power and to scrutinize the ideas and actions of King Srey Sokonthor Bât, Chantraboth thus aspired to offer insights to guide contemporary politics.

In his preface to Chantraboth's book, Hun Sen interpreted its findings as follows:

> Preah Sdech Kân has been continuously recorded in Khmer history as a man who betrayed the King, or a usurper. ... [on the contrary] we can note that Preah Sdech Kân was a Khmer, born in the class of temple-servants, that he was not a man who betrayed the King, or a usurper, as is always said.[60]

Hun Sen suggested the following points be reexamined in order to provide a better understanding of Sdech Kân's actions:

- The manner of doing things and the behavior of King Srey Sokonthor Bât.
- The popular movements throughout the country that joined Sdech Kân's struggle against the King.
- [The fact that] the monks and pagodas that had previously received support, benefits, and privileges from the King and Royal family turned to support and protect Preah Sdech Kân.
- What was the reason that brought people from all classes to rise up to fight the King?
- What kind of problems did Khmer society have in terms of the tenfold conduct of the King, justice, society, agriculture, and economy during the period of King Srey Sokonthor Bât?
- Can Preah Sdech Kân, who escaped his attempted murder by the King just to survive, be considered to have committed an act of betrayal?[61]

---

[56] Ros, *Preah Sdech Kân*, 1. All citations from this book are the author's own translations.

[57] Leang Delux, "History: Hun Sen Finances a Book about Sdach Korn," *Cambodge Soir*, March 29, 2007. When the first printing was exhausted, a second edition was released in 2007; see Bo Proeuk, "Hun Sen-sponsored 'Preah Sdach Korn' Book Needs 2d Edition to Meet Demand," *Reaksmey Kampuchea*, September 25, 2007.

[58] Ros, *Preah Sdech Kân*, 3–4.

[59] The seriousness with which Hun Sen takes allegations of being a traitor to the nation was highlighted by how he warned critics of the January 7 ceremony that anyone accusing him or senior government officials of being a "national traitor" would be arrested. See Cheang Sokha and Rebecca Puddy, "Don't Call Me a Traitor: PM," *Phnom Penh Post*, January 10, 2011.

[60] Hun Sen, "Aromkâtha [Preface]," in Ros, *Preah Sdech Kân*, i.

[61] Ibid., ii.

These points can also be read as outlining a "timeless" scenario centered on the relationship between an unvirtuous king and an emerging *neak mean bon*. Applied to the relationship between the royalist faction and Hun Sen, the points suggest that in the period prior to Hun Sen's actions to limit the royalists' power, there was something problematic about the behavior of the royalist faction. At the same time, Hun Sen enjoyed the unanimous support of the people and of the *sangha*, and such support indicated underlying societal problems stemming from the morally flawed conduct of the royalists. Hun Sen's points, then, suggest that he was justified in curbing the power of the royalist faction by alluding to the imaginary of the *Preah Bat Thommik*. It is because of the royalists' failure to uphold the "tenfold virtues of the king," which define the *Preah Bat Thommik*, that the people and *sangha* rally to protect the *neak mean bon*.

Reassessing the historical Kân also offered the prime minister an opportunity to reinvent his own political identity. Kân provides Hun Sen with a new vision to guide the present era.[62] Kân's political thinking is said to have rested on two conceptual innovations; freedom rights (*setthi seripheap*) and class struggle (*tâsou vannah*). These radical innovations predated the emergence of similar notions in Europe, making Cambodia the birthplace of democratic politics.[63] In Hun Sen's preface, we read:

> Preah Sdech Kân [...] can be considered a brilliant hero in the world, who raised the doctrine and vision of freedom rights, and was the first to speak about and practice this, in the sixteenth century. France, famous as the country of human rights, started discussing freedom rights only in the eighteenth century. Something even more special is how Preah Srey Chettha Preah Sdech Kân raised the theory of class struggle to become the base of building Cambodia. Karl Marx, the father of Communism, raised this thought and wrote down the theory of class struggle only at the end of the nineteenth century.[64]

These two conceptual innovations together make up early democratic beliefs, providing a blueprint for contemporary politics:

> Can the political theory of Preah Srey Chettha Preah Sdech Kân that advances freedom rights and class struggle, which became the base in building the nation, the motherland, be considered to be the first step in history toward democratic beliefs? Also, for my own vision, I note that the doctrine and activity of Preah Srey Chettha Preah Sdech Kân has the characteristics of the first democratic revolution of the people in Cambodian history, thanks to Sdech Kân who liberated them from the class system, letting there be freedom and equality in society [...][65]

The toppling of the unjust monarch results from Kân's championing of freedom rights and class struggle. It constitutes a national democratic revolution, which in

---

[62] Ibid., iii.

[63] Ros, *Preah Sdech Kân*, 271.

[64] Hun, "Aromkâtha," ii–iii.

[65] Ibid., iii.

turn is posited as an integral part of the very fabric of the nation.[66] This particular nationalist vision turns the trinity of "Nation, Religion, and King" on its head. It not only closely knits together the notion of democracy with opposition to a morally flawed royalist faction, but also situates this within broader ideas of equality and social mobility. The leader who dares to challenge the hereditary leader achieves the democratic revolution and embodies the nation's aspirations.

The conceptualization of democracy as a fusion of class struggle and freedom rights refashions a discourse—the discourse of people's democracy (see chapter 4)— that firmly integrates the notion of democracy as part of revolutionary history. Hun Sen invoked both concepts during the PRK, depicting democracy and the securing of freedom rights as the unchanging objective of the Cambodian revolutionary quest pursued through class struggle from the pre-protectorate era onward.[67] Having cast off his previous socialist identity, the changing revolutionary imaginary provided by Sdech Kân allows Hun Sen to reorient the notion of democracy to respond to the novel threat of a reinstated monarchy.

The bringing together of notions of "freedom rights" and "class struggle" also integrates the transformation of regime identity with the transition to a free market economy. In a seeming paradox, Kân is not only credited with having invented Marxist-style class struggle, but also commemorated for having introduced Cambodia's first monetary unit, the *sleung*. The National bank has started reminting the *sleung* coin, thus reminding the nation of Sdech Kân's other face as a proto-capitalist.[68]

In this attempt to reconcile the the Marxist concept of class struggle with freedom rights, now primarily imagined as part of a liberal tradition, Hun Sen echoes and challenges Sihanouk, while inheriting the same paradoxes that Sihanouk once faced. Just like Hun Sen, Sihanouk identified the beginnings of Cambodian socialism with the monarchy—but with Angkorean kings. These were taken to have demonstrated incipient socialism through the traditional pattern of land use, whereby the king was the guardian rather than proprietor of the land, making Cambodians "free men," and through economic and social projects such as irrigation projects and hospitals.[69] The Sdech Kân narrative is a counter-narrative to Sihanouk's, in that it challenges socialism's Angkorean roots by ascribing the beginnings of class struggle to a particular *neak mean bon*. It offers an alternative, moralistic genealogy of just leadership where the emphasis lies on a notion of democracy, which neatly cuts it off from the aristocratic kings who came before and after Sdech Kân.

---

[66] In some of the prime minister's speeches, it is the very death of Srey Sokonthor Bât that marks the national democratic revolution. See Hun Sen, "Educational Achievements in Kompong Thom's Santuk District," *CNV* 121, February 11, 2008.

[67] Hun Sen, *13 Tosâvot nei Domnaoer Kampuchea* [13 Decades of Cambodia's Evolution] (Phnom Penh: Pracheachon, 1991), 76, 280.

[68] "Cambodia Ancient Naga Coin Nordic-Gold Proof-Like Coin," http://www.nbc.org.kh/english/nbc_gallery/ more_info.php?id=4, accessed October 1, 2014.

[69] Sihanouk stated that "we must go back to the past to find the veritable origins of a socialism that did not yet have this name. The installers of this socialism were our Kings of Angkor." Sihanouk, "Pour Mieux Comprendre le Cambodge Actuel," 18.

NATIONAL RECONCILIATION

Next to a particular idea of democracy, the reinvention of Sdech Kân also transmits a distinct version of national reconciliation in contemporary Cambodia. Hun Sen has stated that he has taken the late Lao prime minister Kaysone Phomvihane's way of national reconciliation following the 1975 revolution as a model for the recreation of the Cambodian monarchy, in terms of how Kaysone's new regime dealt with the Lao monarchy that it replaced.[70] This, he has specified, particularly refers to how Kaysone integrated leading royalists—such as former Prime Minister Prince Souvanna Phouma—into the new regime.[71] Through these measures, in Laos, royalists came to lend traditional notions of legitimacy to the new regime.[72] In Cambodia, FUNCINPEC has been weakened by a series of coalition governments with the CPP, while King-Father Sihanouk sometimes appeared more supportive of Hun Sen than of FUNCINPEC. Paradoxically, Laos's transition from monarchy to a people's republic has provided the model for the reverse transition in Cambodia: to a constitutional monarchy from a communist system.[73]

By further inserting the fate of the monarchy into a discourse of national reconciliation, the Sdech Kân narrative supports this agenda. In many of Hun Sen's speeches, the reinvention of Sdech Kân has in different ways been integrated into supporting his claims to be the main architect of peacebuilding in post-conflict Cambodia. Royalists and other members of the political opposition generally identify the signing of the Paris Peace Agreements on October 23, 1991, between the SOC government and the tripartite resistance coalition, as the end of the civil war. Crediting Sihanouk with the successful negotiation of the PPA and pointing to how he presided over the Supreme National Council (SNC), the transitional government during the peace process, the idea of Sihanouk as the father of national reconciliation constitutes a main claim to legitimacy for Second Kingdom royalists that resonates with the promises of the *Putth Tumneay*. Hun Sen, while still regularly referring to Sihanouk as the father of peace and national reconciliation, has increasingly downplayed the importance of the PPA, pointing to how the peace accords were the product of external intervention and to how civil war between the new government and the Khmer Rouge resumed after the PPA's ratification.[74]

---

[70] Author's interview with Hun Sen, September 29, 2011.

[71] With the establishment of the Lao People's Democratic Republic in 1975, Souvanna Phouma became "Counsellor to the Government"; King Savang Vatthana abdicated and was appointed "Counsellor to the President"; former Crown Prince Vong Savang was appointed member of the Supreme People's Assembly; and Prince Souphanouvong, a life-long Communist, was made president of the new republic. Martin Stuart-Fox, *A History of Laos* (Cambridge: Cambridge University Press, 1997), 170.

[72] In a further parallel to contemporary Cambodia, the use of traditional notions of legitimacy became even more pronounced following the collapse of communist ideology in the late 1980s, when the Lao regime turned to employ a Buddhist discourse centered on righteous kings. Today, historical warrior kings have increasingly been promoted as national "ancestors." See: Evans, *The Politics of Ritual and Remembrance*, 70; Evans, "Revolution and Royal Style;" and Grabowsky and Tappe, "Important Kings of Laos."

[73] This is even more paradoxical given that following the Laotian transition, ex-king Savang Vatthana, his queen, and crown prince are believed to have died in a reeducation camp in Houaphan province. Evans, *The Politics of Ritual and Remembrance*, 99–100.

[74] See "Hun Sen's Speech at the Twentieth Anniversary of the Return of Sihanouk from Exile and Sihanouk's Ninetieth Birthday," *CNV* 164, October 30, 2011, in which Hun Sen, while still referring to Sihanouk as the "father of peace," stops at emphasizing "the brilliant

Instead, Hun Sen credits his win-win strategy, whereby defectors from the Khmer Rouge were offered full integration into Cambodian society, with having achieved national reconciliation with the integration of the last Khmer Rouge forces in 1998.[75] The win-win strategy thereby achieves the promises of January 7, 1979, celebrated by the CPP as the "nation's second birthday," when the Kampuchean United Front for National Salvation, out of which the PRK government would develop, overthrew the Khmer Rouge-regime of Democratic Kampuchea with (what is described as) Vietnamese backing.

The reinvention of Sdech Kân advances an idea of the curbing of royal power as integral to building national reconciliation and prosperity. While the win-win strategy constitutes Hun Sen's final defeat of the Khmer Rouge, the Sdech Kân narrative shows how Hun Sen has clipped the royalists' wings, leading to their reintegration into national politics under the leadership of the CPP. The reinvention of Sdech Kân also supports the attribution of post-conflict national reconciliation to Hun Sen's win-win strategy, outperforming Sihanouk. In a number of speeches, Hun Sen has recalled how the war that broke out during Sdech Kân's reign started a period of civil war lasting over three hundred years, until Hun Sen ended the chaos.[76] Here Sdech Kân and Hun Sen, rather than overlapping, are intrinsically linked as instigator and conciliator, respectively, of a defining phase of Cambodian history. Even in courting the people's votes ahead of elections—most recently in 2013—Hun Sen has invoked Sdech Kân in this context of national divisions—then stated that a main achievement of his own leadership has been to bring peace to a divided country.[77] At yet other times, Hun Sen links the 1998 final achievement of the win-win strategy to the July 1997 events.[78] These were justified by Hun Sen as a counter-attack against an alliance between royalists and the Khmer Rouge. The July 1997 events are thereby tied up with the win-win strategy, and together made to define national reconciliation in the Second Kingdom.

---

reflection" of Sihanouk and Monineath in "the creation of [the] policy of national reconciliation and healing."

[75] See. for example, Hun Sen, "Speech at Indonesian Chamber of Commerce and Industry, Jakarta," March 16, 1999, cited in Chhay, *Samdech Akka Moha Sena Padei Techo Hun Sen*, 79. On the win-win strategy, see Ma Yarith, *Yutthosastr Chnea Chnea: 5 Chomnuch robâs Samdech Neayok Rothmontrey Hun Sen* [The win–win strategy: 5 points of Samdech Prime Minister Hun Sen]. (Publisher unknown, 2007).

[76] In other speeches, Sdech Kân brings peace in a straightforward parallel to Hun Sen more than three hundred years later. See Hun Sen, "Inaugurating Buddhist Temple in Serei Suosdei Pagoda."

[77] Hun Sen, "Buddhist Achievements in Santuk," *CNV* 181, March 21, 2013.

[78] For speeches in which Sdech Kân's killing of Srey Sokonthor Bât is linked to the win-win strategy, as the start and end point of civil war, respectively, see, for example: "Address to the Closing Session of the National Conference: 'Peace, National Reconciliation, and Democracy Building: Ten Years after the Paris Peace Agreement,'" *CNV* 45, October 22, 2001; and "Address on the Occasion of the Acceptance of the Honorary Doctorate Degree of Political Science from the University of Ramkhamhaeng, Kingdom of Thailand," *CNV* 46, November 15, 2001. For a speech in which 1998 as the end-point of national division since the time of Sdech Kân is put in relation to the 1997 events, see "Inaugurating Bayon TV/Radio Broadcast Station," *CNV* 110, March 11, 2007.

STATUEMANIA

The intended overlap between Hun Sen and Sdech Kân is perhaps most prominently manifested in the statues of Sdech Kân that dot the Cambodian landscape.[79] The first statue of Kân was made in 2006 by a student at the Royal University of Fine Arts (RUFA), in Phnom Penh. An equestrian statue of Sdech Kân was thereafter commissioned for Srolop from a team of RUFA sculptors by Oknha Sim Vanna, a native of Kompong Cham involved in the development of Srolop, upon instructions from Hun Sen. Subsequently, statues modeled on the one in Srolop were commissioned in Pailin, Preah Vihear, Banteay Meanchey, and Kep provinces, and at the Ministry of Commerce in Phnom Penh. At least two different sculptors were assigned to make those, and there are two main variations: an equestrian and a standing pose. The faces on these Sdech Kân statues clearly resemble Hun Sen's. Indeed, the sculptors for the Srolop statue, on which subsequent statues have generally been modeled, were instructed to make the face similar to the prime minister's.[80] Sculptors from the same team also made an equestrian statue of general Ta Di, erected near Preah Vihear temple, commissioned to resemble Hing Bun Heang, chief of Hun Sen's bodyguard unit.[81] All of these statues have been commissioned by members of the political elite as a means of showing their loyalty to the prime minister.[82] One sponsor of a Sdech Kân statue, Cham Prasidh, who was Minister of Commerce at the time, explained that he had the statue erected in recognition of how the prime minister feels that he shares the same fate as Sdech Kân.[83]

Some time after these sculptures of historical figures made in the likeness of present-day political leaders started emerging, the prime minister declared that sculptures of contemporary leaders were forbidden. In June 2010, Om Yentieng, personal adviser to the prime minister and head of the anti-corruption unit, was chastised in public by Hun Sen for ordering a three-meter-high statue of the prime minister, to be put in front of the anti-corruption unit. The statue was removed, and Om Yentieng had to offer a public apology. The reason for the removal, given by Hun Sen's cabinet chief, Ho Sithy, was that making statues of living people ran counter to Cambodian culture, according to which statuary was said to be associated

---

[79] Also in Thailand and Laos, there are recent domestically produced heroic king statues (in Thailand, statues have proliferated ever since 1908), and in Laos, busts of Kaysone donated by North Korea. See: Grant Evans, "Immobile Memories: Statues in Thailand and Laos," in *Cultural Crisis and Social Memory: Modernity and Identity in Thailand and Laos*, ed. Shigeharu Tanabe and Charles F Keyes (London: RoutledgeCurzon, 2002); Wassana Nanuam and Nauvarat Suksamran, "Monument of Epic Size Rises to the Glory of Thai Kings," *Bangkok Post*, May 2, 2015.

[80] Author's interview, August 2011.

[81] A section of the prime minister's bodyguard unit has been stationed at Preah Vihear.

[82] The statues in Kep and at the ministry of commerce, both erected in 2010, were commissioned by Minister of Commerce Cham Prasidh. A statue was commissioned for Preah Vihear, reportedly by the son of four-star general Kun Kim, deputy-commander-in-chief of the Royal Cambodian Armed Forces (RCAF) and chairman of Hun Sen's advisors. Another statue was commissioned for Banteay Meanchey, reportedly by Ung Oeun, governor of Banteay Meanchey province, and deputy prime minister Yim Chhay Ly.

[83] Author's interview with Cham Prasidh, August 2, 2011.

with honoring the dead.[84] Following this incident, all display or sale of statues of top leaders was ordered stopped.

Statue of Sdech Kân, Pailin (photo courtesy of James Gerrand)

How can we account for the seeming paradox that making portrait-statues of historical figures in the likeness of current political leaders is encouraged, while making portrait-statues that overtly depict contemporary political leaders is forbidden outright? Moreover, Ho Sithy's statement is not entirely true: recent Cambodian statuary has depicted living kings and leaders.[85] Yet a statue of the historical Sdech Kân, with what seems to be the prime minister's face, makes particular claims that go beyond those of a statue plainly representing the PM. Statues present a body arrested in time, and thereby arrest time itself. In this sense, statues as a material culture "transact between life and death/destiny," recalling the two substitute bodies of Hun Sen and Sdech Kân.[86] Portrait-statuary as a genre in Khmer art was, since Angkorean times, bound up with worshipping the merit of the king, as the statue was seen to represent the king as dharma, embodying moral order.[87] The statue served as a bridge between future and past, in that all future kings' dharma in turn was embodied by the maintenance of the statuary and thereby

---

[84] Chun Sakada, "Hun Sen Statue Removed after Dust-up," *Voice of America (Khmer)*, June 18, 2010.

[85] For example, an equestrian statue of king Norodom (r. 1860–1904), bequeathed by the French in 1876, was erected at the Royal Palace; and a statue of king Sisowath (r. 1904–27) was set up on Wat Phnom in 1909. Sihanouk had busts and statues of himself placed around the country during his time in power, and there were even busts of Pol Pot made at S-21 in preparation for a planned cult of personality, new to Cambodian communism, but that never materialized. See: Milton Osborne, *Phnom Penh: A Cultural and Literary History* (Oxford: Signal, 2008), 70; Chandler, *Brother Number One*, 149; and Nic Dunlop, *The Lost Executioner: The Story of Comrade Duch and the Khmer Rouge* (London: Bloomsbury, 2005), 184.

[86] Evans, "Immobile Memories," 174, drawing on Kenneth Gross, *The Dream of the Moving Statue* (Ithaca and London: Cornell University Press, 1992).

[87] Ashley Thompson, "Angkor Revisited: The State of Statuary," in *What's the Use of Art: Asian Visual and Material Culture in Context*, ed. Jan Mrázek and Morgan Pitelka (Honolulu: University of Hawai'i Press, 2008), 187.

the maintenance of the moral order.[88] In modern times, many of these ancient statues continue to be venerated by royal family members and ordinary Cambodians alike, maintaining their association with Khmer royalty and with national political integrity that follows from their "cosmic ordering role."[89] Contemporary worship of statuary, in different ways associated with today's king, is both of statuary as representation of ancient kings, and of the statuary as the incarnation of ancient kings.[90] Worship of such statuary is politically embedded, for instance, the statuary of Sdech Komlong, also known as the Leper King, and Yeay Tep, is sponsored primarily by royal family members.[91]

The recent statuary of Sdech Kân competes with ancient royal statuary to embody memories of the royal past, offering newly manufactured memories belonging to a different imagined lineage—one that uproots the very idea of genealogy. By tapping into this series of connotations, Hun Sen claims the moral ancestry of a rival imagined community, joined with Sdech Kân through the statue to embody national leadership.[92] Just as today's royalty through the intermediary of the statues is "endowed with divine stature," the Sdech Kân statues in some sense confer an association with the immortal and divine.[93] Conversely, and more sinister, a direct depiction of present leaders could suggest if not their death (as claimed by the prime minister's cabinet), then at least their mortality. It is perhaps no coincidence that, as noted above, the other person represented in this iconographic form, through the statue of Ta Di at Preah Vihear, is Hing Bun Heang, chief of Hun Sen's bodyguard unit—the person with the utmost responsibility to protect Hun Sen's personal safety.

The statuary also plays a decisive role in spatially defining the nation. Grant Evans, in discussing Thailand's first statue of a living person—the 1908 Chulalongkorn monument in Bangkok—argues that it represented a changing concept of distance, as the image of the king symbolically stepped closer to the

---

[88] Ibid., 186–87.

[89] Chan Sophea Hang, "Stec Gaṃlaṅ' and Yāy Deb," in Marston and Guthrie, *History, Buddhism, and New Religious Movements in Cambodia*, 113, 125.

[90] Ibid., 113.

[91] A cement replica of Sdech Komlong was erected at Wat Unnalom in Phnom Penh by CPP officials ahead of the 1993 national elections, seemingly to compete with the royal cult—yet, in the words of Hang, the cult turned out to be a "discreet' one. Ibid., 122–23.

[92] The association with royal statuary is an association primarily with national leadership rather than with kingship. This is clearly evidenced by an incident during the Khmer Republic, when the statue of Braḥ Aṅg Saṅkh Cakr, the Leper King, at the Phnom Penh riverfront, was beheaded. That event was interpreted as an attack on Lon Nol, a Republican and the national leader at the time. See John Marston and Elizabeth Guthrie, "The Icon of the Leper King," in Marston and Guthrie *History, Buddhism, and New Religious Movements in Cambodia*, 87–88.

[93] Hang, "Stec Gaṃlaṅ' and Yāy Deb," in Marston and Guthrie, *History, Buddhism, and New Religious Movements in Cambodia*, 113–14. Classical Cambodian portrait-statues typically represented kings, princes, or high dignitaries after their death in their divine aspect. See: George Coedès, "Le Portrait dans l'Art Khmer," *Arts Asiatiques* 7 (1960): 179–98; and Pou, "Dieux et Rois dans la Pensée Khmère Ancienne," 653–69. Thompson explores the conceptual complexities of the portrait-statue in terms of the relationship between king and the god it represented, suggesting that the old Khmer portrait-statue "was and is conceived as the posthumous abode of the person/god embodied within, and as an embodiment of the reign of successive kings." See Thompson, "Angkor Revisited," in Mrázek and Pitelka, *What's the Use of Art*, 203.

people.[94] In today's Cambodia, these statues similarly bring the presence of authority to different corners of the nation. Central authority in the capital defines the right to represent the nation, and it is in this context that the contemporary worship of royal statuary is understood to maintain the substitution between ancient and modern capitals.[95] The erection of a Sdech Kân statue at what has been identified as the ancient capital of Srolop symbolically shifts the nation's symbolic midpoint to Hun Sen's home province. Imagined in the context of new–old struggle with royals, this statue, in particular, provides a counterpoint to the worship of royal statuary in a mirror fashion linked with national reconciliation after the 1997 events.[96] The role of the recent statuary in claiming the right to define the nation's boundaries is perhaps most obvious in the placement of the statue of Ta Di at Preah Vihear temple, the center of a border conflict with Thailand. By establishing an identification between the ancient monument and Hun Sen's network, a link is created between the newer statuary and a royal site that is the focus of much contemporary nationalist sentiment.[97]

FILM, OVERLAP, AND INVULNERABILITY

The Sdech Kân narrative was also intended to be disseminated through the medium of film. In 2009, the popular production company Hang Meas started initial planning, at the request of Hun Sen, according to sources inside the project. Mao Ayuth, then secretary of state for the CPP's Ministry of Information and a veteran filmmaker, was to be its director. The principle roles were cast. The portrayal of Kân fell to one of Cambodia's most popular singers. Search requirements, he explained, had been that the actor should be a "Khmer Angkor"—referring to a particular idea of the appearance of a "real Khmer," defined by characteristics such as having dark skin and being tall and strong—and the singer fits well into this category.[98] Presumably, this selection criterion was intended to show Sdech Kân as truly a "man of the people."

The film project was interminably delayed, so that the only cinematographic portrayal of Kân, as of early 2016, is that of an American fantasy film, "Clash of the Empires." In this low-budget movie filmed in Cambodia, a Salvadorian actor depicts a prehistoric king named Kân. Asked about the choice of character (peripheral in the

---

[94] Evans, "Immobile Memories," in Tanabe and Keyes, *Cultural Crisis and Social Memory: Modernity and Identity in Thailand and Laos,* 155.

[95] Hang, "Stec Gaṃlaṅ' and Yāy Deb," in Marston and Guthrie, *History, Buddhism, and New Religious Movements in Cambodia,* 124–25.

[96] Sihanouk phrased his return to Angkor after the July 1997 events to "pay his respects to the statues" as a metaphor for reestablishing peace and reconciliation in their wake. See Thompson, "Angkor Revisited," in Mrázek and Pitelka, *What's the Use of Art,* 181. In 1998, Sihanouk and Monineath sponsored a pavilion for Yāy Deb shortly before a summit to resolve conflict in the wake of the first national elections following the 1997 events. See Hang, "Stec Gaṃlaṅ' and Yāy Deb," in Marston and Guthrie, *History, Buddhism, and New Religious Movements in Cambodia,* 116.

[97] Thompson traces how the struggle for central authority through identification with monuments was bound up with the representation of the nation and borders at the time of the 2003 anti-Thai riots. See Thompson, "Angkor Revisited," in Mrázek and Pitelka, *What's the Use of Art,* 203–6.

[98] Author's interview, September 2009.

film), the Salvadorian reported that the film crew had asked young Cambodians hired as crew members to name a great Khmer hero—and Kân was their answer. The foreigners on the set were blissfully unaware of any political overtones.[99] The contrast between the projected Kân as the hugely popular, quintessentially Cambodian "Khmer Angkor" star and a Salvadorian wearing a bizarre fur hat adorned with animal horns could not be more stark. Yet, this unexpected twist testifies to the successful spread of the narrative and popularity of Kân.

In 2016, it was announced that the Sdech Kân film directed by Mao Ayuth was to be completed by early 2017. CPP Senator Ly Yong Phat was to provide a budget of $1 million USD, making this the most costly of any Cambodian film to date.[100] Although most of the cast—including the lead actor—has been changed, discussions with members of the initial film set while some production was underway provided fascinating perspectives. The film set up a new stage for the acting out of a narrative that theatrically blurred the metaphorical and the real. Comments by the actor originally selected to star as Kân—the substitute body of Kân in some sense—on the nature of overlap of the two substitute bodies were therefore spine-tingling. Asked whether he considered Hun Sen to be the reincarnation of Sdech Kân, the actor replied:

> Hun Sen *is* Sdech Kân. He thinks he was Sdech Kân in a previous life and Cambodian people think so. Hun Sen is Sdech Kân because they have many things in common. Both were born in Kompong Cham province. Sdech Kân was a temple-servant and Hun Sen used to serve in the pagoda as well. Now everyone loves Sdech Kân and wants to hear about Sdech Kân. But if Hun Sen falls from power, then people will stop caring about Sdech Kân and will hate him.[101]

Hun Sen is accepted as a reincarnation of Sdech Kân for as long as his hold on power proves this claim. But like Sdech Kân, Hun Sen is susceptible to being challenged, and could ultimately fall from power, as a result of which he would be forgotten and even hated. This perspective to some extent transcends the question of whether Hun Sen is the "actual" reincarnation of the king. The crucial challenge for this actor, and for others involved in the film project, was to establish the truth about Sdech Kân. Engaging in a discourse that posited Hun Sen as Kân's substitute allowed them to weigh Hun Sen's rule through an assessment of the historical Kân. For example, one assistant producer critical of the Prime Minister collected his own set of historical materials on Kân, to expose his "true nature" in conversations with others on the set.[102]

Stories of Hun Sen's supernatural abilities circulate in Cambodia and seem to provide one explanation for the foundations of his power, and why it is that he "*is*" Sdech Kân. Invulnerability is a notion that is well-documented as central to social

---

[99] Author's interview, July 2013.

[100] Muong Vandy, and Will Jackson, "Hun Sen and the Man Who Would be King," *Phnom Penh Post*, January 9, 2016.

[101] Author's interview, September 2009.

[102] Author's interview, November 2009.

and political imaginations across Southeast Asia.[103] Being invulnerable is an important characteristic of both the *neak mean bon* and the *Preah Batr Dhammik*.[104] Invulnerability, though, is not reducible to simply an ingredient of these two concepts, but could be said to be a kind of core of imaginings of the foundation of political power in the region. Andrew Turton calls it "a requirement of leadership." As such, it is associated both with unofficial leadership, such as that of millenarian leaders of exceptional merit and with a "state-forming kind of knowledge."[105] Unsurprisingly, the new lead actor of Mao Ayuth's Sdech Kân film is a champion bodybuilder.[106] If Tony Day is right in positing security as the "dominant constraint on the form and role of state in Southeast Asian societies," then the prime minister's aspiration to invulnerability places him at the center of this power, knowledge, and state-forming nexus.[107] But if invulnerability is the desired ideal, the Sdech Kân narrative can be understood primarily in the context of the prime minister's perception of vulnerability. Taken to its logical conclusion, such a parallel brings to mind Sdech Kân's bitter end—decapitation after thirteen years of rule. Indeed, just as the statues, the narrative as a whole may be understood as an attempt to ward off the prime minister's own mortality.

Modeling Just Leadership

Through becoming the substitute body of Sdech Kân, Hun Sen seeks to reconstitute the particular bodies of the royal family as well as kingship as a whole. Though he publicly claims to be the monarchy's defender, Hun Sen makes use of his implied reincarnation of Sdech Kân to remodel the relationship between the nation, Buddhism, and kingship, and to weaken the national leadership role of the monarchy and the royalist faction in Cambodia's Second Kingdom. By drawing on the historical ambiguity between inherited and noninherited leadership that the historical Cambodian monarchy entails, kingship is challenged from within its very discourse, and the importance of genealogy is uprooted. The reinvention of Sdech Kân exalts nonhereditary leadership, which is inserted into a modern discourse of democracy, equality, and even social mobility.

Hun Sen's reincarnation of Sdech Kân can be understood as fundamentally a bid to embody national leadership, rather than kingship as such. As the man of prowess and virtue at the center of the polity, Hun Sen personally represents the nation. In its different forms of expression, his reincarnation as Sdech Kân powerfully delivers the message that Prime Minister Hun Sen is personally the architect of post-conflict national reconciliation, peacebuilding, and democracy in Cambodia, and that these achievements are founded, in turn, on his curbing of royal power. This conception of

---

[103] See, for example: Andrew Turton, "Invulnerability and Local Knowledge," in *Thai Constructions of Knowledge*, ed. Chitakasem Manas and Andrew Turton (London: School of Oriental and African Studies, 1991), 155–82; and Day, *Fluid Iron*.

[104] Turton, "Invulnerability and Local Knowledge," 171; Khing, "Neak Mean Boun," 84–85; and Heng, "In Search of the Dhammika Ruler," in Kent and Chandler, *People of Virtue*, 313. Invulnerability is a particularly democratic form of knowledge in that it is "accessible to all members of a community" (Day, *Fluid Iron*, 160). This goes particularly well with the somewhat similar democratic notion of the *neak mean bon*.

[105] Day, *Fluid Iron*, 160.

[106] Muong and Jackson, "Hun Sen and the Man Who Would be King."

[107] Ibid., 157.

democracy is different from the liberal democratic discourse employed by the Cambodian People's Party program. Presenting a new political identity to fill the shoes of his previous identity as a socialist, Hun Sen turns to the revolutionary figure of Sdech Kân. Through it, he reorients the notion of democracy in order to respond to the novel threat facing his regime in the KOC: the reinstated monarchy.

Has Hun Sen achieved the complete overlap of the two substitute bodies? The narrative testifies to the importance of moral claims in contemporary Cambodian politics by first of all defining Hun Sen as a man possessing merit. Hun Sen's success depends primarily on whether he will be judged to embody the model of just leadership that he invokes. More important clues still might lie in the telling absence of rival rumors and narratives concerning the actual occupant of the throne. In this sense, the throne that Hun Sen claims is vacant.

CHAPTER THREE

ROYALISTS:
BETWEEN EMBODIMENT AND DOCTRINE

In Cambodia, ideas of social organization have evolved along with the institution of the monarchy. Because of this, royalist representation of the nation is key to untangling national imaginings in the Second Kingdom. Historical Cambodian ideas of political representation developed around the monarchy, positing a direct link between the body of the king and the "body politic" of the kingdom. Such ideas were very much alive when, in 1993, a constitutional monarchy was reinstated after a hiatus of more than two decades, and former king Norodom Sihanouk reascended the throne. Royalist party FUNCINPEC gained an electoral victory, and went on to form a coalition government with the CPP. 1993 marked the beginning of lengthy contestation of the mandate of the modern Khmer monarchy and of political royalism. Royalists faced the challenge of defining a way for royalism, as a political party force, to represent the nation. Their task was to transfer regal legitimacy to the political party vehicle, FUNCINPEC, which would compete in elections.

Not only was the monarchy restored in 1993, but also the First Kingdom national anthem *Nokor Reach* ("Royal Kingdom") and national flag (both of which had been replaced upon the 1970 abolition of the monarchy), as well as the national motto, "nation, religion, king" (*cheat, sasana, mohaksatr*). According to You Hockry, newly appointed FUNCINPEC co-minister of interior at the time, Hun Sen suggested that the word "happiness" (*sopheak mongkol*) be added to the motto, to emphasize considerations of welfare and development, but dropped the suggestion following objections from the royalist side.[1] The importance that royalists accorded to the formulaic purity of the motto sprang from their objective to establish the historical coninuity of the monarchy, as eternally bound up with the trajectory of the nation. Echoing how in the immediate postcolonial period Sihanouk discursively used monarchical institutions to bridge pre- and postcolonial Cambodia (and portrayed the colonial era to be an "inauthentic abyss"), Second Kingdom royalists in many ways dismissed the period since the 1970 institution of a republic as an aberration.[2] The coup d'état of 1970 had put the very existence of the nation in peril, and the 1993 return of the royals promised its restoration.[3] To promote this idea, Second Kingdom royalists sought to naturalize the "nation, religion, king" trinity as

---

[1] Author's interview with You Hockry, June 15, 2010.

[2] On the immediate post-colonial period, see Edwards, *Cambodge*, 9.

[3] See, for example, Norodom Ranariddh, *Droit Public Cambodgien* (Perpignan: CERJEMAF/Presses Universitaires de Perpignan, 1998), 189.

an unchanging foundation of Cambodian social order.[4] Yet this enterprise proved exacting, reflecting both the historically contested nature of its configuration and the variety of meanings intended by contemporary royalists anchored in such historical ambiguities.

As the Second Kingdom progressed, political royalism became an increasingly meaningless notion. From the party's erstwhile victory in the 1993 elections, FUNCINPEC support steadily plummeted until it failed altogether to win any seats in 2013. Parallel to this, the mandate of the monarchy was increasingly cemented as a "strict" form of constitutional monarchy, to be contrasted with the larger mandate implied by ideas of the king as the embodiment of the nation. A variety of factors have played a role in royalism's decline. Critical ones, often noted, are the corruption in which FUNCINPEC's leaders have engaged, and their disregard for activists at the party base. Entering into successive coalition governments with the CPP, FUNCINPEC notoriously engaged in rent-seeking behavior that not only discredited the party in the eyes of the public, but also fractured it internally.[5] An underlying lack of political vision gave free rein to opportunism, so that the increasingly marginalized royalists would make themselves useful to the CPP in return for the most limited share of power. Above these contemporary failings towered the memory of Sihanouk's role in the Khmer Rouge's rise to power. What has remained outside the analysis is that these factors played out in the context of a set of tensions that destabilized Second Kingdom royalism from within.

Although Cambodian royalism is now in its death throes, this chapter lays out how a multifaceted struggle to imbue royalist politics with meaning took place in the first two decades of the Second Kingdom. This struggle can be understood to reflect a breaking point, as royalists sought to transfer the legitimacy of the monarchy to the novel framework of a royalist political party within the bounds of a constitutional monarchy. Political royalists made elaborate bids to represent the post-PPA nation. They alluded to historical ideas of embodiment in a contemporary reinvention of incarnate politics. They struggled to develop a doctrinal identity to imbue their claims with the language of ideology. They advanced theories of how democracy in the Second Kingdom necessarily remained tied to the monarchy. Each bid for legitimacy attempted to establish a unique or exclusive link between royalists and the nation.

These negotiations within the royalist camp are central to larger, contemporary renegotiations of the categories making up the Cambodian political landscape. Since historical ideas of political representation in Cambodia developed around the monarchy, contemporary debates within the royalist camp about the nature of representation, entailing ideas of embodiment versus a doctrinal identity, and hereditary versus elected leadership, have brought the renegotiation of these questions to a head. Royalist politics provided an arena for these historically inherited debates to play out in the contemporary setting. Examining these negotiations is also crucial for reassessing the fate of royalist political parties. Long-time FUNCINPEC leader Norodom Ranariddh has typically summed up party achievements under his presidencies (1993–2006, 2015–) as the introduction of

---

[4] FUNCINPEC party statutes pledge to "try hard with all methods to protect the national motto, 'nation, religion, king.'" See FUNCINPEC, *Statutes and Internal Regulations* (I. iv), 2005; and FUNCINPEC, *Statutes and Internal Regulations* (I. iv), 2006.

[5] Compare to Roberts, *Political Transition in Cambodia 1991–99*, 126–30.

liberal democracy and restoration of the constitutional monarchy.[6] Yet, the resurrection and adaptation of historical ideas of royal legitimacy impacted the meaning of these two cornerstones of FUNCINPEC's legitimizing language. A fine-grained study of the reinvention of links to the nation is therefore crucial for analyzing the trajectory of political royalism.

These questions had previously been debated by Sihanouk, as head of the first (and last) post-independence royalist regime, the Sangkum Reastr Niyum, 1955-70. The Sangkum Reastr Niyum would come to supplant Cambodia's constitutional monarchy, introduced in 1947,[7] Royalist political parties looked back to the Sangkum Reastr Niyum as a model for Second Kingdom Cambodia, both since it retained a rosy and nostalgic glow as Sihanouk's self-proclaimed "Oasis of Peace" before the outbreak of civil war, and because it provided a unifying rallying point for royalists, who had scattered in different directions after 1970. Yet, in turning to Sangkum as their model, Second Kingdom royalists had to navigate its inconsistencies and paradoxes. Under the Sangkum Reastr Niyum, the question of the relationship between kingship and a political form of royalism were partly suspended in an ambiguous "monarchy without a king," with Sihanouk acting as head of state after he abdicated the throne. The Sangkum was described as a political "movement" rather than a political party—but nonetheless functioned as a party in elections. The contemporary renegotiation of the role of the Cambodian monarchy and political royalism followed from these historical ambiguities, conserved in the person of Sihanouk. The dilemmas that surfaced centered on a tension between ideas of embodiment and doctrine, which entailed questions of inherited versus non-inherited leadership, merit, and genealogy.

Second Kingdom royalists attempted to establish a meaningful link between political royalism and the nation through four interlinked tensions. First, I look at a productive tension between unity and diversity, seen variously in the tension between the royal family as a unified group versus the diverse political tendencies it embraced, and between the royal family as a "truly national" suprapolitical force versus the necessity for royal family members to take a partisan political stand. Second, I explore a tension inherited from the Sangkum era, centered on the reconciliation of kingship with a political form of royalism. Third, turning to royalist conceptualizations of democracy, I examine a tension between contending visions of royalist democracy as a Sangkum-derived discourse and of royalist democracy founded in a "democratic opposition" identity. Finally, I explore successive attempts at reinventing a Sihanoukist identity from the perspective of a tension between doctrinal identity versus ideas of embodiment. These interconnected tensions engaged in crucial ways with the person and legacy of Sihanouk, both as the leader of the Sangkum Reastr Niyum and as contemporary monarch and King-Father. The failure to work out each of these tensions contributed to the overall failure to establish a link between the nation and political royalism. First, as royalist nationalism came to be strongly associated with national unity under Sihanouk, the

---

[6] See, for example, Ranariddh, under his pen name Sam Nora, "Note of the Day 6: The Contributions of the Royalist Party FUNCINPEC Led by HRH Prince Norodom Ranariddh," 2010, available at http://www.norodomranariddh.org, accessed 10 March 2012.

[7] A constitutional monarchy of sorts can be said to have existed since King Sisowath ascended the throne in 1904. The French Résident supérieur acted as the equivalent of a prime minister, while the king played a ceremonial role and served as conciliator between the people and the government.

historical and contemporary presence of diverse political tendencies within the royal family stood out uncomfortably, and, ultimately, crippled political royalism by placing national unity above partisan political action. Second, the failure to establish a clear mandate of political royalism meant that the very foundation of a party political form of royalism was missing. Third, both contending democratic discourses became increasingly meaningless for asserting a political royalist identity. Fourth, while ideas of embodiment were sidelined, attempts to turn the Sihanoukist legacy into a doctrine ultimately made it susceptible to hijacking by rival political parties. The combined effect was that the very foundation, form, and content of political royalism as a force to represent the nation remained unaccounted for.

UNITY IN DIVERSITY?

The 1993 gathering of the great majority of royal family members in FUNCINPEC in many ways formed a *discontinuity* with the recent past, when members of the royal family had scattered over the diverse terrain of political tendencies. Second Kingdom royalists united from sharply contrasting political backgrounds. While many had joined FUNCINPEC after its 1981 creation by Sihanouk, many had only at times (or, more rarely, not at all) sided with Sihanouk during the two preceding decades. Second Kingdom royalist politics can, in this sense, be understood as an enterprise of uniting a dispersed family from various political camps. Many who had not consistently sided with Sihanouk after his 1970 ouster were given prominent roles post-1993, both in the Royal Palace and in party politics. This included royals who had actively supported the Khmer Republic, such as Sisowath Thomico, long-term aide to Sihanouk in the KOC, and Sisowath Sirirath, ambassador to the United States and permanent representative at the UN (1994–97), FUNCINPEC co-minister of defense (1998–2004), and deputy president of FUNCINPEC (2006–11). Many had been self-identified socialists of different types. In an apparent contradiction, Sisowath Thomico claimed to have joined the Khmer Republic out of Trotskyist convictions.[8] Other senior figures had joined the Khmer Rouge revolutionaries, such as Sisowath Ayravady, who, upon returning to Cambodia in 1997, would serve as Ranariddh's director of cabinet during his presidency of the National Assembly (1998–2006) and work at King Sihamoni's secretariat.[9] The two royal family members who had remained in Cambodia during the People's Republic of Kampuchea—the late Sisowath Sovethvong (Lola) and her sister Sisowath Pongneary (Lolotte)—were both integrated into new royalist politics, even though both had worked for the Heng Samrin regime. Lola was instrumental in aiding the negotiations between Sihanouk and the PRK and later SOC governments leading up to the PPA, while Lolotte was given an important ceremonial role in the Royal Palace and granted the honorific title "Samdech."[10]

---

[8] Author's interview with Sisowath Thomico, May 20, 2010. Even Sihanouk, in his day, reportedly stated that he would have been a leftist if he had not been a member of the royal family. See Osborne, *Sihanouk*, 145–46.

[9] Sisowath Ayravady worked as a translator at the Democratic Kampuchea Ministry of Foreign Affairs, together with her husband, Ngo Pin, later a secretary of state for FUNCINPEC. Sihanouk's son, Norodom Narindrapong, once in line to become king, remained a convinced Pol Potist until his death in 2003. He was not, however, integrated into royalist politics post-1993.

[10] Author's interview with Sisowath Pongneary, September 12, 2011.

Such elasticity is arguably derived from a productive tension between unity and diversity characteristic of the royal family and, with them, royalist politics. The relationship between the part and the whole, particularity and universality, is central to conceptualizations of kingship worldwide.[11] In historical Cambodian conceptualizations of the royal body as one in a series of substitute bodies, the king was at once a part of the whole of the communal body, and, simultaneously, a whole in and of himself—or, rather, Thompson writes, a potential whole.[12] The king's representation of the whole was, ultimately, an ideal-type situation. In the post-independence era, this friction between the part and the whole, now imagined as the nation, took expression in a tension between the royal family acting as a unified faction on the one hand, versus the diverse political tendencies it embraced on the other. The monarchy as a national, suprapolitical force, was set against the taking of a particular political stand, as royalists became political actors within a multiparty framework.[13]

This tension can be understood as a major theme of Second Kingdom royalist politics. The imperative of royal involvement in the nation's shifting political fortunes had prompted family members to follow different political banners during previous decades, when royalist side-taking was often messy and pragmatic. Royalist identity as a unifying force above partisan rivalries was now the chief reason why previous political affiliations were excused, enabling disparate parties to re-gather under one party banner. This was testified to in personal accounts both of motives for leaving the side of royalists led by Sihanouk, and of motives for later reconciliation. The Khmer Republic provides a case in point. Sihanouk's cousin Sisowath Sirik Matak was instrumental in establishing the Khmer Republic in 1970, and prominent royals of today, notably his son Sisowath Sirirath and nephew Sisowath Thomico, would support it. Today, both emphasize that the Khmer Republic was not "Republican" *per se*, stressing instead its anti-Sihanoukist character based on the disapproval of Sihanouk's close ties with the North Vietnamese communists at the time.[14] Thomico's explanation outlines conflicting responsibilities of royals in the early 1970s: "The people fighting against the Lon

---

[11] In medieval Europe, the king's two bodies (the body natural and the body politic) were thought to depend on each other so that they formed "one unit indivisible, each being fully contained in the other." Kantorowicz, *The King's Two Bodies*, 9, cited in Thompson, "The Suffering of Kings," 92.

[12] Thompson, "The Suffering of Kings," 93.

[13] This tension has had to be negotiated by all Southeast Asian monarchies engaged in the making of nation states following the demise of absolute monarchies. For a discussion on the role of actors of royal blood engaging in complex alliances and side-taking in the making of postcolonial Laos, see Søren Ivarsson and Christopher E. Goscha, "Prince Phetsarath (1890–1959): Nationalism and Royalty in the Making of Modern Laos," *Journal of Southeast Asian Studies* 38, no. 1 (2007): 55–81. For an account of how the Thai monarchy has built its legitimacy on promoting a view of itself as suprapolitical, see Thongchai Winichakul, "Toppling Democracy," *Journal of Contemporary Asia* 38, no. 1 (2008), 11–37.

[14] Having left Cambodia in 1958 to study in France, England, and Japan, Sisowath Sirirath was recruited to the Khmer Republic by his father, Sirik Matak. He states his main motivation to have been anti-communism. His cousin Sisowath Thomico on the other hand, returning from studies in Paris, claims to have been a "far-leftist" who disagreed with the Pol Potist analysis of Cambodian society along Maoist lines (in favor of a Trotskyist reading), and considered the Khmer Republic to be a necessary stage on the road to the final revolution. Author's interviews with Sisowath Thomico, May 20, 2010, and Sisowath Sirirath, May 13, 2010.

Nol-regime were Vietnamese. As a Cambodian, as a member of the royal family, I took the decision to stay and fight them. I think that the secret mission of every royal family member is to fight for the country."[15] Thomico perceived it to be his particular responsibility as a royal to take political action—even if that meant fighting the deposed Sihanouk. Though by all accounts Sirik Matak was motivated by a pro-Western orientation and a desire to change economic policies, four decades later, royals once loyal to Sirik Matak maintained that he took sides with Lon Nol also to protect the royal family, who mostly remained in Cambodia during the Republic.[16] In maintaining this they referred to an old and tried royal strategy of covering all bases, intended to ensure that the royal family emerged on the winning side.

The reasoning behind the decision of Sisowath Lola and Sisowath Lolotte to join the Heng Samrin regime displays a similar logic. The two sisters remained in Cambodia under Democratic Kampuchea and were the only royal survivors to remain in the country after 1979. Lola was recruited to work at the PRK Ministry of Foreign Affairs and became deputy of the Kampuchean United Front for National Salvation (UFNS) and member of parliament for Takeo.[17] Lolotte later explained her late sister's decision to work with the government in the following words: "The government needed to assemble all the minorities, including the royal family. She represented the royal family in the *Communauté*. [...] It was the work that mattered to us. Socialism, or not socialism, it was the work, and remaining in the country."[18] This reasserts the royal necessity to remain in the nation, even as a marginalized part of it. Her words highlight how, in the PRK nation, the royal family had been reduced to the status of a minority—a tiny fraction of the national community, one that could never aspire to representing the whole nation. Lolotte thus underscores just how far the monarchy had come from the historical conception of its role, manifested by the discrepancy between their particularity as a family and the national whole.

The shared understanding of this tension arguably aided subsequent reconciliation. According to Lolotte, "Sihanouk forgave everyone everything. [...] When he returned, it was like there had been no problem at all."[19] Sisowath Thomico and Sisowath Sirirath had already been reconciled with Sihanouk in 1979. Thomico's aunt Monineath was Sihanouk's spouse, and Thomico used this family

---

[15] Author's interview with Sisowath Thomico.

[16] Most royal family members remained in Phnom Penh under the Khmer Republic, including Queen Kossamak. Though some suffered imprisonment early on, most lived rather freely until 1973, when a son-in-law of Sihanouk bombed the presidential palace, following which several royal family members were put under surveillance. Sylvia Sisowath, who remained in Cambodia until 1974, stated: "Most of us [members of the royal family] stayed during the Khmer Republic. We had no reason to leave our country. The Republicans were not against the royal family." Author's interview with Sisowath Sylvia, May 26, 2010.

[17] Sisowath Lolotte and Sisowath Lola were reunited in Phnom Penh in September 1979, where they lived together until Lola passed away in 1994. Lolotte was called by Lola to work at the Ministry of Foreign Affairs, where she briefly worked in the political department before changing to work in the ministry's nursery.

[18] Author's interview with Sisowath Pongneary.

[19] According to Lolotte, during the PRK, Sihanouk even sent a representative to look for remaining royals, and the representative found Lola and Lolotte. Testifying to his unchanging concern for them, Sihanouk thereafter regularly sent money to Lolotte. Author's interview with Sisowath Pongneary.

relationship to explain to Sihanouk that he, Thomico, had just chosen "a different path"; later that same year, Thomico was appointed as Sihanouk and Monineath's press attaché.[20] Meeting Sihanouk and Monineath in January 1979 in New York, Sisowath Sirirath accepted Sihanouk's invitation "to unify all the Cambodian overseas forces." Sisowath Sirirath was thus made Sihanouk's representative in Canada and the United States, and would serve as his ambassador to the UN and his chief of protocol.[21]

After 1993, the royal emphasis on unity was paramount. Royal family members shared a belief that they needed to act as a unified faction to serve as a unifying force for Cambodia. This need was only heightened by the discord of the preceding decades. Sisowath Sirirath captured a typical sentiment:

> If you compare with all countries in the world, they only went through a transition between communism and capitalism. Cambodia is different—we went through five different regimes during sixty years. The royal family is a unifying force for Cambodia. Without Sihamoni and Sihanouk, Cambodia would not be a unified country.[22]

Royal family members gathered around Sihanouk's role in the peace process that concluded with the 1991 Paris Peace Agreements. Royalists, together with other members of the political opposition, identify the signing of the PPA on October 23, 1991, between the People's Republic of Kampuchea government and the tripartite resistance coalition as the end date of the civil war. As Sihanouk presided over the signing of the PPA, the idea of Sihanouk as the father of national reconciliation came to constitute a main claim to legitimacy for Second Kingdom royalists.[23] At the conclusion of the peace process, Sihanouk returned to Cambodia as chairman of the Supreme National Council, a large coalition government. According to Ranariddh, the "monarchic principle of a national community without any exclusion" was thereby realized in Sihanouk.[24] With Sihanouk's reinstatement as a constitutional monarch two years later, this suprapolitical role was tied to the constitutional monarchy.

Unity under Sihanouk was seen as a precondition for national unity and, as part of this, the royal family naturally had to come together around him. This neatly illustrates contemporary perceptions of part and whole—the belief that gathering

---

[20] Author's interview with Sisowath Thomico, May 28, 2010.

[21] Author's interview with Sisowath Sirirath, May 25, 2010.

[22] Author's interview with Sisowath Sirirath, May 13, 2010.

[23] Hun Sen has increasingly downplayed the importance of the PPA, instead crediting his "win–win policy" with having achieved national reconciliation. While October 23 was originally a public holiday, the CPP later discontinued that commemoration. In 2009, Hun Sen announced that celebrating the anniversary of October 23 was "meaningless," and that the opposition would be free to do away with the January 7 celebration if it came into power. In the wake of Sihanouk's passing, the CPP-led government in October 2012 redesignated October 23 as a public holiday to commemorate the PPA. See: Yun Samean, "Hun Sen Says Celebrating Oct 23 'Meaningless,'" *The Cambodian Daily*, January 12, 2009; "Government Redesignates October 23 as Public Holiday," *The Cambodia Herald*, October 23, 2012; Ma Yarith, *Yutthosatr Chnea Chnea: 5 Chomnuch robâs Samdech Neayok Rothmontrey Hun Sen* [The Win-Win Strategy: 5 Points of Samdech Prime Minister Hun Sen]. [Publisher unknown], 2007.

[24] Norodom Ranariddh, *Droit Public Cambodgien*, 155.

around Sihanouk would enable him to heal the nation. This also defined ideas of royalist nationalism as bound up with Sihanouk's suprapolitical role. It is difficult to exaggerate how firmly royalist nationalism was thereby tied to the idea of unity and national reconciliation, and raised above partisan politics. This was manifest in Sisowath Ayravady's definition of "nationalism":

> When I think about nationalism, I always look to the past, to what Cambodia as a monarchy has been going through. 1993 was an important date for the sake of nationalism. Sihanouk reunified all political parties or factions. [...] Royalist nationalism truly exists. For at least 70 percent of the people, nationalism is bound up with Sihanouk.[25]

Royalist rallying around Sihanouk as a symbol of national unity was, however, beset by a series of problems. Most glaring was Sihanouk's role in the rise of Democratic Kampuchea, the memory of which towered monumentally over any suggestion that he be a symbol of national unity. Although royals were intent on glossing over the establishment of Democratic Kampuchea—which many of them considered to be the result of a series of tragic but unintended developments that had spiraled out of control—many Cambodians of the older generation associate Sihanouk with the coming to power of the Khmer Rouge.

Furthermore, in spite of the celebration of alleged unity, royal family members had little else but Sihanouk around which to unite. FUNCINPEC quickly became a family affair, offering positions to royal family members eager to be involved, and placing less emphasis on previous political experience. Sisowath Pheanuroth, returning to Cambodia in 1993 after twenty-six apolitical years in France, quickly became vice governor of Phnom Penh. He later explained his political involvement in these terms: "the way to socialize and be part of the family was to be involved in FUNCINPEC. It was a natural way to go."[26] Sihanouk also expanded the royal family by granting royal titles to more distant relatives and in-laws.[27] The common identity as royal family members was projected to hold these individuals together under one political label as "royalists." Royalism, *reach niyum*, was in turn primarily defined as the political thought of different royal family members.[28] This emphasis on the incarnate, however, perpetuated the same tension.

Ever since the brief introduction of party politics, royal family members had encompassed diverse political strands. Indeed, three princes founded the first political parties in the kingdom in 1946. Prince Sisowath Yuthevong, founder of the Democratic Party (DP); Prince Norodom Narindeth, founder of the Liberal Party; and Prince Norodom Montana, founder of the Progressive Democrats, articulated early political programs that differed from Sihanouk's later one.[29] As is discussed below, Yuthevong, in particular, is commemorated by some royals as an early royal

---

[25] Author's interview with Sisowath Ayravady, November 18, 2009.

[26] Author's interview with Sisowath Pheanuroth, June 18, 2010.

[27] For example, Norodom Marie was made a princess (*Preah Ang Mchas*) by Sihanouk in 1993; Sisowath Thomico was made prince; and Sisowath Pongneary (Lolotte) was bestowed the honorific *Samdech*.

[28] Author's interviews with Sisowath Ayravady, Sisowath Pheanuroth, and Sisowath Panara Sirivudh, June 4, 2010

[29] Chandler, *The Tragedy of Cambodian History*, 30.

nationalist. This constitutes an alternative genealogy of royalist nationalism, tracing the origins of indigenous "democratic" thought to Yuthevong rather than to Sihanouk.

This fluidity in royalist party politics persisted beyond 1993, as senior royals joined rival political parties. Asked what Sihanouk thought about this, Thomico remarked: "He had one son who was the leader of FUNCINPEC [Ranariddh], one son in CPP [Chakrapong], and then Narindrapong [another son] supported Pol Pot—what should he say? He accepted it."[30] Meanwhile, royal family members often remained closer to each other across the fault lines of political parties than was apparent. This can be understood partly as a conscious strategy to ensure that royals would not be left out from the winning side. Sitting on all sides of politics ensured royals a backup plan no matter the outcome. In its present incarnation, this strategy is a response to the incongruity of reducing the royal category to political party affiliation.[31]

The problems caused by the tension between the need for royals to portray national unity, and the diversity of their political programs, undermined political royalism, a dynamic which was intensified by Ranariddh's response to this tension. While the themes of peace and national reconciliation are primarily associated with Sihanouk, Ranariddh has tried to recreate similar legitimacy for himself as the one who brought peace and national reconciliation. One example of this is how Ranariddh has justified his acceptance of the 1993 power-sharing formula, whereby state power came to be shared between CPP and FUNCINPEC despite the latter's electoral victory, in terms of emulating his father's example in prioritizing peace and national unity. The power-sharing formula was a main factor enabling the CPP's continued hold on national politics and the gradual marginalization of FUNCINPEC. Ranariddh's explanation, therefore, justifies the single most important move in undermining political royalism. Ranariddh stresses that he agreed to the power-sharing formula at Sihanouk's request, in order to avert civil war following the threat of territorial secession by the movement led by Norodom Chakrapong, his half-brother.[32] While the exact dynamics of this course of events remains debated, Ranariddh's explanation seems largely accurate.[33] The language employed by Ranariddh to outline his decision has, however, a particular resonance. For example, at a 2011 campaign speech for the Norodom Ranariddh Party (which Ranariddh headed after his 2006 ouster from FUNCINPEC), Ranariddh told the audience that it was because of the threatened secession that he agreed to share state power, lest Cambodian territory be split and civil war ensue. Sihanouk, he said, encouraged him to agree, "to save Cambodian people's lives," and if he had not, all those present

---

[30] Author's interview with Sisowath Thomico, May 28, 2010.

[31] It is also consistent with the historical toing and froing of Khmer—and Lao—royals' tributary relations with neighboring powers. I am grateful to Martin Rathie for making this observation.

[32] Compare to Sam Nora, "Note of the Day 23: The So-Called 'Insanity?' of Samdech Krom Preah Norodom Ranariddh," 2011, at http://www.norodomranariddh.org, accessed 12 March 2012.

[33] It is clear that Chakrapong publicly proclaimed a breakaway zone in June 1993, shortly after the elections, and that Sihanouk favored a fifty–fifty power-sharing solution, even before the threatened secession. See, for example, Roberts, *Political Transition in Cambodia 1991–99*, 109–13. Ranariddh is quiet, however, on the role played by the CPP in the threatened secession, alleged by some.

would be dead. For this reason, he stated, "I sacrificed myself for the nation," and "sacrificed the election result which made me the winner."[34] By employing this language, Ranariddh defines royalist nationalism as taking action that will not result in partisan political gain. The prince regally sacrifices selfish political interest for the larger interests of the nation, a decision that reflects how the royals are ultimately responsible for maintaining a suprapolitical conscience for national reconciliation. The consequences of this line of reasoning, however, differ greatly between the monarchy and political royalism. By defining royalist nationalism as opposed to the support of any particular partisan affiliation, Ranariddh eclipses the political party form of royalism.

Norodom Ranariddh gives a press brief on the final election day, May 28, 1993
Phnom Penh (photo courtesy of Roland Neveu)

EMBODIED POLITICS: CONSTITUTIONAL MONARCHY AND POLITICAL ROYALISM

A second tension in royalist politics followed from royalists' failure to agree on the mandate of the reinstated constitutional monarchy, as well as on what role political royalism could and should play. Although such questions have been debated in many democratizing contexts, in Cambodia this debate followed the particular reconfiguration of the problem by Sihanouk's post-independence regime. The Sangkum Reastr Niyum left questions of the mandate of the Khmer monarchy and Khmer political royalism unresolved and preserved in the very body of Sihanouk. The unsettled question of how to reconcile kingship with a political form of royalism became a central paradox for royalists in the KOC. To resolve it, royalists took recourse in historical ideas of embodiment.

---

[34] Author's fieldnotes, NRP election campaign, June 4, 2011, Oudong village, Kompong Speu province.

Historical Khmer conceptualizations of kingship emphasize the inherently incarnate role of the king. The idea of embodiment, rather than the idea of elected leadership, can be understood as the fault line between Western liberal notions of legitimate leadership and historical Khmer ideas of kingship.[35] The organic link between the moral behavior of the king and the welfare of the kingdom was historically conceptualized as a structure that presumed the unity of the physical body of the king and his mystical body, the "body politic." In the Angkorean period, the king was associated with the divine, a link contained in the Brahmanic concept of the *devaraja*.[36] With the spread of Theravada Buddhism, the righteous king was thought of as a *dhamma raja,* a king ruling in accordance with the Buddha's teachings.[37] Ian Harris writes that his benevolent power "was no longer considered so much an expression of his divinity; rather, it was considered a register of how closely he adhered to the eternal laws of existence *(dhamma)*, as discovered and enunciated in the teachings of the Buddha."[38] Khmer Buddhist cosmology posited Khmer royalty as having multiple substitute bodies through the merit they accumulated, including the kingdom and the entire universe. The king was regarded as a repository of merit symbiotically linking, through his person, the state and the cosmos.[39]

French protectorate-era scholars, seeking to define Cambodian political imaginations, first turned the monarch into an incarnation of the *nation*.[40] In the

---

[35] Thompson, "Angkor Revisited," 186–87.

[36] Although *devaraja* later came to denote "God-King" in popular usage, Angkorean inscriptions very rarely describe royals by this term. Instead, they identify the *devaraja* as a sacred, mobile object that the king would bring to his capital. See, for example, Edwards, *Cambodge*, 22; Harris, *Cambodian Buddhism*, 11–12; Hermann Kulke, "The Devarāja Cult: Legitimation and Apotheosis of the Ruler in the Kingdom of Angkor," in *Kings and Cults: State Formation and Legitimation in India and Southeast Asia,* ed. Hermann Kulke (New Delhi: Manohar, 1993), 355; Hiram W. Woodward Jr., "Practice and Belief in Ancient Cambodia: Claude Jacques, Angkor, and the *Devarāja* Question," *Journal of Southeast Asian Studies* 32 no. 2 (2001): 257–58; Hermann Kulke, *The Devaraja Cult* (Ithaca: Cornell University Southeast Asia Program, 1978); and Michael Vickery, *Society, Economics, and Politics in Pre-Angkor Cambodia: The Seventh–Eighth Centuries* (Tokyo: Center for East Asian Cultural Studies for UNESCO, Toyo Bunko, 1998). Pou argues that kings became worshipped as gods *after* their death, which has been misunderstood as their having been considered God-Kings during their lifetime (Pou, "Dieux et Rois dans la Pensée Khmère Ancienne," 667). Because of the important role of statuary in linking the king and the divine, the academic debate on the relationship between the king and divine has largely been carried out in the discipline of art history. Compare to Coedès, "Le Portrait dans l'Art Khmer." Thompson suggests that "A king was associated with a certain god and would be portrayed in that god's image, if not during his lifetime surely after his death. Like the father, the son both worshiped and was to be worshiped in the image of the supreme god" (Thompson, "Angkor Revisited," 185). The contemporary notion, *atitep-khsatr* ("God-King"), was only introduced as part of the New Vocabulary (Jacob, "The Deliberate Use of Foreign Vocabulary by the Khmer," 159).

[37] Harris, *Cambodian Buddhism*, 302.

[38] Ibid., 80.

[39] Ibid. Compare to Thompson, "The Suffering of Kings," 91.

[40] Edwards quotes Étienne Aymonier, writing in 1896, that "the *Nation* has long been accustomed to the idea of not separating its own existence to that of the royal house. The monarch is the living incarnation, the august and supreme personification of *nationality*" (Edwards, *Cambodge*, 13). For Republican France, this idea underpinned its encouragement of the Cambodian monarchy, which would serve as the transmission belt for French imperial control.

1930s, a few Western-educated individuals linked the Western concept of nationalism with indigenous notions of kingship and the Buddhist *sangha* to create a civic religion of loyalty to the nation. Following the Thai counterpart *Chat, Sasana, Phramahakasat* ("Nation, Religion, King"), which had been introduced in neighboring Thailand by King Rama VI (r. 1910–25), the slogan "nation, religion, king" (*cheat, sasana, mohaksat*) first appeared in Khmer usage.[41] The Khmer historical precursors to these notions, *sdech, sangha, srok*, denoted slightly different meanings from their modern counterparts, and their relationship was not fixed in the implied equilibrium and equality of this formula. Yet when Sihanouk ascended the throne in 1941, the unity between nation, religion, and king, allegedly present since time immemorial, was celebrated.[42] Contestation over the relationship between the three components of this trinity would nonetheless persistently color Cambodian politics henceforth. Sihanouk's Sangkum Reastr Niyum tried to settle conflict precisely by promising that it would ensure that the motherland returned to its past glory by giving "the trinity" its "true sense;" this was an enterprise that, however, soon became ambiguous.[43]

In 1955, Sihanouk launched the Sangkum Reastr Niyum, which replaced the multiparty democratic system of 1946–55, and would come to replace the constitutional monarchy, instituted in 1947. Sihanouk had abdicated the throne to become a "full-time politician" as its chairman.[44] His father, Suramarit, ascended the throne, but upon Suramarit's death in1960, no new monarch was appointed. Sihanouk's abdication was made out as a precondition for his political leadership role. Yet, although Sihanouk denied this, his political popularity could not be easily disentangled from his previous kingship, which he retained in all but title in the eyes of most citizens.[45] As chairman of the Sangkum, Sihanouk certainly did benefit from and even encourage popular belief in himself as a God-King embodying the nation.[46] Indeed, Sihanouk made a point of tracing the history of Cambodia in terms

---

[41] Ibid., 118, 169; and Gyallay-Pap, "Reconstructing the Cambodian Polity," in Harris, *Buddhism, Power and Political Order*, 72. On the creation of the three pillars in the Thai context, see Frank E. Reynolds, "Civic Religion and National Community in Thailand," *Journal of Asian Studies* 36 no. 2 (1977), 274–82.

[42] Compare to Gnoc Them's 1950 pamphlet, "Nation, Religion, King," which describes the three words as "very meaningful" in every country and the "foundation of all other words" (Gnoc Them, *Cheat, Sasana, Mohaksatr* [Nation, Religion, King] (n.a, 1950). Gnoc Them (1903–74), schooled in Battambang and Thailand, joined the Tripitaka Commission in the 1930s, was defrocked in 1936, and became the editor of *Kampuja Surya* in 1938. On Gnoc Them, see Edwards, *Cambodge*, 223, 308–9.

[43] Compare to Norodom Sihanouk, *Statuts de Sangkum* (Article 3).

[44] Chandler, *The Tragedy of Cambodian History*, 78.

[45] A contemporary observer wrote that "Sihanouk denies this, calling attention to the number of unemployed kings in the world. Sihanouk's royal blood may have smoothed the path to political success, but it certainly did not ensure it, and Sihanouk today habitually behaves as if he were campaigning for a national election." See John P. Armstrong, *Sihanouk Speaks* (New York: Walker, 1964), 20.

[46] Chandler cites a brochure put out by the Sangkum government: "This abdication was justified by [Sihanouk's] fervent desire to serve better his people by whom *he is worshipped as a God*. In short, he wanted to give his people the necessary strength to fight favoritism and oppression ... and lead them back to the tradition of a glorious past" (Chandler, *The Tragedy of Cambodian History*, 78). This neatly illustrates the conflation between Sihanouk's abdicated and royal stature during Sangkum.

of the Cambodian monarchy, which he equated with the destiny of the Khmer people.[47] The tension between Sihanouk's abdication as a precondition for political activity, at the same time that his legitimacy still rested on his previous kingship, can be understood as a constitutive paradox of Sangkum that left fundamental questions concerning the mandate of the Khmer monarchy unresolved and conserved in the very body of Sihanouk. Throughout the Sangkum era, the regime would build its legitimacy on advancing the idea of supposed organic relations between Sihanouk and the people, a vision that would find doctrinal expression in Sihanouk's Buddhist socialism—the self-professed regime identity. All legitimacy was invested in Sihanouk, although it was not clearly defined on what grounds.

Sihanouk himself consistently emphasized that the Sangkum-era re-organization of authority meant that power was invested in him personally. At the time, Sihanouk did not treat the monarchy as an eternal given, but rather as a temporal framework that might soon outlive its usefulness. He envisaged saving the nation as his own personal mission, while giving an oath never to resume the throne and pledging not to appoint a successor.[48] In 1962, Sihanouk wrote that the arrival of communism in Cambodia would dismantle the institution of the monarchy, and that the Sangkum had been launched in preparation for this envisaged transition.[49] Four decades later, in his memoirs, *Shadow over Angkor*, Sihanouk portrayed Sangkum as a necessary step toward fulfilling the political logic of the constitutional monarchy. Sangkum limited the king's involvement in political affairs, while transcending the constitutional monarchy to bring in a unique system of guided democracy.[50] Sihanouk recognized that he had "in essence abolished the monarchy" with his abdication, and portrayed the task to save the country as his personal mission, even outside the framework of the monarchy. In this sense, Sihanouk's personal importance transcended that of the monarchy as an institution.[51]

---

[47] See, for example, Norodom Sihanouk, "La Monarchie Cambodgienne & La Croisade Royale pour l'Indépendance" [undated, originally in *Réalités Cambodgiennes*, May 24–September 13, 1958].

[48] Sihanouk made this statement with the oath to never resume the throne: "And this I have always said, too, the day when our Monarchy, by order of the popular will or international contingency, ceases to be a harmonious and useful framework, I would not hesitate to take the initiative myself in sacrificing it and orienting the nation toward other roads and assist it to accomplish in peace and without bloodshed the revolution of its choice." Norodom Sihanouk, *Réalités Cambodgiennes*, August 3, 1962: 9.

[49] Ibid.

[50] Sihanouk sums up the transition from absolute monarchy to Sangkum as follows: "In the space of eight years, Cambodia had moved forward from an absolute monarchy to a constitutional monarchy with an elected parliament and on to an original form of guided democracy via the National Congress of the Sangkum. The role of the monarch had been reduced—at my initiative—to a symbolic one. Power of decision was in the hands of the Prime Minister and his cabinet, reinforced by the direct participation of the people." Norodom Sihanouk, *Shadow Over Angkor: Memoirs of His Majesty King Norodom Sihanouk of Cambodia*, ed. and trans. Julio A. Jeldres (Phnom Penh: Monument Books, 2005), 59.

[51] "I knew in my own mind that in taking this stand [the hibernation of the throne] *I was, in effect, abolishing the monarchy in everything but the form. I had faced up to this with my own abdication* [emphasis added]. But the monarchy continued to be the greatest single unifying influence in the country, and a too sudden break would only benefit our enemies [...] the time had not yet come for this [the abolishment of the monarchy]. For the people, the monarchy and Buddhism equaled the nation. Thus, while fighting to retain the monarchy, I opposed choosing a new monarch." Ibid., 61.

Historians' assessments of Sihanouk add context to his possible motives for abdicating the throne and then putting it into "hibernation." Sihanouk's abdication "opened up a new political game" allowing Sihanouk to emerge as a dedicated politician, shirking his royal, ceremonial duties. As the monarchy was now considered an illegitimate institution for political decision-making among the Cambodian political elite, Sihanouk's ambition was to transcend the multiparty elections they supported, and instead win acceptance for a national union government without political parties, in which he could play the leading role.[52] It is unclear to what extent this move was premeditated and tactical, rather than a spontaneous stroke of fortune.[53] Perhaps Sihanouk's idea germinated when, in March 1945, the Japanese removed the French *résident superieur* above him, effectively making Sihanouk both prime minister and head of state until the 1946 return of the French, after which the 1947 constitution revoked those powers.[54] Despite having sworn not to return to the throne himself once he abdicated, Sihanouk was cautious of permitting someone more strong-willed than his father to ascend the throne; this came to determine Sihanouk's decision to hibernate the throne upon his father's death.[55] The hibernation was therefore not so much an attempt to avoid antagonism of different royal factions as an outright attempt by Sihanouk to ensure that he would remain Cambodia's unchallenged leader.[56] Sihanouk called for a referendum for chief of state, which Chandler refers to as a "charade" (given the lack of voting secrecy), which resulted in Sihanouk's overwhelming victory.[57] Upon being elected Cambodia's first non-monarchic chief of state, Sihanouk assumed the constitutional powers of a monarch, while renouncing the monarch's ceremonial responsibilities. Queen Kossamak stayed in the palace as a symbol of the monarchy, but Sihanouk reportedly paid less attention than previously to royal ceremony.[58] Sihanouk organized National Assembly elections in 1955, 1958, 1962, and 1966, yet the powers of the assembly were reduced to near insignificance, while biannual National Congresses were to ensure that decision-making was by consensus under the

---

[52] On this last point, see Chandler, *The Tragedy of Cambodian History*, 79.

[53] Ibid., 78.

[54] Henri Locard, personal communication, April 18, 2015.

[55] Were Ranariddh, Sihanouk's second son, to be appointed king then, as a minor, his powers would have been assumed by a regent. This was not unlikely to be Prince Monireth, an uncle of Sihanouk's whom Sihanouk was wary of promoting, suspecting him of royal ambitions. Moreover, when reaching majority, Ranariddh could provide another counterpoint to Sihanouk. Sihanouk also opposed appointment of his mother, Kossamak, as queen in her own right, in all likelihood over similar caution of increasing her influence. Chandler, *The Tragedy of Cambodian History*, 115–16.

[56] Compare to how, in Spain, the throne was similarly hibernated under Franco because Franco was wary of antagonizing different royalist factions. Franco restored the monarchy in 1947, yet not until 1969 was Juan Carlos appointed as designate monarch, and no king was appointed until after Franco's death in 1975. See Bart Maddens and Kristine Vanden Berghe, "Franco and the Spanish Monarchy: A Discourse Analysis of the Tourist Guides Published by the Patrimonio Nacional [1959–1987)," in *Royal Tourism: Excursions Around Monarchy*, ed. Phil Long and Nicola J. Palme (Clevedon: Channel View Publications, 2008), 82.

[57] Chandler, *The Tragedy of Cambodian History*, 116–17.

[58] Ibid., 117.

direction of Sihanouk.[59] The bases of regime legitimacy were thereby firmly invested in Sihanouk himself.

The Sangkum heritage left Second Kingdom royalists two main challenges. First, they needed to reinstate the value of the reintroduced constitutional monarchy, which had been shown over a twenty-three year hiatus not to be an inalterable, timeless national institution. Second, they needed to give value to FUNCINPEC as the vehicle of political royalism, in spite of the fact that Sihanouk could not act to continue to conflate the royal element and personal political prowess in political leadership.

Both these dilemmas necessitated a rereading of Sihanouk's role during the Sangkum Reastr Niyum era. Royalists turned to historical ideas of embodiment. Sihanouk's leadership role under the Sangkum was derived from the way that he embodied the monarchy, and thereby the nation. After the introduction of a constitutional monarchy, his kingship had to be exercised outside its traditional, absolutist framework. The Sangkum arrangement provided this mechanism, allowing Sihanouk to act out his *royal* role outside the institution of the monarchy. Denying that Sangkum entailed either the abolition in disguise of the monarchy or, tellingly, its "disembodiment," Ranariddh writes:

> [...] one measure needs further examination: the hibernation of the Throne (1960). Hypocritically, some have wanted to see a kind of abolition of the monarchy in disguise, at the initiative of the ex-King himself. Others, in the field of political science, have analyzed it as an act of imprudence which disembodied [*désincarnait*] the monarchical institution and habituated the popular masses to a power without King. To this it is easy to reply that Prince Sihanouk never conceived of the institution of Head of State as an instrument to destroy the monarchy; it was on the contrary about a skillful construction destined to assure its survival, avoiding impasses and conflicts which would have resulted from the appointment of a new monarch. As for the effect on popular opinion of a "monarchy without King," one would, in order to confirm it, need to measure the aptitude of the peasant masses to grasp the juridical subtleties and the constitutional distinction between a monarch and a Head of State—former monarch—holder of all royal prerogatives. This is especially so since the extreme personalization of power—whether as a royal or as a Head of State matters little—that Sihanouk realized must also be considered. Finally, it should be added that the abdication and return to power after a temporary withdrawal [*retrait*] is one of the constants of Khmer history. The reform of 1960 in all respects institutionalized a traditional mechanism.[60]

This passage self-consciously styles the monarchy according to historical ideas of embodiment. Ranariddh outlines an exceptional role given to Sihanouk by virtue of his *royal status*, which allows him even to abdicate and later return. Indeed, a king's periodic absences and much anticipated returns are a distinguishing trait of

---

[59] Sihanouk lost control of the National Assembly, however, in 1966. Unlike in previous elections, he did not choose candidates himself and a strong anti-Sihanouk majority was elected. This was the National Assembly that would dismiss Sihanouk four years later.

[60] Norodom Ranariddh, *Droit Public Cambodgien*, 135.

the Khmer monarchy.[61] As Thompson writes, Sihanouk's 1955 abdication, in keeping with this historical tradition, was predicated on the idea of the king's multiple bodies. In Thompson's reading, the abdication protected kingship that is not elected and never can be (as the substitution of bodies does not follow changing public opinion) from the encounter with democracy; this principle allowed Sihanouk to be elected only after his abdication.[62] In Ranariddh's reading, the abdication allowed Sihanouk to maintain kingship, in a way that transcended the limits of the institutional form of the monarchy. Sihanouk's faithfulness to his ancestral past averted the "fetishism of monarchism as a form of government." His abdication marked, "conforming to historical tradition," that "the royal function could not be reduced by its incumbent to advantages of prestige or interest. [...] During the Resistance, as in all his notes and directives, the Prince-King has taken it as a rule not to reason but on the *functional* necessity of a chief of state, king, or elected president, little does it matter."[63] In this way, Ranariddh attempts to reconcile all of Sihanouk's various capacities after his abdication, with Sihanouk inhabiting multiple substitute bodies. Sihanouk was kingship incarnate in each of these capacities—including as an elected leader.

Since the substitution of bodies is a characteristic that cannot be suspended and reassumed, Ranariddh needed to show that it was consistently maintained by Sihanouk, who, in 1993, again ascended the throne. Sihanouk, as the reinstated constitutional monarch, again embodied the nation. Ranariddh speaks of the monarchy as being constituted by man and action, inseparable from each other.[64] The re-embodiment of the nation was necessarily tied to Sihanouk, who personified it:

> The constitution of 1993 is above all the restoration of the legitimacy of Norodom Sihanouk. But it does not realize the effective return to power of the prince, it only assures the recognition of his work and the restitution *of a symbol where the man and action are inseparable, the monarchy.* [...] History teaches us that restorations are generally a compromise between the past and the integration of revolutionary steps. [...] In certain respects, this analysis, devoid of illusions, holds true for Cambodia. In others not: we need to take note that authority was restored not only as an abstract principle, but *on a personal basis in Sihanouk as an uninterrupted incarnation of the national struggle and fight against oppression.*[65]

Ideas of embodiment were in this way made to define the newly inaugurated constitutional monarchy. Ranariddh traced these ideas to the concept of the God-King, *devaraja*. For Ranariddh, Sihanouk's legitimacy rested in age-old beliefs in the Cambodian king as a God-King:

> Cambodia, traditionally, is a Kingdom. The people of Cambodia are very attached to the royalist system. *But for them, it is* [about] *the Royal Family.* The

---

[61] Thompson, "The Suffering of Kings," 109–11; see also Thompson, "Angkor Revisited," 180–81.

[62] Thompson, "The Suffering of Kings," 109.

[63] Norodom Ranariddh, *Droit Public Cambodgien*, 160.

[64] Ibid., 263.

[65] Ibid., 263–64, emphasis added.

traditional, original concept is that of the God-King. You cannot compare it to the Constitutional Monarchy of the United Kingdom for instance. [...] Even my father, he is very liberal. But, he is seen as a God-King. [...] It is very deeply anchored into the Cambodian mentalities. [...] My father stepped down and he formed his own party: the Sangkum Reastr Niyum. But, [according to] the mentality of Cambodians: God-King, since thousands of years.[66]

As a God-King, Sihanouk's role transcended that of a strictly constitutional monarch along Western European lines. Ranariddh considered the phrase that "the King reigns but does not govern," found in the 1993 constitution, to be "adapted to the socio-political realities of the European parliamentarian monarchies." This formula, he stated, did not correspond to the Cambodian popular mentality, and must therefore be adapted to the Cambodian environment.[67] In response, FUNCINPEC under Ranariddh put forth Sangkum-derived conceptions of democracy particularly suited for Cambodia, informed by ideas of kingship as embodiment of the nation, which will be discussed below.

Embodiment was also advanced to support political royalism. The incarnate nature of the monarchy was projected to bestow legitimacy on all royal family members, who, to some degree, shared in the ability to incarnate the monarchy and thereby stand in for the nation. This is seen in Ranariddh's words, quoted above, in which he argues that Cambodian popular attachment is to royal family members rather than to the monarchy as an institution. Ranariddh has repeatedly phrased his political role in the language of embodiment, while precisely what he claims to embody reflects the shifting Cambodian political context. The notion of embodiment thereby ties together diverse claims to legitimacy, from disparate sources, such as monarchical values, his nationalism, his involvement in the national resistance, his attachment to liberal values, his Western academic credentials, and democratic legitimacy. For example, under the headline "The Bottom of the Problem: Cambodian Legitimacy," Ranariddh asked: "In Cambodian political life, who *incarnates* what in 1997?" He then quoted a "diplomat friend" who listed Ranariddh's multiple sources of legitimacy:

Legitimacy of traditional essence. In a country without points of reference, searching for its roots, he [Ranariddh] incarnates, in the shadow of the king, monarchical values forged by Buddhist tolerance and concern for the common good.

Legitimacy of a national kind. Without any ties of dependence, even to the country that received him in exile [...] He owes neither his past, nor his present power to it [France].

Legitimacy of the resistant who suffered the cowardice of the instigators of the first coup, who fought against the oppression of the terrible years and then against the externally imposed oppression [by Vietnam] [...].

---

[66] Author's interview with Norodom Ranariddh, June 2, 2011, emphasis added.

[67] Norodom Ranariddh, *Droit Public Cambodgien*, 289. Compare to Constitution of Cambodia (Article 7), 1993.

Liberal and Western academic legitimacy. Open to everyone's point of view, respectful of the freedom of expression of all individuals and groups, and of the press [...].

Above all, *democratic legitimacy.* It was the Khmer people and the Khmer people only who in 1992 [sic] gave him its confidence and a mandate after free elections.[68]

While historical ideas of embodiment singled out the king based on merit rather than genealogy or elections, the Cambodian monarchy has evolved to incorporate elective elements framed by genealogical restraints. To justify a role for themselves, Second Kingdom royals stressed genealogical lines. Embodiment needed to be thought of as a hereditary quality, equally for the Crown and for political royalism. While lauding the Crown's elective nature, Ranariddh has also argued against an overemphasis on it, charging that the principle of heredity is at the root of the monarchy.[69] Meanwhile, Ranariddh's royal descent was used to legitimate his leadership of FUNCINPEC, suggesting that the ability to represent the nation incarnate applied to him in particular, as Sihanouk's son. Ranariddh has occasionally made reference to himself as a God-King, and FUNCINPEC under his leadership has portrayed itself as a vehicle to achieve a "union of people and prince," closely mimicking the Sangkum.[70]

Although ideas of embodiment bestowed some legitimacy on Sihanouk, indications are that his imagined incarnation of the monarchy has failed to carry over to the office of the constitutional monarchy or to political royalists.[71] That Ranariddh's repeated claims of national embodiment failed to garner support is unsurprising, given how Sihanouk continued to play a central role in Cambodia as a constitutional monarch and (since his second abdication in 2004) as King-Father— not to mention that Sihanouk bypassed Ranariddh in favor of Sihamoni when designating the new monarch. Deriving his royal claims from Sihanouk, Ranariddh ended up second to a man who often contradicted him in public, sometimes publicly supporting Hun Sen rather than his son. This stemmed from the crisis of reconciling kingship with a political form of royalism, provoked by Sihanouk's personalization of power under the Sangkum. By advancing ideas of embodiment, political royalists hoped to reinstate legitimacy to Sihanouk as well as to themselves. Yet, in perpetuating the idea of Sihanouk as the incarnation of the nation, they have yet to convincingly justify the existence of a political royalist faction.

ROYALIST DEMOCRACY

A third tension placed royalists between two contested conceptualizations of democracy.

FUNCINPEC and the SRP have come together under a democratic banner at crucial points of time, contesting the fundamental "rules of the game," such as

---

[68] Norodom Ranariddh, *Droit Public Cambodgien*, 177–78.

[69] Ibid., 268, 280, 281.

[70] Hughes, "Transforming Oppositions in Cambodia," 308.

[71] On contemporary belief in Sihanouk as a substitute body for the welfare of the kingdom, compare to Kent, "The Recovery of the King."

elections. A shared democratic opposition identity has, at these times, been the basis of claims to represent the nation. Parallel to this, royalists routinely draw on understandings of democracy that differ from both Western liberal democratic understandings and those of the self-identified democratic opposition. Hughes argues that the SRP and FUNCINPEC share a "democratic opposition" identity, opposing the legitimacy of the CPP on the grounds that they view the CPP as authoritarian, and claims that, beside this core identity, FUNCINPEC has as its second core identity "royalism" and the appeal of that royalism to the Sangkum legacy.[72] Yet these two identities did not simply coexist but, instead, created enormous tension due to their competing visions of how to organize society. Both sets of democratic conceptualizations were integrated into FUNCINPEC actors' definitions of "royalism." Rather than mutually exclusive identities, they can be understood as two poles on a continuum, so that the same actor could refer to both at different points in time.

Below, I trace a discourse that framed itself as distinctly royalist by making reference to Sangkum-derived concepts of democracy. It offered unique conceptualizations of democracy in the Cambodian context, which ran directly contrary to the liberal democratic conceptions that Ranariddh has occasionally claimed as the basis for FUNCINPEC identity. Yet these Sangkum-derived concepts were increasingly used to justify cooperation with the CPP, and have become increasingly meaningless for asserting a political royalist identity. This discourse was closely associated with Ranariddh, who, as leader of FUNCINPEC (1993–2006; 2015–), to a large extent defined party political royalism.

Next, I trace a democratic opposition identity. This entails reference to an anti-communist, anti-Vietnamese resistance identity, as suggested by Hughes, but also refers to liberal democratic ideas of relations of accountability between the elected leadership and the electorate, coupled with support for a strictly constitutional monarchy. It was primarily associated with a separate group of FUNCINPEC actors who advocated closer cooperation with the SRP. Yet this vision of royalist democracy also lost meaning as an articulation of political royalism, primarily because Ranariddh outmaneuvred it. Moreover, when Ranariddh was eventually sidelined, the (essentially pro-CPP) elements who took over the party portrayed their rift with Ranariddh in terms of remaining faithful to a shared resistance identity. Royal family members associated with this second stance were prompted to join Ranariddh, in whom they had no further faith, to defend the involvement of royals in politics.

Royalist Democracy as a Sangkum-derived Discourse

A continued allegiance to Cambodian models of kingship, which posit an organic relation between the people and the king, has continuously colored interpretations of democracy in KOC royalist politics.[73] This contrasts with liberal democracy, characterized by the way that the "sovereignty of the nation is assumed to be distributed evenly among the citizens."[74] Ranariddh's main claim to

---

[72] Hughes, "Transforming Oppositions in Cambodia," 307.

[73] See how Ranariddh argues that the 1993 constitution does not exclude organic relations between the king and the people, as it does not specify whether the king is representative of the people, co-sovereign with the people, or an autonomous authority (Norodom Ranariddh, *Droit Public Cambodgien*, 279).

[74] Thompson, "Angkor Revisited," 186–87.

democratic legitimacy has been electoral legitimacy—seemingly in line with liberal democratic imaginings. As FUNCINPEC leader, Ranariddh repeatedly claimed legitimacy by virtue of FUNCINPEC's 1993 victory.[75] Yet, rather than referring his democratic credentials to FUNCINPEC's "democratic" policy agenda that could ensure the equal distribution of sovereignty among citizens, Ranariddh typically alluded to the way that he embodied the aspirations of the national community, in line with historical conceptualizations of the king's representation of the people. Ranariddh used FUNCINPEC's 1993 victory to prove that he, personally, enjoys popular support and that, as a consequence, any idea he launched would be inherently democratic. This overlay is widely made among royalists. Democratic ideas are typically seen as intrinsically linked to royalism, which is proven by the way that the royal party is believed to be supported by the people if there are free and fair elections.[76] This mirrors similar beliefs by the self-identified democrats who judge the will of the people to be obscured by various CPP strategies and, therefore, not adequately represented in elections. Yet royalists differ in that their claims to popular support are derived from ideas of popular representation through organic relations.

In *Droit Public Cambodgien* (Cambodian Public Law), Ranariddh asks the central question: In the Cambodian context, is democracy compatible with the monarchy?[77] He identifies a worldwide trend whereby power and sovereignty have been transferred, first, from personalized authority to absolute, theocratic monarchy; and in a second stage, to the people, marking the transition to a democratic system. This gradually erased the idea of sovereignty by hereditary means. This is not to say that the abolition of the monarchic form of state necessarily must follow. Instead, Ranariddh charges that within a democratic framework the monarchy retains value as a national symbol, the "more irreplaceable the more fragile the country is." For this, he takes the British and the Thai monarchies as examples.[78] In Cambodia, however, the monarchy and democracy are not only compatible, as in Britain and Thailand, but they are also infallibly linked. This stems from what—Ranariddh asserts—is the originally elective nature of the Khmer Crown.[79] Since the 1993 constitution put popular representatives in the body that elects the king, the link

---

[75] Ibid., 178.

[76] This logic is also evident in the following quote by Ranariddh, under his pen name Sam Nora, in explaining why FUNCINPEC, after his ouster from the party leadership, was clearly not a Sihanoukist party: "In that sense, we do not believe that the 'neo-FUNCINPEC' under the current leadership can be considered anymore as a Sihanoukist political party. The voters of the 2008 general elections did not make any mistake. In effect, how a party which pretends to be Sihanoukist could get only two seats in the current National Assembly? [*sic*]" See Sam Nora, "Note of the Day 5: Is the 'Neo-FUNCINPEC Party' a Sihanoukist Party?," 2010, available at http://www.norodomranariddh.org, accessed 1 March 2012. The premise is that, since Sihanouk embodies the aspirations of the people, a failure to attract voters primarily indicates a failure to represent Sihanouk.

[77] Norodom Ranariddh, *Droit Public Cambodgien*, 61. This book, an adaptation of Ranariddh's doctoral thesis, offers his analysis of the Cambodian state and political and judicial institutions from Angkorean times to the present, discussed with reference to notions of the nation, state, sovereignty, democracy, and legitimacy. Its target audience, specifies the title page, was students at Phnom Penh's Faculty of Law and Economics (now the RULE, Royal University of Law and Economics) and at the Royal School of Administration.

[78] Ibid., 61–62, 68.

[79] Ibid., 65.

between the monarchy and democratic practice remains in place. Ranariddh states that this tie explains the history of the Cambodian monarchy from 1950 to 1960, which saw the affirmation of a "modern conception of Khmer democracy," as Sihanouk launched a new solution to the problem of elected versus inherited leadership.

The question in this context was how to ensure that democracy, in terms of the people being the holders of sovereignty, is best realized. In articulating his answer, Ranariddh referred back to the particular articulation of democracy under the Sangkum Reastr Niyum.[80] The Sangkum, known as "Cambodian-style democracy" (*la démocratie cambodgienne*), was specific to Cambodia, yet said to nonetheless possess "global authenticity." Sangkum-style democracy uniquely responded to the "socio-cultural level of development" of Cambodia at the time, which did not correspond to the "preestablished schemes" of Western democracy. Ranariddh offers the assessment that:

> The real problem, in fact, for Sangkum was not to caricature a Western-style democracy for which the democratic phase of our history, which had just come to a close, had demonstrated the dangers and ambiguities, but to integrate the peasant masses, far removed from classical democratic values, into a system listening to the people and to its actual needs. To avoid that the People would continue to be mystified, the Sangkum asserted itself fundamentally as an anti-Party regime, that is, anti-establishment. Hence its hostility to classic "bourgeois" formations, instruments, and beneficiaries of a moderate democracy, which were pushed to dissolve after 1956.[81]

Here, Ranariddh criticizes Cambodia's short experience of parliamentary democracy before the Sangkum, and lauds the dissolution of the "bourgeois formations" of rival political parties as the Sangkum's democratic value.[82]

While accepting the 1993 constitution as a *fait accompli*, Ranariddh and other royalists have repeatedly referred back to the Sangkum-era articulation of democracy, which partly conflicts with the constitution, in advancing a royalist democratic vision. Finding that Sangkum-era political institutions are a valid model for the KOC to duplicate outright, Ranariddh takes FUNCINPEC's 1993 electoral victory as an affirmation that the people support the "political logic" of the Sangkum-era constitution. This political logic can be summarized under the three notions of social opening, national union, and direct democracy, which Ranariddh identifies as a "coherent doctrinal basis" for Sangkum democracy.[83] Yet the contemporary context is radically different from that of Sangkum, when Sihanouk dominated the totality of the political scene. As a consequence, these references have become increasingly void of meaning, and have either been expropriated by the CPP, or used as ill-masked justifications to get some limited share of power.

---

[80] Ibid., 67.

[81] Ibid., 136.

[82] Particularly, the Democratic Party was incorporated into the Sangkum from 1957.

[83] Ibid., 133.

The Social Opening

Ranariddh characterizes the Sangkum-era "social opening" as the integration of "the royal tradition of aiding '*le petit peuple*' within a modernized framework of third-world socialism, but without sharing their [third-world socialisms'] often mystifying nature."[84] He references Sihanouk's *Considérations sur le socialisme Khmer*, a document in which Sihanouk outlines an indigenous Khmer socialism with roots in the Angkorean monarchy.[85] Sihanouk finds proof of this in the great public works that the Angkorean kings realized—supposedly for the benefit of peasants. He quotes King Jayavarman VII's famous dictum, "He suffered from his subjects' illnesses more than his own: because it is the suffering of the public that is the suffering of kings, and not their own suffering."[86] Sihanouk situates his nationalization of industries, collectivization of agriculture, and wide range of communal projects in this context.

The social opening in this sense of provision and protection bestowed by the ruler remained central to Ranariddh's vision of KOC democracy. He considered the constitutional formula "the king reigns but does not govern" to be perilous.[87] "Unaware of 'constitutional nuances,'" Ranariddh writes, "the rural masses in particular will misunderstand that the King is no longer, as before, the dispenser of all benefits and the natural protector against the abuses of the officials." This, he fears, will make them likely to turn away from the monarchy to find help elsewhere, "particularly in political parties which are infinitely more binding than the King in their demands of loyalty or dependence, so that democracy and freedom will suffer from this change."[88]

With the king's abilities to provide circumscribed by the constitutional monarchy, the social opening took expression in how FUNCINPEC under Ranariddh engaged in development activities, framed as directly modeled on Sihanouk's activities in the past. Yet the overwhelming discrepancy in the CPP and FUNCINPEC's ability to provide social services—to the latter's detriment—made FUNCINPEC vulnerable to CPP criticism. Gift-giving practices as an "invented tradition" have ever since the beginning of Cambodia's reform process in the late 1980s emerged as a central CPP strategy for maintaining power through the KOC (as will be discussed below).[89] What has been given less attention is that gift-giving practices, carrying a range of symbolic connotations, directly bore on the viability of political royalism. The social opening was not solely a historical legacy, but an important part of the contemporary reinvention of "royalist democracy." Moreover, while observers have rightly noted that Hun Sen drew on the legacy of Sihanouk in gift-giving, Hun Sen did not stop at this.[90] He took these practices as his basis for explicitly arguing that the CPP was a continuation of Sangkum, outperforming Ranariddh's FUNCINPEC. Such claims gained traction since the idea that the

---

[84] Ibid.

[85] Norodom Sihanouk, *Considérations sur le Socialisme Khmer*, Ministry of Information, 1961. This essay thus preceded Sihanouk's 1965 *Notre Socialisme Bouddhique*, which provided a further elaboration.

[86] Norodom Sihanouk, *Considérations sur le Socialisme Khmer*, 4–5.

[87] Constitution of Cambodia (Article 7), 1993.

[88] Norodom Ranariddh, *Droit Public Cambodgien*, 289.

[89] Hughes, "The Politics of Gifts."

[90] Ibid.

monarchy ought to provide for the people continued to form an important part of democratic legitimacy for the contemporary royalist faction.

The CPP has purported to follow the line of the Sangkum ever since Sihanouk's 1991 return to Cambodia. Five days thereafter, Frings writes, a CPP statement declared that the party professed "domestic and foreign policies in line with the Sangkum Reas[tr] Niyum led by Samdech Preah Norodom Sihanouk." A circular adopted by the CPP standing committee established that "Samdech has expressed great satisfaction with the current political line of our party and state, regarding it as the *continuation of the policy of the SangkumRess[tr] Niyum party* [*sic*] that he led before 1970." The CPP was made out to be the "Little Brother of the Sangkum Reastr Niyum Party," a title said to have been bestowed by Sihanouk himself.[91] Yet, as Frings notes, Sangkum Reastr Niyum's Buddhist socialism was not a Marxist socialist regime.[92] Moreover, the CPP under Hun Sen has challenged both Sihanouk's Buddhist socialism (as argued above) and its contemporary rearticulations by royalist actors (as argued below). Rather, CPP discourse has developed during the course of the KOC to portray the party as the rightful heir to Sangkum Reastr Niyum, primarily in terms of development activities, which the CPP claimed to be modeled on those of the Sangkum-era social opening. This is seen in the following statement by Hun Sen:

> I am now setting aside my time to visit our people like what was done by HM the King in 1940s, 1950s, and 1960s and CPP has always followed that model. I used to mention that we have a great university, that is HM the King and Samdech Preah Reach Akkeamohesei [Queen Monineath] who have always firmly associated themselves with our people and Buddhist parishioners through activities for development.[93]

In fact, Hun Sen has claimed to derive his notion of "people's democracy" from the Sangkum Reastr Niyum, pointing to the shared prioritization of efforts to "rebuild" the country (i.e., development activities).[94] Integral to this is an "art of sharing" resources, part of which involves private donations by party officials to public projects. Hun Sen has portrayed this as the social and political line of the CPP and the KPRP ever since 1979, inherited from the Sangkum Reastr Niyum. This is accompanied by an emphasis that, were the CPP to lose elections, sharing would come to an end, as the people would no longer be able to request help from CPP

---

[91] Viviane K. Frings, "The Cambodian People's Party and Sihanouk," *Journal of Contemporary Asia* 25, no. 3 (1995): 359–60.

[92] Ibid., 360.

[93] Hun Sen, "Inaugurating a Buddhist Hall of Common in Srey Santhor," *Cambodia New Vision* 72, January 2004.

[94] For example, Hun Sen has stated that "There is no other option but to continue with people's democracy under the leadership of CPP—a concept that is similar to *Sangkum Reastr Niyum*. Samdech Preah Norodom Sihanouk led a crusade for independence from French colonialism and rebuilt the country under the time when there were serious threats of wars from countries around us. I am so proud and thankful that Samdech Preah Norodom Sihanouk and Samdech Preah Akka Mohesai always allowed their *Sangkum Reastr Niyum* to be mentioned as predecessor of the Royal Government's efforts in rebuilding the country." Hun Sen, "Keynote Address at the Opening Ceremony of the Samdech Hun Sen's Tree Nursery Station at Tamao Mountain," *Cambodia New Vision* 117, October 2007.

leaders.[95] This could be said to neatly fulfill Ranariddh's prophecy that if support were provided by political parties, people would be required to demonstrate party loyalty to receive social services. Yet FUNCINPEC also demanded political loyalty in order to receive social services, which reinforced the logic of provision as a precondition for political legitimacy. Together with FUNCINPEC's continued reliance on such practices in spite of its insufficient material resources, this weakened the royalist cause.

In addition to the FUNCINPEC party apparatus, royalists also relied on purportedly humanitarian organizations for carrying out the royal function of provision. In this they drew on the intimate historical association between healing and kingship.[96] Ashley Thompson outlines how Jayavarman VII's maxim "the suffering of the people is the suffering of the king," quoted by Sihanouk, above, is derived from a "certain conjunction of the physical health of the people and the social health of the kingdom through the figure of the king." She suggests that "in Cambodia, attempts to heal the king, the community, or the individual subjects of the king inevitably have recourse to complex strategies of integration, embodiment, and substitution between these various co-implicated bodies."[97] The king, then, plays a crucial role in the healing of national community.

The Cambodian Red Cross (Kakâbat Krohom Kampuchea; CRC), then known as the Khmer Red Cross Society (Samokom Cheat Kakâbat Krohom Khmer), was founded in February 1955, shortly before the establishment of the Sangkum.[98] Since its beginning, the CRC received unique recognition from the government as its auxiliary.[99] It has since enjoyed a mandate as a quasi-governmental organization, basing its work on the help of volunteers to distribute aid to victims of natural disasters, soldiers, orphans, and others. But during the civil war from 1979 onwards, four different Red Cross groups operated in the respective occupied zones, illustrating the politicization of the organization.[100] Mirroring his larger role in peacemaking, Sihanouk led the reunification of the CRC between 1992 and 1994.[101]Ranariddh's wife at the time, First Lady Princess Norodom Marie, (née Eng)

---

[95] Hun Sen also states, "it is about the art of sharing, which is a part of the CPP's policy in bringing about development to the country from 1979 to the present. I think this has brought us to a clear political and social line. Sharing resources has been a tradition of CPP since 1979, and it was also done in the time of Samdech Preah Norodom Sihanouk's *Sangkum Reastr Niyum*, or, to be frank, since when the earth exists, because Cambodia also enjoys donation and assistance from the rich countries as well. [...] Judging from what they said, as soon as CPP loses the elections there will be no more sharing and people could not request help from leaders of CPP. This would help our people make political choices in the upcoming elections." Hun Sen, "Inaugurating Junior High School Hun Sen—Srah Banteay," *Cambodia New Vision* 110, March 2007.

[96] Thompson, "The Suffering of Kings," 91.

[97] Ibid., 93.

[98] The organization was renamed the Cambodian Red Cross (CRC) in 1979.

[99] Men Neary Sopheak and Tianji Dickens, *United For Humanity* (Phnom Penh: Cambodian Red Cross, International Committee of the Red Cross and the Federation, 2005), 31.

[100] Ibid., 7.

[101] Ibid., 27.

became CRC president (1994–1998), reestablishing royal control over the institution after a hiatus brought on by the 1970 Khmer Republic.[102]

Envisaging her work for the Cambodian Red Cross as a particularly royal task, Princess Marie would later describe the reunification of all warring factions that it entailed, and its provision of aid, as the very meaning of royalist nationalism in the KOC.[103] Parallel to her work for the CRC, Marie also headed her own organization, Sobbhana. Named after Princess Rasmi Sobbhana, who had originally founded the CRC, it was established by Marie in a refugee camp on the Thai-Cambodian border in 1985 and its activities were expanded nationwide following the peace process.[104] These activities included training on textiles and handicraft, sponsoring girls' education, as well as a variety of health projects. Sobbhana carried out practices associated with the "social opening" alongside FUNCINPEC party structures, engaging the wives of party functionaries in humanitarian work. Accompanied by the wives of high-ranking FUNCINPEC officials, Marie traveled to beneficiary villages where, together with medical practitioners, she educated village women on hygiene and sanitation and handed out medicine. She estimates approximately 200,000 people to have benefited from Sobbhana project activities since 1993. For Marie, the activities of the organization followed a distinctly royal tradition of royals personally exploring and addressing the people's needs. As she explained it, "most of the volunteers belong to FUNCINPEC; they are wives of the ministers, secretaries of state, and undersecretaries of state. I want them to understand only that you have to love your country and especially the people—because they need you. You have to understand and to have been there yourself: that is what I have done." Marie aimed to transpose this royal tradition to the novel party political context.[105]

The political and symbolic importance of such strategies of provision is highlighted by the fact that, following the July 1997 overthrow of Ranariddh, Bun Rany replaced Princess Norodom Marie as president of the Red Cross in 1998. Since then, the Red Cross under Bun Rany has become increasingly publicly exalted.[106] Sobbhana, on the other hand, has drastically reduced its activities. Bun Rany's association with caretaking intersects with the conceptual and historical role of royals on a number of levels. Paralleling the consolidation of power by Hun Sen and his network, it has firmly integrated practices of gift-giving into personalized claims to embody nation-building in line with historical conceptualizations of kingship.

The discourse adopted by the CPP toward the CRC emphasizes ancient Cambodian indigenous roots of mutual aid and solidarity, and credits the CRC with helping Cambodia find her way back to this tradition. In a speech, Hun Sen stated:

---

[102] Presidents of the CRC are Samdech Preah Reach Kanitha Norodom Rasmi Sobbhana (1955–67), Queen Norodom Monineath (1967–70), Chuop Samlot (1971–73), Phlech Phiroun (1974–75, 1979–92), Princess Norodom Marie Ranariddh (1994–1998), and Bun Rany (1998–present). Honorary presidents are Queen Kossamak (1961) and Queen Norodom Monineath (since 1994).

[103] Author's interview with Norodom Marie June 19, 2010.

[104] The name Sobbhana also reflected Norodom Marie's appreciation for Rasmi Sobbhana as a "second mother-in-law" who had taken care of Ranariddh when he was young.

[105] Ibid.

[106] This can be contrasted with the CPP working groups, the backbone of CPP strategies of provision, which remained an open secret, in that they were mentioned in the news but with no public documentation available, and were directly associated with voter mobilization at the local level.

"The Cambodian Red Cross has helped Cambodia by enabling the Cambodian people to express, in an institutionalized way, our ancient culture of helping each other. This is a trait that is found in the core of our civilization, inherited from our forebears, but one we have been unable to nurture in our dark recent history. The CRC has helped all of us reawaken this important trait."[107] This is strikingly similar to how Sihanouk described joint voluntary work as one of the principal characteristics of Khmer socialism: "The ideals of mutual aid and solidarity between all social classes of the Sangkum Reastr Niyum are the motors that drive the people to provide a voluntary effort to serve the Khmer community and nation."[108]

Cambodian Red Cross gift-giving ceremony, with Sihanouk (left), Monineath (center), and Bun Rany (right); Siem Reap, 2009 (photo courtesy of James Gerrand)

Indeed, an important reason for the exaltation of Bun Rany's presidency of the CRC is arguably the distinctly royal overtones of the ability to "stand in for the suffering of the kingdom." If Hun Sen's autobiography is used as "a metaphor for the resurgence of the nation after 'the ashes of Democratic Kampuchea,'" then his wife's caretaking role completes the family metaphor.[109] This division of labor is naturally aided by how Bun Rany worked as a nurse under the DK until withdrawing, in 1979, to raise a family; her experience as a nurse allows her to

---

[107] Hun Sen, "Talk at the Third General Assembly of the Cambodian Red Cross," Chaktomuk Conference Hall, Phnom Penh, quoted in Men and Dickens, *United For Humanity*, 5.

[108] Sihanouk, *Considérations sur le Socialisme Khmer*, 11.

[109] On Hun Sen's autobiography as a metaphor, see Hughes, "The Politics of Gifts," 473–74. The most comprehensive and official narrative of Bun Rany's life to date is in *Red Rose of the Mekong*, which provides an account of Bun Rany's life from childhood to the CRC presidency. Huot Sambath, *Red Rose of the Mekong* (original publisher unknown; reproduced by the *Quiz Times Newspaper*, Ministry of Information, and Attwood Import-Export Co., Ltd., n.d.).

legitimately provide medical advice.[110] Bun Rany is described as possessing characteristics that closely invoke the *srey krop leak*, or the Khmer ideal woman, a discourse that holds widespread legitimacy in contemporary society.[111] Thereby, Bun Rany has become perhaps the foremost example of the "feminization of moral order," a return to traditional social values in terms of gender, which Penny Edwards identifies in contemporary Cambodia.[112] Just as a traditional discourse ties the family's prosperity to female activities, Bun Rany's virtues are relevant to the prosperity of the entire nation.[113] In CRC material, such as songs frequently broadcast on national television, Bun Rany is typically portrayed as motherly with regard to the nation, and often as a "saving mother" (*neak mdae sangkroas*). This portrayal echoes the way that Queen-Mother Monineath was commonly referred to as *Samdech Mae* (Mylady Mother), and then *Samdech Yeay* (Mylady Grandmother), just as the less frequent appeal of Hun Sen as *lok puk* mirrors King-Father Sihanouk's nicknames, *Samdech Euv* (Monsignor Papa), and *Samdech Ta* (Monsignor Grandfather).[114] Indeed, underlining how important it is for the CRC under Bun Rany to be acknowledged as the very same CRC of the royal past, a Royal Decree (*kret*) of May 6, 2002, officially recognized the Cambodian Red Cross as the successor of the original, 1955 organization.[115]

The CRC has produced a number of songs, and these are frequently broadcast on the Bayon TV network, owned by Hun Sen and Bun Rany's daughter Hun Mana. The songs typically employ royal language[116] and acknowledge the royal origin of the organization, characterizing Bun Rany's activities as the continuation of royal work handed down. Several CRC songs paraphrase Jayavarman VII's famous dictum, suggesting a deliberate attempt to insert the first couple's patronage of the organization into the context of kingship and healing. One song declares that:

---

[110] See, for example, the CRC-produced video, "Medical Practitioner and Woman Understands Women," in which Bun Rany gives medical advice to women about to give birth.

[111] See: Judy Ledgerwood, "Politics and Gender: Negotiating Changing Cambodian Ideas of the Proper Woman," *Asia Pacific Viewpoint* 37 no. 2 (1996), 139–52; Roeun Aing Sok, *A Comparative Analysis of Traditional and Contemporary Roles of Khmer Women in the Household: A Case Study in Leap Tong Village* (Phnom Penh: Royal University of Phnom Penh, 2004); and Mona Lilja, *Power, Resistance and Women Politicians in Cambodia: Discourses of Emancipation* (Copenhagen: NIAS Press, 2008), 70.

[112] Edwards, "The Moral Geology of the Present," 227–32.

[113] Ledgerwood, "Politics and Gender," 143. In Khmer Buddhist conceptualizations, a woman's virtue, in itself, is a sign of previous meritorious behavior, and will bring safety, order, and prosperity to her family. In this sense, any woman acts as a substitute for the family, and the first lady, necessarily, for the nation.

[114] Indeed, the CRC can be said to contain a wider "familiarization" of political power, integrating the wives of senior CPP leaders as well as business tycoons (*oknhas*) into its structures. The Central Committee of the Fifth Term of Office (2011–14) thus included as first vice president, Annie Sok An, wife of the Minister of the Council of Ministers Sok An; second vice president, Choeng Sopheap, wife of *oknha* Lao Meng Khin; Nhem Sophanny, wife of National Assembly Vice President Nguon Nhel; Men Pheakdei, wife of late National Police Chief Hok Lundi; and four *oknhas*, namely Ly Yong Phat, Mong Rithy, Kith Meng, and Lim Chhiv Ho (among whom Kith Meng is National Chamber of Commerce president and Ly Yong Phat and Mong Rithy are CPP senators). See *CRC Newsletter* 3 (2011): 45–47.

[115] Cambodian Red Cross, *"Preah Reach Kret Sdey pi Kar Totuol Skoal Kakâbat Krohom Kampuchea"* [Royal Decree on the Recognition of the Cambodian Red Cross], 2010.

[116] Royal language forms a particular register of Khmer, with its own distinct vocabulary reserved for royalty.

Wherever there is a victim, there is *Lok Chumteav Bandit*, president of the CRC, descending to help. *Samdech Techo* and *Lok Chumteav Bandit* are powerful [*sakseth*] gods who save lives, they are like a father and mother. *The suffering of the people is the suffering of both of them,* distributing wealth to help the CRC provide help [emphasis added.][117]

In this song, as in a number of other songs popularized by the CRC, Hun Sen and Bun Rany are described as nothing short of "divinities" (*tevota*).[118] This echoes how historical conceptualizations of healing conflated royal and divine status by positing the king as a substitute body of the Buddha as a healer.[119] The song stretches the saving capacity of the first couple to tell the audience that they are divinities, vested with magical power (*sakseth*)—a form of power associated with royalty.[120]

This illustrates not only the similarity of legitimization between the CPP and the Sangkum, but also FUNCINPEC's failure to reinvent the royalist provision-based identity to its advantage. Provision was envisaged as a cornerstone of royalist democracy and remained a key way in which FUNCINPEC related to the electorate. Both the loss of the CRC presidency and, more generally, that they were outmaneuvered by the CPP as providers of benefits, can be understood to have caused a resulting "democratic deficit" for the royalists.[121] This also testifies to the importance of a material base for realizing this vision of royalist democracy. Without such a base, royals appear to be less-than-royal. Conversely, political actors with the ability to provide can be thought to take on some of the royal aura. This brings up questions of the overall liberty of royalists to pick-and-choose in their legitimizing discourse. With provision deeply engrained in ideas of kingship, their ability to move away from such ideas was constricted. The above quandary was, in this sense, indicative of a larger problem of the viability of transposing royalism to the party political arena.

The National Union

The Sangkum dissolved rival political parties—ending Cambodia's short experience of parliamentary democracy. Ranariddh lauds this as the regime's democratic value, defining the resulting "national union" such that "no political

---

[117] "*Samdech Techo øphirouchon*" [The Progressivist Samdech Techo]. This is later paraphrased: "The people are easily victimized. *Lok Chumteav Bandit* pities and helps victims from her heart, which wants to save the people. Because the suffering of the Khmer subjects is the suffering of both [Hun Sen and Bun Rany]; they need to be saved." Bun Rany was awarded the title *Lok Chumteav Kittipritt Bandit* by the Royal Academy of Cambodia in 2010, while "Samdech Techo" is an epithet for Hun Sen.

[118] See, for example, the songs *Tossânah Monusâthor Krop Chrong Chroey* [A Complete Humanitarian Vision], which states, "Husband and wife are living gods [*tevota ros*] who help victims [...] they descend to help because of pitying their nephews and nieces [...] They will be our mother and father for a long time to come, their hearts will not leave their nephews and nieces"; and *Bândam Lok Chumteav Bandit* [The Advice of Lok Chumteav Bandit].

[119] Thompson, "The Suffering of Kings," 96.

[120] Compare to how in the Lao and Thai contexts the notion of *saksit* is similarly an important criterion for the contemporary cult of royals. Evans, *The Politics of Ritual and Remembrance*, 30, 101–3.

[121] Author's interview with Norodom Marie.

tendency, current of thought, or faction should be excluded from the national community or the political dialogue."[122] Central to Ranariddh's political analysis of the KOC, this reasoning is manifested in his distrust of the current multiparty system, and his advocacy of gathering different political tendencies under one structure.[123]

Ranariddh and other royalists have repeatedly appealed to the idea of a national union to frame FUNCINPEC policies. Ranariddh appealed to the value of consensual politics to justify the sequence of coalition governments formed with the CPP in 1993, 1998, and 2004, claiming to act in conformity with the wishes of Sihanouk.[124] As a reinstated monarch, Sihanouk also repeatedly advocated some variant of a consensus-based national union, although under the guise of a multiparty political system. When the 2003 general elections resulted in the CPP failing to gain the two-thirds majority required to form a government on its own, FUNCINPEC and the SRP formed the "Alliance of Democrats," contesting the election results and each claiming they would refuse to join a coalition government if Hun Sen remained prime minister. King Sihanouk then proposed a tripartite coalition government among the CPP, FUNCINPEC, and SRP. On November 5, 2003, the three parties met and agreed to form a coalition government under Hun Sen as prime minister.[125] The tripartite government, however, never came into being. A senior FUNCINPEC official at the time explains why:

> There was a meeting between Sihanouk, Hun Sen, Ranariddh, and Sam Rainsy. Sihanouk said, "Having an opposition is contrary to Cambodian culture. We should all join together to work towards reunification, like during the Sangkum." Then there was also a very small democratic opposition, but it was included in the Sangkum. Everyone agreed, Hun Sen, Ranariddh, and Sam Rainsy. But after Sam Rainsy left the meeting, he phoned Ranariddh to decline. [...] The opposition wants to stay in opposition![126]

This course of events, though not corroborated by Sam Rainsy, has been reiterated since 2003 by Ranariddh and his loyalists as a critique of Rainsy. The reason is deeper than a simple condemnation of Rainsy allegedly going back on his word. The quote above demonstrates why: it situates Sihanouk's encouragement of a tripartite coalition government in the context of the Sangkum idea of a national union, arguing that a democratic opposition would be contrary to Cambodian culture.[127] Here, democracy in the sense of a conflict of ideas is fraught with danger,

---

[122] Norodom, *Droit Public Cambodgien*, 133–34.

[123] Ibid., 71.

[124] As mentioned above, Ranariddh blames the 1993 coalition government on Chakrapong's threatened secession. Subsequent coalition governments are portrayed as pragmatic measures to solve political crises in conformity with the wishes of Sihanouk. Compare to Sam Nora, Note of the Day, 23.

[125] "World Briefing Asia: Cambodia: Coalition Government," *New York Times*, November 6, 2003.

[126] Author's interview with Noranarith Ananda Yath, June 4, 2011.

[127] The CPP, on the other hand, seems to have favored a two-party solution. Outlining his case against the "5 November '03" agreement, Hun Sen stated that he favored a two-party coalition with FUNCINPEC, since a tripartite coalition government would result in constitutional ambiguities on how to dissolve the government in case of a coalition partner

and the possibility of democratic division is a real threat to contemporary politics. This account offers an alternative explanation of why a joint opposition agenda foundered. When FUNCINPEC proceeded to form a two-party coalition government with the CPP in 2004, marking the end of cooperation with the SRP (which has remained deeply distrustful of FUNCINPEC ever since), Ranariddh received heavy criticism from inside the party.[128] By referring to Sihanouk's suggestion of a national union, the story of these events is turned around to portray the democratic opposition as sowing seeds of discord in a fundamentally non-Cambodian manner.

Yet the reference to a national union, when advanced from a position of political marginalization, carries different meanings and implications than Sihanouk's original ideas. Ironically, while Sihanouk's "national union" was designed to eclipse the threat of political rivals, today's references are primarily attempts to become useful to the dominant CPP. This is underlined by Ranariddh's increasingly vocal opposition to the very idea of a Cambodian political opposition following his ouster from the FUNCINPEC leadership in 2006, when campaigning for his new Norodom Ranariddh Party and attempting to advance it as a potential coalition partner for the CPP. Referring to Sihanouk's 2003 advice, Ranariddh argued that a political opposition runs contrary to Cambodian culture, and branded the existing opposition as the "champion of division".[129] A communication under his pen name, "Sam Nora," thus rejected the possibility of Ranariddh joining the opposition on the dual grounds that Cambodia was said to lack a culture of opposition, and because of the Cambodian opposition being "sterile and incapable [of uniting]."[130]

Ranariddh argued that there are three political forces in Cambodia: the CPP, the royalists, and the "oppositions;" thus juxtaposing the royalists and the opposition.[131] The royalists, divided into "new FUNCINPEC" and the NRP, needed to be reunified in the framework of a "real royalist party" for "Royalists, Sihanoukists, and other Patriots" to represent a second political force. The opposition, on the other hand, consisted of the SRP and the Human Rights Party (HRP). Ranariddh referred to these three forces as the new political "triptych" (*kâmleang noyobay bey*) in Cambodia, recalling the national motto of nation, religion, king.[132] The existence of royalists as

---

leaving, and in regards to the National Election Committee (NEC). See Hun Sen, "A Visit to the Kompong Raing Bridge Construction," *Cambodia New Vision* 73, February 2004.

[128] Sam Rainsy's agreement to sign the 2006 constitutional amendment (which required a simple majority rather than a two-thirds majority for passing bills in parliament and made FUNCINPEC redundant as a CPP coalition partner) is generally understood as an act of revenge following the formation in 2004 of a coalition government between FUNCINPEC and the CPP.

[129] Sam Nora, "Note of the Day 24: Samdech Krom Preah Norodom Ranariddh's Middle Path," 2011, at http://www.norodomranariddh.org, accessed 12 March 2012; Sam Nora, "Note of the Day 1: The Opposition Parties in Cambodia are the Champion of Division," 2010, at http://www.norodomranariddh.org, accessed 1 March 2012.

[130] Sam Nora, "Note of the Day 47: The NRP's Middle Path: Rationale and Justification," 2011, at http://www.norodomranariddh.org, accessed 13 March 2012.

[131] See: Sam Nora, "Note of the Day 14: The Royalists within the National Community (Part 1)," 2010, at http://www.norodomranariddh.org, accessed 10 March 2012; Sam Nora, "Note of the Day 15: The Royalists within the National Community (Part 2)," 2010, at http://www.norodomranariddh.org, accessed 10 March 2012; and Sam Nora, "Note of the Day 38: The Political 'Triptych' in Cambodia," 2011, at http://www.norodomranariddh.org, accessed 13 March 2012.

[132] Sam Nora, "Note of the Day 38," 2011.

a third pole, neither opposition nor ruling party, was said to be unique to Cambodia.[133]

Ranariddh branded his political bid to reunify royalists as "the middle path"—neither joining the opposition nor opposing the CPP.[134] This recalled how, during Sangkum, Buddhist socialism was said to represent a middle path to the Cold War, split between the free world and communism, and between the domestic right and left. Sihanouk cast his middle path as distinctly Buddhist, tied to what was celebrated as age-old national religion safeguarded by Cambodia's historical kings.[135] Ranariddh, on the other hand, defined his middle path as the "participation of the royalists/nationalists in the state powers and administration, in a process of peace, stability, and development, leading towards real national reconciliation and unity."[136] This meant royalists participating in the legislative, executive, and local state governments; this could only be realized through cooperation with the ruling CPP:

> Hence, the quasi magic formula: the political force, represented by the Royalists, Sihanoukists, Patriots, ADDED to the other one, the CPP, to serving, altogether, Cambodia. That one is not servitude, but a real cooperation and collaboration, to resolving altogether, the problems of national interests, in stability, peace and in the framework of a rule of law. The Prince refuses thus the idea of using the Royalists, Sihanoukists and Patriots, to oppose and fight against the ruling Party. Such a way will represent for them and, in a long run, for our country a mortal danger.[137]

This stance of advocating collaboration with the CPP was summed up in NRP's campaign formula, "don't confront—add" (*kom bok—bauk*).[138]

Yet Ranariddh's middle path, which attempted primarily to justify coalitions with the stronger CPP as its junior partner, differs sharply from that of Sihanouk, who exerted firm control over his political adversaries. Indeed, this was the main source of friction as royal family members gathered around Ranariddh after his 2006 ouster, many disapproving of his dependent stance. Other senior royalists, advocating a confrontational stance vis-à-vis the CPP, heavily criticized what they considered to be Ranariddh's subversion of the Sihanoukist idea of a middle path. One of them charged:

> I don't understand Ranariddh's thinking. They [NRP] don't campaign to win. They campaign to be in coalition with the CPP! They call it a middle way. They represent themselves not like a leader, but like a mistress, a second wife. "Honey, I will vote with you for this, but not for that. For that one, I support the

---

[133] Sam Nora, "Note of the Day 24," 2011.

[134] Sam Nora, "Note of the Day 47," 2011.

[135] See: Norodom Sihanouk, "Notre Socialisme Buddhique;" Hughes, "Reconstructing Legitimate Political Authority through Elections?" 40; and John L. S. Girling, *Cambodia and the Sihanouk Myths* (Singapore: Institute of Southeast Asian Studies, 1971), 5.

[136] Sam Nora, "Note of the Day 24," 2011.

[137] Sam Nora, "Note of the Day 47," 2011.

[138] Author's fieldnotes, Ranariddh campaign speech, June 4, 2011, Oudong village, Kompong Speu province.

opposition. For this one, I vote with you, honey." For me, a political party cannot campaign like that. You must campaign to win![139]

The last remnants of the NRP (known between 2008–2010 and 2012–2014 as the Nationalist Party) would eventually dissolve in 2014 into the CNRP, two years after Ranariddh's second resignation from the party presidency—never having been a significant political party.

Direct Democracy and the National Congress

Ranariddh writes this about the Sangkum-era practice of direct democracy: "The third concept, 'direct democracy' is a unique form of Khmer democracy. [...] It is a technique to put the new doctrine into practice and expresses above all a refusal to see power confiscated by the intermediary of officials, whether elected or civil servants."[140] Sangkum understood democracy as an organic unity, with the king as the embodiment of popular aspiration.[141] According to its statutes, the Sangkum, rather than a political party, was the symbol of aspirations of the *"Petit Peuple,"* the "true People of Cambodia." It was "a National Gathering [...] defending the National Union [...] for the return to good traditions which created the grandeur of Cambodia in her glorious past. These traditions are the People's Community with its two natural protectors: Religion and the Throne."[142] The body politic was made out to be a democratic organism whose members would peacefully work toward shared goals in social harmony. The chief mechanism for this was the biannual National Congress, a new version of direct democracy that replaced parliamentary democracy, where members of the Sangkum movement voted on major issues (including complex ones of foreign policy) through a show of hands.[143] The National Congress initiated policies, later turned into laws by the National Assembly, which was reduced to near insignificance. First instituted in 1955, twenty-eight National Congresses were held before 1970.

Ranariddh's contemporary democratic vision transposed Sangkum direct democracy, and the ideas of democracy as organic unity on which it was built. Contrasting the current "representative democracy" with an ideal "direct democracy," Ranariddh charges that, under a system of representative democracy, power is taken from the popular masses and given to a dominant political class.[144] The "nation," as the holder of sovereignty, is nothing but an abstraction, since real power comes to lie with its representatives. This system gives no place to the expression of the people's will, apart from the delegation of power by the vote.[145] The imperfection of representative democracy is manifest in the flaws of elections,

---

[139] Author's interview with anonymous source, July 10, 2011.

[140] Norodom Ranariddh, *Droit Public Cambodgien*, 134.

[141] Hughes, "Transforming Oppositions in Cambodia," 308.

[142] Norodom Sihanouk, *Statuts de Sangkum* (Article 4), 2–3.

[143] Chandler, *The Tragedy of Cambodian History*, 84. See also Norodom Sihanouk, *Statuts de Sangkum* (Section 3).

[144] Ranariddh engages with no political theorists in this discussion. Rousseau, famously associated with developing ideas of direct democracy, is instead later criticized for overlooking how democracy can lead to oppression. See Norodom Ranariddh, *Droit Public Cambodgien*, 70.

[145] Ibid., 66.

its main instrument, as opposed to the referendum, the main instrument of direct democracy. Contrasting the "traps" of elections with the "virtues" of the referendum, Ranariddh charges that elections have scope only to the extent that they testify to a "real consensus" by the governed. Yet, he charges, a real and more widespread consensus can be marked by the attachment to the monarchic principle and "to the one that embodies it," i.e., the king. The monarch is a national symbol and guarantor of the common interest, and his role may in times of crisis temporarily be even greater.[146] The monarch thus steps in for the shortcomings of representative democracy in guaranteeing consensus and national unity.

Ranariddh distrusts the election-focused political party as the basic unit of popular representation, and favors instead the gathering of different political tendencies under one and the same organizational structure. A grouping of various national trends in a single but flexible structure allowing ample space for internal freedom of expression, he deems, is not incompatible with democracy.[147] He warns against the multiplication of political parties, judging that a few parties should be enough to "incarnate" the major national tendencies. The multiparty system has never been the sign of a healthy and efficient democracy, he charges. On the contrary, the multiplication of political parties "without doctrine" endangers real democracy, since partisan secession "in order to impose one's view" does not further increase the democratic spirit.[148]

Such views are anchored in Ranariddh's belief in the organic relationship between the people and the monarch, which cannot be substituted by an elected parliament or executive. Testifying to his view of democracy as organic unity, Ranariddh objects to the liberal democratic rights language in the 1993 constitution. Ranariddh laments that the techniques for assuring that "the Khmer people are masters of the country's destiny" are limited to "classical recipes of representative, liberal, pluralist democracy," with the "corrective" of the National Congress. He further laments that there is no heading in the 1993 constitution that lays out the role and powers of the "Khmer People"—rather, it lays out "the rights and obligations of Khmer citizens."[149]

To correct the shortcomings of the current representative democracy, Ranariddh invokes Sangkum mechanisms to involve ordinary people in public affairs, including the referendum, right to petition, revocation of representatives, and, above all, a National Congress.[150] Though provided for by the 1993 constitution—which set forth that a yearly National Congress, chaired by the king and open to all Khmer citizens, would have the mandate to inform citizens on various matters, to raise issues and requests for the state to solve, and to adopt recommendations for consideration by state authorities and the National Assembly—a National Congress has yet to be convened.[151] FUNCINPEC has persistently campaigned for the king's right to head a National Congress and for the realization of two other constitutional

---

[146] Ibid., 68.

[147] Ibid., 71.

[148] Ibid., 71–72.

[149] Constitution of Cambodia (Chapter III), 1993.

[150] Norodom Ranariddh, *Droit Public Cambodgien*, 67.

[151] Constitution of Cambodia (Chapter XII, Articles 128–30), 1993.

provisions: the king's right to preside over the Supreme Council for Armed Forces, a body not yet created; and the right to preside over the High Council of Magistracy.[152]

Yet the calls for a National Congress today carry different meanings from those of the Sangkum era, and highlight the hollowing out of meaning from political royalism. Whereas the National Congress during Sangkum served as an essential mechanism for communication between a paternalistic ruler and the people, and thereby served also to give a semblance of power-sharing, in the KOC it was invoked as a means of investing the constitutional monarch with some limited powers. The political harmlessness of such claims is perhaps best illustrated by how the reinstatement of constitutional rights to the king emerged as the main point that FUNCINPEC and the NRP could unite around in negotiations about merger in the years following Ranariddh's 2006 ouster. Both the post-2006 FUNCINPEC and the NRP campaigned for the reinstatement of the king's constitutional powers and, as a main part of this, promoted the idea of the National Congress.[153] Asked in a press conference what the two parties had to offer "now that monarchism and Sihanoukism were outdated," the party leaders referred to two unrealized constitutional provisions: that the king should head a Supreme Council for Armed Forces, and that the king should head a National Congress. FUNCINPEC President Keo Puth Reasmey recalled their response as follows: "There are two things to be a royalist that are mentioned in the constitution. We are royalists, if we win the elections we will make sure that the King gets both of these powers."[154] That is, royalism had by then been eroded to refer merely to protecting the constitutional powers of the king. Ultimately, it further helped define the king as a purely constitutional monarch.

Royalism as Democratic Opposition

Appeals to Sangkum-style democracy coexist with parallel appeals to a democratic opposition identity. There were thus two parallel democratic logics invoked by royalist actors. While Ranariddh has associated himself more closely with Sangkum-derived ideas of democracy, another group in FUNCINPEC's leadership advocated for the party to assert itself as an opposition party, and was more willing to ally with the democrats than to form coalition governments with the CPP. This group of royalists was disappointed by Ranariddh's lack of an oppositional stance. They envisaged the royalist political agenda as protecting the multiparty, liberal democratic system, and the constitutional monarchy, where the monarch reigned but did not rule. They took pride in how FUNCINPEC helped achieve the PPA in terms of how it established that Cambodia would be a liberal, multiparty democracy, and outlined the rights of the citizens: and were also proud of the resulting constitution of 1993, which contained provisions to this effect.

Some of these royalists invoked an indigenous democratic legacy, derived not from Sangkum but from the Democratic Party (DP) founded by Prince Sisowath Yuthevong in 1946. The DP posed a formidable challenge to Sihanouk—to the point that Sangkum was set up partly in response to it. A gifted mathematician who had spent more than a decade in France, Yuthevong was seen as an alternative to the

---

[152] Ibid., Articles 287–88.

[153] FUNCINPEC, "Kolokar Noyobay Sângkhep Konâbâk FUNCINPEC," 2006, 6, and author's interviews with Keo Puth Reasmey, June 8, 2010, and You Hockry.

[154] Author's interview with Keo Puth Reasmey, June 8, 2010.

elite around Sihanouk, who was, at the time, still a puppet ruler under the French. Becoming Cambodia's first prime minister, Yuthevong oversaw the drafting of the 1947 constitution, which instituted a constitutional democracy and invested more power in an elected assembly than in the chief of state.[155] In creating a liberal democratic framework through the 1993 constitution, some claimed to have looked back to Yuthevong's framework set out by the 1947 constitution, using it as a model. Sisowath Sirirath phrased it this way:

> Yuthevong [...] wrote the first constitution of democratic Cambodia in 1947. After FUNCINPEC won the elections in 1993 and we drafted the constitution, we took a lot of wordings from Yuthevong's Constitution, such as the line that specifies that Cambodia shall be free, independent, and neutral. We took a lot from Yuthevong. But 90 percent of it has been changed by the CPP since then through amendments. Now more than 200 people are not allowed to demonstrate in the street. We are slowly moving back to another phase. Our newspapers are free and fair in looks only, but you don't see the opposition parties on TV. This is not democratic. There is only one voice. This is not in conformity with our vision.[156]

This can be understood as an attempt to argue for the royalist roots of an indigenous democratic movement, which supports a more general identification with a liberal democratic agenda based not on Sangkum-style national consensus but on a multiparty system, freedom of demonstration, and freedom of press. Invoking Yuthevong's name in this sense invoked shared intellectual origins with the self-identified democratic opposition, which repeatedly makes such demands. Such references to Yuthevong typically contrasted him favorably with Ranariddh, and, at times, Sihanouk. In one example of such a reading, a royal family member criticized Sihanouk and Ranariddh for their "paternalistic" leadership style, before concluding that Yuthevong, because of his work for a multiparty democratic system and constitutional monarchy in Cambodia, was the "pride of the family."[157] References to Yuthevong, therefore, in some sense, offer an alternative genealogy of royalist nationalism.

The tension between these coexisting logics has been a constant source of friction within FUNCINPEC. Ranariddh's ideas of democratic representation founded in ideas of organic relations contrasted sharply with the conflicting vision of FUNCINPEC as a liberal democratic party, promoting relations of strict accountability between the elected and the electorate. Proponents of the latter criticized the hierarchical vision of society envisaged by the circle around Ranariddh, a vision mirrored by FUNCINPEC party structure. While it was by no means a coup by a more liberal democratic faction, the party coup in 2006 that ousted Ranariddh did highlight tensions in the party resulting from Ranariddh's strong grip over party internal affairs. After the resulting implosion of the royalists, politicians who identified with a liberal democratic identity blamed the downfall of political royalism on the failure of FUNCINPEC leaders, especially Ranariddh, to work out a royalist identity based on what they considered to be modern democratic ideas of

---

[155] Chandler, *The Tragedy of Cambodian History*, 30, 35–36.

[156] Author's interview with Sisowath Sirirath, May 13, 2010.

[157] Author's private communication with anonymous source, September 2012.

equality. This exasperation was expressed by one of Ranariddh's long-standing aides:

> So, when you write about royalism, who do you include as a royalist? What does royalism mean now? I don't know what royalism means anymore. In the 1990s, many foreigners were suspicious of royalists, thinking it [royalism] is too pyramidal. I used to explain it as "We are modern democrats who believe in having a King, as well as multiparty, liberal democracy." But in actual fact, there is a contradiction. We do not have the maturity to have a constitutional monarchy like in the UK. The concept for the Prince and others, is still the God-King ... it is so hierarchical. [...] I think there is a contradiction that we cannot overcome, between the idea of a constitutional monarchy and democratic ideas [on the one hand], and the old pyramidal idea, what monarchy means in Cambodia—absolute [on the other]. I don't know what political royalism could mean in Cambodia.[158]

To this disenchanted group, FUNCINPEC's pyramid organization made it a less than democratic party, which, together with a lack of internal discipline, weakened it. FUNCINPEC leaders, they claimed, showcased a liberal democratic identity by virtue of their association with liberal democratic countries where they had spent time in exile, yet failed to substantiate this claim:

> As a political party, FUNCINPEC had a platform but had problems with the daily management and administration, and some visions were not there. The base perspective was to receive some vision from the top. [...] People think that we come from a liberal culture so we are democrats, but I think people from FUNCINPEC knew nothing about democracy or liberalization. They only spoke the word.[159]

This group took practical measures to form alliances with the self-identified democratic parties. In 2003, Norodom Sirivudh, then secretary general of FUNCINPEC, proposed the Alliance of Democrats (AD) between FUNCINPEC and the SRP. The effort to bridge the differences between royalists and self-identified democratic parties was repeated by Sisowath Thomico's 2006 establishment of the Sangkum Jatiniyum alliance. The formation of a joint democratic opposition foundered, however, for several reasons. A decisive one was the power balance within FUNCINPEC, which tilted in favor of Ranariddh. Ranariddh's 2004 decision to call off the AD and form a coalition with the CPP was a turning point for relations between FUNCINPEC and the SRP that permanently ended trust between the two parties, and also alienated and embittered those within FUNCINPEC who identified with a shared democratic opposition identity.[160]

A second main impediment to the formation of a joint democratic opposition was the royalists' fear that the SRP was anti-royalist—either in the sense of being anti-constitutional monarchy (Republican), or anti-Sihanoukist. Royals have been generally convinced that Sam Rainsy holds Sihanouk ultimately responsible for his

---

158 Author's interview with Pok Marina, June 20, 2011.

159 Author's interview with Sisowath Pheanuroth.

160 Author's interviews with anonymous sources, July 12, 2010, and July 10, 2011.

father's death, and that, in spite of his outward support of the constitutional monarchy, Sam Rainsy harbors deeply anti-royalist sentiments in both of the above senses.[161] One senior royal who had previously been the driving force behind cooperation between FUNCINPEC and the SRP thus typically remarked: "Sam Rainsy is still anti-royalist, because Sihanouk killed his father."[162] This conviction has continuously acted to prevent close cooperation between royalists and democrats, even when politicians from the two camps have appeared to have a joint agenda. In 1994, Norodom Sirivudh resigned from his posts as co-deputy prime minister and minister of foreign affairs following Ranariddh's expulsion of Sam Rainsy from the post of minister of Finance.[163] Yet Sirivudh and his aides deny that the two men shared a common agenda, precisely by pointing to Sam Rainsy's perceived anti-royalist stance.[164] Sisowath Thomico similarly claimed to have lost hope of cooperation with the SRP after watching a French documentary in which Sam Rainsy "spoke unjustly of Sihanouk" (though the two would later come together in the CNRP).[165] Trust was further damaged by the publication of books by Sam Rainsy and his sister Sam Emmarane that were highly critical of Sihanouk.[166]

Third, while the two democratic visions were primarily associated with two different sets of actors, these stances were, in reality, more like two end points on a continuum with many royalist actors intermittently associating themselves with either pole. In the wake of his calls for royalists and the SRP to unite, Sisowath Thomico would, as we shall see, attempt to revive Sihanouk's doctrine, elevating Sihanouk's Buddhist socialism to a guiding ideology for the KOC and advocating the implementation of its ideas of direct democracy. His stance manifests how ideas of democracy derived from Sihanouk remained a prominent, if not inescapable, part of royalist discourse and thinking, bringing real difficulty in uniting with the non-royalist democratic opposition.

The Legacy of the Resistance

If a joint "democratic opposition" identity with the SRP was difficult to form, then a "democratic opposition" identity based on the legacy of the PRK-era resistance was more successful. The defection of members of the former KPNLF faction to FUNCINPEC encouraged this dynamic. In 1998, the Son Sann Party, successor to the KPNLF, merged with FUNCINPEC. Former KPNLF fighters generally chose to join FUNCINPEC, following the formation of the first coalition government in 1993; the disintegration of its successor party, the Buddhist Liberal Democratic Party (BLDP); the July 1997 events, which forced actors to take sides between Hun Sen and Ranariddh; and, finally, the implosion of the Son Sann Party

---

[161] Sam Sary helped Sihanouk found the Sangkum Reastr Niyum, but fell out with Sihanouk and died under unclear circumstances in 1962, after having fled Cambodia. See Chandler, *The Tragedy of Cambodian History*, 99–101.

[162] Author's interview with anonymous source, July 10, 2011.

[163] Compare to Roberts, *Political Transition in Cambodia 1991–99*, 156.

[164] Author's interview with Pok Marina, and interview with anonymous source, July 10 2011.

[165] Author's interview with Sisowath Thomico, May 28, 2010. Sisowath Thomico, Sam Rainsy, and Tioulong Saumura studied together at Sciences Po (Paris) in the early 1970s, and were also all activists who would militate against the Khmer Rouge. According to Thomico, they split because Rainsy was more political, while Thomico wanted the struggle to be broader, envisaging it in terms of culture and civilization.

[166] Ibid.

the following year. As a consequence, most of the KPNLF's former leaders also ended up in FUNCINPEC.[167] These KPNLF supporters joined FUNCINPEC because of their shared anti-communist, anti-Vietnamese national resistance identity, as well as for access to patronage structures this connection granted, as seen in the following quote:

Everyone jumped from Son Sann to FUNCINPEC. They didn't want to go to the CPP—that is a different school of thought. They considered FUNCINPEC to be from the national resistance. Going to the CPP, they would climb slowly. In FUNCINPEC, if you are good with Ranariddh, you can jump up.[168]

Similarly, senior royalists generally thought the defunct KPNLF/BLDP/Son Sann Party faction to share with them a democratic identity defined in terms of the anti-communist resistance struggle.[169] They emphasized Son Sann's loyalty to Sihanouk, which they contrasted with the more ambiguous stance of Sam Rainsy. One senior FUNCINPEC official explained the relationship between FUNCINPEC and the parties coming out of the old KPNLF faction this way: "It is like democratic ideas [held by KPNLF/BLDP/Son Sann Party], versus another democratic faction [FUNCINPEC] that emphasizes the role of the king. We are both the successors of the old Democratic Party."[170]

It thus testified to the importance of lingering ties that FUNCINPEC and former KPNLF members considered themselves as sharing a democratic identity, defined as anti-communist, anti-Vietnamese resistance. Within this framework, the difference was typically outlined as FUNCINPEC being royalist and KPNLF "nationalist" (meaning neither monarchist nor anti-monarchist).[171] The KPNLF contained both members loyal and opposed to the monarchy and Sihanouk. Royalists could accept former KPNLF fighters, such as General Dien Del,[172] into their ranks more easily, as their previous opposition was understood (and to some extent, perhaps, redefined) as anti-Sihanoukist (opposing Sihanouk's perceived pro-Vietnamese stance) rather than fundamentally Republican. This tied them to the shared, basic, anti-communist, anti-Vietnamese stance. The more limited role of the contemporary constitutional monarchy ever since Sihamoni's ascension on the throne, in turn, made FUNCINPEC more palatable for former KPNLF fighters.[173] Their support of the monarchy was fundamentally opportunistic, based on the perception that the rural electorate—whose votes they courted—still supported the monarchy. This could not be disentangled from the resistance lens, which prioritized the anti-

---

[167] Author's interview with Huy Vora, April 29, 2010.

[168] Author's interview with Keo Puth Reasmey, June 8, 2010.

[169] Author's interviews with Pok Marina, Keo Puth Reasmey, Norodom Marie, and Ek Sereyvath, May 30, 2011.

[170] Author's interview with Pok Marina.

[171] Author's interviews with Dien Del, June 14, 2010, and Huy Vora.

[172] Dien Del (1932-2013), was a former general in the Khmer National Armed Forces (Forces Armées Nationales Khmères, FANK), the army of the Khmer Republic, who helped establish the KPNLF and was chief of staff of its army, the KPNLAF.

[173] Compare to author's interview with Dien Del: "I prefer Sihamoni to Sihanouk—he correctly does his job. Sihanouk has too much political tactic and always supports the Vietnamese. [...] Sihamoni follows the constitution, I think he is a very good king. The situation of Cambodia now is because of Sihanouk. [...] They [FUNCINPEC leaders] know me, they know that I am not really a royalist, if I said I like the monarchy, but now we have a good king."

communist struggle in whichever shape would be most efficient. General Dien Del expressed this as: "Nationalism is not like before. If you were a nationalist you went to the Republic, now you go to the monarchy. It is the tendency."[174] This opportunism also explained their dislike of Sam Rainsy, who they considered democratic but not monarchist, and therefore alienated from the rural electorate.

On October 18, 2006, Prince Ranariddh was ousted as president of FUNCINPEC at an extraordinary party congress that turned him into the party's "historical leader." The faction behind the ouster alleged incompetence, poor collaboration with the CPP, and absences abroad, and later sued Ranariddh for allegedy embezzling $3.6 million US for the sale of the party headquarters. In interviews, the new FUNCINPEC leadership would explain the development in terms of a divide between former resistance fighters and the circle around Ranariddh, which had disproportionately promoted returnees and (particularly) royal family members at the expense of former resistance fighters.[175] They claimed to want to democratize FUNCINPEC by transferring more powers to its mid- and lower ranks, staffed by many former resistance fighters. While Ranariddh had been party president for life, the presidency now became subject to election, and decision-making powers were transferred to the steering committee. FUNCINPEC leaders accused Ranariddh of having planned to change FUNCINPEC into the "Prince Ranariddh Party," which Ranariddh denied.[176] They portrayed Ranariddh as wanting to create his own party identity, free from the shadow of Sihanouk, comparing him to "an eighteen-year-old who wants to be free from his parents."[177]

What Ranariddh would refer to as the "party coup" was effectively the takeover of FUNCINPEC by a faction that, by all accounts, enjoyed the close support of the CPP. It can also be understood in terms of the tension between royalist and resistance identities, an internal fracturing of FUNCINPEC that lent itself to CPP manipulation. Returning royals, others who returned from Western countries, and former resistance fighters had long competed for power in FUNCINPEC. Relatively few royal family members were involved in resistance activities in the border areas.[178] Yet royal family members returning to Cambodia in the early 1990s came to occupy FUNCINPEC's top positions at the expense of resistance fighters.[179] Moreover, non-royal returnees from the West, who also came to occupy top party

---

[174] Ibid.

[175] Author's interview with Keo Puth Reasmey, June 8, 2010.

[176] Ibid., and author's interview with Noranarith Ananda Yath. According to Keo Puth Reasmey, FUNCINPEC's new president, Ranariddh had prepared to dissolve FUNCINPEC and proclaim a new party. Upon learning about that, another group of people arranged to bring FUNCINPEC under Nhek Bunchhay's control. According to the NRP version, Ranariddh was aware that Nhek Bunchhay was planning to take over FUNCINPEC, and calmly waited for him to act, knowing that he (Ranariddh) would set up his own party thereafter. Keo Puth Reasmey's assessment seems correct: "There were preparations made behind the scenes for both men."

[177] Author's interview with Keo Puth Reasmey.

[178] These included, for example, Norodom Ranariddh, Norodom Marie, Norodom Sirivudh, and Norodom Chakrapong.

[179] You Hockry, as minister of the interior (1993–98, 1998–2003), was, together with Ranariddh, responsible for appointing FUNCINPEC provincial governors, governors of districts, and chiefs of districts, as well as police commissioners. Hockry blamed the low representation of resistance fighters in FUNCINPEC in these positions on those individuals' lower levels of education. Author's interview with You Hockry.

positions, were expected to show deference to royalty in spite of their own high levels of competence and personal wealth. This forced subservience to royalty resulted in disaffection and disloyalty.[180] Ranariddh's 2006 ouster reflected such discontent and testified to the strength of loyalties between former KPNLF and FUNCINPEC resistance fighters. General Nhek Bunchhay, FUNCINPEC's new secretary general instrumental in masterminding Ranariddh's ouster, was backed up by other former military officers and fighters, both from FUNCINPEC and KPNLF. He had been the main point of contact within FUNCINPEC for former soldiers to join the party, and had cultivated their allegiances.[181] Following the split, the new FUNCINPEC leaders claimed to represent previously neglected resistance fighters. For example, Princess Norodom Marie, who remained in FUNCINPEC (at that point she was separated from Ranariddh), stated that Ranariddh had abandoned those who fought with him and she criticized royal family members exiting FUNCINPEC following his ouster for generally not having taken part in the resistance.[182] FUNCINPEC's continued royalist credentials were (additionally) maintained by Keo Puth Reasmey, the party's new president, who was married to Sihanouk's daughter, Norodom Arunreasmey; and by Sisowath Sirirath, second vice president and Arunreasmey's ex-husband. Ranariddh's supporters, meanwhile, formed a new, small party in October 2006, the Norodom Ranariddh Party.[183] During the time when Ranariddh was in self-imposed exile the party was known as the "Nationalist Party," between 2008–10. (After Ranariddh dissolved it into FUNCINPEC in 2012, it was revived under the name "Nationalist Party" by former NRP members between 2012–14).[184] The party enjoyed the support of the majority of politically involved royals, and included both returnees and a few former resistance fighters from FUNCINPEC and KPNLF. It emphasized the role of CPP manipulation in engendering the split.[185]

Royals in the new FUNCINPEC leadership were sidelined in 2008 when Hun Sen announced that Keo Puth Reasmey, Sisowath Sirirath, and Norodom Arunreasmey would not be part of the new government, while Nhek Bunchhay and other non-royal resistance fighters would. By then, the debate was radicalized to center on the involvement versus the noninvolvement of royal family members in politics. Also many royals who associated with a democratic opposition identity saw themselves constrained to take a stance for Ranariddh, who still failed to convince

[180] Hughes, "Transforming Oppositions in Cambodia," 309.

[181] This included Dien Del, who joined FUNCINPEC actively after 1997, and after having turned originally to FUNCINPEC after the failure of the LDP to win seats in 1993. Dien Del later stated: "I would have liked to join FUNCINPEC even before 1997, but some leaders [i.e., Ranariddh] were too proud—they looked down on other people. They didn't connect with our military past. I didn't need that. They had no way to bring the FUNCINPEC military up." Author's interview with Dien Del.

[182] Author's interview with Norodom Marie.

[183] The Khmer National Front Party changed its name to NRP on October 16, 2006.

[184] The Nationalist Party and the NRP have had the same party symbol, a map of Cambodia and the motto "freedom, sovereignty, territorial integrity" (*seripheap, atepethey, boronopheap tek dey*), with the difference being that the NRP symbol featured Ranariddh's picture on top. The name "Nationalist Party" [Konâbâk Cheatniyum] was chosen to invoke Sihanouk's nationalism, as well as to have an acronym similar to the "NRP." Author's interview with Huy Vora.

[185] Author's interviews with Noranarith Ananda Yath and Ngo Pin February 23, 2010.

them. If anything, Ranariddh's ouster seemed to them further proof that Ranariddh was a hopeless card, yet they needed to gather around him more than ever. Meanwhile, the CPP has since exercised an ever larger influence over FUNCINPEC—and over Ranariddh.

DOCTRINE VERSUS EMBODIMENT

One key way to imbue the concept of royalism with meaning has been to turn to Sangkum as a legacy to unite around, reinventing ideas of "Sihanoukism" (*Sihanouk niyum*) and "Buddhist socialism"—Sihanouk's self-professed regime identity.[186] Yet these reinventions highlight tensions as to what extent Sihanoukism and the legacy of Sangkum lend themselves to provide a party political ideological identity, rooted in deeper tensions in the royalist project between embodiment and doctrine. Ranariddh, as outlined above, has referred to Buddhist socialism as his model for democracy in the Cambodian context, tying democracy to the Khmer monarchy. He has consistently argued for these conceptions from the perspective of embodiment, whereby he and other royal family members are in the unique position to incarnate the nation's aspirations. Other royalists have attempted to make Sihanoukism relevant by advocating it as a political ideology. Yet this "disembodiment" of Sihanoukism made it susceptible to being claimed by any political group. This danger was illustrated after 2006 when, following Ranariddh's ouster from FUNCINPEC, royalists divided into three parties: FUNCINPEC, the NRP, and the short-lived Sangkum Jatiniyum Front Party. The ensuing debate came to focus on the content of the Sihanoukist heritage, particularly the tension between embodiment and a doctrinal identity to be distilled from it.

Turning Buddhist Socialism into an Ideology

One of the most outspoken attempts to revive the legacy of Sangkum took place in 2006, as an attempt to save political royalism that was in serious disarray. In March, Ranariddh had resigned as head of the National Assembly after the passage of a constitutional amendment that allowed motions to be passed with a simple majority rather than the previously required two-thirds majority, which had made the coalition between CPP and FUNCINPEC redundant. FUNCINPEC was also plagued by internal divisions, such as the rivalry between Ranariddh and FUNCINPEC Secretary General Nhek Bunchhay. Shortly before Ranariddh's ouster from the FUNCINPEC presidency in October 2006, Prince Sisowath Thomico, Queen-Mother Monineath's nephew and head of Sihanouk's cabinet, announced that he would form a broad coalition political party to unify all royalists in Cambodia, which was to take the ideology of the Sangkum Reastr Niyum as the

---

[186] Over the late 1950s and 1960s, Sihanouk developed the concept of Buddhist socialism in a series of writings published in *Sangkum*, *Kambuja*, and *Réalitées Cambodgiennes*. See, for instance, *Sangkum* 1 (June 1955); and compare to Harris, *Cambodian Buddhism*, 147. Chandler calls Buddhist socialism a "ramshackle ideology" (David P. Chandler, *A History of Cambodia* [Boulder: Westview Press, 2000], 199), and Kershaw (Roger Kershaw, *Monarchy in South-East Asia: The Faces of Tradition in Transition* [London: Routledge, 2001], 55) refers to the "blatant philosophical inconsistency of the doctrine." Observers have also noted Sihanouk's confessed lack of knowledge of political theory, his pragmatism, and how he was influenced by other leaders at the time rather than studies on political thought. See: Chandler, *The Tragedy of Cambodian History*, 87; and Osborne, *Sihanouk*, 135.

basis of its political platform.[187] This, he stated, was intended to resolve the crisis of the involvement of royals in politics and to address deeper problems in Cambodian society rooted in a lack of vision.[188]

In July 2006, Thomico launched the Sangkum Jatiniyum alliance (the "Alliance of the National Community") with four small political parties at the former royal capital, Oudong, a symbolically important location.[189] Over the following weeks, Thomico toured the Cambodian countryside, screening Sihanouk's Sangkum-era films, *Le Cid* and *Twilight*, as well as documentary footage about infrastructure projects undertaken by the Sangkum Reastr Niyum governments.[190] In August, the Sangkum Jatiniyum Front Party held its first congress.[191] Shortly thereafter, a ceremony was organized at Wat Phnom in Phnom Penh where participants swore an oath to sacrifice their lives for Cambodia's independence, sovereignty, and territorial integrity, and "to protect the King and Queen forever."[192]

Thomico attempted to revive an elusive doctrine upon which Sangkum was said to have been founded, arguing that Cambodia had to find a way to develop the country through a coherent ideology. The SJFP reflected Thomico's perception that Cambodia had suffered a loss of political vision, and that contemporary Cambodia was undergoing similar social transitions as during Sangkum. Reviving Sihanouk's ideology was thus intended to procure a political vision and respond to social change. Thomico sought to remind the divided royalist faction what monarchism in Cambodia would mean, and to find a new vision through the values of the Sangkum Reastr Niyum. In particular, he perceived his challenge to be the transformation of the celebration of Sangkum from advocating Sihanouk *as a person* into a project of

---

[187] Sisowath Thomico gave up his royal title in 1970 and fought for the Khmer Republic. Returning to Paris in 1973, Thomico founded the journal *Anuvath*, where he advocated for social and political change in Cambodia. According to Thomico, it was at this time that he first started writing articles about how Sangkum Reastr Niyum and Buddhist socialism could be useful to this end, claiming that: "It was a way for me to have my own revolutionary ideas put in place. It was the way for Cambodia to reach revolution, through the spirit and culture of Cambodia. I was for nonviolence. I thought we would make the revolution peacefully, through ideas. Buddhist Socialism could have been the basis to bring Cambodia to that final goal." Author's interview with Sisowath Thomico, May 20, 2010.

[188] A third reason was to ensure that Ranariddh would have an alternative political party vehicle to FUNCINPEC, if necessary. Ibid.

[189] Oudong, the royal capital from 1618–1866, houses royal stupas from this period. During the Sangkum period, the site was considered so invested with royal power that flying over Oudong was prohibited; see: Sisowath Samyl Monipong, *Voyage au Royaume de la Panthère Longibande* (Paris: Connaissances et Savoirs, 2008), 135; and Yun Samean and Douglas Gillison, "Thomico Announces Alliance with Fringe Parties," *The Cambodia Daily*, July 28, 2006.

[190] Yun Samean, "Thomico Visits Four Provinces, Shows Movies," *The Cambodia Daily*, August 9, 2006.

[191] Yun Samean, "Thomico's New Party Holds First Congress in Capital," *The Cambodia Daily*, August 21, 2006.

[192] Thomico also urged the UN and the international community to monitor the 2007 commune elections and 2008 national elections, and accused FUNCINPEC of inaction when the media broadcast anti-Sihanouk songs from the Khmer Republic in October 2005 (this was around the time that Hun Sen threatened to dismantle the monarchy if Sihamoni did not sign the supplemental border treaty with Vietnam.) Prak Chan Thul and James Welsh, "Thomico, 50 Party Faithful Swear Oath to Country," *The Cambodia Daily*, September 11, 2006.

reminding others of Sihanouk's *political heritage* by explaining the ideology of the Sangkum Reastr Niyum.[193]

Since Thomico was a young high school student during the Sangkum era, he later complemented his understanding of the period with family testimonies and his studies of Sihanouk's writings at the time.[194] He took "Buddhist socialism" to mean that Cambodia could find an indigenous way of thought by turning Buddhist philosophy into a political ideology, which would include ideas of direct democracy and a national union. Thomico perceived the legacy of the Sangkum to be particularly applicable to the social and political context of the Second Kingdom for two reasons. First, Cambodian society desperately needed to find an "indigenous and unique ideology" to guard economic development against the perils of globalization. During Sangkum, Buddhist socialism had represented a middle path to the Cold War split between the free world and communism. In the contemporary context, Thomico turned against models of economic development imposed by international financial institutions, such as the IMF and WTO, which he argued were unsuitable for an emerging economy like Cambodia's. Following a middle path in the present context would mean letting Cambodia find her "own way," while steering clear of unchecked capitalist development. Second, the nation was presently facing a similar societal shift to that of the Sangkum era. In Thomico's view, Sangkum had been a way for Sihanouk to unify the nation through uniting political parties, intellectuals, and the elite. This had entailed reuniting a divided royalty, as the three main political parties during Cambodia's first brief experience with parliamentary democracy had been founded by princes.[195] The present government, Thomico argued, faced a similar conflict of generations, with young people making up a huge majority of the population. As young people are set apart from their elders by a different range of experiences and a higher level of education, Thomico imagined them to have a different vision for Cambodia's political future. He believed this new generation to be at odds with what he described as the government's authoritarian style of governing, and warned that if its demands were not met, Cambodia would experience further conflict. Thomico proposed to solve this by setting up the National Congress provided for by the constitution, which he considered to be a uniquely suitable mechanism for identifying tensions in Cambodian society through exchanging views in open discussion. The contemporary challenge, in his mind, was to modify the Congress so as to find a way to encourage and enable the young generation to speak out, and to mix all different views into one, common vision. And care should be taken to organize the Congress slightly differently from during the Sangkum, to ensure that it really would provide an opportunity for free speech. For Thomico, the lack of dialogue within political parties clearly demonstrated that a common vision could not be articulated through these parties. The mission was, therefore, to generate ideas that could later be developed by political parties. He envisaged the monarchy as an overarching, unifying institution uniquely positioned to set up such a dialogue between different components of Cambodian society.

---

[193] Author's interview with Sisowath Thomico, May 20, 2010.

[194] Ibid.

[195] The Democratic Party, Liberal Party, and Progressive Democrats.

Defining Sihanoukism

Thomico advocated not only the ideology of Sihanouk, but also the man. Shortly after setting up the SJFP, he called for Sihanouk to head a "government of national union." In the ensuing debate, Hun Sen advanced a reading of political royalism that precluded the involvement of royal family members in politics—a concrete bid to settle the debate between the incarnate versus the ideological in royalist politics. Shortly thereafter Ranariddh was ousted as president of FUNCINPEC (which came to be headed by royals junior to him and non-royals), a development widely believed to have had the backing of the CPP. In the ensuing scenario, contestation between the three self-identified royalist parties came to center on the right to define "Sihanoukism" as ideology versus embodiment.

In September 2006, Thomico stated that conditions for free elections had not been met and called for the National Assembly to disband, transferring powers to Sihanouk as prime minister of a government of national union until elections could be held.[196] Hun Sen retorted that these demands equaled a coup against the constitution, and that anyone who wanted to dissolve the National Assembly should "prepare their coffins." He recalled the limits of a constitutional monarchy by separating the monarchy as an institution from the monarchy as the royal family, with these words: "I warn them again that the Monarchy belongs to no one. They should not use its influence for their interests."[197] In early October, president of the National Assembly and CPP honorary president Heng Samrin called for the introduction of a bill barring royals from politics, as a way to ensure their political neutrality.[198] This was supported by Sam Rainsy, who referred to an international model of constitutional monarchy. In early February 2007, Sihanouk asked royal family members to end their involvement in Cambodian politics.[199] A few days later, Prime Minister Hun Sen called on royal family members to submit a legally binding bill that would ban themselves from engaging in politics ahead of the 2008 national elections. This, however, did not happen.[200]

The CPP endeavor to sweep royals out of politics was accompanied by declarations that the party was the "new royalists." Hun Sen claimed this mantle by virtue of safeguarding the constitutional monarchy within its boundaries and ensuring that it is strictly separated from political royalism.[201] In particular, he credited himself with the accomplishment of the PPA framework by allowing

---

[196] Pin Sisovann, "Prince Thomico Plans Petition Asking Assembly To Disband," *The Cambodia Daily*, September 15, 2006; Leang Delux and Soren Seelow, "Formation of a Government of National Union—Thomico is Defending Himself from All Provocation," *Cambodge Soir*, September 25, 2006.

[197] Hun Sen, "Visiting the People in Kompong Chhnang Province," *Cambodia New Vision* 104 (September 2006). See also Pin Sisovann and James Welsh, "Hun Sen Calls for Prince's Party Ouster," *The Cambodia Daily*, September 28, 2006.

[198] Yun Samean, "Assembly Complains of Lengthy Royal Absences," *The Cambodia Daily*, October 5, 2006.

[199] Heng Reaksmey, "Retired King Sihanouk Defends PM Hun Sen," *VOA Khmer*, February 2, 2007.

[200] Chun Sakada, "Hun Sen Says Royalists Should Abandon Politics," *VOA Khmer*, February 5, 2007. See also Lor Chandara and John Maloy, "Royals Could Initiate Political Exit," *The Cambodia Daily*, February 6, 2007.

[201] Compare to Hun Sen, "Graduation Ceremony and Diploma Presentation in CUS," *Cambodia New Vision* 117, October 2007.

Sihanouk to sit at the negotiation table, and by having been the one, benevolently, to allow Sihanouk to return to Cambodia thereafter. Hun Sen also attributed the establishment of the Second Kingdom and consequent national reconciliation to January 7, 1979, stating that Ranariddh, in a letter, has admitted this to be the case.[202] The meaning of "royalism" was thus shifted to refer to the protection of a strict constitutional monarchy.

In the new political landscape after Ranariddh's ouster from FUNCINPEC, meanwhile, there were two self-proclaimed royalist parties, FUNCINPEC and SJFP, as well as a faction loyal to Ranariddh that developed into the Norodom Ranariddh Party. All three claimed Sihanoukist credentials. While the SJFP was founded on the justificatory claim to bring back Sihanouk's Sangkum, Ranariddh boasted about being Sihanouk's son, whereas FUNCINPEC, in turn, was the party originally founded by Sihanouk. To prove its royalist credentials, FUNCINPEC organized a large ceremony for Sihanouk's eighty-fourth birthday, contrary to Sihanouk's expressed wish.[203] FUNCINPEC also attempted to discredit the SJFP by casting it as Republican, referring to Thomico's previous side-taking for the Khmer Republic.[204] To add to the confusion, while Sihanouk was widely believed to have some link to the SJFP—a belief also maintained by Hun Sen—Sihanouk publicly distanced himself from the party, charging that it was anti-royalist and anti-Sihanouk.[205] Although all parties claimed his support, Sihanouk offered no straightforward public support for any of them.[206]

Contestation between the three parties came to center on the possibility of turning Sihanouk's heritage into an ideology. Sihanouk, in his time, had refused references to "ideology," while struggling with the need to create a terminology for his own thinking, which had been dubbed "Sihanoukism." As noted in the introduction, Tep Chhieu Kheng, in a 1968 article entitled "Le Sihanoukisme" in Sihanouk's flagship publication, *Sangkum*, examining what Sihanoukism could possibly mean, concluded that:

> To define the political line of Samdech Euv, the neologism "Sihanoukism" has been forged. Is it a doctrine? A new philosophy? Or a new ideology? In fact, Sihanouk had no part in the formation of the new term. Wary of the establishment mindset, he deliberately avoided words ending in "ism" that express a general trend, a profession of faith which is a little too categorical. [...] If not a doctrine or a philosophy, nor an ideology, what is it? "Sihanoukism" is an attempt, but a successful attempt, to grasp reality, to

---

[202] Hun Sen, "Graduation Ceremony at the Vanda Institute," *Cambodia New Vision* 155, January 2011. Hun Sen has also sometimes likened himself to an adopted son of Sihanouk, seemingly trying to tap into Sihanouk's royal legitimacy. Compare to Hun Sen, "Excerpts on Interpretations Concerning Royal Palace," *Cambodia New Vision* 108, January 2007.

[203] Yun Samean, "F'pec Hosts Contentious Birthday Celebration," *The Cambodia Daily*, October 31, 2006.

[204] Yun Samean, "Ranariddh, Thomico to Form Alliance," *The Cambodia Daily*, November 7, 2006.

[205] Leang and Seelow, "Formation of a Government of National Union."

[206] Author's interview with Khieu Suon, May 12, 2010. Sihanouk referred to the ousting of Ranariddh from FUNCINPEC as a "coup de parti," the meaning of which provoked heated debate among all factions. Vong Sokheng and Charles McDermid, "FUNCINPEC Prince Hails 'Royalist' CPP," *Phnom Penh Post*, November 3, 2006.

capture the fact from life in its authenticity and dynamism. It is also a way of being, a sort of way of life, a *savoire-faire* for the Khmer people and for all placed in the same situation.[207]

This resistance against employing "Sihanoukism" as an ideology was now reiterated by Sihanouk. When Thomico started to claim the Sangkum heritage as an ideology guiding the SJFP, Sihanouk released a statement asking Thomico, the party he would form, and FUNCINPEC never to refer to either "Sihanoukism," "the Sihanoukist ideology," or "the ideals of Sihanouk."[208]

The new FUNCINPEC leadership, however, ignored Sihanouk's historical and contemporary objections to branding Sihanoukism an ideology. FUNCINPEC continued to claim to represent Sihanoukism, referring to it as doctrine. According to Keo Puth Reasmey, FUNCINPEC's new president, Sihanouk could no longer make claims to own Sihanoukism. Sihanoukism should rather be understood as a general theory of leadership:

Sihanoukism—it is not the love of the body of Sihanouk. It is like a theory of leadership of a country. Sihanoukism means neutrality, territorial integrity, sovereignty, and independence. An ideology of how to lead the country. We call it Sihanoukist. We claim it. We see Sihanouk as a principle of party. This is Sihanouk for us—a principle. It is an idea that animates our group. We want to implement Sihanoukism in developing Cambodia, because we saw during his sixteen years in power that Cambodia was prosperous; there was justice, independence, and sovereignty. Khmers had pride. We were not beggars of money from the international community. Prince Sihanouk has developed a theory of how to lead. Cambodia must develop, thinking of sovereignty and independence. That is what Sihanouk has done in the 1960s, we want to take it to implement it again. [...] Only the Sangkum Reastr Niyum had Sihanoukism. [...] Thomico [...] wrote a letter to me, that I should stop using the name of Sihanouk, otherwise it will affect the name of Sihanouk and the Royal Family. [...] I said, "Why did you say so? Sihanoukism does not belong to Sihanouk. It is not the person. It is the idea that Sihanouk has invented to lead the country. If we think it is good, we take it. It is the book, the theory. Like Buddhism, Christianity, Maoism. [...] There is a difference between Sihanouk and Sihanoukism. And if you do not dare to promote Sihanoukism, we do. Sihanoukism will be the spirit in the head of the people." [...] We bring the gospel. Even without Sihanouk, Sihanoukism is still here. It is the principle of the party, one idea that animates us.[209]

This was paralleled by FUNCINPEC leaders' support of the CPP's appropriation of the "royalist" label. Sisowath Sirirath, FUNCINPEC's new second deputy president, thus stated in a press conference that "Now, the most Royalist party is the CPP—without them this country could not be called the Kingdom of Cambodia.

---

[207] Tep, "Le 'Sihanoukisme,'" 8.

[208] Norodom Sihanouk, "Statement," Phnom Penh, June 30, 2006. The statement was in French and referred to *Sihanoukisme*, *l'idéologie Sihanoukiste* and *les idéaux de Sihanouk*.

[209] Author's interview with Keo Puth Reasmey, June 8, 2010.

They are the true royalists, because, without Samdech Hun Sen, how can the monarchy survive?"[210]

Conversely, for the ousted Ranariddh, it became vital to assert Sihanoukism as the possession of an incarnate quality, not reducible to ideology. In a note entitled "Is the Neo-FUNCINPEC party a Sihanoukist party?" Ranariddh defined Sihanoukism as follows:

Sihanoukism is not an abstract concept or simply an ideology. A real Sihanoukism is what our venerated King Father Norodom Sihanouk, the Architect of the November 9th 1953 National Independence, incarnated. The latter is also the guarantor and the fierce defender of the independence, as far as the national sovereignty and the territorial integrity [sic]. Territorial integrity must be perceived as the defence of our land borders (the East, North and West) and sea limits. It should also be a practice of a real national union and concord. It should also be a practice of social justice, in particular that one of the so-called "minor people" [sic]. It is for that reason that the latter continue to adore and to venerate our beloved Samdech Euv, Samdech Ta, and Samdech Ta Tuot.[211] A Sihanoukist party must finally be autonomous and being able to freely conclude any alliance with other political parties. Cooperation with the latter, in particular with the ruling party, to the benefit of our country is neither alienation nor a submission. This is the authentic Sihanoukism.[212]

Sihanoukism was therefore necessarily tied to the person of Sihanouk, evident in the further elaboration offered by Ranariddh:

For the people of Cambodia, Sihanoukism means this. Not only royalty [in general], but that my father is the father of the nation. He preserved the territorial integrity, the sovereignty of the nation, social justice, development, well-being: it is the practical way to approach Sihanoukism, instead of talking about a simple theory. Even Gaullism, what does it mean? De Gaulle for the French people, for the world, he is the liberator of France. What he represents, it is this. We should, in my opinion, continue to have a practical approach to Sihanoukism. I am a Sihanoukist not only because Sihanouk is my father, but because of what he represents for us as Cambodians. In particular, during my father's era, you had war around Cambodia, war in Vietnam, war in Laos, but for fifteen years my father successfully preserved Cambodia in peace. For the people of Cambodia, Sihanoukism is simply like this. But we cannot compare my brother, the King, to my Father ... No one can be compared to my father, and so for the people Sihanoukism is this. It is more a practical way of thinking than a theory.[213]

---

[210] Vong and McDermid, "FUNCINPEC Prince Hails 'Royalist' CPP."

[211] "Samdech Euv," "Samdech Ta," and "Samdech Ta Tuot" are epithets for Sihanouk.

[212] Sam, "Note of the Day 5," 2010. This note of the day, together with the document "Liberal and Advanced Monarchy," were said to form the base of the NRP political platform. Sam Nora, Liberal and Advanced Monarchy (Publisher unknown, n.d.) See also Sam, "Note of the Day 15," 2010.

[213] Author's interview with Norodom Ranariddh, June 2, 2011.

Sihamoni, as a purely constitutional monarch, cannot continue the political leadership of Sihanouk. As the foremost royal political party actor, Ranariddh is uniquely poised to continue the organic link between the people's aspirations and the monarchy. Yet a fundamental problem to Ranariddh's claims to represent Sihanoukism has been how Sihanouk was very much his own presence—although both as a constitutional monarch and King-Father, his liberty to make political statements was circumscribed. Hun Sen has repeatedly drawn attention to this, claiming that some people were more Sihanoukist than Sihanouk himself.[214] This refers precisely to how claims have been made in the name of Sihanoukism—yet these claims have lost force by lacking Sihanouk's corroboration.

Prince Thomico, meanwhile, dissolved the SJFP in 2007 and returned to Sihanouk's side as his head of cabinet. He declared himself to be satisfied that the CPP had picked up Sangkum as its model, emphasizing how the Sangkum provided a national legacy that could be taken up by any political party:

> Before 1970, Cambodia was the most advanced country in the region. We were the first to have an Olympic Stadium. We had beautiful architecture, famous landmarks in Phnom Penh were built. These were the symbols of what the Sangkum Reastr Niyum tried to give to Cambodia. There was the culture of urbanism. Phnom Penh today is in large part a legacy of what Sangkum Reastr Niyum tried to give Cambodia. The parks, the urbanism, the boulevards. Those are the models that have to be looked to by all the political parties. It is not the legacy of one singular party, but the legacy of the nation.[215]

Thomico redefined the role of the Cambodian monarchy to be that of a truly constitutional monarchy, and now envisaged the task of royalists to be giving this novel image and mission to the Cambodian monarchy. Sihanouk, as a reinstated king, still had a political mission, and the public still considered the king as head of the government. The new task for royalist parties was therefore to explain the circumscribed role of the constitutional monarchy to the people.[216] This redefinition reflected, of course, how Thomico's original intentions had been outmaneuvered. It was the end of a process of erasing notions of a unique role to be played by royalty in politics, that had started with Ranariddh's replacement as FUNCINPEC leader by figures without royal ancestry. The replacement eclipsed the inherited ability to embody the nation as a point of reference to legitimize the exercise of politics. While Thomico had tried to reverse this process by making royalism relevant through revival of the Sangkum legacy, he had met a dead end. As an ideology, this legacy was easily appropriated by the CPP and a FUNCINPEC under CPP control, both of which asserted the mandate of the monarchy as strictly constitutional and questioned the involvement of royals in politics.

---

[214] For example, in 2005, rebuking FUNCINPEC demands that more power be given to the Supreme National Border Council (SNBC), headed by Sihanouk, Hun Sen stated that "The problem here is that we have people who have proven themselves more Sihanoukist than the former King himself, or more Royalist than the monarchy." Hun Sen, "Selected Responses to the Press on SNBC," 2005.

[215] Author's interview with Sisowath Thomico, May 20, 2010.

[216] Ibid.

This chain of events candidly exposes royalist inability to transcend Sihanouk's legacy to invent an up-to-date royalist identity, which developed into nothing short of an identity crisis. In the aftermath of these events, one prominent royalist politician expressed his frustration in these words: "We are only the derivatives of Sihanouk. We are the brother, the son, the daughter of Sihanouk ... we are not the reference. When Sihanouk disappears, there will be nothing left."[217] This bleak prophecy has since been proven right.

FROM POLITICAL ROYALISM TO ROYAL IRRELEVANCY

This chapter has outlined a series of attempts to establish credible links between political royalism and the nation, attempts that ultimately failed. The process illustrates how political royalism shifted from being something meaningful at the start of the Second Kingdom, when FUNCINPEC emerged victorious in the first multiparty elections, to something substantially meaningless two decades on. It suggests that this demise was bound up with thoroughgoing problems in transposing the legitimacy associated with the monarchy to a political party form of royalism.

This crisis of representation centered on the transfer of regal legitimacy from the monarchy to a party political form of royalism, in general, and, in particular, from Sihanouk to his son Ranariddh as leader of FUNCINPEC. Ranariddh anchored his claims of representation in historical ideas of embodiment related to the monarchy, attempting to mobilize the electorate around his alleged embodiment of the nation. These ideas modified both of FUNCINPEC's foundational and oft-repeated claims to legitimacy: representation of the principles of liberal and pluralist democracy, and restoration of a constitutional monarchy. FUNCINPEC advocated neither a strictly constitutional monarchy nor a liberal democracy along Western lines, in spite of elements within the party that would have preferred this to be the case. At the most basic level, the decay of a political party form of royalism can be understood in terms of the royalists' failure to modify their claims to representation through embodiment to fit the far more marginalized way in which they actually related to the modern nation, resulting in a wide, actual discrepancy.

In the multiparty liberal democratic state with a constitutional monarchy, Cambodian royalists had to deal with a series of tensions in drawing on regal legitimacy. The first of these was one between royalism as a suprapolitical force versus royalism as pertaining to a particular political party. A tension between a suprapolitical and partisan role is something monarchies in the region, and elsewhere, have had to confront following the end of absolute monarchies. For example, in Thailand, the claim of Thai royals to be unambiguously "above politics" has been crucial to gaining support for the monarch's ability to intervene on the national political scene.[218] In Cambodia, by contrast, royals sought to legitimate their role as party political actors. Yet they tied royalism to a suprapolitical conscience, which eclipsed its party political form.

Second, reconciliation of kingship with a party political form of royalism was problematized by how the Sangkum had uprooted the institutional monarchy and compromised the political involvement of royals. While Ranariddh tried to

---

[217] Author's interview with anonymous source, July 10, 2011.

[218] Winichakul, "Toppling Democracy," 15.

overcome this challenge by alluding to ideas of embodiment and how he had inherited this ability by virtue of his royal ancestry, these claims were not only undermined by the fact that Sihanouk still constituted a formidable presence, but arguably also by changing conceptions of the legitimacy of inherited versus elected leadership. Both the CPP and the self-identified democrats advanced conflicting readings that, in different ways, stressed the legitimacy of elected office.

The failure to agree on the contents and mandate of political royalism helps explain why political royalists took recourse in the legacy of the Sangkum and the notion of Sihanoukism. Caroline Hughes has written that "FUNCINPEC has attempted little in the way of adapting the inherited rhetoric of Sihanoukism to new realities. The party continues to campaign almost exclusively on the notion that Cambodian voters will always vote for the King, as the lynchpin of the nation."[219] This chapter has suggested a more tormented relationship between royalists and Sihanoukism. FUNCINPEC and other royalist parties relied so heavily on a Sihanoukist language that their search for relevance meant the reinvention of Sihanoukism in a myriad of different ways. Sihanoukism provided the language for negotiating change as royalists imbued their reading of the Sangkum era with particular meanings in order to transpose them onto the present era. Yet reflecting the paucity of underlying vision, the resulting bids were increasingly void of meaning and equally unsuited to new realities.

These references meant hugely different things in the contemporary context than during the Sangkum. Ranariddh remodeled Sihanouk's ideas of a national union and middle path to justify cooperation with the ruling CPP. This compromised Ranariddh's royal stance and split FUNCINPEC internally. The hostility to the idea of an opposition entailed the abandonment of a domestic identity as "nationalist opposition."[220] Royalism was left hovering in the middle, neither leader nor opposition. Moreover, FUNCINPEC under Ranariddh continuously referred to the ability to provide as an integral part of democratic legitimacy, in spite of the fact that the party did not have the means to deliver on it. When the royalists were outperformed by the CPP, who had the material base to fulfill this logic, it therefore led to a real democratic deficit. This highlights the importance of a material base for regal legitimacy and, particularly, to back up claims to embodiment. The real ability to provide, and to make decisions, more convincingly supports the claim to embody the nation than do references to intangible, innate ability.

Finally, attempts to inject meaning into royalism through offering an ideological identity highlighted tensions as to what extent Sihanoukism, and the legacy of Sangkum, was able to provide a party political ideological identity, rooted in deeper tensions in the royalist project between embodiment and doctrine. Ranariddh's fear of disembodiment of the Sihanoukist legacy proved well-founded. Ultimately, by turning "Sihanoukism" into an ideology, the new FUNCINPEC (under the influence of the CPP) could claim to represent Sihanoukism in a way that became complicit in separating political royalism from royal family members. The Sihanoukist legacy, as a practical manual for concrete policies, was easily and credibly taken up by the CPP. Meanwhile, Sihanoukism, as a doctrinal identity for the new FUNCINPEC, was

---

[219] Hughes, "Reconstructing Legitimate Political Authority through Elections?" 50.

[220] Hughes, "Transforming Oppositions in Cambodia," 311–12.

ultimately unengaging, as it corresponded neither to a real ability to provide, nor to legitimacy through an inherited ability to embody the nation.

This suggests a failure by royalists to reinvent their identity to make credible claims to representation. Yet it also implies that there were limited options available, other than to draw on historical ideas of kingship that were ultimately ill-matched to their actual political role. The discourse of kingship provided a constraint rather than a resource. In particular, Sihanouk's ideological legacies were, in some sense, hopeless. The string of unsuccessful reinventions of Sangkum and Sihanoukism begs the question of what a successful one could ever have looked like. In this perspective, Sihanouk, from the moment of inventing a modern variant of royalism in the Sangkum, also set a time limit to its life span. The celebration of Sangkum was indicative of a consequent deep crisis of contemporary royalism. Representing the nation became a matter of representing Sihanouk—the irony being that he was, of course, better suited to represent himself.

CHAPTER FOUR

DEMOCRATS: DEMOCRACY AND THE POST-PPA NATION

A main argument of this book is that all Cambodian political parties competing electorally in the KOC have invested significant efforts in claims to be "democratic." Being "democratic" was also the main political identity of a certain set of them. These so-called democratic parties (*konâbâk pracheathipatey*) included the Buddhist Liberal Democratic Party (BLDP); the Son Sann Party; the Khmer Nation Party (KNP), which turned into the Sam Rainsy Party (SRP); the Human Rights Party (HRP); and the Cambodia National Rescue Party (CNRP), into which the SRP and HRP merged in 2012. This chapter examines the national vision of these parties by reassessing the relationship between democratic imaginings and the nation in contemporary Cambodian political discourse. It identifies the nexus between democracy and the nation as central to the "self-identified democrats"—who, for the sake of simplicity, will be referred to in the following pages simply as "democrats"— and explores the consequences for their broader political imaginations and practice.[1]

The democrats have disappointed foreign observers looking for domestic bastions of liberal democratic thought in Cambodia. In academic writing on the Cambodian democratic opposition, notions of "democracy" and "nationalism" are usually treated as opposites. In these accounts, the democratic opposition is understood to carry out double-faced politics—embracing both tendencies that can be called democratic and those that can be interpreted as racist, xenophobic, and ultra-nationalist. Accentuating the distinction between the two, Caroline Hughes argues that, for the SRP as well as FUNCINPEC, the primary identity at home has been that of nationalist resistance, whereas the primary identity abroad has been that of democratic opposition.[2] These contrasting tendencies in party discourse are generally explained by reference to how the democrats are thought to play the "nationalist card," defined as anti-Vietnamese discourse and xenophobia, to triumph over the CPP-led government, which they believe to be tainted by its association with Vietnam. What is read as ultra-nationalist rhetoric has been understood to primarily serve a mobilizing purpose, as "a strategic response to Cambodia's constricted political environment," or, more specifically, an advantageous strategy in

---

[1] There is thus no normative assessment attached to the use of the term "self-identified democrats" or its abbreviation, "democrats," and usage here neither seeks to rebut nor confirm the validity of their democratic claims. This terminology stems only from the fact that while *all* political parties claimed to be democratic, some claimed this as their main identity.

[2] Hughes, "Transforming Oppositions in Cambodia," 311–12.

rural campaigning to connect with the rural electorate.[3] Existing accounts, then, have typically depicted the democrats as an opposition force that capitalizes on xenophobic nationalism and makes inconsistent references to a democratic identity. This interpretation has cemented the notion of "nationalism" as an opportunistic and shallow category in contemporary politics, which stands in straightforward opposition to "democracy" and obliterates any remaining hope for it.

To some extent, the distance between the democratic and the nationalist poles has been bridged by the notion of populism. Kheang Un writes that, to critics, "Rainsy is not a genuine democrat, but rather a populist manipulating democratic processes and norms in order to achieve his political objective: the capture of state power"; while Hughes identifies the opposition as heirs to a populist discourse revolving around the relationship between ruler and ruled and the defense of sovereign territory.[4] The notion of populism suggests that ideas of popular representation are key to SRP discourse, yet stops short of asking why they go to the heart of contemporary opposition—and state—democratic projects.

Contrary to the prevailing understanding put forth by Un, Hughes, and others, that "democracy" and "nationalism" are diametrically opposed in Cambodian politics, these concepts are better thought of as being in tension with one another. A look at the historical emergence of the notion of democracy as well as contemporary examples of "democratic" politics around the globe suggests that the standard scholarly juxtaposition of democracy and nationalism is not necessarily correct. "Democracy" means rule by the people. But in modern times, as Michael Mann writes, democracy has come to mean two things. The first is the ordinary people, the masses; the second is the "nation," or the *ethnos*, an ethnic group. This conflation of the popular masses and the nation spread worldwide alongside ideas of democracy, as democracy began to entwine the *demos*, people, with the dominant *ethnos*, generating multiple conceptions of the nation and the state.[5] The institution of democracy is tied to national forms of exclusion, and the entwining of the *demos* with the dominant *ethnos* has been a hallmark of the spread of democracy.[6] This suggests that surprise at the conflation of the two has more to do with dominant contemporary Western liberal democratic discourses, which no longer celebrate narrow, exclusive notions of the nation, but rather broad, inclusive ones of multiculturalism. While Un and Hughes criticize the assumptions of the Western liberal democratic project informing internationally sponsored Cambodian post-conflict democracy-building, which sees democracy and nationalism as antithetical, they also remain confined by this Western vision, treating the notions as complementary rather than inquiring into how they are mutually supportive.

The conflation in democratic imaginings of representation of the people and representation of the nation has been a feature of successive Cambodian post-independence political projects. Mann argues that two democratic constructions of the people may be distinguished: a stratified people and an organic people. The view

---

[3] For the former position, see Kheang Un, "Configuring Opposition Politics," in Kane and Wong, *Dissident Democrats*, 105; for the latter, see: Hughes, *The Political Economy of Cambodia's Transition*, 129; and Hughes, "Transforming Oppositions in Cambodia," 306.

[4] See: Un, "Configuring Opposition Politics," in Kane and Wong, *Dissident Democrats*, 114; and Hughes, "Khmer Land, Khmer Soul," 54.

[5] Michael Mann, *The Dark Side of Democracy*, 2.

[6] Ibid., 3.

of the people as diverse and stratified underlies liberal conceptions, which posit that the state's main role is to mediate and conciliate among competing interest groups. Organic conceptions, on the other hand, view the people as one and indivisible.[7] Cambodian post-independence state and opposition projects have shared a largely organic conception of democracy, which views the people as one and indivisible, united, and integral.[8] This mass has been imagined as the nation. The notion of democracy has remained tied to ensuring national preservation, while ethnic notions have been variously emphasized or downplayed.

In contemporary Cambodia, all political parties have launched democratic discourses, parallel to appeals to liberal democracy, which share some, if not all, traits of many contemporary discourses of liberal democracy, tying together bids for representation of the people as a mass with a national vision.[9] The CPP is generally understood not to have replaced its abandoned Marxist–Leninism with any other political identity in particular. This chapter demonstrates how Hun Sen has advanced "populism" as a hitherto overlooked regime identity, claiming popular representation through a truly national form of democracy. It then turns to examine the ways in which democrats similarly conflated democracy as representation of the people-as-mass with the people-as-nation, while also emphasizing the ethnic dimension of the nation. Their agenda was not an amalgamation of "democratic" and "nationalist" concerns, but rather represented an intensification of said nexus. This found expression in their core imagining of representing "the people's will." This provides an alternative explanation for why Caroline Hughes finds SRP and FUNCINPEC discourse to "awkwardly" conflate what she considers to be liberal views of the people's will as an "amoral and neutral construct facilitating the delegation of authority," with a view of the people's will as a "moral imperative to liberate the nation from alleged 'traitors.'"[10] Rather than manifesting a liberal discourse to which has been added morally based, xenophobic elements, this conflation arguably stems from a political analysis that is rooted in a more fundamental conflation of notions of democracy and notions of the nation. This chapter lays out the negotiation of this nexus in democratic political imaginings and the implications of acting on these imaginings.[11]

---

[7] Ibid., 55.

[8] Hughes, "Khmer Land, Khmer Soul," 45.

[9] Liberal conceptions that posit the state's main role to be mediation among competing interest groups underlie the liberal democratic conception of elections as expressing the people's will as the aggregate of plural individual choices, whereas organic conceptions of the people in possession of one singular conscience underlie a view of self-determination as the "collective fulfillment of a moral duty," downplaying elections (see: Mann, *The Dark Side of Democracy*, 55; and Hughes, "International Intervention and the People's Will," 544–45). According to this definition, all Cambodian political actors advanced discourses belonging to the second category. Even if applying a minimal and procedural definition of liberal democracy as "a political system where multiple political parties compete for control of the government through relatively free and fair elections" (Foweraker and Krznaric, "Measuring Liberal Democratic Performance," 759–87), particularly CPP and FUNCINPEC discourses, as outlined above, have opposed such a system in different ways.

[10] Hughes, "International Intervention and the People's Will," 539.

[11] This chapter, then, pursues a strict focus on the consequences of imaginings of democracy as popular and national representation, and does not delve specifically into related, prominent aspects of the discourses of self-identified democrats, such as territorial imaginings. See, for example, Harris, "Rethinking Cambodian Political Discourse on Territory," 215–39.

THE CPP'S "PEOPLE'S DEMOCRACY"

In neighboring Thailand, democratic imaginings and national identity emerged in tandem since 1932, the end of the absolute monarchy. Over the decades, the Thai state has developed a democratic ideology that transcends Western-style parliamentary democracy, and conceptualizes democracy, in the words of Michael Connors, as an "ideal psychological, almost spiritual, condition of the people and their capacity to be self-governing."[12] He terms this "democrasubjection," as a disciplining practice of governmentality that has produced a "Thai democracy" that privileges dependent subjects over popular participation. In post-independence Cambodia, punctuated by political discontinuity, there has never been one hegemonic, transforming "national ideology" of democracy such as Connors identifies in Thailand. The notion of democracy (*pracheathipatey*) was firmly integrated in all post-independence political projects and employed to support the nationalist claims of each one of these projects. While there was never one national ideology, these different projects thus still shared the fusion of nationalist and democratic claims. As in Thailand, these articulations of democracy, phrased as distinctly Cambodian, matched democracy with the needs of the "people," largely viewed by the state as well as opposition projects as an "undifferentiated mass of Khmers imbued with a set of inherited and larger than life propensities and dispositions."[13]

Post-independence Cambodia clearly manifests just how closely notions of democracy are bound up with national imaginings, as successive regimes have employed the language of democracy as a bid for identification with the nation. Both Sihanouk and Hun Sen have portrayed their regimes as popular democracies, claiming them to be more truly "Cambodian" forms of democracy than are models built along Western liberal democratic lines, and sneering at the accompanying notion of a "loyal opposition." Sihanouk employed the vocabulary of *pracheathipatey* as a legitimizing language when proclaiming the dissolution of parliament and assuming all powers through the 1952 Royal Mandate, ending Cambodia's brief experience of parliamentarism by reproaching the parliamentarians for "playing with democracy."[14] Similarly, Sihanouk, when abdicating in 1955 to enable the institution of Sangkum Reastr Niyum, which effectively replaced parliamentarianism, spoke of "*the promotion of a truly democratic system* putting an end to a situation in which the powers of government were concentrated in the hands of a small group of privileged people who could not be said to represent the interests of the people, whom they were exploiting. My objective is to make the people themselves exercise these powers [...]."[15] Sihanouk's direct democracy was, by definition, opposed to the concept of a "loyal opposition," making itself out as a national union for all citizens, regardless of their political opinion.[16] Though not formally outlawed, the political opposition was silenced and relegated to clandestine activities.

---

[12] Connors, *Democracy and National Identity in Thailand*, 2.

[13] Hughes, "Khmer Land, Khmer Soul," 45, 48.

[14] Baruch, *La Démocratie au Cambodge*, 6.

[15] Ibid., 10, emphasis added.

[16] Sihanouk established a Sangkum "counter-government" in 1966, tasked with making the opposition stance known to the government (which was required to cooperate with it), but

The Khmer Republic, Democratic Kampuchea, and the People's Republic of Kampuchea made successive bids for the realization of democracy, tied in different ways to their nationalist claims. The Khmer Republic "sought to build a new democratic Cambodia, free from the strictures of the past, and independent of French cultural domination," merging patriotic enthusiasm with democratic ideals in an "experiment in Khmer democracy."[17] For Democratic Kampuchea, relying on selected Marxist–Leninist models, the assimilation of all nationalities into a "classless Kampuchean people" was integral to the achievement of democracy defined along those lines.[18] For the PRK, which emphasized the implementation of Marxism–Leninism as a joint Indo-Chinese agenda, the link to a "national" form of democracy was more tenuous, yet there are indications that such links were attempted. Immediately upon seizing control, the regime built itself by organizing the people down to the local level into the Kampuchean United Front for National Salvation (FUNSK), with the task of popularizing government policies through mass movements.[19]

In contemporary Cambodia, in parallel with his appeals to liberal democracy, Prime Minister Hun Sen claims "populism" as the political identity of his regime, and has advanced the concept of "people's democracy" (*pracheathipatey pracheachon*) as the base of CPP policies and his own political thinking.[20] This has been overlooked by existing scholarship, which typically assumes that Hun Sen has not put forth a self-identified political identity, and focuses on how he is noted to pay half-hearted lip service to liberal democracy, while, in practice, contradicting its principles at will.[21] The notion of people's democracy deviates from a liberal democratic model by claiming popular representation through a truly national form of democracy. Recurrent in public discourse, the notion of "people's democracy" is crucial for reading the nature and direction of democracy under the CPP, in terms of how it construes the Cambodian people, the relationships between people and the political leaders, and the nature of political participation.

---

saw to it that the counter-government followed a pro-Sihanouk line rather than that of the government of the day.

[17] Corfield, *Khmers Stand Up!*, ix.

[18] Heder, "Racism, Marxism, Labeling, and Genocide in Ben Kiernan's *The Pol Pot Regime*," 109.

[19] Slocomb, *The People's Republic of Kampuchea*, 161, quotes Heng Samrin in 1979: "In order to help the people at all levels broaden, deepen, intensify their love of nation, to depend on themselves, to support themselves, to have awareness of mastery over their destiny and the country, to increase solidarity and consensus in activities to push ahead the revolutionary movements of the masses [...] the Central Committee of the Front must open wide and gather the important people, intellectuals, patriotic monks into the Front in all provinces [...]"

[20] Hun Sen, himself, explains people's democracy and populist democracy as interchangeable concepts (author's interview with Hun Sen). A notoriously imprecise concept, "populism" is generally associated with unity among the masses, anti-elitism, and, sometimes, a "trans-class" coalition wherein a charismatic leader appeals to the public with pledges of material redistribution. All of those elements figure, to varying extents, in Hun Sen's definition of his brand of populism, as explored below. Other defining features of Asian populism, such as anti-intellectualism and anti-foreign sentiments, do not figure in Hun Sen's definition; see, for example, Mizuno Kosuke and Pasuk Phongpaichit, *Populism in Asia*.

[21] Compare to: Slocomb, "The Nature and Role of Ideology in the Modern Cambodian State," 395; and Heder, "Political Theatre in the 2003 Cambodian Elections," 161–62.

Hun Sen has offered the following definition of "people's democracy":

What I try to do is to provide the best service for the people, the majority of the people, who are the poor. When we started the struggle to liberate the citizenry, we targeted making the majority of the people rich, after the genocidal regime. From bare hands we made sure that people would live again, enjoying better living conditions. Our policy towards farmers is that we have never taxed them. I have not only told my colleagues not to tax farmers, but also that we must intervene to help the people. We have to build infrastructure for the people, including irrigation, roads, canals, housing, schools, and clinics. People acknowledge that we are the one to end the war by himself.[22] The old generation created the war, but we are the one who put an end to it. Only this opportunity, peace, provides people in general with political opportunities to develop our society economically. These are some of the points related to the basis of our policies—that is, people's democracy.[23]

In this definition, "the people" are conceptualized as being the poor, and, in particular, as the majority rural population. Social and economic development is envisaged as charity, rather than in terms of state accountability (associated with taxation in the liberal tradition). CPP gift-giving practices, which have been demonstrated to insert patronage practices into Cambodia's democratic system in complex ways, are a central part.[24] These include the distribution of donations (small handouts as well as rural infrastructure projects) from the CPP to rural communities, known as *choh moulothan* ("going down to the base"). This strategy originated in the 1980s, when party cadres brought pro-socialist, anti-Khmer Rouge propaganda to the grassroots, until, with the advent of a multiparty democratic system, its meaning changed to party officials distributing donations which were understood to increase in the event of a CPP electoral victory.[25] *Choh moulothan* has been crucial for the CPP's continued hold on power. CPP working groups (task forces made up by party officials) mobilize resources for rural development on the provincial, district, and communal levels to which they are assigned. Though the working groups provide rural infrastructure funding nationwide, they are not financed by the CPP's central budget, but assemble resources from their own networks to provide for their respective areas.[26] Hughes has highlighted how gift-

---

[22] Hun Sen used the pronoun *yung*, which can be variously translated as "we" or "I." That the official translator at this interview chose to translate the sentence as "*we* are the one to end the war by *him*self," was presumably intended to convey some of the ambiguity of this wording, which could apply to either Hun Sen himself, or the FUNSK, from which the CPP leadership emerged.

[23] Author's interview with Hun Sen. This definition corresponds to elaborations in Hun Sen's speeches (e.g., Hun Sen, "Selected Comments at the Graduation and Presentation of Diploma to the Graduates from the Asia-Europe Institute;" and Hun Sen, "Keynote Address," 2007), indicating his consistent use of the term.

[24] See: Hughes, "The Politics of Gifts"; and Kimchoeun Pak, "A Dominant Party in a Weak State."

[25] Un, "Patronage Politics and Hybrid Democracy," 221–22.

[26] In this top-down structure, a high ranking official (prime minister, deputy prime minister, or minister) is responsible for the province-level working group; a lower-rank (minister, secretary of state, or director general) central or provincial official is responsible for the district-level working group; a provincial or district-level official for the commune-level

giving is not merely a transaction that swaps material goods for support, but also has a symbolic dimension as a kind of "invented tradition" that co-opts discursive resources, such as a notion of the meritorious donor, with material ones.[27] The reverberations of gift-giving practices also extend to democracy itself. Cast as part of a larger framework of people's democracy, they are central to the regime's version of democracy as propagated to the general public, and to regime policy-making.

Prime Minister Hun Sen enjoys a joke with farmers at an outdoor meeting in Pursat, August 2009. Seated at his right is Lim Kean Hor, minister of water resources and meteorology (photo courtesy of James Gerrand).

Secondly, Hun Sen's definition of "people's democracy" integrates the economic development that the gift-giving system supports into the regime's peace-building agenda. Economic growth and peace-building go hand in hand. This is why, rather than the PPA, Hun Sen has credited the economic development associated with people's democracy, alongside the win–win strategy, with bringing about real peace and national reconciliation in the wake of Cambodia's lengthy civil war.[28] Similar to how the win–win policy targeted the reintegration into national society of political opponents starting with the Khmer Rouge, people's democracy, through economic mechanisms, serves to integrate all segments of society into a national whole, and preclude opposition to the regime. Hun Sen claims his model for such peace-building through social and technological development from Malay ex-Premier Mahathir, who used rural development and poverty reduction initiatives, rather than

working group; and a commune-level official for the village level working group. Pak, "A Dominant Party in a Weak State," 108–21.

[27] Hughes, "The Politics of Gifts."

[28] Hun Sen, "Selected Comments at the Graduation and Presentation of Diploma to the Graduates from the Asia-Europe Institute."

force, to make the opposition forces join him, then brought his party to successive electoral victories.[29] In Cambodia, these practices include investment in rural infrastructure, such as roads, schools, and health clinics; non-taxation of farmers; and, in particular, the *choh moulothan* initiatives, whereby help is benevolently offered by government officials.[30] Echoing regional discourses of "developmental democracy," development and democracy-building are here different faces of the same coin, as the democratic political program has to respond to the actual needs of the people.[31] Yet by connecting economic growth and peace-building so closely, the very existence of a political opposition is framed as socially divisive and detrimental to socioeconomic development. Oppositional activities act against peace-building efforts and serve to perpetuate conflict—perhaps even provoking a relapse into war. The insertion of a discourse of war into the democratic debate produces an understanding of an integrated national community that rejects the principle of a political opposition.

The notion of "people's democracy" can be understood to provide a discursive and conceptual bridge in regime identity from the PRK to the KOC era of capitalist transformation. Hun Sen first developed the notion in his doctoral thesis on the evolution of Cambodian regimes and state–society relations since the time of the French protectorate, written during the PRK era.[32] In the thesis, a re-reading of Cambodian history using Marxist–Leninist concepts and categories, democracy is firmly integrated as part of revolutionary history, as the unchanging goal of thirteen decades of a Cambodian revolutionary quest. The Cambodian revolution is described as being a single, continuous process lasting for the past 130 years, although it has constantly transformed to respond to various evolving contradictions.[33] Yet in spite

---

[29] Author's interview with Hun Sen. Though there is no dearth of regional models for *choh moulothan*-style initiatives, including Maoism, Ho Chi Minh, and Kaysone Phomvihane, and, in particular, Sihanouk's Sangkum Reastr Niyum, which Hun Sen has described as a "similar concept" to people's democracy (see Hun Sen, "Keynote Address," 2007), Mahathir differed from these in that he also relied on courting the popular vote in a multiparty framework.

[30] Hun Sen has repeatedly stated that no tax will be imposed on farmers for as long as he remains in power. See, for example, Hun Sen, "Visit to Bridge Construction Sites in Kompong Thom."

[31] Examples abound in Hun Sen's speeches of how he puts democracy-building in an explicitly developmental context. See, for example, "The interview given to Radio Free Asia (RFA)," December 2, 2002, *Cambodia New Vision* 59 (December 2002).

[32] Author's interview with Hun Sen, as well as Hun Sen, "Selected Comments at the Graduation and Presentation of Diploma to the Graduates from the Asia-Europe Institute." In the latter speech, Hun Sen describes his doctoral thesis on people's democracy as "software," which one does not forget easily having written it oneself, seemingly casting the thesis as a manual for later political action. Hun Sen's doctoral thesis was entitled *Lokkhânah Pises Day Laek nei Domnaurkar Padevott Kampuchea* [The Special Characteristics of the Evolution of the Cambodian Revolution] and was presented for a Ph.D. in Political Science from the National Political Academy in Hanoi, the CPV-party school, in 1991. Parts of the thesis were published as Hun's book *13 Tosâvot nei Domnaoer Kampuchea* [Thirteen Decades of Cambodia's Evolution].

[33] Following these contradictions, the revolutionary struggle was directed against feudalism and the French during the protectorate era, against capitalist principles within a feudal framework under Sihanouk's Sangkum Reastr Niyum, and against the continued fusion of capitalism and feudalism and US-neocolonialism under the Khmer Republic, until, eventually, the revolution was betrayed by the "Pol Pot group." It was then reoriented under the "people's democratic revolution." Hun, *13 Tosâvot nei Domnaoer Kampuchea*, 61, 108, 149, 172.

of changing circumstances, democracy remained the revolution's goal—from its very first stage in the pre-protectorate era, when the newborn "democratic revolution" (*padevott pracheathipatey*) is said to have been fighting for "democratic freedom" (*seripheap pracheathipatey*). To consider just how far back Hun Sen meant to trace the contemporary notion of "people's democracy," it is instructive to look at the concept's genealogy. The term first appears in the phrase "the people's democratic national revolution" (*padevott pracheacheat pracheathipatey pracheachon*), and refers to how the revolution, gone awfully wrong in the horrors of Democratic Kampuchea (DK), was remade through the December 1978 creation of FUNSK, which participated in the overthrow of the DK.[34] The specific meaning of *padevott [pracheacheat] pracheathipatey pracheachon* is thus defined as the elimination of Pol Pot's "slave mode of production" to create a new political regime with a new mode of production.[35] Yet this people's democracy forms a basic continuity with previous stages of the evolving democratic national revolution as one distinct phase of the *padevott pracheacheat*, linking it back to the very origins of the revolution.[36] The difference from the previous stages of the revolution is primarily that democracy is now a heightened priority. While previously national problems were prioritized and democratic progress was only gradual, in the *padevott pracheathipatey pracheachon*, national problems and democratic progress are resolved together at the same time.

In the Second Kingdom, the notion of "people's democracy" perpetuates this close interlinking of democracy, revolution, and the nation, providing the language to negotiate the quality and contents of the transforming regime. Democracy is made out to form a continuity linking past and future regime practices, evoking a Marxist–Leninist-style progressive trajectory—even though its Marxist–Leninist contents have been wiped away. Whether democracy is intended to retain a revolutionary—if not Marxist–Leninist—aura is a vexed question, but the answer is arguably yes. By referring to a PRK-era notion, Hun Sen puts democracy in an explicitly revolutionary context. Indeed, it would not be far-fetched to think of people's democracy as the latest stage of an evolving Cambodian revolutionary quest towards genuine democracy, in which the Marxist–Leninist stage has been superseded, yet the dialectic moves on undisturbed, so that "people's democracy" handles new, emerging contradictions. This is perhaps most succinctly expressed in the phrase quoted by Ben Anderson, "revolution is continuity," although in a very different sense to that which he proposes.[37] Anderson uses this phrase to refer to the manifestation of what he understands to be a particular Javanese cyclical intuition of history, which, under Sukarno, turned the idea of revolution into one of restoration. Hun Sen's account, on the other hand, posits the revolution as progressing and transforming as it confronts changing realities—so that the only

---

[34] Ibid., 238–39.

[35] Ibid.

[36] The diverse concepts introduced are *padevott pracheathipatey*, for the pre-protectorate era; and *padevott pracheacheat pracheathipatey*, from the Japanese occupation until the remade revolution from 1978 onward, for which the term *padevott pracheathipatey pracheachon* is used. Hun Sen writes that "the character of *padevott pracehacheat* and the character of *padevott pracheathipatey pracheachon* is the same, and they have to be achieved together" to save the nation, eliminate the reactionary leadership, eliminate Chinese ideological influence, and eliminate Pol Potist "slave relations of production." Ibid., 239–40.

[37] Anderson, *Language and Power*, 148, quoting Castles, "Notes on the Islamic School at Gontor," 33.

continuity lies in the notion of revolution itself. One of the clearest examples of such changing revolutionary imagery is the figure of Sdech Kân, discussed above, who is a revolutionary primarily in the sense that he does away with the notion of hereditary leadership, yet ultimately is a king himself. Unsurprisingly, then, Sdech Kân is said to be the very first person to have introduced people's democracy—as the first democratic beliefs in world history.[38] This narrative thus offers a parallel genealogy of the notion. It posits social mobility as a central component of democracy, amplifying the CPP leaders' frequent stress on their simple origins. In advancing this narrative, Hun Sen responds to a new contradiction—posed by the reinstated monarchy which emerged as a novel threat to the CPP in the KOC—in the language of revolution and democracy, if not that of Marxism–Leninism.

By perpetuating revolutionary language with modified meanings, the notion of people's democracy allows the regime to retain a separate identity from Western liberal democracies—thus also responding to a second threat posed by the post-1993 framework. The transformation into a new political and economic system is managed precisely through reorienting the notion of people's democracy to frame the novel regime practices—such as gift-giving—which characterize it.[39] Hun Sen contrasts people's democracy with the "feudal forms of democracy" (*pracheathipatey sâkdephoum*) of capitalists.[40] This serves to guarantee that no Western liberal country can be a democratic model for Cambodia. Yet capitalist development under the regime follows no Marxist model, and, consequently, its language must metamorphose to accommodate the shifting class composition and increasing social stratification resulting from it. Hun Sen addresses this tension by arguing that there must be differences in income for society to function:

> Please don't confuse the people's democracy that we are implementing with that of the Pol Pot regime. Pol Pot used the word democracy in order to make all people live in equality. In order to have them live in equality, they made the rich become poor. Now, we cannot stop the establishment of the middle class [...] we cannot make the rich become poor. We need the rich people to pay tax, and then to take this tax to serve the poor. There is no country in the world where all people live in equality and everyone is the boss. If everyone is the boss, then no one will become a worker. If there are no rich people to build factories, how could we have workers? We need to make use of the rich, so that they use their capital for investment. Then the poor people have work to do, and generate income. [...] We have to try our best to reconcile between them, so that the rich will not become the enemy of the poor, and the poor will not become the enemy of the rich. We have to make a reconciliation so that the rich and poor share with each other, for the sake of national development.[41]

---

[38] Hun, "Aromkâtha," iii.

[39] Hughes traces the practices of gift-giving to the beginning of Cambodia's political and economic reform processes, around 1989, when policies of resource extraction emerged as an imperative for the government. See Hughes, "The Politics of Gifts," 469.

[40] Although the fusion of capitalist and feudal systems may seem odd according to orthodox Marxist analysis, this is in line with Hun Sen's previous analysis of society under Sangkum Reastr Niyum and the Khmer Republic, which were both said to contain capitalist principles within a feudal framework. Hun, *13 Tosâvot nei Domnaoer Kampuchea*, 108, 146.

[41] Author's interview with Hun Sen.

Here, Hun Sen appeals to a middle ground, reminiscent of the Sihanoukist third way, between a full-fledged capitalist system associated with liberal democracies, and the other extreme—extreme communism, such as that under Democratic Kampuchea. Since people's democracy is formulated in opposition to the "democracies of capitalists," this serves to imply a measure of egalitarianism and to conceal resulting tensions.

Serving as a bridge in regime identity from its previous Marxist–Leninism, populism also fills the shoes of this ideology. It is tied to Hun Sen and his rise within the CPP, which was associated with the pushing aside of Marxist–Leninism. As part of this, pragmatic technocrats came to replace Marxist–Leninist ideologues in government.[42] "Populism" and "people's democracy" are referred to as the regime identity not only by the prime minister, but also by those in the government circles close to him, many of whom were part of the technocrats originally rising to power with him during the PRK.[43] Long-time Minister of Commerce Cham Prasidh, who was discovered by Hun Sen six months after joining the PRK Ministry of Foreign Affairs in 1980 and would serve as Hun Sen's private secretary until 1987, states that, although he was devoid of ideology when he joined the PRK, he followed Hun Sen's lead in developing a passion for and devotion to the people. Hun Sen, he asserts, is a populist, and the CPP a populist party—defined as one that does everything to serve the people.[44] Meanwhile, parts of the CPP's leadership that belong to rival networks—including those monitoring the party ideological line— still claim a Marxist–Leninist identity for the party.[45]

This brand of populism can be understood as a kind of supra-ideology, which transcends all other political ideologies and identities. It equates the CPP with the aspirations of the people, and, therefore, incorporates and supersedes any other political identity. This is made clear in the following speech by Hun Sen:

> A true democrat does not have to declare him/herself so. One would neither have to claim oneself to be a true patriot or a true royalist. (If one listens to their campaign) we do not have a place, because they claimed it all—patriot, royalist, Sihanoukist, democrat, human rights activist, etc. What is left for us, then, is populist. In fact, judging from our actions, what we have done so far has truly revealed the nature of populism, which stays as the Cambodian People's Party's true policy. It is part of people's democracy that is included in my doctoral thesis. We never self-proclaim to be so and so, but our actions have clearly defined who we are. Our philosophy is clear, that claiming to be so and

---

[42] Heder, "Political Theatre in the 2003 Cambodian Elections," 159.

[43] Author's interviews with Cham Prasidh (minister of commerce); Im Sethy (minister of education, youth, and sports) 11 August 2011; and Suy Sem (minister of labour) 19 September 2011.

[44] Author's interview with Cham Prasidh.

[45] For example, Ker Bunkheang, deputy head of the CPP Commission for Propaganda and Education, the commission responsible for controlling political thinking within the party, claims the CPP to be Marxist–Leninist. Cham Prasidh, when questioned about this, dismissed it, stating that although the CPP party structure has maintained a committee responsible for Marxist–Leninist education, "the government no more talks about that [Marxism–Leninism]," concluding that now "we have to just dissolve them [the CPP Commission for Propaganda and Education]." Author's interviews with Ker Bunkheang,15 June 2010, and Cham Prasidh.

so is not necessary. We belong to the Cambodian People's Party and have implemented successfully the policy of populism. We devoted our attention to rural roads. By the end of the first decade of the twenty-first century, we are thinking about asphalting the rural roads that we have built (in the past decades). Whether the opposition consents or not is their problem. What we are doing is a true effort for progress.[46]

Here, what the CPP has done equals populism, and populism equals what has been done by the CPP. As invoked by Hun Sen, populism (or people's democracy) means anything that the prime minister says it does. This works by equating the nation and the people with the CPP—or perhaps, given that he is behind the notion of populism, with Hun Sen.[47] Because of this, ideology is made irrelevant. A further strategic reason for avoiding reference to ideology is arguably that this provides less opportunity for critics to hold the regime to its own words by employing the regime's vocabulary for resistance.[48] Yet, arguably, the divide Margaret Slocomb places between "thirty years of ideology" (1955–84) and a "post-ideological" era associated with Hun Sen is meaningful only in a narrow sense.[49] Hun Sen's notion of populism is, in fact, not dissimilar from Sihanouk's Buddhist socialism. Both notions serve to equate the leader with democratic representation of the people and the nation. Largely self-justifying, both Buddhist socialism and people's democracy have been what Sihanouk and Hun Sen said they were. In both cases, facilitating development and providing services have been crucial for cementing the bond between concepts of nation and democracy. There are, therefore, important similarities in terms of notions of democracy as popular and national representation, rather than ideology *per se*, functioning as a core of political discourse.

Recognizing that "people's democracy" is presented by the CPP as a form of populism that guides regime policies helps qualify our understanding of the CPP's stance versus multiparty liberal democracy. Multiparty elections, which are integral to the liberal democratic process, have served as an important legitimizing tool for the CPP.[50] Yet people's democracy construes the Cambodian people, the relationship between the people and the political leadership, and the nature of political participation very differently from liberal democratic theory. The "people" are equated with the majority rural, farming population. The existence of a political opposition is considered socially divisive and detrimental to socioeconomic development and peace-building. This post-Marxist–Leninist identity serves to guarantee that the regime maintains a separate identity from Western liberal democracies, and can therefore provide an alternative reading of practices that

---

[46] Hun Sen, "2010 Rural Development Review," *Cambodia New Vision* 154 (December 2010).

[47] Hun Sen's personal identification with the nation is also highlighted in his statement, "Sometimes people wonder what is Hun Sen really [...]. In communist countries I was called a liberalist and in liberal countries I was called a communist. Finally I had to tell myself Hun Sen is Hun Sen. Hun Sen belongs to the Cambodian people." See "Hun Sen Moves Ahead," *Asiaweek*, May 21, 1999, cited in Slocomb, "The Nature and Role of Ideology in the Modern Cambodian State," 394–95. This quote also demonstrates how "people's democracy" transcends the past communist/liberal dichotomy.

[48] James C. Scott, *Domination and the Arts of Resistance: Hidden Transcripts* (New Haven: Yale University Press, 1990), 103.

[49] Slocomb, "The Nature and Role of Ideology in the Modern Cambodian State," 388.

[50] Hughes, "Reconstructing Legitimate Political Authority through Elections?"

would otherwise be characteristic of the liberal democratic process. For example, Hun Sen repeatedly emphasizes how his right to rule is a consequence of how he has received a majority of the people's votes.[51] Yet such a claim collapses the distinction between people's democracy and liberal democracy, given that Hun Sen has repeatedly made out his electoral support as a consequence of the regime's socioeconomic policies or its direct identification with the people.[52] Moreover, elections have been promoted as proof of Hun Sen's ability to organize them, and Hun Sen has repeatedly abstained from participating in election campaigns, suggesting that he is above the electoral process.[53] Sometimes, the presence of an idea that is in conflict with liberal democracy is clearly manifest, such as in Hun Sen's public disdain for the notion of a loyal opposition. The DIFID tactics (known under its English acronym formed by the constituent parts "divide, isolate, finish, integrate, and develop") were originally applied to the Khmer Rouge as five points making up the win–win strategy.[54] Hun Sen has recognized these as tactics that can equally be employed toward the political opposition in general, and his stress on the need for integration into one, undifferentiated national community has been qualified by an accompanying threat that the word "develop" in DIFID may be replaced with "destroy" if the opposition parties persist in opposing the government.[55]

Contemporary opposition ideas of democratic popular representation must be understood in the context of this regime synthesis of democracy and national identity. Like the regime, the opposition articulates democracy in a way that identifies the will and needs of the people. In opposing the regime, the opposition's democratic imaginings turned precisely against the practices associated with people's democracy, in particular its revolutionary heritage, which they saw in terms of continuity rather than transformation.

DEMOCRATIC OPPOSITION STARTING POINTS

Since the start of the Cambodian post-conflict democratization process, self-identified democrats have turned to the 1991 Paris Peace Agreements and the resulting 1993 constitution for guidance in the democratization process. Political party contestation quickly came to center on contending interpretations of the constitution and manipulation of the electoral system. Such conflicts contradicted a common assumption that the multiparty system would bring about a transformation from disagreements over fundamentals to an electoral contest between policy

---

[51] See, for example, Hun Sen, "Graduation Ceremony at the Vanda Institute."

[52] See, for example, Hun Sen, "Interview with 'Le Point' on July 14, 1998," *Cambodia New Vision* 8 (July 1998).

[53] As noted by Hughes, "The Politics of Gifts," 475. For example, in his "Interview with 'Le Point,'" Hun Sen refers to himself, Chea Sim, and Heng Samrin not as "players" but as "coaches," who, having produced a "winning team," will not be changed and will not take part in the election campaign. "Interview with 'Le Point,'" 1.

[54] Ma, *Yutthosastr Chnea Chnea*, 1.

[55] See, for example, Hun Sen, "Selected Ad-lib Address at the Groundbreaking Ceremony to Build Roads and Bridges in the District of Khsach Kandal, Kandal Province, 14 January 2003," *Cambodia New Vision* 60 (January 2003).

platforms.[56] Concerned with establishing the democratic "rules of the game," democrats called for the correct implementation of the PPA and attempted to establish the political arena as a forum of debate among PPA signatories, where each actor would have voice and weight.

The democrats' analysis that the CPP regime was a communist dictatorship (*omnach phdach kar*)—despite its disavowal of socialism—emanated from an anticommunist, anti-Vietnamese strand of thought. They pointed to the CPP's KPRK and Khmer Rouge origins and argued that the regime had been installed with the help of the Vietnamese Communists.[57] Politically, in their analysis, the communist nature of the CPP regime was demonstrated by the conflation between the CPP and the state; the long hold on power by the executive; the interference of the executive in the legislature and judiciary; and the strong power of the executive over the legislature.

The democrats' charge that the CPP-led state was a puppet under Vietnamese dominion also built on deep-seated perceptions of threat to the very survival of the Cambodian nation and territorial state—a discourse that, in its different incarnations, has been crucially bound up with Cambodia's post-independence political trajectory.[58] The discourse of impending national extinction has been traced back to the French protectorate, which constructed a heritage of "national" culture centered on the cult of the Angkorean era, in which the history of the Cambodian nation ever since was one of gradual decay.[59] Yet Cambodian nationalism emerged not only in response to French colonialism, but was also related to Cambodia's historical experience as a sparsely populated buffer between the Thai and Vietnamese states, suffering repeated invasions and occupations by its neighbors.[60] In the 1830s, Cambodia underwent a forced Vietnamization, which in many ways foreshadowed later French colonialism.[61] To many, the Vietnamese-installed PRK therefore seemed to substantiate the worst nightmares of Vietnamese hegemony, and the resulting fear of national extinction became associated with the noncommunist resistance, and its KOC successors: the self-identified democratic

---

[56] Hughes, "Parties, Protest, and Pluralism in Cambodia," 165–68. Hughes draws on Giovanni Sartori's distinction between conflict over fundamentals and conflict over issues, suggesting that consensus over fundamentals, particularly procedures for resolving conflict, permits peaceful conflict over issues.

[57] Though Marxism–Leninism was dropped at the October 1991 congress at which the Kampuchean People's Revolutionary Party changed its names to the Cambodian People's Party, the CPP still traces its birth to the 1951 creation of the Khmer People's Revolutionary Party, the first Cambodian communist party, an occasion that is commemorated annually.

[58] Compare to Barnett, "Cambodia Will Never Disappear." For an account of how the Khmer Rouge envisaged the revolution's role in this "myth," see Ben Kiernan, "Myth, Nationalism, and Genocide," *Journal of Genocide Research* 3, no. 2 (2001): 187–206. See also Serge Thion, "The Ingratitude of the Crocodiles: The 1978 Cambodian Black Paper," *Bulletin of Concerned Asian Scholars* 12 no. 4 (1980), 38–54; and David P. Chandler, "Seeing Red: Perceptions of Cambodian History in Democratic Kampuchea," in *Revolution and Its Aftermath in Kampuchea*, ed. David Chandler and Ben Kiernan (New Haven: Yale University Press, 1983), 34–56.

[59] On protectorate-era myth-making, see Edwards, *Cambodge*.

[60] Volker Grabowsky, "Lao and Khmer Perceptions of National Survival: The Legacy of the Early Nineteenth Century," in *Nationalism and Cultural Revival in Southeast Asia: Perspectives from the Center and the Region*, ed. Sri Kuhnt-Saptodewo, Volker Grabowsky, and Martin Grossheim (Wiesbaden: Harrassowitz, 1997), 145–65.

[61] See Chandler, *A History of Cambodia*, 123–32.

opposition. Concerned with protecting the territorial boundaries of the Cambodian state, the democrats were particularly preoccupied with Kampuchea Krom—an area historically part of Cambodia, which saw Vietnamese colonists arrive from the 1620s onward and which was partitioned by France to Vietnam in 1949. The democrats took this as an ominous example of how gradual settlement by Vietnamese would result in the loss of Cambodian territory, and aimed to "reclaim" this territory, or, at least, to ensure the safeguarding of the rights of the ethnic Khmers living in that area.[62]

Such fear for national survival informs democrats' understanding of contemporary Cambodian democracy. Many democrats sense an imminent threat to the survival of the Cambodian nation, grounded in both historical and present-day realities. Asked to define his notion of Cambodian "nationalism," prominent democrat Son Soubert (whose father, Son San, was a Khmer Krom) referred to a kind of "self-defense," as opposed to a "call for grandeur."[63] His analysis places contemporary dynamics in the context of Thai and Vietnamese historical expansionism, and is founded in a geopolitical analysis of the predicament of a small country locked in a regional conflict complex. Similarly, Sam Rainsy has offered the following comparison:

> There are two countries that I would like to compare Cambodia to. One is Poland. Poland [once] upon a time disappeared because of two big neighbors, Russia and Germany. You can understand why Polish people are so nationalistic—they fight for their identity, and have lost their country. Cambodia also. Cambodia is squeezed between Thailand and Vietnam, and Cambodia would have lost the country as a nation, had the French not intervened under Napoleon III. After the French left, the process started again. The problem with Thailand on the one hand, with Vietnam on the other hand, resumed. Another comparison is Lebanon. You cannot solve the problem with Lebanon within Lebanon. There is Syria, Israel, Iran. [...] Cambodia is the same. *Democratic or not, it is beyond the issue of democracy for Cambodia. It is the issue of survival for Cambodia* [emphasis added]. It is the balance of power in that region. [...] This is the fate of small countries in the middle of much bigger countries.[64]

The threat to national survival is a problem more fundamental than, and analytically prior to, the question of the implementation of democracy.

Though not synonymous, democrats think that the struggle for national survival and the struggle for democracy are linked. This follows an understanding of democracy that equates it with the people's will. Sam Rainsy has offered the following definition of democracy: "The will of the majority can prevail. You do not

---

[62] On Cambodia's borders, see, for example, Chhak Sarin, *Les Frontières du Cambodge* (Paris: Dalloz, 1966). On contemporary border contestation, see Harris, "Rethinking Cambodian Political Discourse on Territory." On contemporary contestation over the Lao–Cambodian border, see Ian G. Baird, "Different Views of History: Shades of Irredentism along the Laos–Cambodia Border," *Journal of Southeast Asian Studies* 41, no. 2 (2010), 187–213. On Kampuchea Krom, see, for example, Keo Savath, *Jaovay Koy, Virakboros Khmer Kampuchea Krom* [*Jaovay Koy: Khmer Kampuchea Krom Hero*] (publisher unknown, 2006 [1971]).

[63] Author's interview with Son Soubert, 12 March 2010.

[64] Author's interview with Sam Rainsy, 24 April 2012.

oppress people. You cannot go against the will and the interest of the majority."[65] While national survival is the most basic priority, democracy—that is, following the popular will—is a means to ensure it. This view is laid out by Sam Rainsy, as follows:

> Democracy will ensure survival, because the will of the Cambodian people is to survive. So if the will of the Cambodian people prevails, then Cambodia will survive. In order for the will of the Cambodian people to prevail, we need democracy. It is interrelated—definitely democracy and survival is the same battle.[66]

Without democracy, on the other hand, the incumbent CPP would in this perspective continue to cling to power with the backing of Vietnam, compromising chances of survival.

To untangle democratic imaginings of national representation in the KOC, a final twist needs to be considered. The PRK and KOC are considered to differ radically from earlier political entities insofar as Vietnamese attempts at hegemony, through the power Vietnam is believed to exercise over the KPRP-turned-CPP, have penetrated the core of the Cambodian state.[67] This has brought a new set of problems for identifying the people's will in the multiparty democratic setting, and shifted the contemporary democratic agenda. Alleged Vietnamese control over the Cambodian state is imagined to drive a wedge between the will and the interest of the people, thwarting the functioning of democratic institutions and problematizing the task of popular representation. The series of problems and tensions arising from this analysis will be explored later in this chapter. First, however, I will discuss the particular ways in which the KOC's democratic parties, with partly different intellectual genealogies, have envisaged democracy, popular representation, and national survival.

The BLDP, the Son Sann Party, and the Human Rights Party

The first post-PPA "democratic" political party came out of the Khmer People's National Liberation Front (KPNLF), the democratic faction of the tripartite resistance during the 1980s civil war that transformed itself into the Buddhist Liberal Democratic Party (BLDP) ahead of the 1993 elections. Though the party rapidly disintegrated, it is significant as the very first self-identified democratic party in the KOC, with ties to previous democratic projects.[68] After the implosion of the BLDP, a similar agenda was advanced by the Son Sann Party when competing for the 1998 elections. The BLDP political platform included individual freedoms and rights, the rule of law, elections, democracy, private property, and a socially oriented market economy. The party was dominated by Son Sann, one of the founders of the

---

[65] Ibid. Sam Rainsy's perspective provides an alternative to, for example, Hughes, who argues that the "people's will," a core concept of liberal democracy, has been appropriated by the SRP and FUNCINPEC to "exclusionary and xenophobic purposes." See Hughes, "International Intervention and the People's Will," 560.

[66] Author's interview with Sam Rainsy.

[67] Ibid.

[68] The Buddhist Liberal Democratic Party quickly imploded over a split between Ieng Mouly and Son Sann over participation in the 1993 elections. In 1995, Son Sann, Keat Sokun, Son Soubert, Kem Sokha, Thach Reng, and Say Bory were expelled.

Democratic Party, a trusted statesman during the Sangkum Reastr Niyum, and later president of the KPNLF.[69] His close associate, Keat Sokun, later explained Son Sann's idea of democracy as follows:

> Son Sann was very clean and democratic. He taught me that doing politics is easy: just do whatever your subjects want. He taught me two things. Firstly that politics should be to do whatever your subjects want. Secondly, that the economy must be developed from the grassroots, not from the top.[70]

For Son Sann and the BLDP, there was a clear, unambiguous way to establish "what the people wanted"—through parliamentary democracy. This was to be accompanied by social and political development focused on agriculture. The BLDP argued against excessive private sector development and based its envisaged rural development on providing farmers with low interest loans, thus empowering the rural populace through capitalist mechanisms.[71] While the CPP has styled itself as a farmers' party, BLDP politicians charged that the CPP was half-hearted in prioritizing agriculture and failed to empower farmers to be financially independent. Son Soubert, Son Sann's son, later reminisced about a 1994 national assembly debate during which he argued that Cambodia should be developed from its agricultural base:

> Sok An [CPP] said that this is Khmer Rouge ideology. I said, "you traveled around the world, but you did not see that in the developed world the farmers are the rich?" You cannot build a sound economy if it is not based on agriculture.[72]

The BLDP styled itself the latest avatar of an indigenous democratic tradition. This claim was anchored in how the party leadership originated from the KPNLF and the DP. Son Sann was one of the founders of the DP, before becoming Sihanouk's trusted aide and prime minister.[73] The vice president of BLDP, Ieng Mouly, had been an activist for the DP as a student in Cambodia in the early 1970s, thereafter joining Son Sann in France.[74] Both were founding members of the KPNLF.

---

[69] Son Sann served as part of Sihanouk's team at the Geneva Conference negotiations and as governor of the National Bank (1964–68), and held a series of ministerial positions including those of minister of finance, foreign minister, and prime minister. He was also one of the signatories of the PPA.

[70] Author's interview with Keat Sokun, 3 May 2010.

[71] This focus was reflected in the portfolios assigned to the BLDP in 1993: "Rural Development," headed by the late General Thach Reng; "Youth, Sports, and Women's Affairs," headed by Keat Sokun; and "Parliamentary Affairs," under Say Bory.

[72] Author's interview with Son Soubert.

[73] Chandler, *A History of Cambodia*, 188; and Chandler, *The Tragedy of Cambodian History*, 167. After Son Sann retired from government in 1969, he maintained a neutral stance towards the Democratic Party, which was revived during the Khmer Republic. He sought to mediate between the Khmer Republic and Sihanouk. (Compare to Chandler, *The Tragedy of Cambodian History*, 230–31.)

[74] Ieng Mouly had worked with Chau Sau, president of the DP since 1973, a fact that convinced Son Sann to make Mouly a close associate. Author's interview with Ieng Mouly, November 17, 2009.

The BLDP also claimed continuity with the old DP primarily through virtue of being the successor of the KPNLF, the leadership of which formed more of a direct line with the old DP than did that of the BLDP.[75]

In the imagination of the BLDP leadership there was continuity stretching from the DP to BLDP. The DP had championed the idea that political authority needed to be democratically legitimized through a platform that demanded independence and democracy and attacked nepotism and corruption, and DP leaders envisaged the postcolonial state to achieve a "European-type parliamentary system with a maximum of democratic rights," with constitutionalism the foremost political principle of the nation.[76] In between, the KPNLF's main identity had been anti-Vietnamese and anticommunist, with a platform limited to outlining future parliamentary elections and building a market economy. Son Soubert identified continuity between DP and BLDP in terms of a belief in democratic values based on parliamentary democracy and a constitutional monarchy.[77] The BLDP set out to build an identity as the DP's successor party, manifest in its claim when registering the party to be a descendant of the DP. Even the BLDP party symbol, created by Ieng Mouly, suggested a straightforward genealogy: it was a fusion of the symbols of the DP and the KPNLF—an elephant head with three lotuses, symbolizing the three Buddhist gems, or the trinity of nation, religion, king, over Angkor Wat. The search for an earlier democratic identity was also reflected in the party name. According to Ieng Mouly, "Democratic" was meant to reflect that the platform was built around the old DP platform, including the belief in popular rule, whereas "Buddhist" was meant to indicate that it represented the majority-Buddhist people with the connotations of traditional morality that this bestowed.

The name's third keyword, "Liberal," referred to the belief in a liberal democratic system, of which economic liberalization was a key component.[78] Cambodia's ongoing transition to a free market system provided the main impetus to fine-tune the party identity to contemporary realities. The party leaders were concerned about how the emerging free market economy threatened to derail into wild capitalism. The BLDP advocated a social market economy, inspired by a German Christian democratic model. They believed this would prevent the excesses of an unregulated market and accommodate dialogue between leaders of enterprises and workers.[79]

---

[75] Most of the top leadership of the KPNLF came from the DP, including Son Sann (president); former DP prime ministers Huy Kanthoul and Chhean Vam; and Chay Thoul, Thonn Ouk, and Nong Kimny. These were members of an informal committee of "wise men," which Son Sann established as a consulting body. In this committee, only General Saukam Khoy (president of the Khmer Republic in April 1975) had not been a member of the DP. A majority of these leaders did not become members of the BLDP, both because of their by then advanced age, as well as the factionalism that had resulted in Sak Sutsakhan breaking away to found the rival Liberal Democratic Party (LDP) ahead of the 1993 elections. Author's interview with Huy Vora.

[76] Hughes, "Reconstructing Legitimate Political Authority through Elections?," 35 (quoting both); Chandler, *The Tragedy of Cambodian History*, 36, 38, and Michael Vickery, "Looking Back at Cambodia," in *Peasants and Politics in Kampuchea 1941–1981*, ed. Ben Kiernan and Chantou Boua, (London: Zed Press, 1982), 91.

[77] Author's interview with Son Soubert.

[78] Author's interview with Ieng Mouly.

[79] The influence provided to Son Sann and Son Soubert by German Christian and liberal democrats is reflected in their ties to the Konrad Adenauer Foundation, associated with the

The 2008 creation of the Human Rights Party appeared in many ways to be the resurrection of the BLDP. The leadership was the same: Son Soubert and Keat Sokun, who rallied behind Kem Sokha.[80] The reform philosophy was the same, as reflected in the party's four main policies: targeting living conditions, economics, and social affairs; protecting human rights and strengthening citizens' power; abolishing the "dictatorship;" and fostering domestic and international cooperation.[81] It also referred to an identical conception of leadership, reflected in the HRP motto taken from the KPNLF— "to serve, to defend, and to build."[82] The HRP continued the focus on agriculture, carrying itself as a farmer's party, and its leader, Kem Sokha, claimed privileged knowledge of farmers' needs by virtue of his farmer's background.[83]

A New Voice: From the KNP to the SRP

The main voice of the democratic opposition in KOC started as a small circle of people without close ties to the BLDP, the KPNLF, or the DP. The core was a close-knit group of former personal advisers to Sam Rainsy, FUNCINPEC's minister of finance, around whom friends, acquaintances, and urban intellectuals without previous political experience quickly gathered. These included Eng Chhay Eang, Yim Sokha, Yim Sovann, and Ros Chamroeun.[84] Their main political priority, as stated, was fighting communism, and they had therefore supported FUNCINPEC rather than the BLDP, given that FUNCINPEC enjoyed greater popularity and therefore stood a better chance of defeating the CPP.[85] In 1994, Sam Rainsy was expelled from the Ministry of Finance and then removed from the party following a veritable

---

German center-right Christian Democratic Union, and the Friedrich Naumann Foundation, associated with the German liberal Free Democratic Party. Son Soubert was also a member of the Moral Re-Armament movement in the 1970s, a movement with Christian roots that cast off its religious mantle and transformed into a network of people with what Soubert describes as an animating idea of "a process of change, through changing individuals, changing family, and then society." This suggests the broader influence of centrist European ideas of democracy. Author's interview with Son Soubert.

[80] Son Soubert is the son of the late Son Sann. Keat Sokun had supported the KPNLF from Sydney during the PRK, returning to Cambodia to become BLDP minister of Youth, Sports, and Women's Affairs in 1993. Kem Sokha had worked for the KPNLF in the early 1980s, and became a BLDP MP for Takeo in 1993 and party secretary general. He later created the Cambodian Commission of Human Rights in 2002, building his reputation through this independent NGO. All three sided with Son Sann in 1995 and joined in the creation of the Son Sann Party. They were joined by Pen Sovann, the disgruntled former PRK prime minister who spent a decade in solitary confinement in Vietnam without a trial.

[81] "Human Rights Party [Policy]," http://www.hrpcambodia.info/english/?option= com_content&view=aticle&lang=en&id=7&page=Policy, accessed October 26, 2012.

[82] Leaders of the HRP believed themselves to have the backing of most of the old KPNLF supporters, as they view their party as a sort of "resurrected BLDP." Author's interviews with Kem Sokha, 15 March 2010, Son Soubert, and Keat Sokun.

[83] Compare this to "Human Rights Party [Policy]," first point (K1).

[84] Eng Chhay Eang and Yim Sokha had been close friends since adolescence, studying together from high school to university. They supported, first, the KPNLF, then FUNCINPEC, before both becoming assistants to Sam Rainsy in 1993. Yim Sokha recruited his brother, Yim Sovann, a graduate of the Institute of Economics, to join as assistant to Sam Rainsy.

[85] In addition, by 1993, the BLDP had already suffered an internal split. Author's interviews with Eng Chhay Eang 24 March 2010, and Yim Sovann 26 March 2010.

anticorruption crusade, which had set him against the two prime ministers. At first Rainsy planned to return to Paris, where he had lived for most of the last three decades, but he was convinced to stay in Cambodia and set up a new party, whose membership consisted of the friends and former classmates of the core group around him.[86] These university graduates could readily relate to Sam Rainsy's political ideas: support of democracy, freedom of speech, and human rights.[87] In November 1995, they submitted to the ministry of the interior an application to found the Khmer Nation Party. When the party was announced, a number of senior CPP, FUNCINPEC, and other minor party leaders joined.[88] The party changed its name to the Sam Rainsy Party (SRP) in 1998.

Animated by contemporary concerns, the KNP shared with the BLDP a democratic identity strongly equated with anticommunism. Its slightly younger leadership had grown up under the DK and PRK, and these members' political consciousness had been sparked by a bipolar Cold War analysis, which posited a communist system against the free world. Many were motivated by their personal experience of communism, such as Eng Chhay Eang:

> In 1979, I started thinking about the new regime under Vietnamese control. I thought that maybe it [the regime and its living conditions] was the same in all different countries around the world, because we were like a frog in the well. I researched in school and came to know that other countries were different. I found out that there are two different types of countries: communist and free [*seri*]. And we live in a communist country.[89]

Similarly, in his autobiography, Sam Rainsy writes that his love for democracy was ignited when his father, Sam Sary, showed him photos of the Soviet crushing of the 1956 Hungarian uprising, quoting his father's words: "The absence of democracy is intrinsically bound up with the communist Barbary, this dictatorial regime which respects neither individuals nor the people that it purports to represent."[90] Those KNP leaders who had served under the PRK regime were just as prone to make a communist versus noncommunist analysis. Ho Vann had been cultural attaché to the Cambodian Embassy in East Berlin when Germany was reunified. Inspired by how the German people had succeeded in overturning communism without bloodshed, he thought of this as a model for peacefully overturning what he still considered to be a communist system in Cambodia.[91] Kong

---

[86] For example, several members were recruited by Yim Sokha and Eng Chhay Eang from the Faculty of Medicine, leading to a high representation of medical doctors in the party. Yim Sovann also recruited his wife, Ke Sovannaroth, whom he had met at the Faculty of Economics, who would later become the SRP secretary general (2008–13).

[87] The members included Thach Setha, Sok Seng, Kimsuor Phearith, Kuoy Bunroeun, Dam Sith, Yim Sokha, Thun Bunly, Meng Ritha, La Thavudh, Haem Vipea, and Hao Sopheap.

[88] CPP leaders included Kong Korm, Pit Thach, and Sam Sundoeun; FUNCINPEC leaders included Khieu Rada and Nguon Soeu; and minor party leaders included Cheam Channy of the Khmer Neutral Party.

[89] Author's interview with Eng Chhay Eang.

[90] Sam Rainsy, *Des Racines dans la Pierre: Mon Combat pour la Renaissance du Cambodge* (Paris: Calmann-Lévy, 2008), 45–46.

[91] Author's interview with Ho Vann, 26 March 2010. Ho Vann returned to Cambodia in 1996 and joined the KNP.

Korm was another person who claimed to be strengthened in anticommunist resolve by his experience working for the PRK. Korm was recruited to the PRK in February 1979, quickly becoming head of the political department at the Ministry of Foreign Affairs, ambassador to Hanoi (1981–82), member of the KPRP Politburo, and minister of foreign affairs (in 1986). In 1991, he left the KPRP because, in his own words, he "could not live with communism anymore. I had a chance not to live in a communist regime and do things to have a new regime. At that time, I hoped people who came from abroad might help the country install democracy and freedom."[92] Korm was the only high-ranking former CPP official to join the KNP and became its deputy president.

The KNP shared with the BLDP its support for parliamentary democracy, constitutionalism, a constitutional monarchy, and agricultural development as cornerstones of its agenda, but radicalized its analysis to focus on emerging realities, imagined in the economic and moral terms of "corruption." Portraying itself as a reform movement of FUNCINPEC that defended its original principles from the time of anticommunist resistance, the KNP turned against the contemporary FUNCINPEC, which KNP leaders thought had joined paths with the CPP. At the same time, KNP leaders widely perceived their party to represent a "new thinking" with which to confront emerging rampant corruption.[93] These political imaginings connected patriotism (*sneha cheat*) and a democratic conscience (*outdomkote pracheathipatey seri*) with protection of the national interest (*polprayoch cheat*), viewed in terms of territorial integrity and natural resource protection. Deriving from their corruption-centered analysis, the KNP set forth ten core principles (*kol noyobay 10 k*) as its platform, a manifesto on how to develop the country, which included income redistribution, land reform, forest protection, control of illegal immigration, and border encroachment in its anticorruption agenda.[94] In 2003, the ten principles were developed into a list of "100 Practical Measures to be Implemented by a Sam Rainsy Government" under the five rubrics of democracy: justice and human rights, security, improvement of living conditions, a clean and effective government, and national interests and the future of the country.[95] These two documents have served as the SRP's political platforms since.[96]

The Cambodia National Rescue Party

In July 2012, the SRP merged with the HRP to establish the Cambodia National Rescue Party ahead of the July 2013 national elections. With Sam Rainsy as president and Kem Sokha as vice president, the CNRP united groups of democrats

---

[92] Author's interview with Kong Korm, 31 March 2010.

[93] Author's interview with Eng Chhay Eang.

[94] See SRP, "Kol Noyobay 10 Kh Robâs Konâbâk Sam Rainsy" [10 Political Principles of Sam Rainsy Party], undated. The contact person for the drafting of the political principles was the late Chem Chansada, though all active members came together to discuss them. Author's interview with Thach Setha, 6 May 2010.

[95] SRP, "100 measures to be implemented by a Sam Rainsy government," 2003. This document was drafted and approved by the steering committee, after consultation "with international and Khmer experts abroad." Author's interview with Yim Sovann.

[96] Though the party debated updating the "100 measures" and the "10 political principles," it was time after time concluded that they remained as relevant as at the time of writing, suggesting that they were perceived as a conflict over deadlocked "fundamentals." Author's interviews with Tioulong Saumura and Eng Chhay Eang.

with different histories. They shared the points in common outlined above: a reading of democracy that equated it with anticommunism, and which centered on protecting those victimized by capitalist development under the transforming regime.[97]

Sam Rainsy speaks to a rally of CNRP supporters in Freedom Park, Phnom Penh, September 2013 (photo courtesy of James Gerrand)

IDENTIFYING THE PEOPLE'S WILL

The first problem for KOC democrats was how to identify the people's will and needs. This was bound up with a tension permeating democratic debates regarding to what extent leaders could transcend their personal life stories in their bid for popular representation. It would be hard to exaggerate the significance of social mobility as a component of the symbolic contestation of democratic imaginings in the KOC. As noted above, CPP leaders often stress their simple origins to deliver the message that, no matter how elevated they may be at the moment, each was, from the outset, truly one of the people. The Sdech Kân narrative celebrates social mobility as the "true" meaning of democracy. Social mobility thus provides yet another solution as to how to relate the body of the national leader to the body of

---

[97] Despite their partly different intellectual genealogies, the split of democrats into different political parties can hardly be seen in terms of substantial policy differences. Sam Rainsy originally intended to join the BLDP after his expulsion as minister of finance, but was recommended by the BLDP to set up his own political party, both because BLDP was in government and because they perceived Sam Rainsy to be too uncompromising. The creation of the HRP ahead of the 2008 elections, according to Son Soubert, was similarly because of a lack of response from Sam Rainsy when Kem Sokha wanted to join the SRP. According to Keat Sokun, he and Son Soubert supported Kem Sokha in setting up a new party with the intent of creating a balance in the opposition, by having two opposition leaders who would preferably ultimately join up. Author's interviews with Keat Sokun and Son Soubert.

the people—by emphasizing the legitimate leader's birth equality with the people and by claiming leadership credentials on the basis of that leader's social mobility.

In contrast, the Cambodian democratic project's claim to popular representation has been partly undermined throughout its history by its elite-driven nature, entailing fundamental problems of connecting with the rural masses it has purported to represent.[98] KOC-era democrats were similarly alienated from the electorate by their elite and transnational backgrounds. This was compounded by how many in the leadership had escaped the Democratic Kampuchea period of extreme hardship, and the sanction-induced suffering of the PRK-era civil war. The CPP has made a point of portraying the democratic opposition as returnees who, having evaded these experiences—which its own leadership endured together with the people—were oblivious of domestic realities. Exacerbating the democrats' estrangement was CPP penetration of rural areas through the conflation of party and state, which made the local state function effectively as an arm of the CPP.[99] Looking back at the demise of the BLDP, Ieng Mouly later stated:

This is why we failed. We didn't make connections with the local pagodas, with the *achars* [Buddhist lay elders] in the villages. We didn't have the support of the people. We were only an elite group with certain ideas. The CPP, on the other hand, are in power because of their contact with the grassroots. You can say that the CPP only are strong because they wield power and because they have money. But they are in power because they have bases everywhere, on the local level. The government representatives in the village are also CPP representatives. That is why they know what people need and can provide it to them. If they need a school, they can give a school. You can say that they are corrupt, and we, we are not corrupt. But since we don't have any money, we cannot help anyone. You can say that this is the politics of charity in Cambodia. They are corrupt and wealthy, but they give a little to the people, and so they help the people—that is why they have their support. People like us, who have no money, cannot even help the people.[100]

These remarks are important because, beyond the awareness of having foundered because of failing to connect with local power brokers, it manifests the

---

[98] The founders of the Democratic Party were a progressive group of French-educated returnees, and the elite-nature of the party was reflected in its motto, "Use the elite to serve the king and the people." See also: Chandler, *The Tragedy of Cambodian History*, 30; and Corfield, *Khmers Stand Up!*, 10–11. While urban intellectuals rallied to the party because of their ideological commitment to democracy, the difficulty of mobilizing the rural electorate led the DP to employ strategies based on "exploiting networks of local administrative control" and "tapping into customary structures of authority" to attract the rural vote. See Hughes, "Reconstructing Legitimate Political Authority through Elections?" 34–36. See also Baruch, *La Démocratie au Cambodge*, 5, who, although writing from an explicitly pro-Sihanoukist perspective, was perhaps not far off the mark in arguing that the DP interested only a minority of civil servants, but left the people indifferent.

[99] See, for example, Margaret Slocomb, "Commune Elections in Cambodia: 1981 Foundations and 2002 Reformations," *Modern Asian Studies* 38, no. 2 (2004): 447–67.

[100] Author's interview with Ieng Mouly. Though Ieng Mouly's statement can be read as an attempt to justify his subsequent defection to the CPP, for which he served as senior minister at the time of the interview, it is arguably also indicative of more profound tensions in the democratic project.

closeness, or even intersection, of the CPP and democrat worldview resulting from their shared focus on delivering services. In the context of overwhelming poverty, providing services is easily identified as the primary satisfaction of the "people's will." It was deeply problematic for the democratic project, which posited the "people's will" as its very *raison d'être*, that the CPP's penetration to the local level gave the party the capacity to identify and satisfy people's actual needs—an ability the democrats themselves lacked.

The emphasis on birth origin has even been employed for partisan rivalry within the democratic camp. As leader of the HRP, Kem Sokha portrayed himself as a middle ground between the two extremes of the SRP and FUNCINPEC's upper-class, educated leaders from abroad, and the CPP's leaders from humble backgrounds. Kem Sokha referred to his farming origins, and the fact that he had lived in Cambodia during much of the PRK, as proof that he could understand the "real" problems of the grassroots. On the other hand, he argued that Sam Rainsy, with his aristocratic background, would be unable to grasp the situation of farmers; according to Sokha, even Sam Rainsy's engagement with factory workers was inspired by Rainsy's higher education in economics.[101]

Ever since the beginnings of KOC multiparty politics, democrat leaders have been acutely aware of how they were set apart from the general public by their elite status and their transnational life trajectories. In response, they engaged in a range of strategies to identify popular needs by understanding ordinary people's living conditions. When Sam Rainsy and his assistants were expelled from the Ministry of Finance in 1994, their first move was to travel around Cambodia to learn about living conditions in different provinces, before establishing the KNP.[102] Similarly, KNP cofounder and wife of Sam Rainsy, Tioulong Saumura, states that her political interest was awakened by how, when she started to involve politically, "Little by little, I [Saumura] discovered the sufferings of the Cambodian people." Saumura outlines her and Rainsy's dilemma as follows:

> *What our party does is really based on the needs of the people. Because we have no idea about it* [emphasis added]. Cambodian society is very feudalistic. You have a group of people with a very privileged life, who do not even want to interact with the rest of the population. It is like the Indian caste system—you are born in one caste and don't interact with the others. Especially for me, I am Western-educated and returned from abroad. How do I know about their [the people's] needs? I have to listen to them, otherwise I have no idea. When I go to meet the voters, what should I tell them? In the beginning, I didn't know. I just had to listen. We have to listen to people, listen to the way they protest. Then we can find out about their way of life and their priorities. Of course we also try to influence them.[103]

This statement vividly illustrates the difficulties for Saumura, as a returnee who had spent nearly thirty years in France, in identifying the needs of the Cambodian people that she aimed to represent. It suggests that KNP, and later SRP, involvement with protest movements was designed for the specific purpose of

---

[101] Author's interview with Kem Sokha.

[102] Author's interview with Eng Chhay Eang.

[103] Author's interview with Tioulong Saumura.

enabling her and the party leadership to learn about popular needs. A conscious attempt to learn about the people's living conditions, in order to help articulate their voice, guided party leaders in shaping the party agenda.

The significance of KNP involvement with protest movements is exemplified by the manner in which the worker's movement—which now forms a backbone of CNRP support—was effectively created by the young KNP. In late 1995, Saumura was taken to see some KNP female garment workers. This was a wholly new area for Saumura, as she explains: "None of us was a specialist on workers or unions. In France, I always voted right-wing. I always felt very privileged. I had a good education, very high salary [from] working in banking. I was never interested in strikes."[104] Meeting with the workers, Saumura was told stories of mistreatment that defied her wildest imagination. She convinced Rainsy, who was at first reluctant, to join in organizing the four thousand workers at this particular factory by electing representatives and preparing them to strike, as well as promising to pay their wages in the event they lost their jobs.[105] When the representatives indeed were fired, a strike was called. The KNP leaders had the workers march several kilometers from the factory grounds near Pochentong to the Royal Palace, in a singing and dancing procession that, according to Saumura, resembled a feast more than a strike. A petition was handed over to King Sihanouk to demand his arbitration, which was followed by a series of meetings in the Royal Palace involving the workers, Rainsy, representatives of the government, and the Malaysian Embassy (the factory was Malaysian-owned). For Saumura, the significance of this event was that workers—who had been relegated to "slavery"—were reinstated as full citizens. Democracy was, for her, defined by how all members of society were to be given equal status as citizens, which amounted to nothing less than a mental revolution. Saumura particularly recalled one of the workers' representatives with the words, "She was just a simple girl working in a factory—she would never have dreamt of ever being allowed into the Royal Palace. This, I think, is real empowerment. This is true democracy. Probably we haven't realized yet the revolution this triggered in those girls' minds."[106]

The search for the elusive popular will and needs was thus so pervasive a dynamic that it came to determine the selection of issues that would become the cornerstones of the democrats' agenda. Even the shape that the democratic project took—heavily geared toward popular protest—can be understood as a direct consequence of this quest for representation. The KNP's, and later SRP's, promotion of popular protest has been understood to inadvertently offer space for individuals to insert their own agendas.[107] Yet this was far from accidental, but embedded in the very nature of the democratic project, forming a response to a key challenge. "Reading" the people, by identifying their socioeconomic needs, emerged as a fundamental imagining of how to relate to the nation. Enabling change necessitated

---

[104] Ibid.

[105] Particularly noteworthy, in hindsight, is Sam Rainsy's reaction to this suggestion, in Saumura's words: "He didn't want to go. He said, 'What should I say to them?' He wasn't that interested. He didn't see the social worry that could turn into a political movement with repercussions for our party" (ibid.). This neatly illustrates how the process of identifying the people's needs shaped the democratic agenda, in ways not anticipated by the KNP/SRP party leadership itself.

[106] Ibid.

[107] Hughes, "Parties, Protest and Pluralism in Cambodia," 174–75.

that the democrats insert themselves in people's realities to channel their demands. To this end, democratic leaders mobilized their selective knowledge.[108] This strategy of "reading" entailed its own fundamental problem of legibility. It tested to what extent the democrats could purport to read the people's will beyond identifying the straightforward, immediate needs of particular constituencies—a problem that I turn to now.

THE LIMITS OF ELECTORAL DEMOCRACY

Another problem derived from the democrats' national and democratic imaginings was that of designing institutions that adequately represented the people's will. The defense of parliamentary democracy has been a hallmark of successive generations of Cambodian democrats. Yet, in the KOC, consecutive CPP electoral victories posed a formidable intellectual problem for the democratic opposition, making its leaders question the efficacy of elections in guaranteeing democracy.[109] Although elections were the main forum for political competition, they possessed their own limitations.[110] As noted in chapter one, Steven Levitsky and Lucan Way have referred to the contemporary Cambodian regime under the label of "competitive authoritarianism," defined as "civilian regimes in which formal democratic institutions exist and are widely viewed as the primary means of gaining power, but in which incumbents' abuse of the state places them at a significant advantage vis-à-vis their opponents."[111] The democrats are acutely aware of what Steve Heder calls an "electoral system with many un-free and un-fair aspects," which he suggests, "together with the CPP's monopoly of force, its control of the courts, its performance legitimacy, and the patronage resources generated for it by the resumed economic boom, helped along by Hun Sen's benefactions to society," electorally marginalizes the opposition.[112]

The central problem for the democrats was why the majority of Cambodians would vote for a party that, in their eyes, did not promote their objective interest, but instead pursued inequitable development benefiting a minority.[113] Democrats invested significant effort in achieving free and fair elections, to correct this alleged

---

[108] For example, whereas Sam Rainsy and Tioulong Saumura modelled labor organization on Western European practices, they were joined by an emerging group of workers' movement leaders who had learnt to organize labor while studying in the former Soviet Union and Eastern Europe. Progressively, the workers' movement was taken over by these young returnees.

[109] This suspicion is confirmed by recent scholarship. See, for example, Slater, "Can Leviathan be Democratic?"

[110] Karbaum, "Cambodia's Façade Democracy and European Assistance," 111.

[111] Levitsky and Way, *Competitive Authoritarianism*, 5. The following argument confirms Levitsky and Way's contention (p. 16) that competitiveness is an important regime characteristic that affects the behavior and expectations of political actors under less-than-democratic conditions, by demonstrating how elections have served to reshape democratic imaginings and the political game.

[112] Heder, "Cambodia," 113.

[113] On the impact of current government policies on the poor, see also Caroline Hughes and Tim Conway, *Towards Pro-Poor Political Change in Cambodia: The Policy Process* (London: Overseas Development Institute, 2003); and Pou Sothirak, "Managing Poverty in Cambodia," in *Cambodia: Progress and Challenges Since 1991*, ed. Pou Sothirak, Geoff Wade, and Mark Hong (Singapore: Institute of Southeast Asian Studies, 2012), 337–65.

asymmetry.[114] Yet the problem of representation has been seen as one that could not be solved by electoral mechanisms alone, since it stemmed from more fundamental problems at the core of contemporary Cambodian society. Democrats explained what, to them, seemed to be the counterintuitive electoral behavior of Cambodians—persistent re-election of the CPP—by arguing that the CPP-led regime blinded the people of their interests through material and ideological modes of domination.

Sam Rainsy and his supporters have repeatedly argued that the Hun Sen regime, in important respects, continues the politics of the Khmer Rouge movement, with the difference being in its intensity rather than in the nature of the regime. They have summed this up in what is known as the "three k," so named for the three component words of the formula: *khlach* ("fear"), *khlean* ("hunger"), and *khlov* ("ignorance"). Sam Rainsy and other democrats have charged that the CPP regime purposely emulates this model to control the populace.[115] In his 2008 autobiography, *Des Racines dans la Pierre* (Rooted in Stone), Sam Rainsy provides a lengthy elaboration on this issue, identifying the following "Khmer Rouge" trends in contemporary Cambodia: widespread fear, through CPP-led politically motivated intimidation, threats and constraint (forming a weapon of political domination); hunger (charging that the CPP prefers to maintain a "link of subjection" with the people by offering donations rather than creating viable jobs); and ignorance (charging that the CPP does not invest sufficiently in education, purposely resulting in continued high levels of rural illiteracy and the absence of social and political conscience and critical thought).[116]

This understanding of the current social and political order bears, in turn, on the democrats' understanding of contemporary democracy. Sam Rainsy's definition of democracy, quoted above as acting in accordance with the will and the interest of the majority, contains an all-important distinction, and possible tension, between the majority's *will* and *interest*.[117] Asked about the democratic prospects in a scenario in which the people are unaware of their objective interests, Sam Rainsy replied by reference to the "three k:"

> *That* [the three k] *is why it is blurred*. The trick of the Hun Sen regime is to make the people poor, to kill the human spirit. It is a similarity between the Khmer Rouge regime and the Hun Sen regime, which Hun Sen as a former Khmer Rouge can understand. There are three words that characterize the Khmer Rouge regime: *khlach*—fear, *khlean*—hunger, *khlov*—ignorance. This is typical of extreme dictatorship. To make the people afraid, and hungry, because then they [the leaders] can command the people by just giving people a bowl of rice,

---

[114] See, for example, SRP, "100 Measures to be Implemented by a Sam Rainsy Government," nr 6, 8, 11, 12, 14; "Human Rights Party [Policy]," principles 11–14.

[115] See, for example, Charles McDermid and Cheang Sokha, "Gagging MPs Likened to Khmer Rouge," *AsiaViews* 35, no. 3 (2010). See also Sam Rainsy and Rado Tylecote, "'Be Vigilant' on Human Rights, Warns Cambodian Opposition Leader. Special Report: Rado Tylecote Talks with Cambodia's Opposition Leader Sam Rainsy in Phnom Penh," April 24, 2006, http://www.conservativehumanrights.com/media/articles/samrainsy.html, accessed July 1, 2015.

[116] Sam, *Des Racines dans la Pierre*, 228–29.

[117] Author's interview with Sam Rainsy.

because people are so hungry, so poor, and ignorant. *Khlach*, [now] the people are not *khlach* as under the Khmer Rouge, but still, they are afraid of supporting the opposition. *Khlean*—[under Khmer Rouge] they would die of starvation. But Hun Sen's people are making people poor. They lose their land, their fishing zone, they have low salaries, there are commercial monopolies increasing the price of commodities. This is the new system to control the people through the economy, through the basic needs of survival. Then they depend on donations, on handouts, and forget the national issue. So Hun Sen can appear as a good man, giving donations, while he jeopardizes the future of his country. *He blurs the line.* It is why the fight against corruption, the fight to improve living conditions, to allow people to live with job creation, [so that] you depend on your salary, and not on handouts—all these are interrelated. Then the human spirit can thrive because you are not prisoner of your stomach.[118]

In this analysis, there is a rift between the will and interest of the Cambodian people, caused and obscured by the politics of the "three k." This destabilizes the prospect of democracy under the incumbent government—even if free and fair elections were to be guaranteed. Even regular elections would, under these circumstances, fail to democratically express the people's will and genuine interests. Ensuring the smooth functioning of an electoral democracy is therefore not the endpoint of the political game. This analysis has informed party political action and strategy for many years in concrete ways, leading to a strong emphasis on the improvement of general living conditions, anticorruption initiatives, and job creation, as well as demands for guaranteed minimum salaries.[119] These cornerstones of the democratic agenda are not only part of a national economic plan, but also measures to address a democratic deficit imagined to be caused by the "three k," which distorts the popular will. The larger aspiration of this political program is to bridge the artificial rift between the popular will and interest to set the democratic game straight.

The belief that the government purposely keeps the people in poverty is widely shared among democrats. In their analysis, unequal capitalist transformation serves to cement CPP political leadership as an only superficially revamped communist regime. This promotes a "feudal" mentality under which Cambodian people have lived for hundreds of years—hence Sam Rainsy's characterization of the incumbent regime as "neo-feudal" or "feudal-communist."[120] The changing political economy of the Cambodian state is seen to hide larger continuities in terms of the promotion of a subservient popular mentality. Democrats' objections to Cambodia's present development path stemmed not only from how they considered it to disadvantage a large segment of the populace, but as much from how they considered unequal development a political tool to becloud the popular mind.

With the ability of elections to assess the popular will thus uprooted, how the popular will could ever be determined emerged problematized. Among the democratic opposition, there is a widespread conviction that their own group enjoys

---

[118] Ibid.; emphasis added.

[119] Compare to SRP, "100 Measures to be Implemented by a Sam Rainsy Government," Sections II and III; CNRP, "7 Point Policies of the CNRP," publisher unknown, 2013.

[120] See, for example, Sam Rainsy's millennium message in Zainon Ahmad, "Uneasy Boom in Cambodia," *New Straits Times*, February 13, 2000.

the support of the vast majority of people. Why this is not expressed at the polls is explained by a mix of reasons that stem from the "three k," ranging from tangible ones—such as the benefits involved in voting for the CPP—to intangible ones, premised on how the people, kept in poverty and ignorance, are unaware of their actual preferences. In this last line of reasoning, the people are beset by a false consciousness of sorts, as described by leading democrats:

> This government is not popular. [Officials] need the police to help with elections. Village chiefs are appointed by the party, and there are handouts through local government. If people don't support the CPP, they wouldn't benefit. It is a trick that was used by the Khmer Rouge too: fear, starvation, and keeping people ignorant.[121]

> So far, our political platform is still very popular and supported by many. But we could not win anything. Since the CPP control everything, control the National Election Committee (NEC). The courts are not independent. There is intimidation. People do not have access to information. Education is limited and the poor cannot afford newspapers. Only a few people in the towns can know what is going on.[122]

The difficulties encountered by democrats in reading the people's will encouraged a tendency to equate their own agenda with that of the general populace, reflected in their often inflated figures of claimed support.[123] It is in this context that we can understand the exhortation to voters to vote "according to their conscience."[124] Undoubtedly of strategic value, self-confident estimates of popular support arguably also reflect a "democrat" identity that equates the representation of the economic interests of constituencies with enjoying their support. Put differently, there is the expectation that all constituencies whose objective economic interests are promoted by the democrats also support them in turn; or, at least, were they to receive education on the "real" situation, they surely would.[125] More problematically, this highlights a discrepancy in the democrats' assessment of the popular will between self-perception and validation. In this sense, the democrats

---

[121] Author's interview with Son Chhay, 23 March 2010.

[122] Author's interview with Yim Sovann.

[123] Steve Heder notes that the SRP, in 2011, "implausibly claimed to have 500,000 members," quoting Meas Sokchea, "Rainsy Still Atop Party," *Phnom Penh Post*, September 12, 2011; see Heder, "Cambodia," 113.

[124] The CNRP, and, earlier, SRP, have routinely admonished voters to cast their ballot according to their *outdomkote* ("ideal") or *moneakseka cheat* ("national conscience"). See, for example, this video: Sam Rainsy, "Sar Lok Protean Sam Rainsy choun Chompoah Pracheareastr Khmer knong Oukas Boh Chnaot Khum–sângkat nov Tngae 3 Mitona 2012" [Message to the people for the 3 June 2012 commune elections], 2012. This admonition has been documented since the 1990s. See Hughes, "Reconstructing Legitimate Political Authority through Elections?" 36.

[125] The equation of economic interest and political support is seen here: "Development under Hun Sen has made only 2 percent of the people richer—you will see that those 2 percent are those who say they are happy with Hun Sen's economic policies, because their living conditions have improved. But 98 percent say no, we remain poor, and we have become even poorer. [...] We know that the majority of the people are unhappy, so how come the CPP wins a landslide victory? It is through manipulation." Author's interview with Sam Rainsy.

could only convincingly claim to represent a nation in becoming, rather than an actual, accomplished nation.

Democrats' disenchantment with what they considered a fraudulent electoral game and search for alternative solutions to democratically represent the people climaxed in the SRP discourse of 2011–12. In self-imposed exile since 2009, Sam Rainsy took a keen interest in the Arab Spring as a model for "people's power" in Cambodia. In his analysis, growing popular discontent over inequitable development had created the preconditions for a popular uprising.[126] In particular, the Tunisian transition was made out as an inspiration for Cambodia, said to be awaiting a "Lotus Revolution." Sam Rainsy even paid Tunisia a visit to consult with pro-democracy activists in order to assess the possibility of such an insurgency.[127] Hun Sen swiftly retorted that since he had been elected, he would step down only if voted out.[128] Shortly thereafter, the SRP party congress approved a strategy that included "participation in the 2012 and 2013 polls while fighting election irregularities and unfairness according to our means" and "a popular uprising inspired by the Arab Spring and other forms of People Power if the forthcoming elections remain fundamentally biased and continue to seriously distort the will of the people."[129] Rainsy charged that a failure to implement electoral reform could help spark a popular uprising, as the population would stop believing in elections.[130] This demonstrates the democrats' exasperation with the existing electoral game, and, in particular, the extent to which they found themselves challenged by the ways in which elections contributed to the CPP's overall legitimacy.[131] Their priority became stripping the incumbent government of electoral legitimacy, both external and internal. Following the contested 2013 elections, the CNRP (formerly the SRP and HRP) refused to acknowledge the official elections results and demanded reelections. Regardless of their grounds, the fervor with which these demands were made remained premised on a belief in their own party—as representative of a nation in becoming—representing the popular will.

DETERMINING A POLITICAL IDENTITY

A further tension concerned the democrats' political identity, and arose from the intersection of how they projected their political agenda and how they understood that political identity themselves. This incorporated a tension between a localized, interest-based agenda that became distinctive of the democrats' political project, versus a national agenda, which these imaginings emerged from, yet, ultimately, was difficult to project. Although the democratic leaders identified closely with a global democratic agenda, the democratic parties did not prioritize liberal democratic

---

[126] Ibid.

[127] SRP Cabinet, "Sam Rainsy in Tunisia to Prepare People Power in Cambodia," 2011.

[128] "Hun Sen Issues New Warning to the Opposition Regarding the Jasmine Revolution," *Cambodia Express News*, July 22, 2011.

[129] SRP, Fifth Party Congress, 2011, *Resolution IX.*

[130] Author's interview with Sam Rainsy.

[131] Ibid. In fact, Sam Rainsy's pronounced preference for electoral reform stemmed, in part, he told me, from his lack of faith in the material conditions for a popular uprising in Cambodia (i.e., lack of internet access).

orthodoxy, and were ultimately susceptible to appearing fragmentary and personalistic.

In their search to identify the people's needs, guided by their political and economic analysis of Cambodian society, the SRP, in particular, embarked on a process of tracing local grievances to defend the people's interests against the transgressions of transforming communism. In their analysis, Cambodia's economic liberalization, begun at the end of the 1980s, served only the political elite, their business associates, and Vietnam, but victimized the overwhelming majority of the population. While they reacted to new realities stemming from Cambodia's recent development, preexisting perceptions of a threat to national survival resonated powerfully.[132] The regime and SRP political projects were made out to be two different conceptions of development, and the development path taken by the CPP was branded as unjust and a threat to national survival. In particular, the CPP-led government's awarding of land to companies as economic concessions was contrasted with the SRP model of reinstating farmers as owners of the land and, instead, inviting investors to buy farmers' produce for processing. At the fifth SRP congress, in 2011, the party pledged to "return to the Khmer people all the goods that have been stolen from it." Land, the property of the nation, was to be returned to the Khmer people, its "true owners," and individuals and private companies that forcibly seized land were declared "enemies of the Khmer people."[133] Sam Rainsy claimed that "this faulty development is in conflict with the Khmer people and kills the nation."[134] The SRP would, by contrast, realize "a true development for the people," which included protecting its property, annulling land concessions, and giving land property rights to every citizen.[135]

The democrats embarked on a process of tracing local grievances stemming from Cambodia's current development path, seeing each as a representative part of the ailing nation. In what can be understood as a parallel discourse to royalist conceptualizations, which play with the idea of the royal body as a stand-in for the nation, every local suffering "victim" was seen as a microcosm of the "victim" nation. For the SRP leadership, there was no conceptual gap, as they perceived the conflict over fundamentals in society to continuously manifest in local issues. The SRP reframed rural grievances into national issues during protests in Phnom Penh. The process of tying local grievances to national imaginings was effortless—from the macro-perspective of the leadership, they were local manifestations of a national drama. Caroline Hughes has argued that ideas of innocence and guilt were useful in negotiating participation in urban protest movements with close links to the SRP because they "linked the problems of the individual" (motivated by a variety of grievances) "into a plurality of narratives with great mobilizational power."[136] While

---

[132] Compare this to Frank H. Golay, Ralph Anspach, M. Ruth Pfanner, and Eliezer B. Ayal, *Underdevelopment and Economic Nationalism in Southeast Asia* (Ithaca: Cornell University Press, 1969). In Aceh, Edward Aspinall has similarly found claims about unjust exploitation of natural gas to reinforce a pre-existing "discourse of deprivation" that infuses Acehnese identity. See Edward Aspinall, "The Construction of Grievance: Natural Resources and Identity in a Separatist Conflict," *Journal of Conflict Resolution* 51, no. 6 (2007): 952.

[133] SRP, Fifth Party Congress, 2011, *Resolution II*.

[134] Ibid., *Author's Field Note*.

[135] Ibid., *Resolution IV*.

[136] Hughes, "Mystics and Militants," 53–55.

the framing of specific interest-based and local issues as national ones certainly served a mobilizational purpose, this framing was arguably a direct consequence of the particular democratic imaginings of the party leadership. From this followed also the reverse tendency—to dismantle the national agenda into the identification of distinct interest groups, each to be represented separately in order to cater to its needs.[137]

This national–local nexus stemmed from how democratic contestation was imagined to remain over the fundamental "rules of the game," the constitution and electoral organization. For example, land seizures were understood in terms of how they ultimately amounted to a violation of the 1993 constitution.[138] This had important consequences in terms of how the democrats related to a liberal democratic agenda. Observers have noted the discrepancy between the SRP political program and discourse, and liberal democratic ideology.[139] Yet, from the point of view of the party leadership, there was no contradiction. The conflict over fundamentals was seen as the national manifestation of a global search for democracy, and they expected Cambodia to join what they imagined to be a worldwide democratizing trend. This identification was reflected in the SRP's affiliation with international liberal democratic associations, which it maintains as a constituent part of the CNRP.[140] The concern for translating democratic concerns into Cambodian realities overshadowed any strict measure of the party agenda against liberal democratic orthodoxy, which was considered out of tune with Cambodian realities. Asked about the nature of SRP's democratic beliefs, Sam Rainsy replied:

> This [question] is too sophisticated. I think the base is—do you believe in the human spirit or not? […] If you are strong, you are in the position to lead the people to stand up against something which is not good. But this "perversion of democracy" is just too intellectual, it is discussing for the sake of discussing.[141]

This passage shows Sam Rainsy's weariness of (primarily foreign) accusations of straying from the liberal democratic path. It also indicates that the democratic struggle was thought to go beyond that of implementing an ideology or doctrine. Most democrats imagined democracy to be concerned with more basic questions of

---

[137] One striking example of this tendency is how, at the establishment of the KNP, Sam Rainsy suggested that Tioulong Saumura form a separate women's party. She declined, pointing out that women make up a majority of the population. Author's interview with Tioulong Saumura. This is indicative of a more thoroughgoing tendency to split the political agenda into representation of particular interest groups, doing little service to the development of one overarching political identity.

[138] See, for example, "Cambodia Marks Constitution Day," *Cambodia Herald*, September 24, 2012.

[139] See Un, "Configuring Opposition Politics"; and Hughes, "Khmer Land, Khmer Soul."

[140] First the SRP, and now the CNRP, is a member of the Council of Asian and Liberals and Democrats (CALD) and of the Liberal International, and Sam Rainsy is a member of the general council of the Transnational Radical Party. Sam Rainsy has emphasized the SRP's belonging to a "world liberal family." See "Sam Rainsy Meets with Liberals across Scandinavia," *Liberal International Newsletter* 228, 2011.

[141] Author's interview with Sam Rainsy.

the relationship between the people and the political leadership. Another SRP (currently CNRP) MP, Ho Vann, expressed it this way:

> Everyone has an *ideology*, but sometimes you need to change the *mentality* because of great obstacles. We have to help "le petit peuple" to fight against the rich people who abuse them. [We have to tell them that] you have rights, to liberty, to justice, to land, to be confident. It is not about Communism or Democracy. It is the habit, the habit of how to live, and how to think. Now it is like that of the communists. I don't want to speak about ideology, but about the habit.[142]

Similarly to the SRP, the HRP combined a proclaimed belief in liberal democratic values with a twist adjusting these to Cambodian realities. Kem Sokha has claimed the basis of his democratic thinking to be drawn both from Buddhist theory and from global liberal democratic discourses. According to Sokha, he therefore routinely included three elements in public speech: Cambodian and international history, Buddhist morality, and "international theory" (referring to liberal democratic theory).[143]

Ho Vann's statement shows that since the democrats did not recognize their opponents as contenders in the democratic game, they envisioned that social and political change would instead occur through a change of popular attitudes. Building a "culture of citizenship" was conceived as an antidote to the "beggar mentality" believed to be promoted by the incumbent government:[144]

> The SRP is trying to empower people as citizens. Not as subjects, not as beggars. Hun Sen promotes a beggar mentality. A beggar cannot afford to be critical. But a citizen is by definition critical, because he is part of the power.[145]

This discourse of citizenship reflected the belief that the citizenry, if allowed to develop critical thinking, would free themselves from the blurred vision that the policies of *khlach, khlean, khlov* had imposed on them. Democrats pledged to move from an "elective democracy" to a "participative democracy," defined as a system "where citizens continually participate in a decision-making process affecting their daily life."[146]

---

[142] Author's interview with Ho Vann; emphasis added.

[143] Author's interview with Kem Sokha.

[144] This reframes Hughes's distinction between a "mystic" approach, which emphasizes individual change, and a "militant" one, which "aims to ensure the triumph of innocence over the guilt through the reclamation of the agencies of state from the brutal and greedy by the innocent and oppressed" (Hughes, "Mystics and Militants," 54–55). While she acknowledges that most reform activists are influenced by both, the SRP agenda corresponds to the one she dubs as "militants." The above argument suggests that a crucial part of the SRP agenda has been to engender change by creating preconditions for the development of individual critical thinking among citizens, collapsing this distinction.

[145] Author's interview with Sam Rainsy.

[146] SRP, "100 Measures to be Implemented by a Sam Rainsy Government," nr 2. As part of this, the SRP advocated measures of a "direct democracy" type, including the promotion of referenda, and the holding of a national congress as a forum for the people to learn about national issues, raise problems, and make suggestions. SRP measures 3 and 5.

Yet the changes needed in Cambodian popular mentality to achieve this culture of citizenship were understood to be profound. Typically, democrat leaders envisaged their own role as that of teachers, and often invoked Western state-society relations as a source of inspiration:

> To change the system peacefully, you need to change the mentality of the people. In Cambodia, it is like in the traditional, ancient states. We need to educate them and say: you are the people, the masters of the country's destiny. Every day, I have to educate the people that I meet to make them change their mentality. If we speak about democracy, they understand nothing. That is my opinion—we need to change people's mentality and especially that of the youth. We need to educate them about anticorruption, how to fulfill their tasks as citizens. I have the technique, I am a pedagogue.[147]

> We have to change the mentality of the people. We think that the obstacle to social development in Cambodia is corruption. All political leaders became corrupt when they were in power. In other countries, they do not allow impunity, but here, yes. So we learn something from developed countries, civilized countries. We should build a new generation of political leaders. Like children when they are small: my son came to Japan with me, now he still looks for trash bins in the street to throw litter, because he got used to it because of the law there.[148]

> I think Cambodian people are learning what democracy is all about. We have the exposure to Western thinking and try to introduce it to our members. Then it is up to them to decide, not us.[149]

This didactic element is not surprising. It is common among regional democratizing elites to envisage democratization as a change of mentality. Many have drawn on Western democratic theory to introduce new notions of citizenship, in order to remold the relationship between populations and the state. Typically, such democratic notions did not emulate a Western model in a straightforward manner. In neighboring Thailand, for instance, Connors finds that democratic ideology has transcended the focus on procedures and form of Western political science, instead conceptualizing democracy as an ideal psychological condition of the people and their ability to govern themselves.[150] In contemporary Cambodia, the democrats' emphasis similarly lay on empowering the people for self-mastery over applying a Western liberal democratic model by the book. In Thailand, such notions came to underpin "democrasubjection," what Connors describes as the employment of elite-defined liberal democracy as a disciplining practice. Though the two differ in important respects, the Thai case also shares certain family resemblance to the Cambodian democratic project. Elites are needed to steer the process of this change of mentality; and the common good, which the ideal citizens are envisaged to work toward, remains elite-defined. In this sense, democratic elites have primarily

---

[147] Author's interview with Ho Vann.

[148] Author's interview with Yim Sovann.

[149] Author's interview with Son Chhay.

[150] Connors, *Democracy and National Identity in Thailand*, 1–2.

represented a nation in becoming, rather than an existing one; a future nation that they have actively tried to create and shape.

The fuzziness this bestowed on defining the brand of democracy championed by democrats was compounded by how capitalist economic development under the alleged "communist" CPP confounded political labeling. In the words of Tioulong Saumura:

> You cannot position us within the framework of the Western left and right scale. You can say that we are conservative, because we are happy with Buddhism being the state religion. [...] We are also liberal and capitalists, in our work for human rights, and in supporting a market economy. We see profit as the engine for human as well as economic development. You could also say that we are also socialist, in that we champion social justice—the reallocation of the fruit of economic growth on a social basis, which liberals and the most extreme right-wing would not like, and we champion workers' rights.[151]

As much political contestation has come to revolve around the degree of state intervention in the market, the CPP has declared the democrats to be interventionist and, by extension, socialist or even communist. Former BLDP Vice President Ieng Mouly, turned CPP senior minister, remarked: "We are all capitalists. We either have capitalism with state intervention, or laissez-faire capitalism. It is now HRP and SRP that think that the state should intervene more. The old communists support laissez faire more, because some of them are rich."[152] Hun Sen has intermittently insinuated that Sam Rainsy's accusations that the CPP-led regime is communist ought to apply to himself, as Sam Rainsy is the one to suggest that the state should interfere in the free market through centralized price-setting.[153]

This quasi-socialist identity was hesitantly adopted. Several SRP leaders described the party as reluctantly socialist, solely because the CPP-led government had failed its task of providing for the populace. The discussion about political labels is significant because it shows that democrats consider that contesting fundamentals has distorted the political landscape to the extent that Western-derived notions could not be applied without qualification.[154] Consequently, the opposition had to correct fundamentals before moving on with a further agenda. Asked to define the party identity of the SRP, MP Son Chhay replied:

> It is so difficult to answer, because we are missing a kind of responsibility of the CPP, because of government corruption. Protecting and taking care of farmers,

---

[151] Author's interview with Tioulong Saumura.

[152] Author's interview with Ieng Mouly.

[153] Compare to: Hun Sen, "Selected Comments at the Graduation and Presentation of Diploma to the Graduates from the Asia–Europe Institute"; Hun Sen, "First Cambodian Bio Energy's Ethanol Factory," *Cambodia New Vision* 129, November 2008.

[154] Recognizing the potential diversity of tendencies within the SRP, once fundamentals had been established, Son Chhay foresaw how, in the future, the SRP was likely to split into several groups, including socialists, liberals, and greens. These groups would represent different ways of democracy, according to Western "rules of the game." Chhay's prediction reflected an expectation of a Western-style political landscape in which develop, but necessarily out of the SRP, since other parties followed political logics that would not allow them to develop according to Western-style directions.

workers, and unions should be their task. To look at it, our party is kind of socialist then. But as a contrast, we are liberal in our approach.[155]

Far more serious than Western-derived political labeling, in terms of developing a political identity carrying domestic weight, was how to make the democratic project appear as something more than a protest movement. The CPP regularly accuses the democratic parties of having little more on their political agenda than simply criticizing the government. The focus on local grievances compounded the risk of the democrat project appearing fragmentary. It is in this context that the CPP strategy of pushing opposition parties to rename themselves after their party leaders should be understood, as this made them appear personalistic. In 1998, Sam Rainsy lost the name "Khmer Nation Party" to his then (pro-CPP) deputy Kong Mony by a court order, and thereafter Rainsy's party adopted the name "Sam Rainsy Party" to avoid losing another party name in the future.[156] In a parallel fashion, the BLDP party name was claimed by two rival factions from 1995 until, according to Keat Sokun, CPP Minister of Interior Sar Kheng suggested to rename it the "Son Sann Party" ahead of the 1998 elections.[157] While the name change worked better for the SRP than it did for the already moribund Son Sann Party (in terms of bringing party stability), SRP party officials were conscious of its disadvantage—it made the party appear "undemocratic" to foreign observers and marginalized to the domestic electorate.[158] Sam Rainsy has tried to counter this by making a point of invoking his name as a stand-in for national values. Discussing the rise in support for the SRP in the 2012 senate elections, Sam Rainsy remarked:

> Hun Sen had been told by his advisors that the SRP with Sam Rainsy abroad would go down the drain, the party would just disintegrate, because they thought the SRP was a one-man show. [...] But the senate elections are a demonstration that the party holds well, and that there are millions of Sam Rainsys in Cambodia. A Sam Rainsy is any person who believes in the values we are talking about—the desire for freedom, the desire for justice, and the desire for human dignity.[159]

The democratic opposition parties have consistently had to counter perceptions of themselves as the factional groupings of single individuals. In contrast, the very name of the CPP purports to represent the Cambodian people. Little wonder, then, that uniting in one party political vehicle in 2013, the democrats would choose the name of Cambodian National Rescue Party. As noted by Sebastian Strangio, the party name echoes that of the Kampuchean United Front for National Salvation, the precursor to the CPP that toppled Democratic Kampuchea in 1979.[160] By choosing it, the CNRP makes a rival claim to represent the Cambodian general populace, and

---

[155] Author's interview with Son Chhay.

[156] Roberts, *Political Transition in Cambodia 1991–99*, 176–77.

[157] Ibid., 178; and author's interview with Keat Sokun.

[158] To counter this, party officials frequently volunteer to explain the change of party name. Compare this to, for example, the author's interviews with Yim Sovann, Thach Setha, and Uch Serey Yuth, all of whom volunteered to explain the change of party name.

[159] Author's interview with Sam Rainsy.

[160] Sebastian Strangio, *Hun Sen's Cambodia* (New Haven: Yale University Press, 2014), 123.

provides an alternative version not only of who the nation's savior is—but also who it is that the nation needs to be saved from.

NATION, RELIGION, KING: TRANSFORMING POST-RESISTANCE IDENTITIES

The democratic identity in the KOC was articulated in a process intertwined with ideas of the appropriate role of the Cambodian monarchy; in this way, it developed in tandem with royalist ideas. Never straightforwardly correlated with a royalist or republican stance, the tension between limiting the powers of the monarchy and at the same time defending it has run through the democratic project throughout the post-independence period. As successors to a shared civil war resistance identity, this tension continued into the KOC when democrats and royalists came together in a joint democratic opposition identity over the contestation of fundamentals. Yet democratic and royalist identities also developed in different directions, cementing themselves as two separate discourses in novel ways. Restricting prospects for cooperation, this would ultimately work out to the disadvantage of royalists.

Under the PRK, the KPNLF and FUNCINPEC, operating outside the country, were, although maintaining separate political identities, united in their shared anticommunist, anti-Vietnamese agenda that subsumed differences under an overarching resistance identity. In the KOC, political party contestation continued to center on a conflict over fundamentals, revolving around contending interpretations of the constitution and electoral organization.[161] The civil war resistance identity was transformed into a shared democratic opposition identity, uniting the opposition now competing under royalist and democratic banners when there was the perception that those fundamental "rules of the game" had been violated, such as following the 1997 violent overthrow of First PM Ranariddh, and repeatedly following national elections.[162] Royalists shared the core "democratic" starting points, outlined above, which upheld the PPA and constitution as a yet-to-be-implemented framework for national politics. Yet, as has been argued, there was also a rift among royalists between those who stressed a distinct role for the monarchy and royalists, and those who identified more closely with a democratic opposition identity.

It would be misguided to take the shared focus on fundamentals to equate the projects of democrats and royalists, even in the limited context of these demands. Even while fighting over the same democratic "rules," in terms of contending interpretations of the constitution and electoral organization, this was argued by virtue of competing logics. By and large, royalists saw these shared concerns through a prism that, ultimately, assigned the monarchy the task of resolving the issues in this quandary. For democrats, the PPA had value as a framework that prepared for the drafting of the constitution and the establishment of a multiparty liberal democratic system. For royalists, the PPA primarily proved Sihanouk, as president of the Supreme National Council (SNC), to be the father of national

---

[161] Hughes, "Parties, Protest, and Pluralism in Cambodia," 167–68.

[162] The SRP, FUNCINPEC, and Son Sann Party jointly contested the 1998 elections results, and the SRP and FUNCINPEC contested the 2003 elections together, resulting in the creation of the "Alliance of Democrats." In 2008 and 2013, the dynamics were different, as FUNCINPEC was by then under strong CPP influence.

conciliation, without whom the contending factions could not have been reunited, and subsequent elections not held.

The shared contestation over fundamentals is best understood as but the latest reimagining of an essentially ambiguous relationship between the democrats and the Cambodian monarchy. From the outset, while democratic discourse targeted the power of an absolute monarchy, it has been a parallel, potentially compatible discourse to that of royalism, which, in its centrist articulations, envisaged the monarchy, if strictly constitutional, as part of its democratic project.[163] Following the ambiguities with which the Cambodian monarchy evolved (particularly Sihanouk's political dominance during Sangkum as an abdicated monarch), the Cambodian democrats' positioning vis-à-vis the monarchy developed in a similarly ambiguous fashion. In this process, the personal stance of Son Sann became particularly formative for democratic identity. A founder of the DP, Son Sann resigned from the party leadership following Sihanouk's 1952 coup, which overthrew the Democrat cabinet, and later joined the Sangkum upon its formation. Known to be scrupulously honest, Son Sann maintained an integrity that unnerved Sihanouk, who nonetheless appointed him to a series of governmental positions in successive Sangkum governments. Son Sann is generally understood to have been personally loyal to Sihanouk, sometimes distancing himself from the DP (which continued to operate until 1957 and again 1970-75) and in spite of his periods of estrangement from Sihanouk this appears to be an image he was eager to project.[164] During the PRK shared resistance, a wedge was driven between royalists and democrats by the fact that the KPNLF, headed by Son Sann, included former Republican activists who remained fervently anti-Sihanoukist, making up most of the cabinet and army.[165] The KPNLF was understood as a Republican movement by observers—and by Sihanouk as well.

It is beyond the scope of this chapter to assess the balance between those neutral to the monarchy and Republican tendencies in the KPNLF. What is of interest is the language employed by contemporary political actors, emanating from the KPNLF and involving the BLDP, HRP, FUNCINPEC, and NRP, when interpreting their past political involvement. While they vigorously attempted to downplay how many of them had moved back and forth between the democratic and royalist camps, the reinterpretations by different politicians also laid out the discursive boundaries they placed on democracy. First, former KPNLF leaders generally refer back to the KPNLF political identity as "democratic." In their accounts, Son Sann remained unfailingly loyal to Sihanouk throughout the civil

---

[163] While the DP center supported a constitutional monarchy, the party also incorporated anti-royalist rightist and leftist elements.

[164] Son Sann, who had served as Sihanouk's minister in 1951–68, offered to mediate between Sihanouk and Lon Nol during the Khmer Republic, although this never came to pass. Upon Son Sann's death in 2000, a state funeral was held, attended by Sihanouk.

[165] While the movement was riveted by internal divisions, the 1985 split between Son Sann and Sak Sutsakhan was not primarily a conflict of a Republican versus a Sihanoukist group, as understood by some, but instead appears to have been rooted in personal conflicts of interest. To a limited extent, the split also went back to how some felt that Son Sann had orchestrated the 1952 coup de force against then Prime Minister Huy Kanthoul. Regardless of the cause of the original split, when this crystallized into a 1993 split between the Liberal Democratic Party (LDP) under Sak Sutsakhan and the BLDP under Son Sann, most of those who joined the LDP were young returnees from France and the United States who leaned toward republicanism. Author's interviews with Ieng Mouly, Dien Del, Huy Vora, and Keat Sokun.

war—even the creation of the KPNLF allegedly came about with the intention of handing over the movement to Sihanouk.[166] The former leadership claims that the Republican image of the KPNLF was orchestrated by external actors, and it did not even know why the KPNLF was perceived as Republican throughout the civil war.[167] Second, "democratic" was not taken to entail a predetermined choice between royalism and Republicanism. While the group that previously surrounded Son Sann continued to stress the compatibility between democracy and the constitutional monarchy, the former Republican-leaning elements argued the same compatibility between being a democrat and a Republican. In both cases, these actors claim to have been "democratic" by following popular preference.[168] For democrats supportive of the monarchy, their emphasis on "democracy" meant that their support of the monarchy was derived from following popular opinion, rather than unconditional support of the monarchy *per se*. Republicans, on the other hand, explained their stance in terms of the monarchy lacking popular support.

This reasoning was also offered to account for political action in the Second Kingdom. When the Son Sann Party dissolved to merge with FUNCINPEC, an important reason for the merger was the shared resistance background called on again following the July 1997 events, which made it critically important to take sides between Hun Sen and Ranariddh. Assumed popular support for the monarchy was also a crucial consideration, quoted by previously staunch Republicans joining camps with the royalists.[169] Former Republican general and cofounder of the KPNLF, Dien Del, having joined FUNCINPEC and later the Norodom Ranariddh Party, justified his moves by how noncommunist nationalism now necessarily meant a union between democrats and royalists, given strong popular support for the monarchy.[170] In such statements, the imperative of following the popular will was indistinguishable from strategic calculations. They also reflected former Republicans' easier acceptance of a weakened monarchy, which was further facilitated by Sihamoni's 2004 ascension to the throne which gave Cambodia a strictly constitutional monarch. Their republicanism was made out, perhaps reinvented, as primarily anti-Sihanoukist, rather than anti-monarchical *per se*.

---

[166] Author's interviews with Son Soubert and Ieng Mouly.

[167] Author's interviews with Son Soubert, Ieng Mouly. and Dien Del. Particularly, the date of proclamation of the KPNLF on October 9, the date of proclamation of the Khmer Republic, was, in hindsight, believed to have given Sihanouk the wrong signal. According to Son Soubert, it was their Thai hosts who made the group proclaim the creation of the front on October 9, 1979, after having refused it on October 5, Son Sann's birthday. Son Soubert claimed this to have been orchestrated by the international community, wanting to set up the resistance in such a way as to be able to rely on people from as many different backgrounds as possible. According to Son Soubert, Son Sann never understood why Sihanouk thought the KNPLF to be "Republican" rather than "democratic," and it was not until after Son Sann's death that Sihanouk alerted Soubert to this issue. Yet Republicans in the KPNLF were certainly aware of the symbolic significance of the date. According to Dien Del, former Republican prime minister In Tam, who rejoined Sihanouk after 1979, purposely informed Sihanouk about the day of the creation of the KPNLF to make him distrustful of the front.

[168] Author's interviews with Kem Sokha and Dien Del. Admittedly, such statements by former Republicans who had defected to royalist parties could be seen as a later invention to justify their changing allegiance. Yet arguably, the very language they chose to employ is significant in the distinction they establish between "democratic" and "Republican."

[169] Author's interviews with Huy Vora and Dien Del.

[170] Author's interview with Dien Del.

By the same token, this set of political actors evaluated royalist parties as either democratic or non-democratic, based on their perceived extent of representation of and responsiveness to grassroots voices. Son Soubert outlined the difference among different royalist projects as follows:

> FUNCINPEC is not democratic—it does not work from the base, it does not listen to the grassroots. If royalists are democratic—then they are ok. Some royalists are democratic, not all. We have to go along *in the way of the people*. Prince Thomico is a democrat. Sihanouk was a democrat when he set up the National Congress.[171]

The ties between royalists and democrats thus reflected lasting bonds from the resistance, thought to constitute a shared identity variously conceptualized as "democratic" or "nationalist." The close interaction between Prince Thomico's Sangkum Jatiniyum Front Party and the group of former BLDP leaders before the establishment of HRP is one such example of a strong connection.[172] The blurring between royalists and democrats was evident in the fluidity between the factions, which was also found at the level of the top leadership. Kem Sokha joined the BLDP rather than FUNCINPEC, statedly because Son Sann (and not Ranariddh) accepted his request to meet.[173] Meanwhile, Sam Rainsy and his close associates came out of FUNCINPEC. Conversely, several of the royalists who remained close to the democratic parties had belonged to the KPNLF and/or sided with the Khmer Republic, and now returned to the royalist side of the divide—perhaps out of a newborn sense of family loyalty. The fact that previous staunch Republicans joined them also testifies to the strength of shared resistance identities, relative to forging links with a new generation of democrats dominating the SRP.[174]

The SRP shifted the democratic identity to one that was more openly in conflict with that of the royalists. The decline of trust between the SRP and FUNCINPEC followed its own distinct trajectory, mirroring power machinations between Ranariddh and Hun Sen. When Ranariddh called off the Alliance of Democrats in 2004 to re-enter a coalition government with the CPP, trust was fundamentally ruined, marking the end of prospects for cooperation; this was later compounded when Ranariddh agreed to have Sam Rainsy exiled. When, in 2006, Sam Rainsy, after being allowed back in Cambodia, signed the constitutional amendment requiring a simple majority rather than a two-thirds majority to pass laws in the National Assembly, this was understood as his revenge against Ranariddh.

---

[171] Author's interview with Son Soubert.

[172] According to Keat Sokun, the SJFP was set up by Thomico as a party to be taken over by Ranariddh, and changed into the Norodom Ranariddh Party. Ranariddh wanted Son Soubert or Keat Sokun to act as vice president and they were both initially involved in the party, but when it became evident that the SJFP had failed, they decided instead to support Kem Sokha in setting up the HRP.

[173] Author's interview with Kem Sokha.

[174] In the KOC, there have been some attempts at commemorating the shared resistance heritage. This has included a yearly commemoration at a stupa in Kien Svay district, Kandal province, where the names of KPNLF fighters who fell during the resistance are inscribed. But see also Brendan Brady and Kouth Sophak Chakrya, "KPNLF Commemoration: Former Resistance Leaders Stand by Antagonism towards Vietnamese," *Phnom Penh Post*, March 6, 2009.

Similar to the group around Son Sann, Sam Rainsy's political views did not differ greatly from royalists who identified closely with a shared democratic agenda.[175] Yet the attitudes of SRP members differed from the Son Sann group. A majority became politically involved specifically because of their support for Sam Rainsy's agenda. They associated more closely with global liberal democratic identities than the former resistance did, and, in this spirit, they supported a constitutional monarchy along Western European lines. Political royalism seemed outdated to them, and they treated such an idea with disinterest.

The single most important factor shaping the SRP's (and now CNRP's) relationship to royalists was Sam Rainsy's family's tormented relationship to Sihanouk. Both Sam Rainsy's and Tioulong Saumura's fathers—Sam Sary and Nhiek Tioulong—had been close allies of Sihanouk, and their families were closely socially linked with the royal family.[176] A prominent politician and deputy prime minister in Sihanouk's government in the 1950s, Sam Sary suffered a fall from grace and became embroiled in a public confrontation with Sihanouk, a conflict that would seal his fate. Most likely recruited by Thai anti-Sihanouk interests, Sary escaped underground to join the Republican "Khmer Serei," led by Son Ngoc Thanh, and then disappeared. Royalists have understood Sam Rainsy to blame Sihanouk for his father's disappearance and death, privately citing Rainsy's perceived vindictive ulterior motives to preclude any closer cooperation.[177] The extent to which this hampered contemporary collaboration was made apparent by Sihanouk's attempts to restore Sam Sary's reputation when trying to unite the opposition. In April 2003, ahead of national elections, Sihanouk released a royal communiqué referring to the incident that caused Sam Sary's fall of grace as a misunderstanding; in it, he called Sam Sary "a great and genuine patriot" who had given proud service to Sihanouk and the nation during the first years of Sihanouk's reign and of Sangkum.[178] Royalist suspicions of lingering rancor appeared to be confirmed by the publication of Sam Rainsy's 2008 autobiography, *Des Racines dans la Pierre* (Rooted in Stone), which was sharply critical of Sihanouk. In the book, Rainsy tried to restore his father's reputation, and outlined his father's painful quest to placate a relentless Sihanouk. He described how his father's escape could not contain Sihanouk's fury, and how Sihanouk continued to persecute the family, forced Rainsy's grandfather and uncle to resign from politics, and imprisoned Sam Rainsy's mother before having the whole family thrown out of Cambodia in 1965.[179] "Too much power can become

---

[175] Sam Rainsy and Norodom Sirivudh had been ousted at the same time in 1995, and maintained friendly links. It was Norodom Sirivudh who proposed the 2003 "Alliance of Democrats" between the SRP and FUNCINPEC. As noted, Sisowath Thomico, Tioulong Saumura, and Sam Rainsy had also militated together against the Khmer Rouge.

[176] To name but some examples, Ketty Tioulong, Saumura's sister, married Norodom Chakrapong (Sihanouk's son) in 1965. Sam Emmarane, Rainsy's sister, danced in the Royal Ballet and served as a lady-in-waiting at Suramarit's coronation.

[177] Author's interviews.

[178] See letter from Norodom Sihanouk, April 26, 2003, in Sam Emmarane, *Cambodge: Histoire d'une Vengeance Royale (1958–1965)* (Paris: Thélès, 2009), 14. A second letter from Sihanouk, dated April 28, 2003 (ibid., 14–15), confirms the important role played by Sam Sary in the Royal Crusade for Independence (1952–53), the Geneva Conference of 1954, and the first years of Sangkum, and concludes with Sihanouk's intention to give Sam Sary justice for all he had done for the nation and for Sangkum.

[179] Sam, *Des Racines dans la Pierre*, 52–56, 43. For Sihanouk's account of the "London incident," see *Réalités Cambodgiennes*, January 20, 1959, partly reproduced in Sam, *Cambodge*, 57.

perversity," Rainsy concluded.[180] His later assessment in his 2013 autobiography, *We Didn't Start the Fire*, that it was not Sihanouk who ordered Sam Sary killed, but Son Ngoc Thanh—who intercepted letters from Sam Sary to Sihanouk seeking reconciliation—would only appear after Sihanouk's death.[181]

Rainsy's sister Emmarane took an even tougher stance in her 2009 book, *Cambodge: Histoire d'une Vengeance Royale (1958-65)* (Cambodia: Story of a Royal Revenge (1958-65)), in which she set out to map Sam Sary's fall from grace and the horrific consequences for his family. The principal cause of Cambodia's tragic recent history, she argued, was the participation of Sihanouk in national politics, particularly his claim to incarnate Cambodia and personify the nation.[182] Her assessment of the Sangkum could hardly be more damning in its mockery:

> Once upon a time there was Cambodia, a country blessed by heaven, where everyone could live happily and where everyone knew that the price to pay was to ignore the political and social problems of the country. There reigned a skillful and charismatic Prince. A demagogue, he practiced toward his people politics marked by *paternalisme bon enfant*. A majority of the people were peasants with little education and used only to hearing the prince, whom they venerated like a God-King and gave the name Samdech Euv (Monseigneur Papa). He vested himself with sacred, personal, and political power, which provoked a vivid reaction from the intellectual elite of the country. To channel it, he created the Sangkum Reastr Niyum (People's Socialist Community) destined to be the only political party, born of the dissolution of others, except the Democratic Party and Pracheachon. The opponents of the princely regime were thrown into prison or subject to intimidations. He showed his faith in Buddha, but to his adversaries he ignored magnanimity and compassion taught by our Master.[183]

Emmarane's book, like Rainsy's first one, was taken by royals as proof of how inflamed the question of Sam Sary's fall from grace and subsequent death remained for the Sam family. They confirmed royalist suspicion of the Sam family to be anti-royalist, finalizing a rift between SRP-brand democratic and royalist identities.

The SRP, and now CNRP, advocates a constitutional monarchy, while remaining largely silent on any royal mandate beyond this.[184] Their debates on what a constitutional monarchy looks like are fundamentally tied up with their relations with royalists. In *Des Racines dans la Pierre*, Sam Rainsy reappraised his father as a consistent supporter of a *constitutional monarchy*—thereby dismissing allegations of republicanism, and claiming a pro-monarchist heritage. Rainsy set out to prove that Sam Sary remained resolutely loyal to the constitutional monarchy until his death. Rather than against the monarchy as such, Sary's criticisms were directed at Sihanouk's "antidemocratic" stance, that is, his near-personalistic rule during the

---

[180] Sam, *Des Racines dans la Pierre*, 58–59.

[181] Sam Rainsy, *We Didn't Start the Fire: My Struggle for Democracy in Cambodia* (Chiangmai: Silkworm Books, 2013), 21.

[182] Sam, *Cambodge*, 70–71.

[183] Ibid., 15–16.

[184] Out of the SRP's "100 Measures," only number five mentions the monarchy, advocating a national congress presided over by the king. The ten principles remain silent on the topic. The CNRP's seven points do not refer to the monarchy.

Sangkum when the national congress and Buddhist socialism outflanked parliamentary democracy. Instead, Sary envisaged Cambodia as a real parliamentary democracy and a constitutional monarchy along the lines of Thailand or Great Britain—the key to which was forming an opposition loyal to the crown.[185] An exit by the king from politics would confer upon him "a great symbolical, immutable power for the whole nation" and make him a unanimously respected, suprapolitical arbiter of conflicts.[186] In fact, Sary was said to have sought to ensure the survival of the monarchy through diversifying its basis of support beyond that of the personal popularity of Sihanouk, by educating young royals to enable them to take on leadership roles based on their formation, rather than birthright.[187]

Yet the meaning of constitutional monarchy was not straightforward in the KOC. Supporting a constitutional monarchy in its early days primarily meant defending the very existence of the *reintroduced* monarchy, and this was high on both FUNCINPEC's and the BLDP's (as the then-democratic alternative) agendas. Yet the contours of this constitutional monarchy were always fuzzy. Most crucially, while royalists pledged their support of the reintroduced constitutional monarchy, they did not envisage it limiting their political involvement, as argued above. Whereas a more purely constitutional monarchy has been in place since Sihamoni's 2004 ascension to the throne, the CPP pushed the idea of a "constitutional monarchy" further increasingly vocally from 2006 onwards, to include the overall end of royals' political involvement. The CPP's call for a bill to bar royals from politics and make them politically neutral to ensure that they would enjoy the respect of the people was supported by Sam Rainsy, who referred to an international model of constitutional monarchy—underscoring his fundamental suspicion of royal involvement in politics.[188]

Reassessing his father as an advocate of constitutional monarchy is thus in accord with Sam Rainsy's contemporary objective to limit the political mandate of royals, argued on pro-monarchic grounds. Rainsy's claim that Sary, after his fall from Sihanouk's grace, represented the democratic opposition, made Rainsy the direct successor to his agenda. This is part of a competing national historiography to the Sihanoukist one, which emphasizes the importance of the 1954 Geneva conference over Sihanouk's Royal Crusade for Independence in achieving national

---

[185] Sam, *Des Racines dans la Pierre*, 47.

[186] According to Sam Emmarane, Sam Sary opposed Sihanouk's political influence since he considered Sihanouk to be king even *after* his abdication. See Sam, *Cambodge*, 19.

[187] From a 1959 letter from Sam Sary to Sihanouk quoted by Emmarane, in which Sary argues for giving princes a special education that will replace the inequality of birth with their superior intellectual and moral formation. He pleads with Sihanouk: "Your present politics builds the prestige of the monarchy only on your personal popularity without a solid and durable base. Father of independence, don't be the destroyer of the monarchy." See Sam, *Cambodge*, 223.

[188] Sam Rainsy stated that: "I want to see Cambodia with a strong and noble monarchy respected by all people. [...] I want Cambodia to have a monarchy like in Thailand, Spain, Belgium, Sweden, Netherlands, Norway, Denmark, Japan and so on. In those countries their people pay very high respect to the monarch and to the royal family. However, most countries have a stipulation for this respect—members of the royal family are not involved in politics. [...] For people to respect the royal family, the royal family must not participate in politics. If you want people to look to you as the symbol of national reconciliation and national dignity you must not dabble in politics." See "Cambodian Opposition Joins Calls For Royalty To Quit Politics," *DPA*, October 4, 2006.

independence.[189] Sam Rainsy has drawn attention to how his father, as a representative at the Geneva conference, was one of the main architects of Cambodian independence.[190] This further points back to a common legacy between Sam Sary and Nhiek Tioulong as "artisans of national independence" who sat together at the negotiation table at the Geneva conference, before "marching together for more than twenty years"—something Sam Rainsy underlines in his autobiography. In this vein, some SRP (now CNRP) MPs trace their party ideas from Sam Sary and Nhiek Tioulong:

> I think the ideas of the party came from Sam Sary and Nhiek Tioulong, through Sam Rainsy and Tioulung Saumura. They have similar biographies and objectives. At the moment we are just taking their ideas. Both tried for independence from the French colonisers. Maybe Nhiek Tioulong was too loyal to king Sihanouk. Sam Sary was freer.[191]

SRP and now CNRP identity is strongly defined by contemporary realities, prioritized over establishing continuity with earlier political projects, and this particular historiography has not been widely disseminated. Still, an understated yet pervasive self-perception among the party leadership contrasts its democratic agenda with a Sihanoukist one.

DEMOCRACY AS A CORE OF CAMBODIAN POLITICAL DISCOURSE

This chapter has sketched a different layout of the democratic discursive field in contemporary Cambodia than is generally understood by scholars and observers, by examining how discourses of democracy conflate popular and national representation. It challenges the dominant understandings: that the CPP mainly pays halfhearted lip service to liberal democratic values, and that the democratic opposition carries out double-faced politics, embracing democratic tendencies on the one hand and ultra-nationalist ones on the other. This chapter reorients these understandings by showing how the CPP-led regime and democrats alike have launched democratic discourses that fuse democracy as representation of the people and of the nation.

This suggests that the nexus between democracy as representation of the people and the nation may be understood as a sort of core of contemporary political discourse, which can be employed as a prism for bids to political representation, rather than "ideology" *per se*. Populism under Hun Sen can be understood as a "supraideology," which transcends appeals to other political ideologies and identities. Meanwhile, democrats do not primarily conceptualize their political project in terms of ideology, but in more fundamental terms of salvaging democracy and the nation. This highlights difficulties in Slocomb's branding of the post-1985 era (when Hun Sen ascended to the post as PM) as "post-ideological," contrasting

---

[189] Still, the KNP was founded on November 9, the day of independence from France in 1953 that concluded the Royal Crusade for Independence.

[190] Sam, *Des Racines dans la Pierre*, preface. Emmarane also emphasized Sam Sary's role in the 1954 Geneva conference. Sam, *Cambodge*, preface.

[191] Author's interview with Kong Korm.

sharply with a previous era of "ideology" (1955–84).[192] There are important similarities in regime projects both before and after this divide, anchored in the continued centrality of this nexus. Hun Sen's notion of "people's democracy" is not dissimilar from Sihanouk's Buddhist socialism. Both notions served to equate the leader with the nation and with democracy. Largely self-justifying, both were primarily what Sihanouk and Hun Sen defined them as. One could argue that only the language of ideology is missing from Hun Sen's brand; yet even Sihanouk, in his days, was suspicious of the label "ideology."

The self-professed CPP-regime identity under Hun Sen builds on notions of democracy and the nation, to which that of revolution can be added. These three notions serve as a bridge from the Marxism–Leninism of the PRK era to the KOC, in which a socialist identity has been abandoned, and large-scale capitalist transformation is under way. While "people's democracy" bestows continuity in terms of positing democracy as the goal of what Hun Sen has referred to as a 130-year-old Cambodian revolution, today carried on by the CPP, it serves to substitute the previous Marxist–Leninist identity, yet retains a dialectic analysis of changing contradictions in society. This revolutionary democratic language is adapted to confront new challenges posed by the monarchy (through a discourse of equal opportunity), and a changing political economy (through opposing "feudal" forms of democracy said to be practiced by capitalists, while themselves engaging in capitalist development). People's democracy serves to guarantee that the regime can retain an identity distinct from Western liberal democracies.

The democrats do not differ from the incumbent regime in tying democracy to popular and national representation, but only in the way that they do so. Since both the Cambodian nation and democracy are considered to be aching under mutating communism, they have but one and the same cure. The cure's composition, however, has been problematized by a number of factors. Identifying the will of the people has been difficult, given the democrat leaders' elite and transnational backgrounds, and lack of everyday closeness that the CPP-dominated local state enjoys. Regime ideological and material domination is perceived to have distorted elections to the point that these have not been representative of the people's will. While local grievances are considered manifestations of a larger victimization of the nation, democrats have been susceptible to appearing as a protest movement without a national agenda. This is compounded by the way democrats also imagine themselves to be locked in a struggle larger than one between competing "ideologies," calling for a more basic change in popular mentalities. Moreover, the creation of democratic identity through tracing a democratic genealogy was never a priority, at the same time as the democrat identity has increasingly evolved to contest political royalism. This set of problems and tensions has permeated democratic claims to national representation.

---

[192] Slocomb, "The Nature and Role of Ideology in the Modern Cambodian State," 388.

CHAPTER FIVE

REASSESSING POLITICAL CONTESTATION IN THE KINGDOM OF CAMBODIA

During the two decades following the Paris Peace Agreements, Cambodian political parties remained locked in bitter conflict as they refused to recognize each other as legitimate contenders. The 1991 PPA was intended to transform the military conflicts of the civil war into an amicable political competition within a multiparty framework, with elections serving as the basis for collegial power-sharing. This effort, a veritable political "shotgun wedding," failed.[1] Multiparty politics have instead exacerbated conflicts of identity, leading political parties to mobilize around politicized identities.[2] Meanwhile, political parties do not primarily phrase their programs using the language of ideology, and policy differences between parties are obscure to voters.[3]

This book sheds new light on the continuous failure of Cambodian political parties to reconcile. Ever since the 1993 reintroduction of a multiparty democratic system, Cambodian politics revolves around a contestation concerning different articulations of the nation. To make politics mean something in post-PPA Cambodia, all political party actors have turned to the nation as the most important part of the answer. Competing constructions of the nation and its representation define political identities. The diverse projects that they advocate all appeal to an overarching Cambodian national identity, thought to unite the populace in the "deep, horizontal comradeship" of an "imagined community."[4] Yet, political actors equate the nation exclusively with their own political projects, so that the "imagined communities" they advance are rival ones. These imagined communities are elite declared, supposed, and desired versions of the Khmer nation. They are *competing* communities insofar as each strives to make a particular understanding of the characteristics and contours of the nation hegemonic; they are *unfinished* insofar as they are continuously subject to practices of reimagination of their particular histories. Rather than a battle over ideology or policy platforms, contestation over national representation involves questions of embodiment and incarnation; of the elected leader versus genealogy and the moral requirements of leadership.

---

[1] Croissant, "The Perils and Promises of Democratization through United Nations Transitional Authority," 661; and Roberts, *Political Transition in Cambodia 1991–99*, 47.

[2] Hughes, "Parties, Protest, and Pluralism in Cambodia," 167.

[3] Un, "Patronage Politics and Hybrid Democracy," 222; and Öjendal and Lilja, "The Never-Ending Hunt for Political Legitimacy in a Post-Conflict Context," in Öjendal and Lilja, *Beyond Democracy in Cambodia*, 303.

[4] Anderson, *Imagined Communities*, 7.

This reassessment of political contestation in the KOC has important consequences on a number of levels. I explore these below, first, with regard to the implications for reassessing internal legitimizations, the role and status of elections, democratic debates, and how these have provided resources and constraints on Cambodia's democratization. Second, I assess the implications for tracing continuity and change in Cambodian elite-level political imaginings, and place the ways in which these transformed from the PRK era in relation to changing political realities. Third, I discuss how this leads us to reconsider the very categories in which political contestation takes place, by examining contemporary ideas of ideology, doctrine, and embodiment. This is followed by a discussion on the popular appeal and acceptance of these elite-level imaginings. In conclusion, implications from a Southeast Asian perspective are drawn out.

LEGITIMACY, DISCOURSES OF DEMOCRACY, AND CAMBODIA'S DEMOCRATIZATION

Many international policymakers continue to assume that holding elections with proper procedures of electioneering is the hallmark of internal legitimacy.[5] Cambodia proves this assumption to be wrong: elections alone were not sufficient to settle questions of internal legitimacy. All competing political party actors within the electoral framework turned to strategies of establishing unique bonds with the nation as the ultimate means of legitimation. While this served to mobilize votes and thereby ensure success within the electoral framework, it also served as an alternative basis of legitimation that went beyond the electoral process *per se*.

The contending sources of legitimacy all aspired to be "democratic" in the sense that they were firmly integrated into contending democratic imaginings and phrased in the language of democracy (*pracheathipatey*). This state of affairs brings us to reassess Cambodian political debates. Cambodian political parties did not merely pay occasional lip service to liberal democracy, while deviating from it in practice. They also advanced alternative articulations of democracy. While these discourses certainly addressed and had a crucial bearing on notions and issues contained in liberal democratic discourse, they were also engaged in a parallel debate over the proper organization of national society and the ideal relationship between the people and the political leadership. The SRP and FUNCINPEC, Hughes has noted, have denied the CPP the status of an equally "democratic" contender, and refused to admit the CPP into the legitimizing "democratic" arena.[6] The above case studies show that flaunting a democratic identity was so crucial that Hun Sen and the CPP also constructed their own so-called democratic arena, inaccessible to political contenders, to retain distinctiveness and legitimacy. Moreover, in spite of intermittent attempts by some to create a common arena, the SRP (now CNRP) and FUNCINPEC ended up creating largely separate ones, each casting their own political project as the only truly democratic one. The reshaping of democratic identities was a more far-ranging and important dynamic than hitherto believed.

Since political parties turned to the nation to imbue politics with meaning, they all relied on democratic imaginings that were tied up with national ones. Each of these discourses referred to national imaginings that accorded their own political party or party actors a unique role in fulfilling the nation's democratic aspirations. This can be understood as a consequence of how the KOC era has been at least

---

[5] Hughes, "Reconstructing Legitimate Political Authority through Elections?" 32.

[6] Hughes, "Transforming Oppositions in Cambodia," 302.

nominally democratic. Political imaginings were therefore readily phrased in the language of democracy. Another reason goes further into the national project, and relates to how national imaginings define the political community, the boundaries of which any democracy needs to establish. National and democratic imaginings, therefore, readily partner. As Michael Mann has shown, the conflation of the popular masses and the nation spread worldwide with ideas of democracy.[7] This book shows that, in contemporary Cambodia, the main political parties, in line with a historical pattern, share a largely organic conception of society, making the people out as an undifferentiated mass. This view of Cambodian society is in resonance with the Andersonian imagined community characterized by a sense of deep, horizontal comradeship. By characterizing the nation in this way, contemporary competing political parties have been able to claim to represent a homogenous, indivisible people. Each party, however, claimed to represent the people in a vastly different manner. The CPP's notion of people's democracy assumed the uniform needs and desires of the people. While this could have been unsettled by parallel notions of social mobility, those notions rather served to reverse the hierarchical order, although a hierarchy nonetheless remained in place. An organic conception of the people underlay the royalist portrayal of the people as one body, indivisible from the monarchy, which enabled the embodiment of the people—also by Hun Sen. Democrats, in turn, separated the population into different interest groups, but nevertheless assumed that the will of the people was harmoniously consonant. This assumption was doubtlessly aided by the fact that the democrats represented a nation with hazy contours still coming into its own, rather than one that was fully formed.

Charting these domestic political discourses is not an idle intellectual exercise, but helps to reframe ongoing political change in Cambodia. The bulk of scholarship on Cambodia's political development employs democracy as a stable benchmark following universal understandings of what democracy entails, in order to analyze Cambodia's democratization following the introduction of a multiparty democratic system—in particular, why liberal democracy has failed to consolidate.[8] The domestic elite imaginings discussed in this book, however, provide both resources and constraints to political change in Cambodia, which help put these debates into perspective. The shared "organic" view of the people arguably underlies political party leaders' views of democracy as what Hughes has called "comprising the co-optation of the broader population into elite-determined political trajectories."[9] The national articulations associated with the incumbent CPP corresponded to actual practice, as it was linked to the de facto curbing of royal power, at the same time as the notion of "people's democracy" addressed real practices of regime–people interactions. The national articulations by royalists and democrats, in turn, defined the nature and boundaries of their demands for "democratic reform."

---

[7] Mann, *The Dark Side of Democracy*, 2.

[8] See, for example: Brown and Timberman, ed., *Cambodia and the International Community*; Karbaum, "Cambodia's Façade Democracy and European Assistance"; Croissant, "The Perils and Promises of Democratization through United Nations Transitional Authority"; Peou, *Intervention and Change in Cambodia*; Roberts, *Political Transition in Cambodia 1991–99*; Sanderson and Maley, "Elections and Liberal Democracy in Cambodia"; and Un, "State, Society, and Democratic Consolidation."

[9] Hughes, *The Political Economy of Cambodia's Transition*, 126.

If democratic legitimacy is considered in terms of procedural democratic legitimacy, these bids for legitimacy were not democratic. Different political party actors did seek to harness legitimacy to ensure success within the electoral framework. Yet their legitimizing discourses cannot be said to add up to procedural democratic legitimacy. This is not, primarily, because of their content. Discourses that include ethnic chauvinism and stereotyping of insiders and outsiders of the national community are part of election campaigns worldwide. Rather, as noted by Hughes, whether these contending sources for legitimacy add up to, or are at least compatible with, procedural democratic legitimacy is a question of whether they are used to mobilize support *within* the confines of the election process or whether they are used to *trump* it.[10]

In Cambodia, contending sources for legitimacy have been employed by all political parties to undermine the legitimacy of electoral politics. This was not a straightforward rejection of the electoral process—a process that all political parties, indeed, gave support to in different ways. The CPP has, after all, decided to stick with elections, which remain crucially important for the party's (and Prime Minister Hun Sen's) legitimacy. Royalists and democrats, meanwhile, by regularly contesting election processes while claiming to advocate for more fair and free elections, clearly and publicly give value to the electoral process. Nonetheless, the preceding chapters have outlined an ambiguous relationship to elections across the political spectrum, compromising and attenuating the legitimacy of electoral politics. Through his reincarnation as Sdech Kân, Hun Sen replaces the ailing monarchy and plunges himself into a series of associations, ultimately representing the nation. While the narrative celebrates elected, non-hereditary leadership, it is firmly tied to the person of the prime minister, posited as the legitimate national leader by virtue of his personal merit, and is part of the personalization of symbolic and political power given to the prime minister. His leadership role can therefore be understood to be confirmed by, but is not reducible to, the legitimacy bestowed by elections. On their part, Ranariddh and other royalists have spoken out against representative democracy and the institution of the political party as a basic unit of popular representation. Ranariddh has criticized elections as the instrument of representative democracy, charging that these have scope only to the extent that they reflect a popular consensus. Democracy, here, stands to signify organic unity and national consensus, unfailingly tied to the Cambodian monarchy. The democrats, meanwhile, not only believe that electioneering practices are skewed and election results therefore biased, but, moreover, often charge that the people have been blinded to their real interests by CPP material and ideological domination. Therefore, while the intention of the democrats is to reform the electoral system, electoral reform alone has been deemed insufficient to achieve democratic representation. Meanwhile, their reading of the people's will has depended on their own efforts to identify the people's objective interests rather than on poll results. Support for the electoral process was therefore neither straightforward nor unconditional, but qualified, contingent, and derivative.

This analysis suggests a different interplay between external demands for democratization and the Cambodian domestic realm than is commonly understood. Changing perceptions and realities of democracy in the Cambodian context of post-conflict reconstruction are generally analyzed in terms of the Western-led

---

[10] Hughes, "Reconstructing Legitimate Political Authority through Elections?" 32.

democracy-building project, initiated in the early 1990s, which was, according to Öjendal and Lilja, largely "imposed, enforced, inserted, and disconnected" and, consequently, "to some extent artificial."[11] The discursive landscape laid out above manifests the contest over what democracy must mean in Cambodia today, which is not primarily representative of a process of "localization" of external demands for democratization. That the Western-led democracy-building project has by no means defined contemporary realities is a point made elsewhere by writers pointing to Cambodia's failure to achieve liberal democracy.[12] But the story does not end here. While faced with an international discourse in support of liberal democracy, with which they interacted in different ways, domestic actors contested the meaning and nature of democracy quite on their own terms. This shows an even greater discrepancy between liberal democratic language and domestic political party agendas. As repeatedly argued, Cambodian elites were not democrats at heart, in the sense that they did not endorse liberal democratic principles.[13] But neither did they purport to be. Yet democracy, articulated on quite different terms, remained an important language for negotiating political developments and change.

These domestic discourses also testify to the importance of moral claims in party political contestation in contemporary Cambodia. We know that politics, religion, and moral order are interwoven in Cambodia today.[14] So far, however, scholarship on processes to recover moral order in Cambodia has been mainly concerned with popular, rural imaginations, and the efforts by party political actors to reshape these have escaped serious attention.[15] A key assumption of the international community involved in the peace and democracy-building project in Cambodia was that elections would gradually erode different moral claims to power.[16] On the contrary, contending moral claims to power remain important within and beyond the multiparty electoral system. Hun Sen's challenging the royalist parties on moral grounds demonstrates a rivalry over a morally based political identity, shifting party political contestation to a moral arena. Suitability for national leadership is determined on moral grounds, which weighs heavier than results at the polls. The "remaking of moral worlds," which scholarship has traced in the aftermath of decades of violent conflict, thus goes straight to the heart of party political contestation.

CONTINUITY AND CHANGE

Accounting for (the lack of) democratic outcomes post-PPA, scholars have typically stressed that Cambodian political culture, understood to be based on absolutist notions of power, rigid social hierarchies, and patronage systems, is

---

[11] Öjendal and Lilja, *Beyond Democracy in Cambodia*, 2.

[12] Heder, "Political Theatre in the 2003 Cambodian Elections," 162.

[13] Ibid., 155; and Gainsborough, "Elites vs. Reform in Laos, Cambodia, and Vietnam," 38.

[14] See: Marston and Guthrie, ed., *History, Buddhism, and New Religious Movements in Cambodia*; Kent and Chandler, eds., *People of Virtue*; Harris, "Buddhist Sangha Groupings in Cambodia"; Kent, "Purchasing Power and Pagodas"; Heng, "The Scope and Limitations of Political Participation by Buddhist Monks"; Gyallay-Pap, "Reconstructing the Cambodian Polity"; and Edwards, "The Moral Geology of the Present."

[15] See, for example: Guthrie, "Khmer Buddhism, Female Asceticism, and Salvation"; Ledgerwood, "Buddhist Practice in Rural Kandal Province"; Satoru, "Reconstructing Buddhist Temple Buildings, and Zucker, "The Absence of Elders."

[16] Hughes, "Reconstructing Legitimate Political Authority through Elections?" 32.

unreceptive to and incompatible with Western-style democracy.[17] In these analyses, such phenomena—absolutist notions of power, rigid social hierarchies, and patronage systems—are typically considered to stem from a traditional conception of power. Martin Gainsborough identifies elite political culture as the most important factor (besides money politics) for the lack of commitment to liberal values in contemporary Cambodia, Vietnam, and Laos. Understanding elite political culture to be informed by elitism and paternalism, he argues that this impacts the character of elections in all three countries, where power holders "treat voting less as a contest of alternatives than as a chance for the citizens to confirm the intrinsic merits of their leaders."[18] Taken together, the elite imaginings reconstructed above offer empirically solid evidence in support of Gainsborough's assertion that elections are treated by Cambodian politicians as confirmation of the intrinsic merit of leaders, though in greatly varying ways. They also point to how an organic view of the people is shared across the political spectrum.

Yet, going to the trouble of tracing Cambodian political elite imaginings in a precise, nuanced way problematizes rather than confirms current understandings of the workings of political culture in Cambodia. Not only are there important differences among competing political actors, but concepts also turn out to be malleable and political actors to be gifted with an astonishing capacity for innovation. This calls into question what Gainsborough pins down as "cultural assumptions about the proper relationship between the state and its citizens, or between rulers and the ruled," in favor of an emphasis on how such culturally embedded notions are picked up and remolded for political gain.[19] Caroline Hughes and Joakim Öjendal have called for a reassessment of the role of "culture" in Cambodian political life, challenging scholarship to engage with "the ways in which Cambodians understand the process of reform and link this understanding to internally reproduced notions of 'culture.'"[20] This book takes up their invitation by outlining how Cambodian political actors negotiate the interplay of culture and power by linking their agendas to competing reinventions of culturally transmitted notions. The insistent message that has asserted itself through these pages is that political elites dynamically manipulate historically inherited notions, selectively reviving and reinventing these to promote vastly different political orders. Their sheer diversity indicates the presence of many competing historical logics in a cultural and political context marked by discontinuity, so that no single one could be deemed more "traditional" than another. This highlights not only the adaptability and flexibility of Cambodian political culture, but also the presence of competing cultural notions that are neither static nor homogenous. Such a picture is more in line with how Steve Heder, invoking the richness and complexity of historical models, has argued that "traditional" in the Southeast Asian context would mean today's men of prowess embracing the global model of liberal democracy.[21] Rather

---

[17] See: Mehmet, "Development in a War-torn Society," 676; Kim, "From Peace Keeping to Peace Building," 4; St. John, "Democracy in Cambodia," 415; and Blunt and Turner, "Decentralisation, Democracy, and Development in a Post-Conflict Society."

[18] Gainsborough, "Elites vs. Reform in Laos, Cambodia, and Vietnam," 39.

[19] Ibid., 38.

[20] Caroline Hughes and Joakim Öjendal, "Reassessing Tradition in Times of Political Change: Post-War Cambodia Reconsidered," *Journal of Southeast Asian Studies* 37, no. 3 (2006): 417.

[21] Heder, "Political Theatre in the 2003 Cambodian Elections," 155.

than contemporary Cambodian elections being representative of a traditional political culture, as in Gainsborough's analysis, Heder finds them to radically deviate from historical models and instead serve as "a cosmetic cover for an ugly metamorphosis," whereby election violence displays unchecked bureaucratic might.[22]

Confirming this latter interpretation, the contemporary political projects here discussed typically imbued supposedly traditional notions with novel meanings to serve contemporary purposes. While the redefinition of cultural notions was partly constrained by their historical meaning, there was also space for their renegotiation. This closely corresponds to the way that Hughes and Öjendal write of culture and tradition as "landscapes of struggle in which certain historical features are embedded, preventing the free play of interpretation, but in which, equally, space is available for differences of perspective, emphasis, and engagement to meet in conflict and negotiation, and to combine over time to comprise significant trajectories of change."[23]

Cambodian political party actors reinvented historical concepts to respond to changes pertaining to the contemporary era. Each sought to reconcile particular tensions and contradictions specific to the KOC period. For the CPP and Hun Sen, this tension centered on the mandate and nature of legitimate leadership in a post-socialist context, while building on their revolutionary legitimacy of the recent past. For royalists, their central dilemma was how to reconcile the reinstated constitutional monarchy with political royalism. Democrats, in turn, struggled to represent a nation that did not yet exist, by voicing the will of a people who they considered to be blinded by CPP ideological and material domination. To confront these new challenges, the political parties reinvented national imaginings and corollary bids for representation, which consequently differed in important ways from the PRK era.

The CPP invented a complex post-socialist identity. This replaced the self-professed Marxist–Leninist regime identity of the PRK that observers have noted to have been particularly hollow ever since the mid-1980s leadership shift, when Hun Sen's rise to power eclipsed the orthodox Khmer Hanoi faction. Heder has consequently categorized the resulting PRK regime as an "ideological fake, constructed on insincere play-acting and theatrics, and a cover for rising personalized networks of Cambodian bureaucratic, military, and economic power." This came about as Hun Sen oversaw a shift from (attempted) bureaucratic socialism to nascent authoritarian crony capitalism by the end of the regime.[24] Apprehensive of communism and the Vietnamese presence, Hun Sen sidelined veterans who had undergone extensive ideological training in the Democratic Republic of Vietnam and who genuinely believed in Marxism–Leninism. Regarding these as quixotic idealists, he replaced them with a group of pragmatic technocrats—many of whom, today, hold important government positions.[25] In 1991, the notion of revolution and the remaining pretense of socialism was publicly

---

[22] Ibid., 162.

[23] Hughes and Öjendal, "Reassessing Tradition in Times of Political Change," 419.

[24] Heder, "Political Theatre in the 2003 Cambodian Elections," 158–59.

[25] Ibid., 159; and Gottesman, *Cambodia after the Khmer Rouge*, 212–16.

dropped.[26] Still, in working out a CPP post-socialist regime identity in the KOC, notions of revolution and democracy remained central—in novel ways. The CPP under Hun Sen continues to posit these notions as interdependent, while remodeling their contents. The revolutionary language was never dropped—it merely lay dormant for a while. The notion of "people's democracy" serves as one such discursive and conceptual bridge in regime identity.

Democracy, during the PRK, was understood as the Cambodian revolution's unchanging goal. The precise notion of "people's democracy" referred to the 1979 defeat of the Khmer Rouge and the PRK regime that then came to be established. People's democracy, then, in its contemporary incarnation, is nothing less than the latest stage of the evolving Cambodian revolutionary quest toward genuine democracy. This provides another take on Anderson's phrase "revolution is continuity."[27] The contemporary Cambodian revolution invoked by the regime is a revolution that has outlived Marxism–Leninism; it is a revolution that is devoid of Marxist–Leninist content. In line with a Marxist–Leninist dialectical analysis, it tackles emerging contradictions in society, yet the solutions offered are not Marxist–Leninist. The notion of "people's democracy" now engages with the newly introduced nominally liberal democratic framework and capitalist transformation under CPP direction. It serves to guarantee that the regime can maintain a separate political identity from Western liberal democracies, at the same time that it frames practices of gift-giving and patronage as central to the new economic system. None of this is Marxist–Leninist, yet these practices are phrased in the language of revolution and democracy. Similarly, Sdech Kân constitutes another such changing revolutionary imaginary. Kân was a revolutionary in the sense that he did away with the notion of hereditary leadership. Yet he was ultimately made king himself—and as a king, he is hardly an orthodox Marxist–Leninist hero. This narrative engages with a second contradiction in contemporary society: the restoration of the monarchy and the return of royalists to the national political stage. The Sdech Kân story ties the revolutionary imaginary to a distinct articulation of democracy, by positing social mobility and nonhereditary leadership as central components.

The resulting CPP identity contained layers of continuity, as it was based on notions of democracy and revolution that interacted strenuously with the socialist discourse from which they originally emanated. It also reflected thoroughgoing change, as these notions were employed in new ways to engage with novel realities. KOC-era rearticulations of notions of ideology can be understood to be more intimately bound up with actual political developments than their articulations during the preceding PRK regime ever were. In 1989, the year that the PRK crumbled, Hun Sen asserted that the external appearance of his regime should be understood as a mere costume.[28] Two decades later, the outward presentation of Hun Sen's regime communicates important messages about ongoing political developments. This is not to say that emerging narratives and self-professed tenets

---

[26] Heder, "Political Theatre in the 2003 Cambodian Elections," 159; and Gottesman, *Cambodia After the Khmer Rouge*, 345. On PRK-era KPRP historiography, see Viviane K. Frings, "Rewriting Cambodian History to 'Adapt' It to a New Political Context: The Kampuchean People's Revolutionary Party's Historiography (1979–1991)," *Modern Asian Studies* 31, no. 4 (1997): 807–46.

[27] Anderson, *Language and Power*, 148.

[28] Heder, "Political Theatre in the 2003 Cambodian Elections," 159.

should be understood at face value as strictly defined ideology guiding political practice. Just as during the PRK, these narratives and ideological constructs act as a cover for (and, as demonstrated, even promote) the politics of personalized networks. Yet, unlike during the PRK era, this ideological facade is not instructed by the Vietnamese, but defined by the incumbent power holders themselves. Whereas notions of revolution and democracy struck a false note in their PRK-era articulations, their KOC-era rearticulations are more representative of actual intent and political practice than (a to a large extent externally defined) socialism ever was. The revolutionary language was reinvented to support Hun Sen's increasingly personal hold on power and to champion regime practices particular to a new capitalist economy—it was actively used to negotiate change. The use of the language of democracy seeks to influence a domestic understanding of what democracy means in the contemporary Cambodian context.

As for political actors coming out of civil-war-era resistance factions, their political identities changed substantially from their PRK-era articulations. In contradistinction to Hughes, who has stressed the similarities between FUNCINPEC and the SRP's (now part of the CNRP) shared dual identities as democratic opposition, internationally, and nationalist resistance, domestically, this book has outlined how royalists engaged in political contestation from within the parameters of a separate, royalist identity.[29] As we have seen, FUNCINPEC and political parties such as the NRP and SJFP first and foremost self-identified and portrayed themselves to the electorate as *royalist*. This is important both because the wide-ranging differences between the self-identified royalists and the self-identified democrats provide an explanation for their failure to come together as one political force, and because it allows for exploration of the negotiation of separate royalist and democrat identities.

For royalists, establishing historical continuity was crucial. On a basic level, they attempted to establish nation, religion, and king as a foundation of the social order in a way that gave meaning to political royalism. Their most celebrated model to this end was Sihanouk's Sangkum Reastr Niyum, which they claimed as the blueprint for their contemporary political project. Yet royalist politics was characterized not by continuity, but by discontinuity. The Sangkum Reastr Niyum was an ideology for people in power, not for an opposition movement. Ironically, considering the increasingly desperate references to the Sangkum Reastr Niyum, it was precisely the rupture of the Sangkum that proved impossible to overcome. Sihanouk's Sangkum arrangement—designed to be politically expedient to Sihanouk at the time—had disarmed the Khmer monarchy and nullified royalists' political ambitions. Royalists failed to move on from this paradox. Trying to reinvent a (from their point of view) golden age that was impossible to resurrect, baffled royalists were at a loss. As a result of this incongruence, their political bids were all phrased in Sihanoukist language, yet referred to vastly different things from those advocated by Sihanouk during the Sangkum.

Tracing these "Sihanoukist" reinventions is important because they unmask problems internal to royalist politics. Although this language was also used to frame distinct political moves, no consensus was reached among royalists on the form, nature, or contents of Sihanoukism. Sihanoukism could consequently not survive its originator, let alone offer an authoritative bid for remodeling ideas of legitimacy.

---

[29] Hughes, "Transforming Oppositions in Cambodia," 311–12.

The failure to revive Sihanoukist language in a meaningful way was therefore bound up with the decay of the party political form of royalism.

In contrast to royalists, democrats were unconcerned with establishing continuity with their ideological predecessors. They self-consciously styled their political project to be finely attuned to changing realities. They turned against the CPP, which they understood to represent merely a transformation of communism, supported by alleged Vietnamese control over the contemporary Cambodian state. This understanding guided their attempts to "read" the will of the people, while the peculiarities of Cambodia's electoral democracy blurred the line of how this reading was to be assessed. This is important because it shows the shifting challenges pertaining to their political project, as compared to earlier democratic projects. Parliamentary democracy, the cornerstone of successive Cambodian democratic projects, emerged significantly problematized since electoral results were not considered to adequately reflect the popular will and interest.

IDEOLOGY, IDENTITIES, AND REPRESENTATION OF THE NATION

The categories that defined competing national visions were also disputed. Contemporary political contestation does not only use the language of ideology that spread with the idea of the nation.[30] Transnational ideologies—such as liberalism and communism—were once important motors of nationalist struggles across Southeast Asia,[31] and they left an indelible mark on Cambodia.[32] In contemporary Cambodia, however, transnational ideologies have lost much of their power. This is less noticeable in the case of democrats, whose liberal democratic identity is influenced by the "transnational networks, movements, and horizons" Sidel identifies as drivers of nationalism throughout Southeast Asia.[33] Even Cambodian democrats, however, consider it their mission to transcend the implementation of liberal democratic ideology. Indeed, contemporary actors routinely employ categories other than ideology to express national political imaginings, such as historical ideas of embodiment. Western-derived political notions readily partner with other such claims to representation. Notions seemingly phrased in the language of ideology, such as Sihanoukism, differ substantially from the concept of ideology in the Western sense. Moreover, the very notion of political ideology and its applicability to contemporary political contestation was debated within the KOC, and was held up as a contrast to the idea of representation through embodiment.

Embodiment continues to have relevance in contemporary Cambodian society, as has been noted by scholarship on statuary and spirit performances. It has also received some attention for its role in Sihanouk's kingship and FUNCINPEC discourse.[34] Extending far beyond these realms, however, the debate over embodiment goes to the core of contemporary political contestation, as it remains

---

[30] Anderson, *The Spectre of Comparisons*, 29.

[31] John T. Sidel, "Liberalism, Communism, Islam: Transnational Motors of 'Nationalist' Struggles in Southeast Asia," *The Newsletter* 32 (2003): 23.

[32] Heder, "Racism, Marxism, Labeling, and Genocide in Ben Kiernan's *The Pol Pot Regime*."

[33] Sidel, "Liberalism, Communism, Islam," 23.

[34] See: Thompson, "Angkor Revisited," 203–6; Thompson, "The Suffering of Kings," 108–10; Hang, "Stec Gaṃlaṅ' and Yāy Deb"; Kent, "The Recovery of the King"; Hughes, "Transforming Oppositions in Cambodia," 307–8; and Hughes, *The Political Economy of Cambodia's Transition*, 119.

an important claim to political legitimacy. Since Cambodia's first elections in 1946 and up through the postcolonial period, the question of whether political contestation was to be based on ideology or embodiment remained unresolved. In contemporary Cambodia, this tension has come to a head. Ideology and embodiment are not mutually exclusive. Claims of embodiment are accompanied by appeals to a doctrinal identity, both by royalist actors and by Hun Sen. Yet whether doctrine is used to accompany claims of embodiment, such as for Hun Sen, or to supplant these, as is, increasingly, the case for royalists, seems to be the defining difference. The doctrine-and-embodiment combination has been successful, testifying to the relevance of claims of embodiment.

The sidelining of embodiment claims in royalist discourse in favor of a doctrinal identity would seem to indicate acceleration toward the use of the language of ideology or doctrine to discuss politics. Hand-in-hand with democratization, this trend might appear to be chipping–away at the discourse of embodiment. Yet the continued salience of embodiment is evidenced by both Ranariddh's repeated use of the language of incarnation and Hun Sen's claims to it. That embodiment failed as a strategy for royalists, who were historically associated with such ideas, does not therefore mean that the idea of embodiment was necessarily anachronistic or redundant in the KOC. Rather, the royalist failure can be traced to the Sangkum paradox, which tied legitimacy to the body of Sihanouk, as well as to the royalists' lack of a material base to back up their embodiment claims, so that their claims were exposed as fictional. By contrast, Hun Sen's claims had a truer ring to them, given his overwhelming dominance over the body politic. This suggests the need for a material base to support claims of national embodiment.

The allegiance to embodiment as a form of political representation helps to explain why political party actors did not predominantly phrase their programs in the language of ideology, and why political parties' policy differences, views, and ideologies did not appear well-defined to voters. It also explains the continued role of individual strongmen, rather than political parties, as mobilizers of opinion.[35] These strongmen were holders of legitimacy, firmly invested in their individual bodies, and only by extension did this personal legitimacy reflect on the political party with which they were associated. Because of the continued personal nature of claims to political legitimacy, legitimacy-building was not primarily associated with party-building. This, in turn, helps to account for the continuous weakening of the institution of political parties as objects of popular loyalty.[36]

Attention to categories of contestation operating parallel to "ideology" and policy also shows Cambodian contemporary politics to be heavily preoccupied with a debate between inherited and elected leadership. An age-old standoff in Cambodia, this issue gathered new urgency after 1993. The debate has arguably been at least temporarily settled in favor of elected leadership. Hun Sen's narrative of Sdech Kân exalted the idea of social mobility and the designation of the leader on the basis of relative merit rather than hereditary right. While royalists made appeals to genealogical lines, these turned out to have little or no legitimacy. Ranariddh's attempt to link democracy to the Cambodian monarchy by pointing to the latter's elective nature shows how the idea of elected leadership had become widely

---

[35] Hughes, "Dare to Say, Dare to Do," 121.

[36] Compare to: Hughes, "Parties, Protest, and Pluralism in Cambodia," 170; and Hughes, *The Political Economy of Cambodia's Transition*, 117.

hegemonic. Yet, while these claims could perhaps support the legitimacy of a constitutional monarchy, they did not support that of political royalism.

Both Hun Sen and royalists advanced the idea of elected leadership in a broader sense than that of liberal democratic multiparty elections. The designation of leadership was not primarily determined by results at the polls, but through a different nomination process. The election of the monarch, as royalists like to point out, is through the throne council. In the case of Hun Sen as Sdech Kân, his achievements single him out as the national leader. His leadership role is confirmed by national election results, but not reducible to a mere consequence of these. Elected leadership is also firmly tied to the possession of moral qualities. The Sdech Kân narrative constitutes, ultimately, a claim to possess merit: the moral qualities of Hun Sen designate him as personally chosen to leadership. The weakening of political royalists, on the other hand, can be traced to widespread corruption preempting any credible counter-narratives from royalists in moral terms.

This analysis is not intended to mystify contemporary Cambodian political discourse by suggesting that it has yet to catch up with a "modern" vocabulary of politics. Rather, it testifies to selective attempts by contemporary actors to vest their political projects in historical arguments that enjoy widespread social legitimacy, while subtly manipulating their contents. Hun Sen's reincarnation of Sdech Kân can be understood as a bid to articulate an interpretation of legitimate leadership to define the present era and negotiate future developments, a concern that goes beyond that of convincingly aspiring to be a *neak mean bon* or *Preah Bat Thommik*. Ranariddh's belabored claims to embodiment attempted to shift the basis of such claims to follow genealogical lines.

PUBLIC APPEAL

This book has outlined the elaborate ways in which members of Cambodia's political elite attempt to make their particular readings of the nation hegemonic. Hughes has written about how successive regimes from 1955 onward have articulated a "hazy vision of 'Khmerness.'"[37] The visions outlined here were hazy in the sense that they retained a fantastical aspect, in that they reflected elite visions and attempts to manipulate public discourse, rather than an accomplished reality. On the other hand, they were clearly anchored in and bound up with real political developments and ongoing political processes. Hun Sen's narrative was complicit in circumscribing the role of the monarchy and political royalists, and was accompanied by other political moves to the same effect. The changing ideas of the monarchy advanced by royalists, meanwhile, reflected and were employed to negotiate these real changes.

One of the most striking paradoxes to emerge from this study is how all these discourses were articulated from above, while purporting to represent grassroots concerns. It is also notable how self-contained some of the debates were; they never completely filtered down to grassroots awareness. These case studies illustrate how far removed elite imaginations still are from the needs and views of ordinary people, and the extent to which these debates remain, ultimately, an intra-elite struggle. A major reason for this is the sheer ignorance of the elite regarding the preferences of the electorate. Hughes has drawn attention to the "social and political opacity of

---

[37] Hughes, "Reconstructing Legitimate Political Authority through Elections?" 45.

Cambodia's post-war rural electoral heartland."[38] Referring to Cambodian voters as the "silenced majority," she writes that "very little is known about the demographics of Cambodian voter preferences in terms of class, gender, or ethnicity, or the motivations for voting," so that "political parties continue to operate blindly in this key site of democratic politics." From the first democratic elections in 1993, voters were discouraged from speaking openly about their political preferences, in order to preclude security problems and spare international democracy promoters from having to engage with local level political party structures. Introduced by international democracy supporters, this strategy of silence has been promoted by Cambodian political parties, including the political opposition, which support it as a strategy to avoid intimidation by the CPP.[39] The restrictive and unfair aspects of Cambodia's electoral system have further obscured popular political preferences, making it difficult for politicians to assess the popular will.

The imaginings of the nation and strategies of its representation outlined in this book can be understood as a consequence of this opacity, which has added up to a veritable crisis of representation. The distance between political parties and the general public, which Hughes has referred to as "the politics of nonrepresentation," has catalysed the emergence of strategies of purported national representation.[40] These attempts at "reading Cambodia" are made equally by the democrats, royalists, and the CPP. All party actors continually face the dilemma of how to make national democratic politics meaningful in a context of overwhelming rural poverty, in which a majority of the electors find themselves on the low end of a deep socioeconomic divide, and are relatively uneducated. The "real problem" for Sangkum, Ranariddh writes, was not to caricature Western democracy, but to integrate the peasant masses, which were far removed from classic democratic values, into a system that listened to people and their real needs.[41] These words could have been spoken by any political party representative about the contemporary context. To make their projects relevant, politicians picked up on new exigencies that they expected to resonate with the times, and to some extent attempted to follow changing public attitudes. This strategy can be seen in Hun Sen's emphasis on social mobility and equal opportunity. Royalists placed their hopes on what they believed to be the people's nostalgic yearning for Sihanouk and his Sangkum Reastr Niyum, and envisaged its institutions to be uniquely placed to address today's popular concerns. The democrats tailored their agenda to champion the rights of those they considered to be victimized by Cambodia's current development path. In this sense, these discourses are also elite fantasies of the elusive Cambodian nation. Ultimately, though, they were constrained, if not straitjacketed, by particular ideological heritages and historiographies, and articulated as attempts to direct the masses into elite-defined trajectories.

The other half of the story presented in these pages, one that remains unwritten, is the renegotiation of these elite-level discourses in Cambodian society. As different segments of society interact with them, they are subject to reinterpretation, renegotiation, and, perhaps, resistance. It is true that tracing these nationalist discourses says little about how successful they are as legitimizing

---

[38] Hughes, "Transforming Oppositions in Cambodia," 298.

[39] Ibid., 303–4.

[40] Hughes, "Parties, Protest, and Pluralism in Cambodia," 170.

[41] Norodom, *Droit Public Cambodgien*, 136.

attempts. Yet tracing them out in a fine-grained manner is necessary groundwork for even starting to assess how ordinary Cambodians relate to their nation and its leaders. First of all, we need to have the precise and nuanced understanding of elite discourses that this book seeks to offer, in order to approach the question of their wider societal resonance. For now, what emerge are the shared limitations circumscribing all claims to popular representation and to consequent "democratic legitimacy." By offering the point of view of political elites, this book invites further study of the making of the Cambodian nation at the intersection of elite and grassroots discourses and imaginations.

IMPLICATIONS IN SOUTHEAST ASIAN PERSPECTIVE

The findings of this book add to the criticism by Southeast Asian scholars of the assumption in "globalization literature" that there has been a general move to a post-Westphalian world order, where allegiance to nation states has been replaced by globalism and cosmopolitanism. In Southeast Asia, these assumptions have been shown to be erroneous, as notions of nations, sovereignty, and bordered territories prevail.[42] In Cambodia, the reintroduction of multiparty elections—one of the main effects of globalization—has resulted in the heightened importance of *national* imaginings.

The Cambodian case is only one among a variety of multidirectional political trajectories that the promotion of procedural democracy has produced in the Southeast Asian region.[43] Here, electoral processes have been indigenized with vastly different results. Robert Taylor's classic edited volume on the indigenization of elections in Southeast Asia tentatively suggested that indigenization processes in the final case crippled rather than empowered electorates, undermining the potential for popular empowerment promised by elections. According to Taylor, the meaning and role of elections in any society can only be gathered through contextualizing the election process, as the same political structures can be interpreted in vastly different ways. Various meanings are attached to the electoral process across the region, and set in the context of each country's political economy.[44] This analysis rings true for Cambodia, where domestic elites attached multiple meanings to the role and mandate of the new electoral process. Since all domestic elites ultimately diminished the importance of elections, then all, if popular empowerment is defined as "the people" being able to exercise its will at polls, contributed to the defanging of popular empowerment. Yet, there was also

---

[42] See: Öjendal, "Democratization amidst Globalization in Southeast Asia," 361; Claire Sutherland, *Soldered States: Nation-Building in Germany and Vietnam* (Manchester: Manchester University Press, 2010); David Brown, "Ethnic and Nationalist Politics in Southeast Asia," in *Contemporary Southeast Asia*, ed. Mark Beeson (New York: Palgrave Macmillan, 2009), 143–56; and Sri Kuhnt-Saptodewo et al., *Nationalism and Cultural Revival in Southeast Asia*.

[43] See, for example: Robert H. Taylor, ed., *The Politics of Elections in Southeast Asia* (Cambridge: Woodrow Wilson Center Press and Cambridge University Press, 1996); Kok Wah Loh and Öjendal, *Southeast Asian Responses to Globalization*; Edward Aspinall and Marcus Mietzner, eds., *Problems of Democratization in Indonesia: Elections, Institutions, and Society* (Singapore: Institute of Southeast Asian Studies, 2010); Aurel Croissant, "From Transition to Defective Democracy: Mapping Asian Democratization," *Democratization* 11, no. 5 (2004), 156–78; and John T. Sidel, "Siam and Its Twin?: Democratization and Bossism in Contemporary Thailand and the Philippines," *IDS Bulletin* 27, no. 2 (1996): 36–52.

[44] Robert H. Taylor, "Introduction: Elections and Politics in Southeast Asia," in Taylor, *The Politics of Elections in Southeast Asia*, 8–9.

considerable diversity among the competing national constructions within Cambodia, each entailing its own intrinsic possibilities of popular empowerment and/or disempowerment, if understood more loosely in terms of how these envisaged popular political involvement. This suggests that the weakening versus strengthening of electorates must be located in exact processes of contestation.

The reintroduction of multiparty elections in Cambodia was thus not the presumed milestone on the road to democratization, but related in a much more complex manner to political change. As a consequence thereof, a "democratic" stance shifted in Cambodia to be bound up with scepticism toward elections. In neighboring Thailand, a "pro-democratic" stance is similarly sceptical of electoral democracy. The urban, educated middle class typically considers rural voting behavior to be determined by patron–client relations, and therefore opposes electoral democracy, judging it "undemocratic."[45] In Cambodia, the presumed effects of patronage incentives on voting behavior have similarly led democrats to highlight the shortcomings of electoral democracy. However, this has produced political strategies quite different from those of their Thai counterparts. The Cambodian democrats actively sought to channel the demands of the general populace, whereas in Thailand, democrats seek to prevent self-expression. This highlights that sharply different political imaginations may develop under similar conditions, resulting in varying democratic outcomes.

The Cambodian case also highlights the importance of monarchies, and royalist ideas more generally, in defining democracy in the region. In contemporary Cambodian politics, the specter of the monarchy remains vigorous.[46] Roger Kershaw suggests that Southeast Asian monarchies "may offer special assets to a polity in transition towards democracy."[47] Monarchies can promote democracy by restraining the excesses of either the power elite or the excesses of "an open democracy." He finds that the separation of the monarchy from the legislature, and the unique ability of a monarch to represent continuity with the past, are critical to the success of regional monarchies in democracy promotion.[48] Empirical cases obviously diverge from the analytical model, but Kershaw identifies this "rosy ideal" as "clearly confirmed" in the case of Thailand, followed next by Cambodia, where the main factor precluding the monarchy from realizing its potential to act as a moderating

---

[45] On Thailand, see: Anek Laothamatas, "A Tale of Two Democracies: Conflicting Perceptions of Elections and Democracy in Thailand," in Taylor, *The Politics of Elections in Southeast Asia*, 201–23; Winichakul, "Toppling Democracy"; and Andrew Walker, *Thailand's Political Peasants: Power in the Modern Rural Economy* (Madison: University of Wisconsin Press, 2012).

[46] Even in Thailand, where the monarchy arguably has played an unrivaled role in shaping Thai democracy since the end of absolute monarchy in 1932, harsh *lèse majesté* laws and a view of the royal family as standing above politics have largely precluded unbiased scrutiny thereof. Some exceptions are: Winichakul, "Toppling Democracy"; Kevin Hewison, "The Monarchy and Democratization," in *Political Change in Thailand: Democracy and Participation*, ed. Kevin Hewison (London: Routledge, 1997), 58–74; Paul M. Handley, *The King Never Smiles: A Biography of Thailand's King Bhumibol Adulyadej* (New Haven: Yale University Press, 2006); Duncan McCargo, "Network Monarchy and Legitimacy Crises in Thailand," *Pacific Review* 18, no. 4 (2005), 499–519; and David Streckfuss, "Kings in the Age of Nations: The Paradox of Lese Majeste as Political Crime in Thailand," *Comparative Studies in Society and History* 37, no. 3 (1995): 445–75.

[47] Kershaw, *Monarchy in South-East Asia*, 159.

[48] Ibid., 159, 162.

force is how it is subject to the "whims of a well-organized power elite."[49] Yet the findings of this book show that the Cambodian monarchy has a more complex role in "democratization"—a role that is derived from the political stance and perceptions of the Cambodian monarchy and royalists themselves, rather than the repressive force of the incumbent power.

These findings are in line with a literature that has outlined a similarly complex, even problematic role of the monarchy and royalist ideas in the region, particularly in terms of promoting an anti-electoral view of democracy. Thailand is a case in point. Kershaw lauds the Thai monarchy as having an "extraordinarily creative function," in which the King has facilitated democracy not only by restraining its "excesses" but also by mobilizing his authority to actively intervene in politics, so that the monarchy has emerged "somewhat above the level of" constitutional monarchy in European states.[50] His analysis, however, omits the most noteworthy influence of Thai royalists—the way that they have undermined electoral democracy by supporting a discourse that casts electoral government as corrupt and monarchical government as "clean politics," with the morally authoritative monarch towering above other political institutions.[51] In Cambodia, royalists displayed a similar distaste for electoral politics, which they undermined in the name of a politics of consensus and national reconciliation. In contrast to their Thai counterparts, however, the Cambodian royals did not exert their influence from a position "above politics"—which has been identified as crucial to the Thai royals' power to intervene on the national political scene.[52] Instead, in the KOC, a long-standing debate of whether Cambodian royals were "above politics" or part of it, was resumed. Royalists tried to assert themselves as party political actors while simultaneously building on earlier discourses of regal legitimacy bestowing the moral high ground. Compared to their Thai counterparts, they therefore faced a formidable task, since they had to justify their political involvement as party political actors. The Cambodian example, therefore, puts the Thai royals' "success story" in perspective. It highlights how deeply problematic it was for a contemporary Southeast Asian monarchy of a Theravada Buddhist tradition to relate to the electoral democratic framework—if engaging in it as a party political force.

Discourses of Buddhist kingship also influence contemporary ideas of leadership. In Thai democracy, the moral character of the leader is considered an important element of leadership, transcending policies and ideas—perceptions closely associated with historical ideas of kingship.[53] In Thailand, as disillusion with electoral politics has grown, the monarch's moral authority has come to be considered superior to that of elected officials.[54] In Cambodia, on the other hand, although royalist political discourse has reinforced the importance of moral legitimacy, royalists failed to imbue these moral claims with meaning. The

---

[49] Ibid., 160, 164.

[50] Ibid., 160, 162.

[51] Winichakul, "Toppling Democracy."

[52] Ibid., 15.

[53] Ibid., 18; and Duncan McCargo, ed., *Reforming Thai Politics* (Copenhagen: NIAS Press, 2002), 5.

[54] The current Thai constitutional monarch, Bhumibol, is widely perceived as a *dhammaraja*, a righteous king with particular moral power, *barami*. See Winichakul, "Toppling Democracy," 21.

Cambodian case demonstrates the adaptability of discourses of moral legitimacy associated with the monarchy, which do not necessarily remain confined to royals, and which can work to their detriment.

This book thus sheds light on processes of reconfiguration of legitimacy through changing conceptualizations of historical kingship observed throughout Southeast Asia. In the region, the revival of ideas of kingship has been understood as part of a larger move toward "retraditionalization." Cambodia differs from its neighbors in three respects. First, this renegotiation of kingship took place within the framework of a reinstated constitutional monarchy, which was unique in Southeast Asia. Second, various meanings of kingship and legitimate leadership were offered by competitors in a multiparty democratic system. This differed from Laos and Vietnam, one-party states where reinventions were tied to the party state and met no political party opposition. Third, unlike Sihanouk, Vietnam's last emperor, Bao Dai, and the Lao kings of the modern era, had almost no personality cult—the last king of Laos, Savang Vatthana, even openly opposed the idea.

Against this backdrop, the Cambodian case can add to the regional debate in several important respects. The Cambodian example highlights certain characteristics of employing historical kingship as a model. Laos and Vietnam—communist one-party states—have used ideas of kingship to provide a political identity after the end of the Cold War, in a bid to appropriate earlier, regal legitimacy.[55] In both these countries, the royal families had long been outmaneuvered, prominent royal family members exiled or killed, and royalists extinguished as a political force. The scholarly debate has therefore centered on making sense out of attempts to transfer earlier, "exhausted" regal legitimacy to contemporary political actors of a post-communist brand, who replace monarchies and face no serious political challenge. The CPP's reinvention of ideas of kingship in Cambodia, by contrast, took place in the context of circumscribing a reinstated monarchy and royalist political party. The Cambodian example thereby uniquely shows how ideas of kingship can be used to trump a king on the throne. Kingship, or ideas thereof, is not something absolutely, or even primarily, tied to the monarch. It rather serves as a historical model of leadership and is therefore very flexible. This explains the ease with which such ideas have been appropriated by communist projects in the region. Grant Evans has argued that, in Cambodia and Laos, "because of the historically close relationship in these countries between kingship and Theravada Buddhism, any cult of personality drifts dangerously in the direction formerly occupied by the former monarch."[56] In Cambodia, legitimizations did, indeed, drift toward kingship as the historical model of leadership. Yet, this shift was hardly dangerous for the Cambodian regime—although Cambodia is a country with an actual reinstated monarch—let alone, then, this suggests, would it be dangerous for the Laotian and Vietnamese regimes, which face no such challenges.

Since kingship is a flexible historical model of leadership, it is best understood not as one indivisible entity but rather as an aggregate of components specific to each historical context. In Cambodia, kingship is bound up with ideas of embodiment, inherited versus elected leadership, and moral achievement and merit. Disaggregating kingship opens up the research agenda to reinventions of kingship in other Southeast Asian contexts. Distinguishing among what qualities of kingship are emphasized in

---

[55] See: Grabowsky and Tappe, "Important Kings of Laos"; and Jellema, "Returning Home."

[56] Evans, *The Politics of Ritual and Remembrance*, 31.

different reinventions is necessary to chart their meanings and outcomes. Although once underway these reinventions will follow distinctly national trajectories, all indications are that they are influenced by regional models. Hun Sen has referred to Laos under former President Kaysone as a major influence. Uniquely Cambodian, Hun Sen's reinvention nevertheless highlights the role of regional flows of ideas and political models in contemporary Southeast Asia.

EPILOGUE

On the eve of Cambodia's fifth national elections (July 28, 2013), popular singer Nop Bayarith took the stage in front of Wat Botum in central Phnom Penh to perform "The Youth's Will" (*Chanthea Yuveachon*), the chief election campaign song of the CPP. The refrain blasted:

> We, good and virtuous Khmer sons and daughters, have to continue to safeguard our ancestral heritage. Do not let the love of Angkor cool down!
> We, good and virtuous Khmer sons and daughters, have to work hard to make Cambodia ever more famous in the era of the iron hands of Techo [Hun Sen].
> Stand up, let's gather together, shoulder to shoulder, let's come together as one.
> The nation needs us. Do not ignore it, young boys and girls, [but act] in accordance with the meaning of the win-win strategy.

The performance culminated in Bayarith's emotional exclamation, "I am excited and proud to be born Khmer, especially during the era of Techo Hun Sen."

Ubiquitously reproduced in national media, "The Youth's Will" was a piece of campaign propaganda that made it clear to the electorate that it was the Cambodian nation, and the different proposed versions, representations, and contours thereof, that was being voted on in the 2013 elections. The message of "The Youth's Will" was that a vote for the CPP equaled a vote for the true Khmer nation. The music video accompanying the song reinforced this point, as images of Angkor and the historical monuments of Phnom Penh were interspersed with scenes from new landmarks created under CPP-led development. Finally, the song was temporally specific: it was set in the "era of the iron hands of Techo." Governance under Hun Sen was turned into a distinct epoch of national history.

The enlistment of famous popular singers into the CPP's election campaign showed its clear awareness of a second defining feature of the 2013 elections: that the kingdom's youth would play a decisive role in determining which version of the nation would be sanctified by winning the popular vote. Young men and women constituted a crucial demographic group: more than 50 percent of Cambodians were estimated to be under the age of twenty-four in 2012, and up to 70 percent were under 35. On the final campaign night, Wat Botum park was starlit by an array of Cambodia's most famous performers offering their public support to the CPP in a pop concert broadcast on national television. Still, the ranks of youth supporters quickly thinned out, while Freedom Park—the designated Phnom Penh rally point for opposition party CNRP—which offered no such entertainment, brimmed with young supporters.

The following day, the nation held its breath as some 69 percent of registered voters cast their ballots. The CPP, under the leadership of Hun Sen, appeared poised to enjoy a landslide victory, having consolidated its power during the previous mandate period to an unprecedented extent. The official election results, released by the National Election Committee, were therefore a surprise to most observers: the CPP suffered a sharp drop in support, winning 48.83 percent of votes, while the CNRP came in a close second, at 44.46 percent. The CNRP refused to acknowledge the official results, citing election irregularities, and claimed to be the real winner of the elections.

The July 2013 elections signal a sea change in the Cambodian political landscape. For the first time since the 1993 reintroduction of multiparty elections, the steady increase in the CPP's vote counts has been broken.[1] Hun Sen's strategy of *Samkok,* or divide and rule, intended to marginalize political challengers, has arguably provoked an impressive backlash.[2] Whilst making political royalism a spent force, this strategy also marginalized the democratic opposition parties SRP and HRP to the point that those parties saw themselves forced to merge into the CNRP party vehicle. Competition between different visions of the nation has now crystallized into a polarized duel between two contending blocs, offering the first credible challenge to the CPP's hold on power. The election results suggest growing discontent with a Cambodia beset by land disputes, economic disparity, youth unemployment, and labor migration abroad. Regardless of whether the dynamics set in motion by the 2013 elections will lead to long-term change or will be stifled in the cradle, 2013 will stand out as a landmark year.

What do the competing versions of the Cambodian nation look like? The debates that this book has identified stand out today in sharp relief. It therefore seems important to end this book by spelling out how they can increase our understanding of the developments now underway.

At the most basic level, the elections came to revolve around the question of continuity or change. This agenda was set by CNRP leaders, who in campaign meetings asked supporters: "change or no change?" (*daur min daur*), only to receive a resounding call for "change" (*daur*). The CPP response and platform was a dogged rejection of change, stubbornly defended by the corresponding campaign slogan "no change" (*min daur*). The CNRP battlecry for "change" did not go unheard by voters— but a change for what?

Firstly and most obviously, the notion of change pitted the CPP backwards look against the future-oriented vision of the democratic opposition. For the CPP, Cambodia is already on a revolutionary path toward democracy—by now a quiet and predictable path, not to be upset by new initiatives. This the party continued to articulate primarily with reference to the Khmer Rouge, just as "people's democracy" in its most narrow sense is portrayed as putting an end to the Khmer Rouge regime and creating a new political regime thereafter. The message, continuously transmitted during the election campaign, was that the nation's trajectory from the horrors of Democratic Kampuchea to present-day development depended on there having been no changes in national leadership after the end of the Khmer Rouge.[3] This discourse assumed a new flavor as novel technologies were

---

[1] The CPP tally increased from 38.2 percent in 1993 to 41.4 percent in 1998, 47.3 percent in 2003, and 58.1 percent in 2008.

[2] *Samkok* refers to the period of the Three Kingdoms in third century China, a period of division that has been popularized in Cambodia through a number of popular television programs.

[3] Cp. Sok Eysan's speech for the CPP in the TVK debate, July 24, 2013.

used to transmit it. Trucks drove around Phnom Penh showing films of the horrors of the Khmer Rouge regime, including documentary footage as well as the 1984 Hollywood-blockbuster "The Killing Fields." As in previous elections, a civil war not dissimilar in style to events in the 1970s was portrayed as an inevitable consequence of regime change.

The CPP intensified its didactic emphasis on past achievement in the wake of the garment workers' demonstrations of early January 2014, which provoked a violent crackdown against oppositional activities. At this crucial time for winning the allegiance of irreverent youth, a spot was repeatedly shown on national television in which a fictive father admonished his child, a garment worker, to be "a good child in society," positively contrasting the life of today's youth with his own life after the liberation from the Khmer Rouge in 1979.[4] The series of juxtapositions was read out: "If you are now a garment worker, then thirty-five years ago you would have been a forced laborer. If you now have new clothes, then thirty-five years ago you would have only one set of clothes to wear. If you now eat chicken, then thirty-five years ago you would have been starving. If you now suffer a little bit, then thirty-five years ago I almost died of suffering. If you now have the right to claim a high salary, then thirty-five years ago I worked without any rights." The father admonished the child "not to forget her birth origins" (*som kaun min phlech komnaoet*). The spot ended with the tag line "From a good father so that his child will become a good child in society."

The CPP attempt to mobilize youth against change appears in hindsight as one of the party's major mistakes. Campaigning against change, in general, is a counterintuitive message when dealing with youth—the message is listless, conservative, and lacking in vision. What is more, the battle for the Cambodian youth is for a youth that has no memories of Democratic Kampuchea, and who are neither frightened of a return of social instability nor grateful for liberation in 1979. The future-oriented vision of CNRP speaks with a different authority than that of the CPP to today's youth, who are engaged in creating a new nation.

A second pivotal issue revolving around the question of "change" is the ability of an individual to single-handedly concentrate the nation's ambitions in himself. In the election campaign, Hun Sen continued to frame political support as allegiance to him personally, based on his singular ability to represent the nation. This was reflected in the CPP's main campaign slogan, a direct appeal to loyalty to Hun Sen phrased as: "If you love, if you pity, if you like, if you trust Samdech Hun Sen, vote for the Cambodian People's Party. Voting for the Cambodian People's Party means voting for yourself." In line with the trend of an increasing concentration of political and symbolic power to Hun Sen, the slogan expressed the personalization of power to the prime minister at the expense of the CPP as a party—pursued ever more overtly. The CNRP message, meanwhile, was the direct opposite. Voting for the CNRP was time and again said to represent a vote for oneself, one's family, and all Khmers—rather than for the individual politicians, Sam Rainsy or Kem Sokha, according to the CNRP's advertising which depicted the two party leaders as secondary.[5]

---

[4] This spot was repeatedly shown on Cambodian Television Network (CTN), for example, on January 18, 2014.

[5] Cp. Kem Sokha's speech for the CNRP in the TVK debate, July 24, 2013.

The election results therefore seem to denude Hun Sen's claim to embody the nation's aspirations, suggesting that there was little substantiation under the facade. The CNRP lost no time in framing the CPP's loss of support as the prime minister's individual failure, noting how no one in the top CPP troika (Hun Sen, Heng Samrin, and Chea Sim) won in their home constituencies, which kindled CNRP calls for Hun Sen to step down. Hun Sen himself appears to have succumbed briefly to depression, to the point that senior politicians reported having been encouraged by outside powers to come together to raise his spirits.[6] Hun Sen's reaction appears rooted in a genuine belief in his own ability to personally channel the nation's ambitions. In a February 2014 speech, Hun Sen remarked, "They talk about the same 'face.' If I have the same face, what's the matter?"[7] Though dejected, Hun Sen's words nevertheless indicated that he will continue to pursue the beaten path. In April 2015, Hun Sen announced his intention to run for reelection as premier in 2018, and, following Chea Sim's death the following month, he was elected CPP president.

Third, the idea of change posited two competing models of the political economic order. The gift-giving practices that define Hun Sen's "people's democracy" were aggressively called into question by the CNRP, which made a concerted effort to bring down their legitimacy and appeal in its campaign. This was expressed in the ubiquitous CNRP campaign slogan: "My gasoline, my motorbike, my money, my morale, save my nation. Change! Change! Change!" The slogan referred to how CNRP campaign rally participants rode their own motorbikes and spent their own hard-earned money on gasoline, thus expressing their unselfish commitment to the nation's future. Its target was CPP rally participants, who received money for their participation (reportedly US$5 per day) and typically toured in trucks provided by the party, which were gaily embellished with colored lights and equipped with video screens and bombastic dance music. The CNRP slogan was printed on stickers and distributed to campaign rally participants, many of whom plastered them onto their motorbikes. The slogan's power lay in tying the rejection of gift-giving practices to the general call for change. Change was portrayed as constituted by citizens taking pride in spending their *own* resources for acting on their political conscience, rather than offering political allegiance in return for financial and material support.

In its campaign discourse, the CNRP encouraged the electorate to receive any gifts offered by the CPP, but to stop short of voting for the party. The typical CNRP narrative had it that many people collected the US$5 daily stipend from the CPP for campaigning for the party, only to bring this money to the donation boxes that the CNRP used to collect donations from rally participants in onsite tents at Freedom Park. According to CNRP lawmaker Mu Sochua, the party typically collected US$30,000 per rally day through these donation boxes.[8] The CNRP encouraged voters to take whatever they could get from the CPP. This reflected a willingness to accept the electorate's dependence on gift-giving rather than to condemn it, but to transform the act of receiving gifts into a subversive, covert rejection of the gift-giver (the CPP).

---

[6] Author's personal communication, November 2013.

[7] Khy Sovuthy, "Hun Sen Says His Face as Good as Any; Situation is Normal," *The Cambodia Daily*, February 11, 2014.

[8] Author's interview with Mu Sochua, November 20, 2013.

To counter the CPP model of handing out financial support as gifts, the CNRP mobilized its discourse on rights to argue on behalf of claiming guaranteed salaries and cost-of-living relief. The CNRP campaigned on a seven-point policy program centered on guaranteeing personal income, with three out of seven points guaranteeing minimum salaries for civil servants and workers and pensions for all individuals aged 65 years and above. The program also promised guaranteed minimum prices for rice, free medical care for the poor, equal education opportunities, youth employment, and price reductions for oil, fertilizer, and electricity, as well as lowered loan interest rates.[9] This program was to be funded by a set of measures including cutting back on corruption, taxing economic land concessions and gambling revenues, and raising licensing fees for the extraction of gold, oil, coal, and gas, although the CNRP did not exert itself to estimate how much revenue would be raised through these measures.

The two parties have reached sharply different conclusions about what the electoral results indicate regarding the parties' respective political-economic models. From the perspective of the CNRP leaders, their dramatic electoral gains stemmed from popular discontent with low living standards. The goal of the CNRP was to transform this discontent into an effective political movement to make people renounce gift-giving practices. Initially, in the CNRP analysis, supporters were motivated by an attempt to secure more personal income, such as promised by the party's seven-point platform. Once people were involved in the CNRP campaign, such initial motives transformed into a changed political consciousness whereby political participation was prized over the promised receipt of benefits.[10] Existing discontent presented an opportunity to educate the people, making their political imaginings conform to elite-defined liberal democracy. The CPP leaders interpreted their own sharp decline in electoral support very differently. According to them, people had developed an indifferent attitude toward the provision of infrastructure under the CPP, such as roads, bridges, and hospitals (much of it, in reality, funded by foreign aid), which they had started to take for granted. A vote for the CNRP, on the other hand, was understood as a vote to obtain more money to put in one's own pockets. This was what had motivated an electorate that had become apathetic about new and improved infrastructure, even though the government's providing such infrastructure forms a cornerstone of people's democracy.[11]

These respective analyses form the basis of the two parties' post-election strategies. The CNRP continues to focus on raising minimum salaries, framing this as a *right*. For example, at a demonstration on International Human Rights Day in December 2013, Sam Rainsy charged that four basic human rights were still lacking in Cambodia: the right to life, the right to decent and dignified living conditions, the right to freedom, and the right to elect political leaders. Salaries, he stated, were integral to both the second and third of these, as minimum salaries would guarantee that workers could live in a decent manner and enjoy freedom.[12] The CPP, by contrast, increased the scale of its gift-giving. A review of four different publications shows that the number of times gift-giving and other ceremonies were mentioned

---

[9] CNRP, *7 Point Policies of the CNRP* (Publisher unknown, 2013).

[10] Author's interview with Mu Sochua.

[11] Author's personal communication with senior CPP leaders, November–December 2013.

[12] Author's notes from Sam Rainsy speech on International Human Rights Day, December 10, 2013, Phnom Penh.

increased in the post-election period.[13] The recipe for recovery was more and better of the same, since the party reasoned that, if voters' main priority was to increase the amount of money they could pocket, it mattered little on what terms. Although there appears to be an element of truth to the analyses of both parties, the CPP gift-giving model is caving in, primarily due to the vast income discrepancy that it supports. Whether voters challenged it because they perceive that they have simply not received enough, or because of a full-scale rejection of the model, this discontent gave the CNRP the momentum to encourage the development of a rights-based political conscience.

The gains of the CNRP can thus be understood as a consequence of how it has, for the time being, successfully managed in its own favor the contradictions inherent in the Cambodian democratic project. For in rewriting democracy as defined by the basic structure of relations between the people and its leaders, and aggressively pushing for a change of mentality from one of receiving benefits to actively earning one's living, the party has offered a clear representation of the democratic agenda.

In pinning down its seven point plan, the CNRP seems to have produced a successful reading of the Cambodian people and their overhanging needs. CNRP grassroots mobilization is best understood as an attempt to channel popular demands for better living conditions. It has taken place through a mixture of championing a rights-based conscience, as well as practices of gift distribution (defended on the basis that these do not discriminate in a partisan political way), which again demonstrate a partial convergence with CPP practices, stemming from the shared focus on provision. The CNRP leadership's eagerness to integrate popular views otherwise wildly inaccessible to it was demonstrated by the People's Congresses set up during the post-election negotiation process with the CPP, where CNRP supporters were invited to take the stage and articulate their desired course of action.

The CNRP's post-electoral response conformed in all respects to the logic of the democratic project, and its priority of bringing down the electoral legitimacy of the CPP. The validity of the official 2013 election results is a thorny issue. International and local NGOs have raised serious questions about the announced results, asserting that the election process suffered from numerous flaws, but an independent and transparent investigation did not take place. An Electoral Reform Alliance (ERA) December 2013 report listed problems with the voter registry, such as excluding eligible voters but including invalid or duplicate names; widely distributing temporary official identification cards for voting; and failing to update the number of seats per constituency to accurately reflect population changes.[14] Meanwhile, while the central problem for democrats had previously been why the majority of the people would vote for a party that went against their objective interests—explained by democrats by asserting that the CPP explicitly misled the public—they were now swift to conclude that the people had finally voted in line with their interests (i.e. for the˙ CNRP). This sea change was explained by the

---

[13] Author's personal communication with Steve Heder, December 10, 2013. The publications Heder reviewed are: the Hun Sen cabinet newsletter, *Cambodia New Vision*; the CPP-friendly *Deum Ampil News*; *Cambodia Express News*; and *Kampuchea Thmey*. There were more mentions of gift-giving and other ceremonies during October and November 2013 compared to the same period in 2012.

[14] The Electoral Reform Alliance (ERA), "Joint Report on the Conduct of the 2013 Cambodian Elections," November 2013.

emergence of a young generation of voters who, having nothing to lose, felt no fear (*khlach*); who, through rapid access to information channels such as social media, were increasingly well-informed (putting an end to *khlov*); and who, consequently, were urged on, rather than held back, by their hunger (*khlean*). On election night the CNRP swiftly proclaimed itself the winner shortly after the voting stations closed, only to withdraw this statement later in the evening. Only an hour after the CNRP declaration, Minister of Information Khieu Kanharith just as hastily announced on Facebook preliminary results declaring a CPP victory. These results would later be confirmed as official. Observers have in vain urged the CNRP to produce evidence to support its renewed assertion—made again two days after the election—that it, rather than the CPP, was the real victor. The conviction with which CNRP's claims were made appears rooted not in evidence, but in an intuitive belief that the people had at long last voted for their own gain—eliminating the divide between their will and their interests—and that the CNRP had won because they ought to have won as the party representing the popular interest. A few weeks after the elections, CNRP discourse would change to demand merely a limited investigation into election-day and ballot-counting problems. That the party was ultimately content with only a minor probe suggests that vagueness could, for the party, be constructive.

Doubtlessly, the 2013 elections represented the best electoral performance of the democrats since the reintroduction of multi-party politics. Their faith in the ability of elections to carry the people's voice thus boosted, electoral reform for the future has emerged as a significant priority for the CNRP. Refusing to take up their seats in the National Assembly, CNRP made the reform of the National Election Committee (NEC) a cornerstone of demands for a political settlement. The July 22, 2014, agreement, which ended a year-long political impasse, achieved just that NEC reform: suggesting that the CNRP had staked everything on electoral reform ahead of the next general elections, in 2018. The deal also meant an agreement was reached between Sam Rainsy and Hun Sen to establish a "culture of dialogue." Hailed as the beginning of a new era in Cambodian politics, the culture of dialogue was based on the different political parties for the first time recognizing each other as legitimate contenders in the electoral arena. Politics was to shift from a conflict over fundamentals to a contest over issues.

The culture of dialogue has been supported by a discourse of Khmer unity, which peaked at the April 2015 Angkor Sangkran festival, amidst the symbolically charged Angkor monuments. Though organized by the Union of Youth Federations of Cambodia (UYFC), headed by Hun Sen's son Hun Many, this Khmer New Year festival was attended jointly by Hun Sen and Sam Rainsy. Suggesting that the word "opposition" should now be replaced by the "sweeter-sounding" "party out of government," Hun Sen asserted that, "We must stay together because, at the very least, *we have the same Cambodian blood.*" An unprecedented one million locals were reported to have attended the festival, which the unlikely pair toured together, inspecting cultural exhibits, handicraft stalls, and shows.[15]

According to Hun Sen, Cambodia has entered a new political stage in its history, as the "culture of dialogue" has replaced a "culture of revenge."[16] Echoing these words, Sam Rainsy has hailed the culture of dialogue as a new, "truly democratic"

---

[15] Mech Dara and Alex Willemyns, "Hun Sen, Sam Rainsy Ring in New Year Together," *The Cambodia Daily*, April 15, 2015.

[16] "Hun Sen to Seek Fifth Term as Cambodia's Prime Minister," *RFA Khmer*, April 29, 2015.

culture, which is to be established not only as a new practice but also a new *mindset*, to replace the old one of war, conflict, and killing. Cambodia, he said, is at a "turning point."[17] Elaborating her vision of the newfound culture of dialogue, CNRP MP Mu Sochua has written that "in a culture where mistrust and fear divide us, the nascent culture of dialogue alleviates political tensions, it encourages people at different ends of the conflict to find a middle way. [...] The 22 July Agreements between the two political parties representing the people at the National Assembly should be seen beyond a political deal but as a breakthrough for inclusive democracy." She concluded that "there must be a shared vision and a common agenda to end the years of mistrust and antagonism."[18]

Tellingly, key to the culture of dialogue has been an overhaul of political discourse. A "code of conduct," to be disseminated among grassroots activists, set forth what words party members are allowed to use during public speeches, forbidding some of the most common political language.[19] The CNRP was to refrain from phrases such as "communist dictator," "Vietnamese puppet," and "person who sells the nation," whilst the CPP was to cease threatening arrest, imprisonment, and civil war.

Democrats stand divided over the culture of dialogue, which critics consider a political trick, designed to break forcibly the political deadlock. When Hun Sen threatened to kill the culture of dialogue if CNRP members continued to criticize the CPP, Sam Rainsy responded that criticism would be toned down, quoting the "new mindset and culture of dialogue" according to which "we must respect our competitor."[20] Criticism, banned from the culture of dialogue, has no place in the new democratic culture of agreeable political competition. The CNRP has had little choice but to accept the CPP's bid for "reconciliation"—and doubtlessly aspires to push rhetoric as far as possible into favorable political realities. Yet criticism is bound to reappear, and for as long as it is not allowed to be part of a conflict over issues, indications are that Cambodian politics will soon enough return to a conflict over fundamentals.

The years 2012–13 brought decisive if predictable developments to the Cambodian monarchy and political royalism, which followed the downward trajectory that this book has traced. Two events stand out as watersheds. Each an endpoint in its own way, these may at first glance appear to be contradictory. In October 2012, just before his 91st birthday (according to the Cambodian way of counting age), King-Father Sihanouk passed away in Beijing, causing an enormous outburst of public commotion in Cambodia. Despite this dazzling display of popular affection for Sihanouk, in the 2013 national elections royalist parties for the first time failed to win any seats.

These dual events—Sihanouk's death and the electoral obliteration of royalist parties—provide decisive testimony for the argument put forward in this book: that the devotion and reverence which Sihanouk nurtured and enjoyed is shockingly

---

[17] "Sam Rainsy Defends 'Culture of Dialogue' with Ruling Cambodian People's Party," *VOA*, May 15, 2015.

[18] Mu Sochua, "Nurturing the Culture of Dialogue," *Phnom Penh Post*, February 16, 2015.

[19] Kuch Naren, "Parties Agree to Code of Conduct for 'Culture of Dialogue,'" *The Cambodia Daily*, May 9, 2015.

[20] Hul Reaksmey and Alex Willemyns, "Rainsy: Sokha Will Heed PM's Warning," *The Cambodia Daily*, April 30, 2015.

useless in winning support for political royalism. Beyond Sihanouk, a *concept* of royalism is not deeply anchored in Cambodia. Royalists' celebration of Sihanouk served to strengthen the personal legitimacy of the King-Father. Yet this has contributed only marginally, if at all, to the legitimacy of their own political project. The death of Sihanouk, which reinforced and accentuated affection for him, has, therefore, paradoxically, left the royalists weakened, and out of steam.

The eradication of royalists from the parliamentary political scene in all likelihood completes the long and steady decline of political royalism, in hindsight commenced at the time of FUNCINPEC's erstwhile 1993 electoral victory (if not already in 1955). The ultimate meaninglessness of royalism as a political project can be traced back to the contradictions previously identified, namely, those between: national unity and partisan political action; kingship and political royalism; contending conceptualizations of royalist democracy; and the Sihanoukist legacy conceptualized as embodiment versus a doctrinal identity. The failure to resolve these has resulted in the now flagrant meaninglessness of royalism, hollowness of the backward gaze to the Sangkum-era, and overt loss of an independent stance vis-à-vis the CPP.

With political royalism obliterated, the monarchy might appear well placed to take on the reconciliating role that has been called for from across the political spectrum. Any such expectations have been swiftly preempted. In the election aftermath, when the just-elected CNRP lawmakers resolved to boycott the National Assembly, the king urged them to join its opening session—which the CPP had declared would nonetheless go ahead—to express "national unity."[21] Despite subsequent calls by the CNRP, civil society groups, and monks for a delay until negotiations between the two parties had produced a solution (two rounds of petitions were delivered claiming to represent about 500,000 citizens), the king proceeded to convene the opening of the parliament in the absence of the CNRP parliamentarians-elect, issued a Royal Decree appointing Hun Sen as prime minister, and asked him to form a new government.[22] Sihamoni's actions differ sharply from those of Sihanouk's, who, when confronted with a similar situation in 2003, refused to preside over a disputed National Assembly until an agreement had been reached. According to Sisowath Thomico, the CPP coerced Sihamoni to take what could appear as a partisan stand, in order to split the people and the king from each other. The CPP and Royal Palace, he noted, would now be equated with each other in the eyes of the public.[23] When voices were again raised asking for the king's intervention to help mediate a political solution following the CPP's January 2014 crackdown on oppositional activities and its ban on assembly, the Royal Palace released a statement that asked people not to "exploit" the names of the king and the Queen-Mother for political ends.[24] It is clear that Sihamoni does not wish to take up the role as a mediator, anymore than he wished to be a king.

---

[21] Vong Sokheng and Meas Sokchea, "CNRP, Take Your Seats: King," *Phnom Penh Post*, September 19, 2013.

[22] May Titthara and Kevin Ponniah, "Petitions Piling Up for King," *Phnom Penh Post*, September 23, 2013.

[23] Colin Meyn, "King Convenes Opening of Contested National Assembly," *The Cambodia Daily*, September 23, 2013.

[24] Colin Meyn and Hul Reaksmey, "Leave King out of Politics, Royal Cabinet Demands," *The Cambodia Daily*, January 24, 2014.

It seems paradoxical that the monarch should refuse a mediating role at a time when the nation appeared more divided than ever since reunification, and when the display of popular allegiance to the monarchy after Sihanouk's death has made its abolition—previously threatened by the CPP—a political impossibility. It appears that Sihamoni and the Queen-Mother support the CPP out of a genuine conviction that only the CPP can act as guardian of the monarchy and of Sihanouk's legacy. According to palace sources, the monarch and his mother consider the CNRP covertly republican and wish to prevent the party from coming to power.[25]

The strong stance in favor of the CPP taken by the monarch and Queen-Mother has highlighted division in the royal family, to some extent along the lines of the division between the Norodom versus Sisowath branches of the family. The Queen-Mother has been known to deplore the fact that nearly all members of the Sisowath branch support the CNRP. Indeed, the polarization of the political landscape prompted several prominent Sisowath politicians, formerly part of FUNCINPEC, to express their support for the CNRP. The only royal to join the CNRP leadership rank, Sisowath Thomico, did so to the dismay of the Royal Palace. One Sisowath royal recounted hearing Sihamoni ridiculing the CNRP protesters at a royal palace ceremony by imitating them shouting their slogan, "change! change! change!" A change of the status quo was precisely what the monarch wanted to avoid. To the Sisowath royal, however, his attitude reflected a disconnect from popular aspirations.[26]

Ranariddh, meanwhile, has made it clear that he remains unable to overcome the contradictions that have rendered his political project fruitless so far. In March 2014, Ranariddh launched a new party, the *Sangkum Reastr Reachea Tepetey* (Community of Royalist People Party), a clear reference to his father's *Sangkum Reastr Niyum*. This party offers yet another reminder of Ranariddh's inability to refresh his political identity. Announcing his intention to re-enter politics, Ranariddh cited as his main inspiration an admonition by Sihanouk on October 30, 2011 (on the occasion of the twentieth anniversary of Sihanouk's return from exile and his ninetieth birthday—a last grand appearance), for the monarchy to be politically neutral. Ranariddh understood this admonition to urge all royalists to come together as one force. This statement now provided the motivation for his return to politics with the stated mission to turn royalists (*neak reachniyum*), Sihanoukists (*neak Sihanoukniyum*), and real nationalists (*neak cheat niyum pit brakâd*) into a *national* political force that was to take an active part in solving major national problems and help the CPP and CNRP overcome the political impasse that had developed, achieving national reunification.[27]

Ranariddh's justification for the new party—a party that, to all appearances, was a transparent CPP-backed attempt to draw voters away from the CNRP—was a case in point. Although the reasoning seemed self-evident to the prince, it posed a flagrant contradiction. In response to Sihanouk's call for the suprapolitical stance of

---

[25] This is despite frantic CNRP attempts to reassure the monarchy of its support. After the July elections, Sam Rainsy headed a delegation to the Royal Palace, where he expressed his support for the throne—the "symbol" and "soul" of the nation—and his belief that the monarchy should be strengthened for the stability of the country. Meas Sokchea and Shane Worrell, "Rainsy's Royal Audience," *Phnom Penh Post*, August 2, 2013.

[26] Author's personal communication, January 2014.

[27] Heng Reaksmey, "Prince Ranariddh to Form New Royal Political Party," *VOA Khmer*, February 25, 2014.

royals, Ranariddh created yet another royalist political party. Again exposing Ranariddh's readiness to be involved in politics at all costs, this also reflects the contradictions entailed in contemporary royalism itself, that is, the difficulty of transposing royalism to the party political system. As the Cambodian monarchy steps into the twenty-first century, these lingering post-independence dilemmas are no closer to being solved, while the monarchy—and with it these dilemmas—steadily becomes less relevant.

To a greater extent than ever, the waning voices of those royalists who remain now primarily validate the CPP. In January 2015, Ranariddh reassumed the FUNCINPEC presidency, dissolving the Community of Royalist People Party. Echoing the language of national reconciliation, Ranariddh pledged ever closer cooperation with the CPP under Hun Sen by uniting royalists with them.[28] Ranariddh's reassumption of the FUNCINPEC presidency—in which, according to the prince, he was encouraged by Hun Sen—is best understood as a consequence of CPP concerns.[29] The 2013 elections made evident that eliminating royalism from the party political system paradoxically endangers the CPP, by creating a united opposition and with it a real possibility of political change. Hun Sen doubtlessly anticipated reversing this situation by bringing the royalist party back to life. The CPP is keenly aware that FUNCINPEC enjoys next to no popular support. Ranariddh's reemergence, then, was an attempt to mobilize whatever popular allegiance he may still command to disrupt the advances of the CNRP. The main role of royalism in Cambodian politics will now be to split the opposition vote, an enterprise that is likely to be masterminded by Hun Sen. Yet such attempts are likely to draw only a minimum of attention, as the CPP's co-option of royalists ultimately backfires. As royalists have lost their independent stance, they have also lost the capacity to gain legitimacy for the CPP, which a more subtle political positioning could perhaps have achieved.

Ranariddh and his followers have staked their fortunes on the political expediency of their reappearance on the stage for Hun Sen. Tellingly, at the time of the 2013 elections, a senior advisor to Ranariddh confided to me in private conversation that Hun Sen and Ranariddh were now "closer than ever before," and passed on, with not a little pride, the detail that Hun Sen had referred to Ranariddh as his "blood brother."[30] According to the advisor, Hun Sen had promised Ranariddh a political comeback by 2018 at the latest. It thus came as little surprise when Ranariddh reappeared at the helm of FUNCINPEC. Yet, indications are that Ranariddh's third way will continue to attract minimal interest in the polarized political landscape of contemporary Cambodia. Ranariddh's faith in his ability to exercise political influence with the blessing of Hun Sen was itself central to his political demise. Still, as pointed out by a disgruntled former Norodom Ranariddh Party parliamentary candidate, Ranariddh and the circle around him place their remaining hopes in the possibility that Hun Sen needs him.

Behind these developments lurk the tensions destabilizing royalism. First, the diverse political tendencies within the royal family have divided it at a crucial point

[28] Mech Dara and Alex Willemyns, "Ranariddh Named Funcinpec President—Again," *The Cambodia Daily*, January 20, 2015.

[29] Alex Willemyns, "Prince Says FUNCINPEC to Work Closely with CPP," *The Cambodia Daily*, January 3, 2015.

[30] Author's interview, July 2013.

of time, and the majority of its members have had their voices stifled. Political royalism has been crippled by placing national unity above partisan political action, which is claimed as the rationale behind both the palace's reluctance to play a role in the post-election period and Ranariddh's uninspiring political agenda. Second, the mandate of political royalism remains as unaccounted for as ever. The Royal Palace has dismissed political royalism as incompatible with kingship, and uses this to chastise royals who express a political stance—in particular, those who favor the CNRP. Third, the two contending discourses of royalist democracy have both finally and irreversibly demonstrated themselves meaningless for asserting a political royalist identity. Those advocating a "democratic opposition" identity now look toward the CNRP, having abandoned all hopes for a separate royalist initiative. Ranariddh, on the other hand, has continued on his established path of a "third way" in clear reference to the Sangkum model, but this is widely understood to serve the CPP and is not associated with an independent political royalist identity. Fourth, attempts to reinvent a Sihanoukist identity by turning the Sihanoukist legacy into a doctrine has allowed this identity to be taken up by the CPP. For instance, on November 9, 2013, the sixtieth anniversary of independence, the CPP announced itself as "Sihanoukist." In a political landscape divided by two strong parties, it is this voice that carries weight.

It is thus unsurprising that, in the aftermath of Sihanouk's death, Hun Sen has stepped up claims to regal and moral legitimacy, legitimacy that Sihamoni has not denied him. In the run-up to July elections, Sihamoni told an assembled audience in Preah Sihanouk province that Hun Sen's leadership had produced many positive results for the Cambodian nation (*cheat*), both in the spiritual realm (*puttheachakr*) and as a kingdom (*anachakr*), thus morally sanctioning Hun Sen's leadership over these three "traditional" pillars of the ideal political order.[31] Sihamoni referred particularly to the donations and public services received by the province, including pagodas and shrines (in support of *puttheachakr*), and schools, hospitals, and infrastructure projects (in support of *anachakr*). By according spiritual-regal legitimacy to Hun Sen on the basis of the distribution of development projects framed as gifts, Sihamoni endorsed these foundational practices of Hun Sen's "people's democracy"—reminiscent of Sihanouk's "social opening"—as practices according legitimate leadership over the nation, Buddhist realm, and the kingdom. This statement was felt even more keenly given that Prince Sisowath Thomico campaigned in Preah Sihanouk province as the CNRP MP candidate.

Sihanouk's death has provided Hun Sen with the opportunity to intensify his claim to genuinely regal, or superior to regal, status in the kingdom, without facing the muted counterpoint to such claims that Sihanouk's mere presence on the planet still offered during his final years. Carrying himself as a contender to Sihanouk's royal family line—the modern-day Sdech Kân—Hun Sen spread the message that he finally and irrevocably outshone the royal family line. Having witnessed the strength of popular allegiance to Sihanouk that the outpouring of public grief at Sihanouk's death evidenced, Hun Sen placed renewed emphasis on his assertion that he is the god-son of Sihanouk. Hun Sen continues to lay claims to belong to an alternative

---

[31] "Preah Mohaksatr Mean Preah Reach Bânhchaul Sârsaoer pi kar Doek Noam Dâ Troem Trauv robâs Samdech Techo knong Kar Øphivodth Brotes" [The King Expresses his Admiration for Samdech Techo's Correct Leadership in National Development], *DAP-news*, July 10, 2013.

royal genealogical line that is based not on bloodline, but on spiritual affinity and moral prowess.[32]

At Sihanouk's February 4, 2013, cremation ceremony, Hun Sen's claims stood out in sharp relief. Traditionally, the deceased monarch's successor lights the funeral pyre, a role most recently performed by Sihanouk at the 1960 cremation of his father, Suramarit. At Sihanouk's cremation, however, it was Hun Sen who lit the pyre—after Sihamoni failed in the attempt. According to eyewitnesses, events transpired as related—and as planned: the cremation was achieved electrically. A newspaper article in the daily *Deum Ampil-news* (DAP), entitled "The Spiritual Power of Hun Sen at the Cremation of Samdech Preah Norodom Sihanouk," outlined what was described as a "historical" event at the lighting of the royal funeral pyre.[33] The Queen-Mother had first received the flame to light the pyre, but the pyre lit only briefly and then went out. Sihamoni then attempted to light the pyre, but it again went out shortly after catching fire. This was repeated a third time when the Supreme Patriarch of the Thammayut order, Bour Kry, made an attempt. Brahmin priests then poured alcohol to stimulate a fire, but to no avail. At this point, something "unbelievable, fantastic, and wondrous" happened: Hun Sen bowed down to pray and pay his respects, in the most determined and confident way possible, and when he then lit the pyre, it caught fire quickly, burning until only the royal ashes remained.[34]

The significance of this event was clear to the DAP journalist. The event "truly showed the strong, skillful, and potent spiritual power (*bon barami*) and magical power (*sakseth*) of Samdech Techo, who as a leader is the most glorious and illustrious (*oudong oudom*) individual, and who is full of priceless virtue (*mohakunatoas*), so that he was able to light the funeral pyre." It followed from Hun Sen's unremitting determination to protect the king, the throne, and the royal family, and, the article seemed to suggest, gave further proof that Sihanouk had designated Hun Sen as his worthy successor. Yet, at the same time, the event also testified to the moral—and, by consequence, physical and concrete—superiority of Hun Sen over Sihanouk. "As a wondrous person that Samdech Preah Norodom Sihanouk fought but could not win over, there is only Samdech Techo Hun Sen, strongman of Cambodia," the journalist asserted. It is hard to imagine this ultimate defeat illustrated in a more evocative way than by Hun Sen alone being able to reduce the body of Sihanouk to ashes.

A second article by Soy Sopheap, DAP's head, underlined the overriding theme: that Hun Sen's spiritual strength as Sihanouk's god-son was ultimately able to command Sihanouk to leave this world. [35] In the words of the article, only

---

[32] This does not exclude the possibility that Hun Sen himself experiences such an affinity. According to a family member, Hun Sen never dreamed about his own father after his death (Hun Neang passed away in 2013), but dreamed twice about Sihanouk after his passing.

[33] Kuch Sovann, "Barami Robâs Samdech Techo Nov Pel Thvay Preah Phloeng Samdech Preah Norodom Sihanouk" [The Spiritual Power of Hun Sen at the Cremation of Samdech Preah Norodom Sihanouk], *Deum Ampil-news*, February 13, 2013.

[34] Ibid.

[35] Soy Sopheap, "Preah Mohaksatr Samdech Mae, Samdech Sanghareach Teang 2 Thvay Preah Phloeng 4 Loek Min Chheah, Loek Ti 5 Samdech Techo Buong Suong Som, Toep Thvay Preah Phloeng Chheah" [The King, the Queen-Mother, and Both Supreme Patriarchs Light the Fire Four Times Without it Catching Fire, the Fifth Time Samdech Techo Prays, Then it Catches Fire], *Deum Ampil-news*, February 13, 2013.

Sihanouk's god-son (*botr toa*) Hun Sen had the magic power (*ritheanupheap*) to have the resolve (*athithan*) to request Sihanouk's soul (*Preah reach vinjeankon*) to allow him to light the cremation fire, and the spiritual power (*bon barami*) to make the King-Father's soul accept him. The narrative of the cremation shows, then, that the ultimate value of Hun Sen inheriting Sihanouk's moral prowess is that he emerges more powerful than Sihanouk, and more so than any royal contenders to power from Sihanouk's blood line.

Upon the publication of these media accounts, Hun Sen made an official interpretation of the meaning of what he referred to as the "miracle"—the fact that only he was able to light the funeral pyre—to preclude alternative interpretations from spreading.[36] He denied that the "miracle" might have resulted from lacking technology—the technological equipment at the cremation was said to have been perfect—and attributed it solely to the spiritual (*barami*) and magic power (*ritheanupheap*) of Sihanouk, that had been able to prevent the fire from catching—until Hun Sen lit the pyre. The fact that he could light the pyre, Hun Sen suggested, stemmed from a shared history between the two in a previous life, which had tied them together also in this life. Neatly framing the trajectory of Sihanouk's sometimes formidable presence in the Second Kingdom into a beginning and an end under the PM's oversight, Hun Sen recalled how he had accompanied Sihanouk ever since travelling with Sihanouk from Beijing back to Cambodia on 14 November 1991, on the brink of the Second Kingdom, until the funeral pyre, turning Sihanouk into ashes. Attributing the "miracle" to a deliberate act by Sihanouk, Hun Sen claimed the Queen-Mother as his source.[37] The spiritual superiority of Hun Sen was thereby granted—or at least never denied—by the royal family itself.

While Sihanouk's ability to incarnate the nation was always contested during his lifetime, his epitaphs paint him as Cambodia's last God-King. This indicates that Sihanouk's attempted national embodiment will define the way he is written down in history, but also that this claimed quality has failed to carry over either to the constitutional monarch or to political royalists. It remains to be seen with what words history will record Hun Sen's representation of the nation. In the final instance, it is the nation—if understood as the Cambodian people—that will have to provide these judgments, and to decide on how to define its relations with its future leaders. There are no lack of visionaries in Cambodia, where imaginations quickly crystallize into reality.

---

[36] "Samdech Techo Bâk Sray Øpphoutheto Neanea Dael Kaoet Laoeng Knong Preah Reach Pithi Bon Ning Pithi Thvay Preah Phloeng Preah Borom Ratanakkot" [Samdech Techo Interprets Different Miracles that Took Place at the Royal Cremation of the Late King-Father], *Deum Ampil-news*, February 14, 2013; Li Selea, "Samdech Hun Sen Bâk Sray Pi Øpphoutheto Nov Thngai Thvay Preah Phloeng Preah Borom Sâp Samdech Preah Mohaviroksatr" [Samdech Hun Sen Interprets the Miracle at the Royal Cremation of the King-Father], *Deum Ampil-news*, February 14, 2013.

[37] Meas Sokchea, "Miracle Cremation: PM Hun Sen," *Phnom Penh Post*, February 15, 2013.

BIBLIOGRAPHY

Abdoul-Carime, Nasir. "Réflexion sur le Régime Sihanoukien: La Monopolisation du Verbe par le Pouvoir Royal." *Péninsule* 31 no. 2 (1995): 77–97.

Aberbach, Joel D., and Bert A. Rockman. "Conducting and Coding Elite Interviews." *PS: Political Science and Politics* 35 no. 4 (2002): 673–76.

Alagappa, Muthiah. "Introduction." In *Political Legitimacy in Southeast Asia: The Quest for Moral Authority*, ed. Muthiah Alagappa, 1–8. Stanford: Stanford University Press, 1995.

———. "The Anatomy of Legitimacy." In *Political Legitimacy in Southeast Asia: The Quest for Moral Authority*, ed. Muthiah Alagappa, 11–30. Stanford: Stanford University Press, 1995.

———. "The Bases of Legitimacy." In *Political Legitimacy in Southeast Asia: The Quest for Moral Authority*, ed. Muthiah Alagappa, 31–53. Stanford: Stanford University Press, 1995.

Anderson, Benedict. "Cacique Democracy in the Philippines: Origins and Dreams." *New Left Review* 169 (1988): 3–31.

———. *Language and Power: Exploring Political Cultures in Indonesia*. Ithaca: Cornell University Press, 1990.

———. *Imagined Communities: Reflections on the Origin and Spread of Nationalism*. London: Verso, 1991.

———. *The Spectre of Comparisons: Nationalism, Southeast Asia, and the World*. London: Verso, 1998.

———. "Western Nationalism and Eastern Nationalism: Is There a Difference that Matters?" *New Left Review* 9 (2001): 31–42.

Armstrong, John A. *Nations Before Nationalism*. Chapel Hill: University of North Carolina Press, 1982.

Armstrong, John P. *Sihanouk Speaks*. New York: Walker, 1964.

Ashley, D. W. *Pol Pot, Peasants and Peace: Continuity and Change in Khmer Rouge Political Thinking, 1985–1991*. Bangkok: Indochinese Refugee Information Center, Institute of Asian Studies, Chulalongkorn University, 1992.

Asia Foundation. *Democracy in Cambodia – 2003: A Survey of the Cambodian Electorate*. Phnom Penh: Cambodia, 2003.

Aspinall, Edward. "The Construction of Grievance: Natural Resources and Identity in a Separatist Conflict." *Journal of Conflict Resolution* 51 no. 6 (2007): 950–72.

Aspinall, Edward, and Marcus Mietzner, ed. *Problems of Democratization in Indonesia: Elections, Institutions and Society*. Singapore: Institute of Southeast Asian Studies, 2010.

Baird, Ian G. "Different Views of History: Shades of Irredentism along the Laos–Cambodia Border." *Journal of Southeast Asian Studies* 41 no. 2 (2010): 187–213.

Barker, Rodney S. *Political Legitimacy and the State*. Oxford: Clarendon, 1990.

Barnett, Anthony. "Cambodia Will Never Disappear." *New Left Review* 180 (1990): 101–25.

Baruch, Jacques. *La Démocratie au Cambodge*. Bruxelles: Éditions Thanh-Long, 1967.

Berry, Jeffrey M. "Validity and Reliability Issues in Elite Interviewing." *PS: Political Science and Politics* 35 no. 4 (2002): 679–82.

Bhabha, Homi. "Dissemination: Time, Narrative and the Margins of the Modern Nation." In *Nation and Narration*, ed. Homi Bhabha, 291–322. London: Routledge, 1990.

Blunt, Peter, and Mark Turner. "Decentralisation, Democracy and Development in a Post-Conflict Society: Commune Councils in Cambodia." *Public Administration and Development* 25 no. 1 (2005): 75–87.

Bourdier, Frédéric. *The Mountain of Precious Stones: Ratanakiri, Cambodia*. Phnom Penh: Center for Khmer Studies, 2006.

Brown, David. "Ethnic and Nationalist Politics in Southeast Asia." In *Contemporary Southeast Asia*, ed. Mark Beeson, 143–56. New York: Palgrave Macmillan, 2009.

Brown, Frederick Z., and David G. Timberman, ed. *Cambodia and the International Community: The Quest for Peace, Development, and Democracy*. New York: Asia Society; Singapore: Institute of Southeast Asian Studies, 1998.

Carothers, Thomas. "Struggling with Semi-Authoritarians." In *Democracy Assistance: International Cooperation for Democratization*, ed. Peter Burnell, 210–25. London: Frank Cass, 2000.

Chhak, Sarin. *Les Frontières du Cambodge*. Paris: Dalloz, 1966.

Chaloemtiarana, Thak. *Thailand: The Politics of Despotic Paternalism*. Ithaca: Cornell Southeast Asia Program Publications, [1979] 2007.

Chandler, David P. "Seeing Red: Perceptions of Cambodian History in Democratic Kampuchea." In *Revolution and Its Aftermath in Kampuchea*, ed. David Chandler and Ben Kiernan, 34–56. New Haven: Yale University Press, 1983.

———. *The Tragedy of Cambodian History: Politics, War and Revolution Since 1945*. New Haven, CT; London: Yale University Press, 1991.

———. *Brother Number One: A Political Biography of Pol Pot*. Oxford: Westview Press, 1999.

———. *A History of Cambodia*. Third ed. Boulder, CO: Westview Press, 2000.

———. "Songs at the Edge of the Forest: Perceptions of Order in Three Cambodian Texts." In *At the Edge of the Forest: Essays in Honor of David Chandler*, ed. Anne R. Hansen and Judy Ledgerwood, 31–46. Ithaca: Cornell Southeast Asia Program Publications, 2008.

Chatterjee, Partha. *The Nation and Its Fragments: Colonial and Postcolonial Histories*. Princeton: Princeton University Press, 1993.

———. "Anderson's Utopia." *Diacritics* 29 no. 4 (1999): 128–34.

Chhay, Yiheang, ed. *Samdech Hun Sen: Tossânah Noyobay Aphirok Selobah Aphivoddh Sangkom neung Chomrieng 115 Bot* [*Samdech Hun Sen: Political Thought, Arts Conservation, Social Development and 115 Songs*]. Phnom Penh: Im Savoan, 2005.

———, ed. *Samdech Akka Moha Sena Padei Techo Hun Sen: Neayok Rothmontrey Brosaut Chenh pi Trokaul Kâsekâr* [*Samdech Akka Moha Sena Padei Techo Hun Sen: Prime Minister Born to a Farmer's Family*]. Phnom Penh: Ponleu Pech, 2007.

Coedès, George. "Le Portrait dans l'art khmer." *Arts Asiatiques* 7 (1960): 179–98.

Cohen, Erik. *Thai Society in Comparative Perspective: Collected Essays*. Bangkok: White Lotus Books, 1991.

Condominas, George. "A Few Remarks about Thai Political Systems." In *Natural Symbols in South East Asia*, ed. G. B. Milner, 105–12. London: School of Oriental and African Studies, 1978.

Connor, Walker. *Ethno-nationalism: The Quest for Understanding*. Princeton: Princeton University Press, 1994.

Connors, Michael Kelly. *Democracy and National Identity in Thailand*. London: RoutledgeCurzon, 2003.

Corfield, Justin. *Khmers Stand Up!: A History of the Cambodian Government 1970–1975*. Clayton, VIC: Center of Southeast Asia, Monash University, 1994.

Craig, Cairns. "Benedict Anderson's Fictional Communities." In *The Influence of Benedict Anderson*, ed. Alistair McCleery and Benjamin A. Brabon, 21–40. Edinburgh: Merchiston Publishing, 2007.

Croissant, Aurel. "From Transition to Defective Democracy: Mapping Asian Democratization." *Democratization* 11 no. 5 (2004): 156–78.

———. "The Perils and Promises of Democratization through United Nations Transitional Authority – Lessons from Cambodia and East Timor." *Democratization* 15 no. 3 (2008): 649–68.

Davies, Philip H. J. "Spies as Informants: Triangulation and the Interpretation of Elite Interview Data in the Study of the Intelligence and Security Services." *Politics* 21 no. 1 (2001): 73–80.

Davis, Erik W. "Imaginary Conversations with Mothers About Death." In *At the Edge of the Forest: Essays in Honor of David Chandler*, ed. Anne R. Hansen and Judy Ledgerwood, 221–48. Ithaca: Cornell Southeast Asia Program Publications, 2008.

Day, Tony. *Fluid Iron: State Formation in Southeast Asia*. Honolulu: University of Hawai'i Press, 2002.

De Bernon, Olivier. "Le Buddh Daṃnāy: Note sur un Texte Apocalyptique Khmer." *Bulletin de l'École Française d'Extrême-Orient (BEFEO)* 81 (1994): 83–100.

———. "La Prédiction du Bouddha." *Aséanie* 1 (1998): 43–66.

Dryzek, John S., and Leslie Holmes, ed. *Post-Communist Democratization: Political Discourses Across Thirteen Countries*. Cambridge: Cambridge University Press, 2002.

Dunlop, Nic. *The Lost Executioner: The Story of Comrade Duch and the Khmer Rouge*. London: Bloomsbury, 2005.

Ear, Sophal. "The Political Economy of Aid and Regime Legitimacy in Cambodia." In *Beyond Democracy in Cambodia: Political Reconstruction in a Post-Conflict Society*, ed. Joakim Öjendal and Mona Lilja, 151–88. Copenhagen: NIAS Press, 2009.

Edwards, Penny. "Imagining the Other in Cambodian Nationalist Discourse Before and During the UNTAC Period." In *Propaganda, Politics, and Violence in Cambodia*, ed. Stephen Heder and Judy Ledgerwood, 50–72. Armonk: M. E. Sharpe, 1996.

————. "Making a Religion of the Nation and its Language: The French Protectorate (1863–1954) and the Dhammakay." In *History, Buddhism, and New Religious Movements in Cambodia*, ed. John Marston and Elizabeth Guthrie, 63–85. Honolulu: University of Hawai'i Press, 2004.

————. *Cambodge: The Cultivation of a Nation, 1860–1945*. Honolulu: University of Hawai'i Press, 2007.

————. "Between a Song and a *Prei*: Tracking Cambodian History and Cosmology through the Forest." In *At the Edge of the Forest: Essays in Honor of David Chandler*, ed. Anne R. Hansen and Judy Ledgerwood, 137–62. Ithaca: Cornell Southeast Asia Program Publications, 2008.

————. "The Moral Geology of the Present: Structuring Morality, Menace and Merit." In *People of Virtue: Reconfiguring Religion, Power and Moral Order in Cambodia*, ed. Alexandra Kent and David Chandler, 213–37. Copenhagen: NIAS Press, 2008.

Ehrentraut, Stefan. "Perpetually Temporary: Citizenship and Ethnic Vietnamese in Cambodia." *Ethnic and Racial Studies* 34 no. 5 (2011): 779–98.

The Electoral Reform Alliance (ERA). *Joint-Report on the Conduct of the 2013 Cambodian Elections*. Phnom Penh: Cambodia, 2013.

Eng, Soth. *Aekâsar Mohaboros Khmer* [Documents on the Great Khmer Heroes]. Vol. 1, episodes 7–10; vol. 2, episodes 11–19. Paris: Association Culturelle Pierres d'Angkor, [1969] 1985.

Escoffier, Claire F. "Les Lao au Cambodge: Une Cohabitation Harmonieuse?" In *Ethnic Groups in Cambodia*, ed. Hean Sokhom. Phnom Penh: Center for Advanced Study, 2009.

Evans, Grant. *The Politics of Ritual and Remembrance: Laos Since 1975*. Chiang Mai: Silkworm Books, 1998.

————. "Immobile Memories: Statues in Thailand and Laos." In *Cultural Crisis and Social Memory: Modernity and Identity in Thailand and Laos*, ed. Shigeharu Tanabe and Charles F Keyes, 154–82. London: RoutledgeCurzon, 2002.

————. "Revolution and Royal Style: Problems of Post-Socialist Legitimacy in Laos." In *Elite Cultures – Anthropological Perspectives*, ed. Chris Shore and Stephen Nugent, 189–206. London: Routledge, 2002.

Finlayson, Alan. "Ideology, Discourse and Nationalism." *Journal of Political Ideologies* 3 no. 1 (1998): 99–118.

Foweraker, Joe, and Roman Krznaric. "Measuring Liberal Democratic Performance: An Empirical and Conceptual Critique." *Political Studies* 48 no. 4 (2000): 759–87.

Freeden, Michael. "Is Nationalism a Distinct Ideology?" *Political Studies* 46 no. 4 (2002): 748–65.

Frings, Viviane K. "The Cambodian People's Party and Sihanouk." *Journal of Contemporary Asia* 25 no. 3 (1995): 356–65.

————. "Rewriting Cambodian History to 'Adapt' it to a New Political Context: The Kampuchean People's Revolutionary Party's Historiography (1979–1991)." *Modern Asian Studies* 31 no. 4 (1997): 807–46.

Gainsborough, Martin. "Elites vs. Reform in Laos, Cambodia, and Vietnam." *Journal of Democracy* 23 no. 2 (2012): 34–46.

Geertz, Clifford. *The Interpretation of Cultures: Selected Essays*. New York: Basic Books, 1973.

Gellner, Ernest. *Nations and Nationalism*. Oxford: Blackwell, 1983.

Girling, John L. S. *Cambodia and the Sihanouk Myths*. Singapore: Institute of Southeast Asian Studies, 1971.

Golay, Frank H., Ralph Anspach, M. Ruth Pfanner, and Eliezer B. Ayal. *Underdevelopment and Economic Nationalism in Southeast Asia*. Ithaca: Cornell University Press, 1969.

Gottesman, Evan. *Cambodia After the Khmer Rouge: Inside the Politics of Nation Building*. New Haven, CT; London: Yale University Press, 2003.

Grabowsky, Volker. "Lao and Khmer Perceptions of National Survival: The Legacy of the Early Nineteenth Century." In *Nationalism and Cultural Revival in Southeast Asia: Perspectives from the Center and the Region*, ed. Sri Kuhnt-Saptodewo, Volker Grabowsky and Martin Grossheim, 145–65. Wiesbaden: Harrassowitz, 1997.

Grabowsky, Volker, and Oliver Tappe. "Important Kings of Laos: Translation and Analysis of a Lao Cartoon Pamphlet." *The Journal of Lao Studies* 2 no. 1 (2011): 1–44.

Guérin, Mathieu, Andrew Hardy, Nguyen Van Chinh, and Stan-Tan Boon Hwee. *Des Montagnards aux Minorities Ethniques: Quelle Intégration Nationale pour les Habitants des Hautes Terres du Viêt Nam et du Cambodge?* Paris: L'Harmattan; Bangkok: IRASEC, 2003.

Guthrie, Elizabeth. "Khmer Buddhism, Female Asceticism, and Salvation." In *History, Buddhism, and New Religious Movements in Cambodia*, ed. John Marston and Elizabeth Guthrie, 133–49. Honolulu: University of Hawai'i Press, 2004.

Guthrie, Elizabeth, and John Marston, ed. *History, Buddhism and New Religious Movements in Cambodia*. Honolulu: University of Hawai'i Press, 2004.

Gyallay-Pap, Peter. "Reconstructing the Cambodian Polity: Buddhism,   Kingship and the Quest for Legitimacy." In *Buddhism, Power and Political Order*, ed. Ian Harris, 71–103. Abingdon; New York: Routledge, 2007.

Hammer, Peter, ed. *Living on the Margins: Minorities and Borderlines in Cambodia and Southeast Asia*. Phnom Penh: Center for Khmer Studies, 2009.

Handley, Paul M. *The King Never Smiles: A Biography of Thailand's King Bhumibol Adulyadej*. New Haven, CT: Yale University Press, 2006.

Hang, Chan Sophea. "Stec Gaṃlaṅ' and Yāy Deb." In *History, Buddhism, and New Religious Movements in Cambodia*, ed. John Marston and Elizabeth Guthrie, 113–26. Honolulu: University of Hawai'i Press, 2004.

Hansen, Anne R. "Khmer Identity and Theravada Buddhism." In *History, Buddhism, and New Religious Movements in Cambodia*, ed. John Marston and Elizabeth Guthrie, 40–62. Honolulu: University of Hawai'i Press, 2004.

———. *How to Behave: Buddhism and Modernity in Colonial Cambodia, 1860–1930*. Honolulu: University of Hawai'i Press, 2007.

———. "Gaps in the World: Violence, Harm and Suffering in Khmer Ethical Narratives." In *At the Edge of the Forest: Essays on Cambodia, History and Narrative in Honor of David Chandler*, ed. Anne R. Hansen and Judy Ledgerwood, 47–70. Ithaca: Cornell University Southeast Asia Program Publications, 2008.

Harris, Ian. "Buddhist Sangha Groupings in Cambodia." *Buddhist Studies Review* 18 no. 1 (2001): 73–106.

———. *Cambodian Buddhism: History and Practice*. Honolulu: University of Hawai'i Press, 2005.

———. *Buddhism Under Pol Pot*. Phnom Penh: Documentation Center of Cambodia, 2007.

———. "The Monk and the King: Khieu Chum and Regime Change in Cambodia." *Udaya* 9 (2008): 81–112.

———. "Rethinking Cambodian Political Discourse on Territory: Genealogy of the Buddhist Ritual Boundary (Sīmā)." *Journal of Southeast Asian Studies* 41 no. 2 (2010): 215–39.

Heder, Steve. "Cambodia's Democratic Transition to Neoauthoritarianism." *Current History* 94 (1995): 425–29.

———. "Racism, Marxism, Labeling and Genocide in Ben Kiernan's *The Pol Pot Regime*." *South East Asia Research* 5 no. 2 (1997): 101–53.

———. "Cambodia." In *Language and National Identity in Asia*, ed. Andrew Simpson, 288–311. Oxford: Oxford University Press, 2007.

———. "Political Theatre in the 2003 Cambodian Elections: State, Democracy and Conciliation in Historical Perspective." In *Staging Politics: Power and Performance in*

Asia and Africa, ed. Julia C. Strauss and Donal B. Cruise O'Brien, 151–72. Richmond: I. B. Tauris, 2007.

———. "Cambodia: Capitalist Transformation by Neither Liberal Democracy Nor Dictatorship." *Southeast Asian Affairs* 2012: 103–15.

Heder, Stephen, and Judy Ledgerwood, ed. *Propaganda, Politics, and Violence in Cambodia: Democratic Transition Under United Nations Peace-keeping.* Armonk; London: M. E. Sharpe, 1996.

Heng, Monychenda. "In Search of the Dhammika Ruler." In *People of Virtue: Reconfiguring Religion, Power and Moral Order in Cambodia*, ed. Alexandra Kent and David Chandler, 310–18. Copenhagen: NIAS Press, 2008.

Heng, Sreang. "The Scope and Limitations of Political Participation by Buddhist Monks." In *People of Virtue: Reconfiguring Religion, Power and Moral Order in Cambodia*, ed. Alexandra Kent and David Chandler, 241–56. Copenhagen: NIAS Press, 2008.

Hewison, Kevin. "The Monarchy and Democratization." In *Political Change in Thailand: Democracy and Participation*, ed. Kevin Hewison, 58–74. London: Routledge, 1997.

Hinton, Alexander. "Khmerness and the Thai 'Other': Violence, Discourse and Symbolism in the 2003 Anti-Thai Riots in Cambodia." *Journal of Southeast Asian Studies* 37 no. 3 (2006): 445–68.

Hopf, Ted. "The Limits of Interpreting Evidence." In *Theory and Evidence in Comparative Politics and International Relations*, ed. Richard Ned Lebow and Mark Irving Lichbach, 55–84. New York: Palgrave Macmillan, 2007.

Hughes, Caroline. "Dare to Say, Dare to Do: The Strongman in Business in 1990s Cambodia." *Asian Perspective* 24 no. 2 (2000): 121–51.

———. "Khmer Land, Khmer Soul: Sam Rainsy, Populism, and the Problem of Seeing Cambodia." *Southeast Asia Research* 9 no. 1 (2001): 45–71.

———. "Mystics and Militants: Democratic Reform in Cambodia." *International Politics* 38 no. 1 (2001): 47–64.

———. "Transforming Oppositions in Cambodia." *Global Society* 15 no. 3 (2001): 295–318.

———. "International Intervention and the People's Will: The Demoralization of Democracy in Cambodia." *Critical Asian Studies* 34 no. 4 (2002): 539–62.

———. "Parties, Protest and Pluralism in Cambodia." *Democratization* 9 no. 3 (2002): 165–86.

———. *The Political Economy of Cambodia's Transition, 1991–2001.* Richmond, VA: Curzon, 2002.

———. "The Politics of Gifts: Generosity and Menace in Contemporary Cambodia." *Journal of Southeast Asian Studies* 31 no. 3 (2006): 469–89.

————. "Reconstructing Legitimate Political Authority through Elections?" In *Beyond Democracy in Cambodia: Political Reconstruction in a Post-Conflict Society*, ed. Joakim Öjendal and Mona Lilja, 31–69. Copenhagen: NIAS Press, 2009.

Hughes, Caroline, and Tim Conway. *Towards Pro-Poor Political Change in Cambodia: The Policy Process*. London: Overseas Development Institute, 2003.

Hughes, Caroline, and Joakim Öjendal. "Reassessing Tradition in Times of Political Change: Post-War Cambodia Reconsidered." *Journal of Southeast Asian Studies* 37 no. 3 (2006): 415–20.

Hun, Sen. *13 Tosâvot nei Domnaoer Kampuchea* [*13 Decades of Cambodia's Evolution*]. Phnom Penh: Pracheachon, 1991.

————. "Aromkâtha [Preface]." In *Preah Sdech Kân*, ed. Ros Chantraboth, i–iii. Phnom Penh: Bânnakear Angkor, 2007.

Huot, Sambath. *Red Rose of the Mekong*. [Unknown publisher.] Produced by the Quiz Times Newspaper; Ministry of Information; Attwood Import-Export Co., Ltd. [n.d.]

Hutchinson, John. *The Dynamics of Cultural Nationalism*. London: Allen & Unwin, 1987.

Itzigsohn, José, and Matthias vom Hau. "Unfinished Imagined Communities: States, Social Movements, and Nationalism in Latin America." *Theory and Society* 35 no. 2 (2006): 193–212.

Ivarsson, Søren, and Christopher E. Goscha. "Prince Phetsarath (1890–1959): Nationalism and Royalty in the Making of Modern Laos." *Journal of Southeast Asian Studies* 38 no. 1 (2007): 55–81.

Jacob, Judith J. "The Deliberate Use of Foreign Vocabulary by the Khmer: Changing Fashions, Methods, and Sources." In *Cambodian Linguistics, Literature and History: Collected Articles*, ed. Judith J. Jacob and David A. Smyth, 149–66. London: School of Oriental and African Studies, 1993.

Jacobsen, Trudy. *Lost Goddesses: The Denial of Female Power in Cambodian History*. Copenhagen: NIAS Press, 2008.

Jellema, Kate. "Returning Home: Ancestor Veneration and the Nationalism of Đổi Mới Vietnam." In *Modernity and Re-enchantment: Religion in Post-Revolutionary Vietnam*, ed. Philip Taylor, 57–89. Singapore: ISEAS, 2007.

Jordens, Jay. "Persecution of Cambodia's Ethnic Vietnamese Communities During and Since the UNTAC Period." In *Propaganda, Politics and Violence in Cambodia*, ed. Stephen Heder and Judy Ledgerwood, 134–58. Armonk, NJ: M. E. Sharpe, 1996.

Kane, John, Haig Patapan, and Benjamin Wong ed. *Dissident Democrats: The Challenge of Democratic Leadership in Asia*. New York; Basingstoke: Palgrave Macmillan, 2008.

Kantorowicz, Ernst H. *The King's Two Bodies: A Study in Mediaeval Political Theology*. Princeton: Princeton University Press, 1957.

Karbaum, Markus. "Cambodia's Façade Democracy and European Assistance." *Journal of Current Southeast Asian Affairs* 30 no. 4 (2011): 111–43.

Keng, Vannsak. *Principes de Creation des Mots Nouveaux*. Série Grammaire et Philologie, vol. 1, tome 1. Phnom Penh: Faculté des Lettres, 1964.

Kent, Alexandra. "Purchasing Power and Pagodas: the Sīma Monastic Boundary and Consumer Politics in Cambodia." *Journal of Southeast Asian Studies* 38 no. 2 (2007): 335–54.

———. "The Recovery of the King." In *People of Virtue: Reconfiguring Religion, Power and Moral Order in Cambodia*, ed. Alexandra Kent and David Chandler, 109–27. Copenhagen: NIAS Press, 2008.

Kent, Alexandra, and David Chandler, ed. *People of Virtue: Reconfiguring Religion, Power and Moral Order in Cambodia*. Copenhagen: NIAS Press, 2008.

Keo, Savath. *Jaovay Koy, Virakboros Khmer Kampuchea Krom* [*Jaovay Koy: Khmer Kampuchea Krom Hero*]. [Publisher unknown.] [1971] 2006.

Kershaw, Roger. *Monarchy in South-East Asia: The Faces of Tradition in Transition*. London: Routledge, 2001.

Khin, Sok, ed. and trans. *Chroniques Royales du Cambodge. De Bañā Yāt à la Prise de Laṅvaek: De 1417 à 1595*. Paris: École Française d'Extrême-Orient, 1988.

Khing, Hoc Dy. "Neak Mean Boun, 'Être de Mérites', dans la Culture et la Littérature du Cambodge." *Péninsule* 56 (2008): 71–106.

Kiernan, Ben. *How Pol Pot Came to Power: A History of Communism in Kampuchea, 1930–1975*. London: Verso, 1985.

———. "Myth, Nationalism and Genocide." *Journal of Genocide Research* 3 no. 2 (2001): 187–206.

Kim, Sedara. "From Peace Keeping to Peace Building: Cambodia Post-Conflict Democratization." Political Studies Association, 2007. www.psa.ac.uk/2007/pps/Kim1.pdf (Accessed October 29, 2012).

Kim, Sedara, and Joakim Öjendal. "Decentralization as a Strategy for State Reconstruction in Cambodia." In *Beyond Democracy in Cambodia: Political Reconstruction in a Post-Conflict Society*, ed. Joakim Öjendal and Mona Lilja, 101–35. Copenhagen: NIAS Press, 2009.

Kuhnt-Saptodewo, Sri, Volker Grabowsky, and Martin Grobheim. *Nationalism and Cultural Revival in Southeast Asia: Perspectives from the Center and the Region*. Wiesbaden: Harrassowitz, 1997.

Kulke, Hermann. *The Devaraja Cult*. Data Paper 108. Ithaca: Cornell University Southeast Asia Program Publications, 1978.

———. "The Devarāja Cult: Legitimation and Apotheosis of the Ruler in the Kingdom of Angkor." In *Kings and Cults: State Formation and Legitimation in India and Southeast Asia*, ed. Hermann Kulke, 327–81. New Delhi: Manohar, 1993.

Laothamatas, Anek. "A Tale of Two Democracies: Conflicting Perceptions of Elections and Democracy in Thailand." In *The Politics of Elections in Southeast Asia*, ed. Robert H. Taylor, 201–23. Cambridge: Woodrow Wilson Center Press and Cambridge University Press, 1996.

Leclère, Adhémard. "Le Sdech Kân." *Bulletin de la Société des Études Indochinoises (BSEI)* 59 (1910): 17–55.

———. *Histoire du Cambodge Depuis le 1ᵉʳ Siècle de Notre Ère, d'Après les Inscriptions Lapidaires: Les Annales Chinoises et Annamites et les Documents Européens des Six Derniers Siècles.* Paris: Paul Guethner, 1914.

Ledgerwood, Judy. "Politics and Gender: Negotiating Changing Cambodian Ideas of the Proper Woman." *Asia Pacific Viewpoint* 37 no. 2 (1996): 139–52.

———. "Buddhist Practice in Rural Kandal province, 1960 and 2003. An Essay in Honor of May M. Ebihara." In *People of Virtue: Reconfiguring Religion, Power and Moral Order in Cambodia*, ed. Alexandra Kent and David Chandler, 147–68. Copenhagen: NIAS Press, 2008.

———. "Ritual in 1990 Cambodian Political Theatre." In *At the Edge of the Forest: Essays on Cambodia, History, and Narrative in Honor of David Chandler*, ed. Anne R. Hansen and Judy Ledgerwood, 195–220. Ithaca: Cornell University Southeast Asia Program Publications, 2008.

Ledgerwood, Judy, and Kheang Un. "Global Concepts and Local Meaning: Human Rights and Buddhism in Cambodia." *Journal of Human Rights* 2 no. 4 (2003): 531–49.

Levitsky, Steven, and Lucan A. Way. *Competitive Authoritarianism: Hybrid Regimes after the Cold War*. New York: Cambridge University Press, 2010.

Lewitz, Saveros. "Note sur la Translittération du Cambodgien." *Bulletin de l'École Française d'Extrême-Orient (BEFEO)* 55 (1969): 163–69.

Lilja, Mona. *Power, Resistance and Women Politicians in Cambodia: Discourses of Emancipation*. Copenhagen: NIAS Press, 2008.

Lilja, Mona, and Joakim Öjendal. "The Never-Ending Hunt for Political Legitimacy in a Post-Conflict Context." In *Beyond Democracy in Cambodia: Political Reconstruction in a Post-Conflict Society*, ed. Joakim Öjendal and Mona Lilja, 297–312. Copenhagen: NIAS Press, 2009.

Lizée, Pierre P. *Peace, Power and Resistance in Cambodia: Global Governance and the Failure of International Conflict Resolution*. Basingstoke: Macmillan, 1999.

Loh, Francis Kok Wah, and Joakim Öjendal, ed. *Southeast Asian Responses to Globalization – Restructuring Governance and Deepening Democracy*. Copenhagen: NIAS Press, 2005.

Lon, Nol. *Le Neo-Khmerisme*. Phnom Penh: [publisher unknown], 1974.

Maddens, Bart, and Kristine Vanden Berghe. "Franco and the Spanish   Monarchy: A Discourse Analysis of the Tourist Guides Published by the Patrimonio Nacional [1959–1987)." In *Royal Tourism: Excursions Around Monarchy*, ed. Phil Long and Nicola J. Palme, 80–106. Clevedon: Channel View Publications, 2008.

Mann, Michael. *The Dark Side of Democracy: Explaining Ethnic Cleansing*. Cambridge: Cambridge University Press, 2005.

Marston, John. "Democratic Kampuchea and the Idea of Modernity." In *Cambodia Emerges from the Past: Eight Essays*, ed. Judy Ledgerwood, 38–59. DeKalb, IL: Center for Southeast Asian Studies, Northern Illinois University, 2002.

———. "Clay into Stone: A Modern-day Tapas." In *History, Buddhism, and New Religious Movements in Cambodia*, ed. John Marston and Elizabeth Guthrie, 170–92. Honolulu: University of Hawai'i Press, 2004.

———. "Cambodian Religion since 1989." In *Beyond Democracy in Cambodia: Political Reconstruction in a Post-Conflict Society*, ed. Joakim Öjendal and Mona Lilja, 224–249. Copenhagen: NIAS Press, 2009.

Marston, John, and Elizabeth Guthrie. *History, Buddhism, and New Religious Movements in Cambodia*. Honolulu: University of Hawai'i Press, 2004.

———. "The Icon of the Leper King." In *History, Buddhism, and New Religious Movements in Cambodia*, ed. John Marston and Elizabeth Guthrie, 87–89. Honolulu: University of Hawai'i Press, 2004.

McCargo, Duncan, ed. *Reforming Thai Politics*. Copenhagen: NIAS Press, 2002.

———. "Network Monarchy and Legitimacy Crises in Thailand." *Pacific Review* 18 no. 4 (2005): 499–519.

McGrew, Laura. "Re-establishing Legitimacy through the Extraordinary Chambers in the Courts of Cambodia." In *Beyond Democracy in Cambodia: Political Reconstruction in a Post-Conflict Society*, ed. Joakim Öjendal and Mona Lilja, 250–296. Copenhagen: NIAS Press, 2009.

Mehmet, Ozay. "Development in a War-torn Society: What Next in Cambodia?" *Third World Quarterly* 18 no. 4 (1997): 673–86.

Men, Neary Sopheak, and Tianji Dickens. *United For Humanity*. Phnom Penh: Cambodian Red Cross, International Committee of the Red Cross and the Federation, 2005.

Ministry of Education. *Sâttheanukrom Khemara Yeanokâm* [*Fundamental Khmer Dictionary*]. [Publisher unknown], 1973.

Mizuno, Kosuke, and Pasuk Phongpaichit. *Populism in Asia*. Singapore: NUS Press; in association with Kyoto: Kyoto University Press, 2009.

Mortland, Carol. "Khmer Buddhists in the United States: Ultimate Questions." In *Cambodian Culture Since 1975: Homeland and Exile*, ed. May Ebihara, Carol Anne Mortland and Judy Ledgerwood, 72–90. Ithaca: Cornell University Press, 1994.

Norodom, Ranariddh. *Droit Public Cambodgien*. [Perpignan]: CERJEMAF/Presses Universitaires de Perpignan, 1998.

Norodom, Sihanouk. *Shadow Over Angkor: Memoirs of His Majesty King Norodom Sihanouk of Cambodia*, ed. and trans. Julio A. Jeldres. Phnom Penh: Monument Books, 2005.

Öjendal, Joakim. "Democratization Amidst Globalization in Southeast Asia: Empirical Findings and Theoretical Reflections." In *Southeast Asian Responses to Globalization—Restructuring Governance and Deepening Democracy*, ed. Francis Kok Wah-Loh and Joakim Öjendal, 345–372. Copenhagen: NIAS Press, 2005.

Öjendal, Joakim and Mona Lilja, ed. *Beyond Democracy in Cambodia: Political Reconstruction in a Post-Conflict Society*. Copenhagen: NIAS Press, 2009.

————. "Beyond Democracy in Cambodia: Political Reconstruction in a Post-Conflict Society?" In *Beyond Democracy in Cambodia: Political Reconstruction in a Post-Conflict Society*, ed. Joakim Öjendal and Mona Lilja, 1–30. Copenhagen: NIAS Press, 2009.

Osborne, Milton. *Sihanouk: Prince of Light, Prince of Darkness*. Honolulu, HI: University of Hawaii Press, 1994.

————. *Phnom Penh: A Cultural and Literary History*. Oxford: Signal, 2008.

Ottaway, Marina. *Democracy Challenged: The Rise of Semi-authoritarianism*. Washington, DC: Carnegie Endowment for International Peace, 2003.

Ovesen, Jan, and Ing-Britt Trankell. "Foreigners and Honorary Khmers. Ethnic Minorities in Cambodia." In *Civilizing the Margins: Southeast Asian   Government Policies for the Development of Minorities*, ed. Christopher R. Duncan, 241–269. Ithaca: Cornell University Press, 2004.

Pak, Kimchoeun. "A Dominant Party in a Weak State: How the Ruling Party in Cambodia has Managed to Stay Dominant." PhD Dissertation, Australian National University, 2011.

Pak, Kimchoeun, Horng Vuthy, Eng Netra, Ann Sovatha, Kim Sedara, Jenny Knowles, and David Craig. "Accountability and Neo-Patrimonialism in Cambodia: A Critical Literature Review." Working Paper 34. Phnom Penh: Cambodia Development Resource Institute, 2007.

Peou, Sorpong. *Intervention and Change in Cambodia: Towards Democracy*. New York: St Martin's Press, 2000.

Poethig, Kathryn. 2006. "Sitting between Two Chairs: Cambodia's Dual Citizenship Debate." In *Expressions of Cambodia: The Politics of Tradition, Identity, and Change*, ed. Leakthina Chan-Pech Ollier and Tim Winter, 73–85. London: Routledge, 2006.

Pou, Saveros. *Dictionnaire Vieux Khmer-Français-Anglais*. Paris: CEDORECK, 1992.

————. "Dieux et Rois dans la Pensée Khmère Ancienne." *Journal Asiatique* 286 no. 2 (1998): 653–69.

Pou, Sothirak. "Managing Poverty in Cambodia." In *Cambodia: Progress and Challenges Since 1991*, ed. Pou Sothirak, Geoff Wade and Mark Hong, 337–65. Singapore: Institute of Southeast Asian Studies, 2012.

Reynolds, Craig J. *Thai Radical Discourse: The Real Face of Thai Feudalism Today*. Ithaca: Cornell University Southeast Asia Program Publications, 1987.

————. *Seditious Histories: Contesting Thai and Southeast Asian Pasts*. Seattle, WA: University of Washington Press, 2006.

Reynolds, Frank E. "Civic Religion and National Community in Thailand." *Journal of Asian Studies* 36 no. 2 (1977): 267–82.

Richards, David. "Elite Interviewing: Approaches and Pitfalls." *Politics* 16 no. 3 (1996): 199–204.

Roberts, David W. *Political Transition in Cambodia 1991–99: Power, Elitism and Democracy.* Richmond, VA: Curzon, 2001.

———. "Democratization, Elite Transition, and Violence in Cambodia, 1991–1999." *Critical Asian Studies* 34 no. 4 (2002): 520–38.

Roepstorff, Andreas, and Nils Bubandt. "General Introduction: The Critique of Culture and the Plurality of Nature." In *Imagining Nature: Practices of Cosmology and Identity*, ed. Andreas Roepstorff, Nils Bubandt and Kalevi Kull, 9–26. Aarhus: Aarhus University Press, 2003.

Roeun, Aing Sok. *A Comparative Analysis of Traditional and Contemporary Roles of Khmer Women in the Household: A Case Study in Leap Tong Village.* Phnom Penh: Royal University of Phnom Penh, 2004.

Ros, Chantraboth. *Preah Sdech Kân.* Phnom Penh: Bânnakear Angkor, 2007.

Saing, Hell. *Neak Padevott Klaeng Klay* [*The False Revolutionary*]. Phnom Penh: Ed. Ariyathor, 1972.

Sam, Emmarane. *Cambodge: Histoire d'une Vengeance Royale (1958–1965).* Paris: Thélès, 2009.

Sam, Rainsy. *Des Racines dans la Pierre: Mon Combat pour la Renaissance du Cambodge.* Paris: Calmann-Lévy, 2008.

———. *We Didn't Start the Fire: My Struggle for Democracy in Cambodia.* Chiangmai: Silkworm Books, 2013.

Sanderson, John, and Michael Maley. "Elections and Liberal Democracy in Cambodia." *Australian Journal of International Affairs* 52 no. 3 (1998): 241–53.

Sar, Sartun. *Vappathor neung Areythor Khmer* [*Khmer Culture and Civilization*]. Part II. [Publisher unknown], 1970.

Satoru, Kobayashi. "Reconstructing Buddhist Temple Buildings: An Analysis of Village Buddhism after the Era of Turmoil." In *People of Virtue: Reconfiguring Religion, Power and Moral Order in Cambodia*, ed. Alexandra Kent and David Chandler, 169–94. Copenhagen: NIAS Press, 2008.

Schedler, Andreas, ed. *Electoral Authoritarianism: The Dynamics of Unfree Competition.* Boulder, CO; London: L. Rienner Publishers, 2006.

Scott, James C. *Domination and the Arts of Resistance: Hidden Transcripts.* New Haven; London: Yale University Press, 1990.

Sidel, John T. "Siam and its Twin?: Democratization and Bossism in Contemporary Thailand and the Philippines." *IDS Bulletin* 27 no. 2 (1996): 36–52.

———. "Liberalism, Communism, Islam: Transnational Motors of 'Nationalist' Struggles in Southeast Asia." *The Newsletter* 32 (2003): 23.

Sisowath, Samyl Monipong. *Voyage au Royaume de la Panthère Longibande.* Paris: Connaissances et Savoirs, 2008.

Skidmore, Monique. *Karaoke Fascism: Burma and the Politics of Fear.* Philadelphia, PA: University of Pennsylvania Press, 2004.

Slater, Dan. "Can Leviathan be Democratic? Competitive Elections, Robust Mass Politics, and State Infrastructural Power." *Studies in Comparative International Development* 43 no. 3–4 (2008): 252–72.

Slocomb, Margaret. *The People's Republic of Kampuchea, 1979–1989: The Revolution after Pol Pot*. Chiang Mai: Silkworm Books, 2003.

———. "Commune Elections in Cambodia: 1981 Foundations and 2002 Reformations." *Modern Asian Studies* 38 no. 2 (2004): 447–67.

———. "The Nature and Role of Ideology in the Modern Cambodian State." *Journal of Southeast Asian Studies* 37 no. 3 (2006): 375–95.

Smith, Anthony D. *The Ethnic Origins of Nations*. Oxford: Oxford University Press, 1986.

Smith, Frank. *Interpretive Accounts of the Khmer Rouge Years: Personal Experience in Cambodian Peasant World View*. Madison, WI: Center for Southeast Asian Studies, University of Wisconsin, 1989.

Springer, Simon. *Cambodia's Neo-Liberal Order: Violence, Authoritarianism, and the Contestation of Public* Space. Abingdon; New York: Routledge, 2010.

Stengs, Irene. *Worshipping the Great Moderniser: King Chulalongkorn, Patron Saint of the Thai Middle Class*. Singapore: NUS Press, 2009.

St. John, Ronald Bruce. "Democracy in Cambodia – One Decade, US$5 Billion Later: What Went Wrong?" *Contemporary Southeast Asia: A Journal of International and Strategic Affairs* 27 no. 3 (2005): 406–28.

Strangio, Sebastian. *Hun Sen's Cambodia*. New Haven: Yale University Press, 2014.

Strauss, Julia C., and Donal B. Cruise O'Brien. "Introduction." In *Staging Politics: Power and Performance in Asia and Africa*, ed. Julia C. Strauss and Donal B. Cruise O'Brien, 1–14. Richmond, VA: I. B. Tauris, 2007.

Streckfuss, David. 1995. "Kings in the Age of Nations: the Paradox of Lese Majeste as Political Crime in Thailand." *Comparative Studies in Society and History* 37 no. 3 (1995): 445–75.

Stuart-Fox, Martin. *A History of Laos*. Cambridge: Cambridge University Press, 1997.

Sutherland, Claire. *Soldered States: Nation-Building in Germany and Vietnam*. Manchester: Manchester University Press, 2010.

Tambiah, Stanley Jeyaraya. *World Conqueror and World Renouncer: A Study of Buddhism and Polity in Thailand Against a Historical Background*. Cambridge: Cambridge University Press, 1976.

Tan, Michelle. "Passing over in Silences: Ideology, Ideals and Ideas in Thai Translation." *Journal of Southeast Asian Studies* 43 no. 1 (2012): 32–54.

Tanabe, Shigeharu. "Introduction: Imagined and Imagining Communities." In *Imagining Communities in Thailand: Ethnographic Approaches*, ed. Shigeharu Tanabe, 1–19. Chiang Mai: Mekong Press, 2008.

Tansey, Oisín. "Process Tracing and Elite Interviewing: A Case for Non-Probability Sampling." *PS: Political Science and Politics* 40 no. 4 (2007): 765–72.

Tauch, Chhoung. *Sdech Kân Chrek Reach* [*Sdech Kân the Usurper*]. Paris: Ed. Association des Écrivains Khmers à l'Étranger, 1995.

Taylor, Robert H. "Introduction: Elections and Politics in Southeast Asia." In *The Politics of Elections in Southeast Asia*, ed. Robert H. Taylor, 1–11. Cambridge: Woodrow Wilson Center Press and Cambridge University Press, 1996.

Taylor, Robert H., ed. *The Politics of Elections in Southeast Asia*. Cambridge: Woodrow Wilson Center Press and Cambridge University Press, 1996.

Tejapira, Kasian. "Commodifying Marxism: The Formation of Modern Thai Radical Culture, 1927–1958." PhD dissertation, Cornell University. Ann Arbor, MI: University Microfilms, [1992] 1994.

Thion, Serge. "The Ingratitude of the Crocodiles: The 1978 Cambodian Black Paper." *Bulletin of Concerned Asian Scholars* 12 no. 4 (1980): 38–54.

Thompson, Ashley. "The Future of Cambodia's Past: A Messianic Middle-Period Cambodian Royal Cult." In *History, Buddhism, and New Religious Movements in Cambodia*, ed. John Marston and Elizabeth Guthrie, 13–39. Honolulu: University of Hawai'i Press, 2004.

———. "The Suffering of Kings: Substitute Bodies, Healing, and Justice in Cambodia." In *History, Buddhism, and New Religious Movements in Cambodia*, ed. John Marston and Elizabeth Guthrie, 91–112. Honolulu: University of Hawai'i Press, 2004.

———. "Angkor Revisited: The State of Statuary." In *What's the Use of Art: Asian Visual and Material Culture in Context*, ed. Jan Mrázek and Morgan Pitelka, 179–213. Honolulu: University of Hawai'i Press, 2008.

Tranet, Michel. *Le Sdach Kan*. Phnom Penh: Atelier d'Impression Khmère, 2002.

Turton, Andrew. "Invulnerability and Local Knowledge." In *Thai Constructions of Knowledge*, ed. Chitakasem Manas and Andrew Turton, 155–82. London: School of Oriental and African Studies, 1991.

Un, Kheang. "Patronage Politics and Hybrid Democracy: Political Change in Cambodia, 1993–2003." *Asian Perspective* 29 no. 2 (2005): 203–30.

———. "State, Society and Democratic Consolidation: The Case of Cambodia." *Pacific Affairs* 79 no. 2 (2006): 225–45.

———. "Configuring Opposition Politics: Sam Rainsy and the Sam Rainsy Party." In *Dissident Democrats: The Challenge of Democratic Leadership in Asia*, ed. John Kane and Benjamin Wong, 105–28. London: Palgrave Macmillan, 2008.

———. "The Judicial System and Democratization in Post-Conflict Cambodia." In *Beyond Democracy in Cambodia: Political Reconstruction in a Post-Conflict Society*, ed. Joakim Öjendal and Mona Lilja, 70–100. Copenhagen: NIAS Press, 2009.

Van den Berghe, Pierre. *The Ethnic Phenomenon*. New York: Elsevier, 1979.

Vickery, Michael. "Looking Back at Cambodia." In *Peasants and Politics in Kampuchea 1941–1981*, ed. Ben Kiernan and Chantou Boua, 89–113. London: Zed Press, 1982.

————. *Society, Economics, and Politics in Pre-Angkor Cambodia: The Seventh–Eighth Centuries*. Tokyo: Center for East Asian Cultural Studies for UNESCO, Toyo Bunko, 1998.

Von Heine-Geldern, Robert. *Conceptions of State and Kingship in Southeast Asia*. Data Paper 18. Ithaca: Cornell University Southeast Asia Program, 1956.

Walker, Andrew. *Thailand's Political Peasants: Power in the Modern Rural Economy*. Madison: University of Wisconsin Press, 2012.

White, Lynn. *Legitimacy: Ambiguities of Political Success or Failure in East and Southeast Asia*. Singapore: World Scientific, 2005.

Winichakul, Thongchai. "The Quest for 'Siwilai': A Geographical Discourse of Civilizational Thinking in the Late Nineteenth and Early Twentieth-Century Siam." *Journal of Asian Studies* 59 no. 3 (2000): 528–49.

————. "Toppling Democracy." *Journal of Contemporary Asia* 38 no. 1 (2008): 11–37.

Wollman, Howard, and Philip Spencer. "'Can Such Goodness Be Profitably Discarded?' Benedict Anderson and the Politics of Nationalism." In *The Influence of Benedict Anderson*, ed. Alistair McCleery and Benjamin A. Brabon, 1–20. Edinburgh: Merchiston Publishing, 2007.

Woodward, Hiram W., Jr. "Practice and Belief in Ancient Cambodia: Claude Jacques, *Angkor*, and the *Devarāja* Question." *Journal of Southeast Asian Studies* 32 no. 2 (2001): 249–61.

Zucker, Eve. "The Absence of Elders: Chaos and Moral Order in the Aftermath   of the Khmer Rouge." In *People of Virtue: Reconfiguring Religion, Power and Moral Order in Cambodia*, ed. Alexandra Kent and David Chandler, 195–212. Copenhagen: NIAS Press, 2008.

Newspaper articles

Ahmad, Zainon. "Uneasy Boom in Cambodia." *New Straits Times*, February 13, 2000.

Bo, Proeuk. "Hun Sen-Sponsored 'Preah Sdach Korn' Book Needs 2d Edition To Meet Demand." *Reaksmey Kampuchea*, September 25, 2007.

Brady, Brendan, and Kouth Sophak Chakrya. "KPNLF Commemoration, Former Border Resistance Leaders Stand by Antagonism towards Vietnamese." *Phnom Penh Post*, March 6, 2009.

Cheang, Sokha, and Rebecca Puddy. "Don't Call Me a Traitor: PM." *Phnom Penh Post*, January 10, 2011.

Chun, Sakada. "Hun Sen Statue Removed After Dust-Up." *Voice of America (Khmer)*, June 18, 2010.

————. "Hun Sen Says Royalists Should Abandon Politics." *Voice of America (Khmer)*, February 5, 2007.

Heng, Reaksmey. "Retired King Sihanouk Defends PM Hun Sen." *Voice of America (Khmer)*, February 2, 2007.

Hul, Reaksmey. "Hun Sen Suggests Expanding Dual-Citizen Ban beyond NEC." *The Cambodia Daily*, December 17, 2014.

Hul, Reaksmey and Colin Meyn. "Ranariddh Plays to Old Politics with New Party." *The Cambodia Daily*, March 17, 2014.

Hul, Reaksmey and Alex Willemyns. "Rainsy: Sokha Will Heed PM's Warning." *The Cambodia Daily*, April 30, 2015.

Khy, Sovuthy. "Hun Sen Says his Face as Good as Any; Situation is Normal." *The Cambodia Daily*, February 11, 2014.

Kuch, Naren. "Parties Agree to Code of Conduct for 'Culture of Dialogue.' " *The Cambodia Daily*, May 9, 2015.

Kuch, Sovann. "Barami robâs Samdech Techo Nov Pel Thvay Preah Phloeng Samdech Preah Norodom Sihanouk" [The Spiritual Power of Hun Sen at the Cremation of Samdech Preah Norodom Sihanouk]. *DAP-news*, February 13, 2013.

Leang, Delux. "History: Hun Sen Finances a Book about Sdach Korn." *Cambodge Soir*, March 29, 2007.

Leang, Delux, and Soren Seelow. "Formation of a Government of National Union – Thomico is Defending Himself From All Provocation." *Cambodge Soir*, September 25, 2006.

Li, Selea. "Samdech Hun Sen Bâk Sray Pi Øpphoutheto Nov Thngai Thvay Preah Phloeng Preah Borom Sâp Samdech Preah Mohaviroksatr" [Samdech Hun Sen Interprets the Miracle at the Royal Cremation of the King-Father]. *DAP-news*, February 14, 2013.

Lor, Chandara, and John Maloy. "Royals Could Initiate Political Exit: Hun Sen." *The Cambodia Daily*, February 6, 2007.

May, Titthara, and Kevin Ponniah. "Petitions Piling up for King." *Phnom Penh Post*, September 23, 2013.

McDermid, Charles, and Cheang Sokha. "Gagging MPs Likened to Khmer Rouge." *AsiaViews*, December 21, 2010.

Meas, Sokchea. "Rainsy Still Atop Party." *Phnom Penh Post*, September 12, 2011.

———. "Miracle Cremation: PM Hun Sen." *Phnom Penh Post*, February 15, 2013.

Meas, Sokchea, and Shane Worrell. "Rainsy's Royal Audience." *Phnom Penh Post*, August 2, 2013.

Mech, Dara, and Alex Willemyns. "Dual Citizens May Be Banned from Prime Minister Role." *The Cambodia Daily*, March 11, 2014.

———. "Ranariddh Named Funcinpec President – Again." *The Cambodia Daily*, January 20, 2015.

———. "Hun Sen, Sam Rainsy Ring in New Year Together." *The Cambodia Daily*, April 15, 2015.

Meyn, Colin. "King Convenes Opening of Contested National Assembly." *The Cambodia Daily*, September 23, 2013.

Meyn, Colin, and Hul Reaksmey. "Leave King out of Politics, Royal Cabinet Demands." *The Cambodia Daily*, January 24, 2014.

Mu, Sochua. "Nurturing the Culture of Dialogue." *Phnom Penh Post*, February 16, 2015.

Muong, Vandy, and Will Jackson. "Hun Sen and the Man Who Would be King." *Phnom Penh Post*, January 9, 2016.

Nanuam, Wassana, and Nauvarat Suksamran. "Monument of Epic Size Rises to the Glory of Thai Kings." *Bangkok Post*, May 2, 2015.

Norodom, Sihanouk. "Notre Sangkum." *Le Monde*, October 8, 1963.

Pin, Sisovann. "Prince Thomico Plans Petition Asking Assembly To Disband." *The Cambodia Daily*, September 15, 2006.

Pin, Sisovann, and James Welsh. "Hun Sen Calls for Prince's Party Ouster," *The Cambodia Daily*, September 18, 2006.

Prak, Chan Thul, and James Welsh. "Thomico, 50 Party Faithful Swear Oath to Country." *The Cambodia Daily*, September 11, 2006.

Soy, Sopheap. "Preah Mohaksatr Samdech Mae, Samdech Sanghareach Teang 2 Thvay Preah Phloeng 4 Loek Min Chheah, Loek Ti 5 Samdech Techo Buong Suong Som, Toep Thvay Preah Phloeng Chheah" [The King, The Queen-Mother and Both Supreme Patriarchs Light the Fire Four Times without it Catching Fire, the Fifth time Samdech Techo Prays, Then it Catches Fire]. *DAP-news*, February 13, 2013.

Vong, Sokheng, and Charles McDermid. "Funcinpec Prince Hails 'Royalist' CPP." *Phnom Penh Post*, November 3, 2006.

Vong, Sokheng and Meas Sokchea. "CNRP, Take your Seats: King." *Phnom Penh Post*, September 19, 2013.

Willemyns, Alex. "Prince Says Funcinpec to Work Closely with CPP." *The Cambodia Daily*, January 3, 2015.

Yun, Samean. "Thomico Visits Four Provinces, Shows Movies." *The Cambodia Daily*, August 9, 2006.

———. "Thomico's New Party Holds First Congress in Capital." *The Cambodia Daily*, August 21, 2006.

———. "Assembly Complains of Lengthy Royal Absences." *The Cambodia Daily*, October 5, 2006.

———. "F'pec Hosts Contentious Birthday Celebration." *The Cambodia Daily*, October 31, 2006.

———. "Ranariddh, Thomico To Form Alliance." *The Cambodia Daily*, November 7, 2006.

———. "Hun Sen Says Celebrating Oct 23 'Meaningless'." *The Cambodia Daily*, January 12, 2009.

Yun, Samean and Douglas Gillison. "Thomico Announces Alliance with Fringe Parties." *The Cambodia Daily*, July 28, 2006.

[Unknown author.] "World Briefing Asia: Cambodia: Coalition Government." *New York Times*, November 6, 2003.

[Unknown author.] "Cambodian Opposition Joins Calls For Royalty To Quit Politics." *DPA*, October 4, 2006.

[Unknown author.] "Hun Sen Moves Ahead." *Asiaweek*, May 21, 1999.

[Unknown author.] "Burma: The End of an Era or a Dynasty's Beginning?," *The Irrawaddy*, January 28, 2011.

[Unknown author.] "Hun Sen Issues New Warning to the Opposition Regarding the Jasmine Revolution." *Cambodia Express News*, July 22, 2011.

[Unknown author.] "Cambodia Marks Constitution Day." *Cambodia Herald*, September 24, 2012.

[Unknown author.] "Government Redesignates October 23 as Public Holiday." *Cambodia Herald*, October 27, 2012.

[Unknown author.] "Samdech Techo Bâk Sray Øpphoutheto Neanea Dael Kaoet Laoeng Knong Preah Reach Pithi Bon Ning Pithi Thvay Preah Phloeng Preah Borom Ratanakkot" [Samdech Techo Interprets Different Miracles that Took Place at the Royal Cremation of the Late King-Father]. *DAP-news*, February 14, 2013.

[Unknown author.] "Preah Mohaksatr Mean Preah Reach Bânhchaul Sârsaoer pi Kar Doek Noam Dâ Troem Trauv robâs Samdech Techo knong Kar Øphivodth Brotes" [The King Expresses His Admiration for Samdech Techo's Correct Leadership in National Development]. *DAP-news*, July 10, 2013.

[Unknown author.] "Hun Sen to Seek Fifth Term as Cambodia's Prime Minister," *Radio Free Asia (Khmer)*, April 29, 2015.

[Unknown author.] "Sam Rainsy Defends 'Culture of Dialogue' With Ruling Cambodian People's Party." *Voice of America*, May 15, 2015.

Magazines

Hun, Kim Sea. "Picharana Deumbei Yol pi Takkavichea [A Synthesis of Logic]." *Kampuja Suriya*, 1967.

Hun, Sen. "Interview with 'Le Point' on July 14, 1998." *Cambodia New Vision* 8 (July), 1998.

Norodom, Sihanouk. *Réalités Cambodgiennes*. August 3, 1962.

———. "Pour Mieux Comprendre le Cambodge Actuel." *Le Sangkum: Revue Politique Illustrée*, August 1, 1965.

———. "Notre Socialisme Buddhique." *Kambuja*, November 15, 1965.

Tep, Chhieu Kheng. "Le 'Sihanoukisme'." *Le Sangkum: Revue Politique Illustrée*, December 1968.

[Unknown author, transcriber.] "The Interview Given to Radio Free Asia (RFA)," December 2, 2002, *Cambodia New Vision* 59 (December), 2002.

Lecture

Phongpaichit, Pasuk, and Chris Baker. 2008. "The Spirits, the Stars and Thai Politics." Presented at the Siam Society, Bangkok, Thailand, December 2, 2008, http://pioneer.netserv.chula.ac.th/~ppasuk/spiritsstarspolitics.pdf (Accessed 5 January, 2011).

Songs

Bândam Lok Chumteav Bandit [The Advice of Lok Chumteav Bandit]. Cambodian Red Cross.

Samdech Techo Øphirouhchon [The Progressivist Samdech Techo]. Cambodian Red Cross.

Tossânah Monusâthor Krop Chrong Chroey [A Complete Humanitarian Vision]. Cambodian Red Cross.

Videos

Cambodian Red Cross. "Medical Practitioner and Woman Understands Women." [n.d.].

Electoral debate. *TVK*, July 24, 2013.

Heng, Reaksmey. "Prince Ranariddh to form new royal political party." *VOA Khmer*, February 25, 2014.

Sam, Rainsy. "Sar Lok Protean Sam Rainsy choun Chompoah Procheareastr Khmer knong Oukas Boh Chnaot Khum–sângkat nov Tngae 3 Mitona 2012" [Message to the people for the 3 June 2012 commune elections]. 2012.

Websites

"Human Rights Party [Policy]." http://www.hrpcambodia.info/english/?option =com_content&view=aticle&lang=en&id=7&page=Policy (Accessed October 26, 2012).

National Bank of Cambodia. "Cambodia Ancient Naga Coin Nordic-Gold Proof-like Coin." http://www.nbc.org.kh/english/nbc_gallery/more_info.php?id=4 (Accessed October 1, 2014).

Speeches

Hun, Sen. "Speech at Indonesian Chamber of Commerce and Industry." *Jakarta*, March, 1999.

———. "Address to the Closing Session of the National Conference: 'Peace, National Reconciliation and Democracy Building: Ten Years after the Paris Peace Agreement.'" *Cambodia New Vision* 45 (October), 2001.

———. "Address on the Occasion of the Acceptance of the Honorary Doctorate Degree of Political Science from the University of Ramkhamhaeng, Kingdom of Thailand." *Cambodia New Vision* 46 (November), 2001.

———. "Selected Ad-lib Address at the Groundbreaking Ceremony to Build Roads and Bridges in the District of Khsach Kandal, Kandal Province, 14 January 2003." *Cambodia New Vision* 60 (January), 2003.

———. "Inaugurating a Buddhist Hall of Common in Srey Santhor." *Cambodia New Vision* 72 (January), 2004.

———. A Visit to the Kompong Raing Bridge Construction." *Cambodia New Vision* 73 (February), 2004.

———. "Selected Responses to the Press on SNBC." *Cambodia New Vision* 89 (June), 2005.

———. "Selected Comments at the Graduation and Presentation of Diploma to the Graduates from the Asia-Europe Institute." *Cambodia New Vision* 90 (July), 2005.

———. "Visit of Samdech Hun Sen and Bun Rany to the Former Royal City of Sanlob Prey Nokor in Kompong Cham." *Cambodia New Vision* 97 (February), 2006.

———. "Inaugurating Buddhist Temple in Serei Suosdei Pagoda." *Cambodia New Vision* 99 (April), 2006.

———, "Visit to Bridge Construction Sites in Kompong Thom." *Cambodia New Vision* 100 (May), 2006.

———. "Selected comments: 'Visiting the People in Kompong Chhnang Province'." *Cambodia New Vision* 104 (September), 2006.

———. "Opening Junior High School Bun Rany–Hun Sen Memot." *Cambodia New Vision* 108 (January), 2007.

———. "Excerpts on Interpretations Concerning Royal Palace." *Cambodia New Vision* 108 (January), 2007.

———. "Inaugurating Junior High School Hun Sen – Srah Banteay." *Cambodia New Vision* 110 (March), 2007.

———. "Inaugurating Bayon TV/Radio Broadcast Station." *Cambodia New Vision* 110 (March), 2007.

———. "Selected Comments at Ceremony to Award Diplomas for Graduates of Vanda Accounting." *Cambodia New Vision* 117 (October), 2007.

———. "Keynote Address at the Opening Ceremony of the Samdech Hun Sen's Tree Nursery Station at Takeo's Phnom Tamao." *Cambodia New Vision* 117 (October), 2007.

———. "Graduation Ceremony and Diploma Presentation in CUS." *Cambodia New Vision* 117 (October), 2007.

———. "Educational Achievements in Kompong Thom's Santuk District." *Cambodia New Vision* 121 (February), 2008.

———. "First Cambodian Bio Energy's Ethanol Factory." *Cambodia New Vision* 129 (November), 2008.

———. "New achievements – Hluong Preah Sdej Kan City." *Cambodia New Vision* 141 (November), 2009.

———. "2010 Rural Development Review." *Cambodia New Vision* 154 (December), 2010.

———. "Graduation Ceremony at Vanda Institute." *Cambodia New Vision* 155 (January), 2011.

———. "Speech at the 20th Anniversary of the Return of Sihanouk From Exile and Sihanouk's 90th Birthday." *Cambodia New Vision* 164 (October), 2011.

———. "Buddhist Achievements in Santuk." *Cambodia New Vision* 181 (March), 2013.

Documents

Cambodian Red Cross. *Preah Reach Kret Sdey pi Kar Totuol Skoal Kakâbat Krohom Kampuchea* [*Royal Decree on the Recognition of the Cambodian Red Cross*]. Phnom Penh: Cambodian Red Cross, 2010.

———. *CRC Newsletter, Year 3, Issue 3*. Phnom Penh: Cambodian Red Cross, 2011.

CNRP. *7 Point Policies of the CNRP*. [Publisher unknown], 2013.

The Constitution of the Kingdom of Cambodia. 1993.

FUNCINPEC. *Lokkhâttikah neung Bât Bânhea Phtei robâs Konâbâk FUNCINPEC* [*FUNCINPEC Party Statutes and Internal Regulations*]. [Publisher unknown], 2005.

———. *Kolokar Noyobay Sângkhep Konâbâk* [*A Summary of the Party's Political Principles*]. [Publisher unknown], 2006.

———.-*Lokkhâttikah neung Bât Bânhea Phtei robâs Konâbâk FUNCINPEC* [*FUNCINPEC Party Statutes and Internal Regulations*]. [Publisher unknown], 2006.

Gnoc, Them. *Cheat, Sasana, Mohaksatr* [*Nation, Religion, King*]. [Publisher unknown], 1950.

Liberal International. *Liberal International Newsletter, vol. 228: Sam Rainsy Meets with Liberals Across Scandinavia*. London: Liberal International, 2011.

Ma, Yarith. *Yutthosastr Chnea Chnea: 5 Chomnuch robâs Samdech Neayok Rothmontrey Hun Sen* [*The Win–Win Strategy: 5 Points of Samdech Prime Minister Hun Sen*]. [Publisher unknown], 2007.

Norodom, Sihanouk. "Considérations sur le Socialisme Khmer." Imprint by Ministry of Information, 1961.

———. "La Monarchie Cambodgienne & La Croisade Royale pour l'Indépendance." Imprint by Ministère de l'Éducation Nationale & Direction des Services Pédagogiques, [n.d.]. [Originally in *Réalités Cambodgiennes*, May 24–September 13, 1958].

———. *Statuts de Sangkum Reastr Niyum*. Phnom Penh: Ministère de l'Information, [n.d.].

———. *Statement, 30 June*. Phnom Penh, 2006.

Sam, Nora. *Note of the Day 1: The Opposition Parties in Cambodia are the Champion of Division*. [Publisher unknown.], 2010.

———. *Note of the Day 5: Is the 'Neo-FUNCINPEC Party' a Sihanoukist Party?*. [Publisher unknown.], 2010.

———. *Note of the Day 6: The Contributions of the Royalist Party FUNCINPEC Led by HRH Prince Norodom Ranariddh*. [Publisher unknown.], 2010.

———. *Note of the Day 14: The Royalists within the National Community (Part 1)*. [Publisher unknown.], 2010.

———. *Note of the Day 15: The Royalists within the National Community (Part 2)*. [Publisher unknown.], 2010.

———. *Note of the Day 23: The So-Called 'Insanity?' of Samdech Krom Preah Norodom Ranariddh*. [Publisher unknown.], 2011.

———. *Note of the Day 24: Samdech Krom Preah Norodom Ranariddh's Middle Path*. [Publisher unknown.], 2011.

———. *Note of the Day 38: The Political 'Triptych' in Cambodia*. [Publisher unknown.], 2011.

———. *Note of the Day 47: The NRP's Middle Path: Rationale and Justification*. [Publisher unknown.], 2011.

———. *Liberal and Advanced Monarchy*. [Publisher unknown.], [n.d.].

Sam, Rainsy and Rado Tylecote. "'Be Vigilant' on Human Rights, Warns Cambodian Opposition Leader. Special Report: Rado Tylecote Talks with Cambodia's Opposition Leader Sam Rainsy in Phnom Penh." Conservative Party Human Rights Commission, April 24, 2006. http://www.conservativehumanrights .com/media/articles/samrainsy.html (Accessed July 1, 2015).

Sam Rainsy Party. *Kol Noyobay 10 Kh robâs Konâbâk Sam Rainsy* [*10 Political Principles of Sam Rainsy Party*]. [Publisher unknown.], [n.d.].

———. *100 Measures to be Implemented by a Sam Rainsy Party Government*. Phnom Penh: Sam Rainsy Party, 2003.

———. *Resolutions Adopted at the Fifth Party Congress*. 2011.

Sam Rainsy Party Cabinet. *Sam Rainsy in Tunisia to Prepare People Power in Cambodia*. 2011.

Author's Interviews

Cham Prasidh, August 2, 2011, Phnom Penh.

Dien Del, June 14, 2010, Phnom Penh.

Ek Sereyvath, May 30, 2011, Phnom Penh.

Eng Chhay Eang, March 24, 2010, Phnom Penh.

Ho Vann, March 26, 2010, Phnom Penh.

Hun Sen, September 29, 2011, Phnom Penh.

Huy Vora, April 29, 2010, Phnom Penh.

Ieng Mouly, November 17, 2009, Phnom Penh.

Im Sethy, August 11, 2011, Phnom Penh.

Keat Sokun, May 3, 2010, Phnom Penh.

Kem Sokha, March 15, 2010, Phnom Penh.

Keo Puth Reasmey, June 8, 2010, Phnom Penh.

Ker Bunkheang, June 15, 2010, Phnom Penh.

Khieu Suon, May 12, , 2010Phnom Penh.

Kong Korm, March 31, 2010, Phnom Penh.

Mu Sochua, November 20, 2013, Phnom Penh.

Ngo Pin, February 23, 2010, Phnom Penh.

Noranarith Ananda Yath, June 4, 2011, Phnom Penh.

Norodom Marie, June 19, 2010, Phnom Penh.

Norodom Ranariddh, June 2, 2011, Phnom Penh.

Pok Marina, June 20, 2011, Phnom Penh.

Sisowath Pongneary Monipong (Lolotte), September 12, 2011, Phnom Penh.

Sam Rainsy, April 24, 2012, Paris.

Sisowath Ayravady, November 18, 2009, Phnom Penh.

Sisowath Panara Sirivudh, June 4, 2010, Phnom Penh.

Sisowath Pheanuroth, June 18, 2010, Phnom Penh.

Sisowath Sirirath, May 13 and 25, 2010.

Sisowath Sylvia, May 26, 2010.

Sisowath Thomico, May 20 and 28, 2010, Phnom Penh.

Son Chhay, March 23, 2010, Phnom Penh.

Son Soubert, March 12, 2010, Phnom Penh.

Suy Sem, September 19, 2011, Phnom Penh.

Thach Setha, May 6, 2010, Phnom Penh.

Tioulong Saumura, May 18, 2010, Phnom Penh.

Uch Serey Yuth, April 23, 2010, Phnom Penh.

Yim Sovann, March 26, 2010, Phnom Penh.

You Hockry, June 15, 2010, Phnom Penh.

Some interviewees asked to remain anonymous:

Anonymous, July 12, 2010.

Anonymous, July 10, 2011.

Author's Field Notes

NRP ELECTION campaign event, June 4, 2011, Oudong.

SRP Fifth Party Congress, September 11, 2011, Phnom Penh.

Sam Rainsy speech on International Human Rights Day, December 10, 2013, Phnom Penh.

INDEX

A

Alagappa, Muthiah, 14, 16, 17
Alliance of Democrats (AD), 93, 100
Anderson, Benedict: on concept of nation, 3; criticism of, 3n11; on imagination of politics, 28n125; Imagined Communities, 1, 2; on nationalism, 3, 17n65, 27–28; on revolution, 125, 170; on Western concepts in the Asian and African contexts, 31
Angkor Wat temple, 1
Annie Sok An (wife of Sok An), 91n114
Aymonier, Étienne, 75n40

B

Bao Dai, Emperor of Vietnam, 179
Barnett, Anthony, 25
Bhabha, Homi, 4n16
Bhumibol Adulyadej, King of Thailand, 20
Bour Kry, 193
Buddhist Liberal Democratic Party (BLDP): in coalition government, 6; disintegration of, 7, 101; failure to connect with people, 139–40; identity of, 35, 134; political platform, 132–34; rival factions in, 152; split of the KPNLF into Liberal Democratic Party and, 154n165
Buddhist Socialism, 31n139, 95, 105–7, 128
Bunchhan Mul, 45n29
Bun Rany (wife of Hun Sen): marriage, 51; in media, portrait of, 90–91; as mother of nation, 91; as president of Cambodian Red Cross, 89, 89n102, 90, 90fig; visit to Srolop Prey Nokor, 47–48

C

Cambodge: Histoire d'une Vengeance Royale (Sam Emmarane), 158
Cambodia: 1960 referendum for chief of state, 78; civil war, 5; "claims of qualification to rule" in postcolonial, 40n4; constitutions and constitutional amendments, 6, 94n128, 99; democracy in, 19, 92; feudalistic nature of society, 140; first monetary unit, 55; French protectorate, 24; impact of globalization on, 176; modern political discourse, 28; moral geography of, 22; national independence of, 4, 25; national minorities, 2–3; nation and race concepts, 32, 75–76; political culture, 32–33, 94, 168; political regimes in, 25, 53, 167–68; popular mentality, 150; "post-ideological" era, 30; print media, 32; representation in United Nations, 5; statuary in, 59–61; threat to survival of, 131; as unfinished imagined community, 2, 4–5; Vietnamese occupation of, 26; Vietnamization of, 130–31; voters in, 9, 175; young population in, 181
Cambodia National Rescue Party (CNRP): in 2013 election campaign, 7, 146, 182, 183, 184–86; as democratic opposition party, 35, 117, 137–38, 152; gift-giving practices, 184; identity of, 160; post-election strategy, 185, 186; raise of popularity, 182; support of royal family by, 190n25
Cambodian People's Party (CPP): business leaders in, 91n114; coalitions with FUNCINPEC, 93–94n127; decline of support, 182, 185; democratic identity and, 164; democratic rhetoric, 18; diversity within, 151n154;

economic platform, 151; in election campaigns, 181, 184; external legitimacy of, 15; foreign relations, 15; gift-giving practices, 86, 122; Hun Sen as leader of, 13; idea of kingship and, 179; identity of, 13, 151–52, 161, 169, 170; legitimation of, 15–16, 87, 87n94; Marxist-Leninist identity, 127, 127n45, 130n57; origin of, 5; political regime of, 7, 130; popular image of, 13; populism of, 12, 128; post-election strategy, 185–86; relations with Norodom Ranariddh Party, 95; resistance to change, 183; as royalist party, 110–11; social basis of, 139

Cambodian Red Cross (CRC), 88, 89, 89n102, 90fig, 91–92

Cambodia's Second Kingdom. *See* Kingdom of Cambodia (KOC) (1993–)

Cham Prasidh, 58, 58n82, 127, 127n45

Chandler, David, 23

Chatterjee, Partha, 3n11

Chay Thoul, 134n75

Chea Sim, 40, 184

Chhean Vam, 134n75

Choeng Sopheap, 91n114

choh moulothan ("going down to the base") initiatives, 122, 124, 124n29

Chulalongkorn, King of Siam, 20

Chuop Samlot, 89n102

class struggle: concept of, 55

Coalition Government of Democratic Kampuchea (CGDK), 5

coalition governments, 5, 6, 93, 93n124, 95–96

Communist Party of Vietnam (CPV), 21

competitive authoritarianism, 142

conflict over fundamentals: vs. conflict over issues, 130n56

Connors, Michael, 120, 150

constitutional monarchy: advocacy of, 158; in historical perspective, 67n7; ideas of embodiment and, 74, 79–82; limits of, 108; nature of Cambodian, 80–81; political parties' debates on, 158–59

culture of dialogue, 187–88

D

Day, Tony, 63

democracy. *See also* royalist democracy: of capitalists, feudal forms of, 126, 126n40; characteristics of, 18–19, 63–64, 85, 118–19, 166–67; conceptualization of, 54–55, 83; as condition for national survival, 132; as core of political discourse, 160; debates over meaning of, 20; monarchy and, 84–85, 154, 178; national imaginings and, 120; nationalism and, 117–18; peasant masses and, 175; in revolutionary history, 55, 125; Sam Rainsy's definition of, 143; scholarly literature on, 19; social mobility and, 138; Son Sann's idea of, 133; in Thailand, 177

Democratic Kampuchea (DK), 6, 15, 25, 31n139, 35, 57, 121, 125, 183

democratic legitimacy, 18–19, 166

democratic opposition, 83, 99, 100–101, 117

Democratic Party (DP), 17, 72, 134, 139n99

democratic revolution (padevott pracheathipatey), 125, 125n36

democratization: Third Wave of, 19

democrats: in 2013 election, 187; coalition between royalists and, 13; criticism of CPP government, 130, 144, 145, 145n125; in culture of dialogue, 188; monarchy and, 154, 155; vs. nationalists, 118; as opposition force, 118; on participative democracy, 149–50; political agenda of, 119, 172; political identity of, 146–47, 151–53, 161; popular support of, 144–45, 165; republicanism of, 155; rivalry within, 140; royalists and, 153; search for people's will, 145; on social change, 149, 185–87; split into different political parties, 138n97; on threat to Cambodian nation, 131; view of democracy, 148–49

Dien Del, 102, 103, 104n181, 155, 155n167

DIFID tactics, 129

direct democracy: idea of, 96, 96n144; vs.
  representative democracy, 96–97
dual citizenship, 10–11

E

Ear, Sophal, 16
economic development, 123–25
Edwards, Penny, 23, 24, 29, 29n130, 91
elections: of 1993, 6; of 2013, 181–82,
  186; elites and, 176–77; internal
  legitimacy and, 164; limitations of,
  142; meaning and role of, 176; moral
  claims to power and, 167; motives for
  voting during, 9–10, 174–75; political
  parties' attitude to, 166; reintroduction
  of multiparty, 177
electoral behavior of voters, 142–43
electoral democracy, 142
Electoral Reform Alliance (ERA), 186
elites, 175–76
embodiment: vs. doctrine, 105, 108, 176;
  notion of, 65, 74–76, 81, 172–73;
  Sihanouk and, 76–82
Eng Chhay Eang, 135, 136
Evans, Grant, 60

F

freedom rights, 55
Frings, Viviane K., 87
FUNCINPEC (Front Uni National pour
  un Cambodge Indépendant, Neutre,
  Pacifique et Coopératif): in 1993
  election, 6; claims for legitimacy, 113;
  conceptualization of democracy and,
  83; contestation of 1998 election
  results, 153n162; corruption among
  leaders of, 66; decline of, 49; demand
  for political loyalty, 88; development
  activities of, 86; expulsion of
  Ranariddh from, 103, 104, 108; on
  extension of power of Supreme
  National Border Council, 112n214;
  identity of, 12, 13, 92, 100, 102–4,
  109, 117; legitimacy of, 14; non-
  democratic image of, 156; in political
  coalitions, 5, 7, 56, 94, 101, 105;

politics of representation, 12; problem
  of management, 100; pursuit to
  establish National Congress, 97–98;
  relations with Sam Rainsy Party, 156;
  resistance fighters in, 101–2; royal
  family members in, 72, 103;
  Sihanoukism and, 84n76, 114; struggle
  over leadership in, 103n176; tensions
  within, 99
FUNSK. *See* Kampuchean United Front for
  National Salvation

G

Gainsborough, Martin, 168, 169
garment workers' demonstrations, 183
German Christian democratic model, 134,
  134–35n79
Gerrand, James, 59fig, 90fig, 138fig
gift-giving practices, 86, 122–23, 126n39,
  184
Gyallay-Pap, Peter, 21n83

H

Harris, Ian, 45, 45n29, 75
Heder, Steve, 7, 14, 32, 40n4, 46,
  142, 169
Heng Samrin, 40, 108
hibernation of throne, 78–79
Hing Bun Heang, 58, 60
Hluang Preah Sdech Kan Cultural
  Historical Site, 50
Ho Sithy, 58, 59
Ho Vann, 136, 149
Huffman, Franklin E., 38
Hughes, Caroline: on behavior and
  rhetoric of political parties, 11, 118,
  147, 149n144; on culture and tradition
  in political life, 168, 169; on gift-giving
  practices, 126n39; on Khmer regimes,
  26, 174; on political legitimacy, 17; on
  politicized identities, 10, 12, 117; on
  representation of popular will, 119,
  174–75
Human Rights Party (HRP), 35, 94, 117,
  135, 138n97, 149
Hun Many, 187

Hun Sen: appointment as prime minister, 189; association with King Jayavarman VII, 44; autocratic regime of, 7n24, 8, 170, 171, 183; on Cambodian Red Cross, 90; coming to power, 6, 39; consolidation of power, 49; on constitutional monarchy, 108; controversy over statue of, 58–59; on CPP policy, 87, 88n95; at cremation ceremony of Sihanouk, 193–94; on culture of dialogue, 188; on democracy, 55, 87, 87n94; disappointment of 2013 election results, 184; divide and rule strategy, 182; economic policy, 123–24; on electoral process, 129; leadership style, 41–42, 174; legitimacy claims, 173, 192–93; meeting with farmers, 123fig; as member of resistance, 52n54; as member of triumvirate, 40; merit of, 64; national leadership of, 12, 13, 41, 63–64; on people's democracy, 121–22, 121n20, 123–24, 124n32; personal identification with nation, 128n47; personal life of, 51–52; on political development in Cambodia, 48–49; political identity of, 54; political style of, 15; political thinking of, 31; on populism, 121, 127–28; as prime minister, 30; publications of, 124; Ranariddh and, 191; as reincarnation of Sdech Kân, 62, 63, 166, 174; relations with Sihanouk, 109n202, 194; response to allegations of treason, 53n59; rhetoric of, 122n22; royalists and, 54, 174; Sam Rainsy and, 11, 187; Sdech Kân narrative and, 39, 40, 46–49, 51–52, 52n55, 54, 60, 62; spiritual superiority of, 194; supernatural abilities of, 62–63; as supporter of royalists, 191; support of research on Sdech Kân, 49–50; visit to Srolop Prey Nokor, 48; win-win strategy of, 57
Huy Kanthoul, 134n75

I

ideology: concept of, 28–29, 30; vs. embodiment, 105, 108, 173, 176; vs. nationalism, 27, 28; Sihanouk's view of, 30; in Thailand, 29; translations of, 29, 29n129
Ieng Mouly, 133, 134, 139, 151, 155n167
imagined community: concept of, 3–4, 5

J

Jacob, Judith, 34–35n160
Jayavarman VII, King of Cambodia, 86, 88
Jellema, Kate, 21

K

Kambuja Suriya (newspaper), 32, 33
Kampuchean People's National Liberation Front (KPNLF), 5, 101–2, 132, 134, 134n75, 154–55, 155n167
Kampuchean People's Revolutionary Party (KPRP), 5. *See also* Cambodian People's Party (CPP)
Kampuchean United Front for National Salvation (FUNSK), 57, 121, 125
Karbaum, Markus, 7n24
Kaysone Phomvihane, 56
Keat Sokun, 133, 135, 135n80, 152
Kem Sokha, 15, 37, 135n80, 138n97, 140, 149, 156
Keng Vannsak, 29n129
Kent, Alexandra, 46
Keo Puth Reasmey, 37, 98, 103n176, 104, 110
Ker Bunkheang, 127n45
Kershaw, Roger, 177, 178
Khieu Chum, 45n29
Khieu Kanharith, 187
Khmer Empire, 6n23
Khmer language: as official language in education, 32; in political discourse, 32–33; transcription and transliteration, 38
Khmer Nation Party (KNP), 7, 117, 136, 137, 141, 152. *See also* Sam Rainsy Party (SRP)
Khmer Red Cross Society. *See* Cambodian Red Cross (CRC)
Khmer Republic, 6n23, 60n92, 70n16, 121

Khmer Rouge regime. *See* Democratic Kampuchea (DK)

Kim Sedara, 16

Kingdom of Cambodia (KOC) (1993–): characteristic of state, 7–9, 8n26; democracy-building project, 8; establishment of, 6; national motto, 39; outline of study of, 35–37

Kingdom of Cambodia (KOC) (1953–70), 6n23, 153, 163–64, 170

kingship: ideas of embodiment and, 179–80; impact on ideas of leadership, 178; Khmer conceptualizations of, 75; popular understanding of, 23; in Southeast Asia, ideas of, 20–21, 179; Theravada Buddhism and, 25, 42, 45, 45n29, 75, 179; virtue and, 42–43

Kompong Cham province, 51

Kong Korm, 136–37

Kong Mony, 152

Kossamak See Sisowath Kossamak, Queen of Cambodia

Kun Kim, 58n82

L

Lao People's Revolutionary Party (LPRP), 21

Laos: ideas of kingship in, 21, 179; king statues in, 58n79; national reconciliation in, 56

leadership: concept of, 43, 174; inherited vs. elected, 173–74; inherited vs. non-inherited, 44, 63

Leclère, Adhémard, 41

legitimacy: concept of, 22–23; key elements of, 14–15; modern vs. traditional, 20; scholarly research on, 16; sources of, 81–82, 166; in Southeast Asia, problem of, 14; use of traditional notions of, 56n72

legitimation of nation, 16–17

Levitsky, Steven, 7, 8n26, 142

Liberal Democratic Party (LDP), 154n165

Liberal Party, 72

LICADHO (Cambodian League for the Promotion and Defense of Human Rights), 11

Lilja, Mona, 9, 18, 19

Lim Kean Hor, 123fig

Lon Nol, 154n164

Lý Dynasty, 21

Ly Yong Phat, 62

M

Mann, Michael, 118, 165

Mao Ayuth, 61, 62, 63

Marston, John, 16

Marxist-Leninism, 127

McGrew, Laura, 16

Men Pheakdei, 91n114

monarch: as personification of nation, 75, 75n40

monarchy: democracy and, 84–85, 154, 178; elective elements in, 82; hibernation of throne, 78; in political representation, 65; restoration of, 65; in Southeast Asia, role of, 177; as suprapolitical force, 69

moral geography, 23

moral legitimacy, 178–79

moral power, 23–24

MOULINAKA (Movement for the National Liberation of Kampuchea), 6

Mu Sochua, 184, 188

N

Nagaravatta (journal), 29, 32

nation: as common identity, 4; concept of, 2, 24–25; homogeneous nature of, 3; as imagined community, 1, 2; Sihanouk's personification of, 80; Theravada Buddhism and, 23, 25

"nation, religion, king" trinity, 65–66, 76

National Committee of Khmerization, 34

National Congress, 96–98

National Election Committee (NEC), 11, 187

nationalism: in Cambodian history, 1, 130; contemporary, 26–27; criticism of conception of, 3n11; definition of, 72; vs. democracy, 118; Dien Del on, 103; global spread of, 28; vs. ideology, 27, 28; origin of, 1, 17n65

Nationalist Party, 104, 104n184

national reconciliation, 56, 57
national union, 92–94
neak mean bon (man of merit), 42–46, 54–55, 63
Neveu, Roland, 74fig
Nhek Bunchhay, 49, 103n176, 104, 105
Nhem Sophanny, 91n114
Nhiek Tioloung, 157, 160
Nong Kimny, 134n75
Nop Bayarith, 181
Norodom, King of Cambodia, 59n85
Norodom Arunreasmey, 104
Norodom branch of royal family, 190
Norodom Chakrapong, 73
Norodom Marie Ranariddh, 88–89, 89n102, 104
Norodom Monineath, Queen-Mother of Cambodia, 90fig
Norodom Montana, 72
Norodom Narindeth, 72
Norodom Ranariddh: 1997 removal from power, 6, 39; on democracy, 82–86, 92–98; Droit Public Cambodgien (Cambodian Public Law), 84, 84n77; expulsion from FUNCINPEC, 103, 104, 108; founder of Community of Royalist People Party, 190–91; on hibernation of throne, 79; on his sources of legitimacy, 73, 81–82, 84; as leader of FUNCINPEC, 66, 82, 112, 191; on monarchy, 71, 80–81; on organic relations of King and people, 83n73; pen name of, 84n76; political career of, 47, 104–5, 156; political style of, 15; on power-sharing, 73; press brief on election day in 1993, 74fig; publications of, 84; question of dual citizenship of, 10–11; relations with Hun Sen, 191; resignation from Presidency of National Assembly, 47, 49; on Sihanoukism, 111, 112
Norodom Ranariddh Party (NRP), 35, 73, 95, 96, 109
Norodom Rasmi Sobbhana 89, 89n102
Norodom Sihamoni, King of Cambodia, 45, 189, 192
Norodom Sihanouk, King-Father of Cambodia: abdication of, 44, 76–77, 76n46, 80; on abolition of monarchy,

77; acceptance of power-sharing, 73–74; as advocate of national union, 93–94; at Cambodian Red Cross giving ceremony, 90fig; on Cambodian socialism, 55, 55n69; "counter-government" of, 120n16; cremation ceremony, 193–94; criticism of, 110; death of father, 188; Dien Del on, 102n173; as father of national reconciliation, 45, 56, 71; as God-King, 81; as head of state, 78; legacy of, 113; legitimacy of, 77, 80–81; loss of control on National Assembly, 79n59; memoirs of, 77; neutrality to political parties, 109; as non-monarchic chief of state, 78; political regime of, 71–72, 76, 120; promise not to resume the throne, 77n48; relations with Sam Rainsy, 157; return to throne, 6, 65, 80; royal family and, 70, 70n19, 76n45; vs. Sihanoukism, 110; statues of, 59n85; title of, 46n33; on transition from absolute monarchy, 77n50–51; view of ideology, 30
Norodom Sirivudh, 49, 100, 101, 157n175
Norodom Suramarit, King of Cambodia, 76

O
O'Brien, Donal Cruise, 46
Öjendal, Joakim, 9, 16, 18, 19, 168, 169
omnach (political power), 23
Om Yentieng, 58
Oudong (former royal capital), 106n189

P
Pach Choeun, 29n130
Pang Khat, 45n29
Paris Peace Agreements (1991), 56, 71, 71n23, 129, 130, 153–54, 163
people's democracy: as CPP regime identity, 126–27, 170–71; vs. democracy of capitalists, 126–27; genealogy of concept of, 125; Hun Sen on, 121–24; vs. liberal democracy,

128–29; notion of, 121, 124, 125, 161, 165, 170; Sdech Kân and, 126
People's Republic of Kampuchea (PRK), 5, 26, 121, 136–37, 170–71
people's will, 119n9, 138, 141
performative politics, 46
Phlech Phiroun, 89n102
political identities, 12, 14
political ideology: notion of, 31
political language: foreign vocabulary, 34–35n160; Khmerization of, 32, 34; neologisms, 33–34, 34n159; Sihanoukist phraseology, 34, 34n157
political legitimacy. *See* legitimacy
political parties: appeal to liberal democracy, 119; characteristic of, 10; coalitions of, 95–96; conception of society shared by, 165; identities of, 12–14, 13, 164, 171; vs. individual strongmen, 173; legitimization of, 15; political strategies of, 163, 169, 175; rhetoric of, 11
political royalism: concept of, 31, 189; decline of, 66; as democratic opposition, 98, 99; destabilization of, 191–92; evolution of, 65–68, 113–14; idea of embodiment and, 81, 82; meaning of, 100, 109; as political self-identification, 31;
politics of nonrepresentation, 175
Pol Pot, 59n85
populism, 121, 127, 128, 160
portrait-statuary in Khmer art, 59–60, 60n93
power: concepts of, 23–24
power-sharing, 73
Preah Bat Thommik (Dharmic King or Just Ruler): concept of, 43–44
Progressive Democrats, 72
Provisional Government of National Union and National Salvation of Cambodia (PGNUNSC), 35
Pung Chhiv Kek, 11
Putth Tumneay (Predictions of the Buddha) prophecy, 43

R

Ranariddh. *See* Norodom Ranariddh

Rasmi Sobbhana. *See* Norodom Rasmi Sobbhana
Rathie, Martin, 73n31
revolution, 124, 124n33, 125–26, 161, 170
Ros Chamroeun, 135
Ros Chantraboth, 49, 50n46, 52, 53
royal body: conceptualizations of, 69, 69n11
royal family, 69, 70–71, 72
royalism. *See* political royalism
royalist democracy, 82–85, 92
royalist identity, 69, 171
royalist nationalism, 72
royalists: in Cambodia and Thailand, 178; challenges of, 79; democrats and, 153; eradication from parliament, 188–89; failure to reinvent identity, 115; influence of, 178; as political actors, 68, 69, 113; political views of, 69–70, 69n14; proposal of coalition party of, 105–6; as protection of power of king, 98; Sihanoukism and, 114
royal statuary, 60n92

S

Sak Sutsakhan, 154n165
Sam Emmarane, 101, 158
Sam Rainsy: anti-royalism of, 100–101; aristocratic background, 140; attempt to form coalition government, 93; autobiography of, 157; on constitutional monarchy, 158, 158n188; criticism of Hun Sen regime, 143–44; on culture of dialogue, 187, 188; on democracy, 132, 136, 143; education of, 101n165; exile of, 156; as founder of Khmer Nation Party, 7, 148n137, 152; interest in Arab Spring, 146; on national survival, 131; political career, 11, 135–36, 138n97, 156; on political persecution of his relatives, 157–58; political style of, 15; as populist, 118; public speaking, 138fig; relations with Sihanouk, 157; royal family and, 157, 157n176, 190n25; travel around Cambodia, 140; workers strikes and, 141n105

Sam Rainsy Party (SRP): characteristic of, 152; contestation of election results, 153n162; cooperation with FUNCINPEC, 13, 156; as democratic party, 117, 149; economic platform, 147; foundation of, 7; identity of, 117, 148, 160; political platform, 137, 137n95–96; promotion of culture of citizenship, 149
Sam Sary, 157, 158, 158n187, 160
Sangkum Jatiniyum alliance ("Alliance of the National Community"), 100, 106
Sangkum Jatiniyum Front Party (SJFP), 35, 106, 109, 112, 156n172
Sangkum Reastr Niyum (People's Socialist Community), 25, 45, 67, 76, 85, 87, 171, 175
Sangkum Reastr Reachea Tepetey (Community of Royalist People Party), 190
Sar Kheng, 152
Sartori, Giovanni, 130n56
Savang Vatthana, King of Laos, 56n71, 179
sdech: origin and meaning of word, 44
Sdech Kân: book on, 52–53; cinematographic portrayal of, 61–62; conceptualization of democracy and, 54–55, 170; as controversial historical figure, 39, 53; death of, 63; Hun Sen on, 54; idea of reincarnation of, 40, 62; introduction of people's democracy by, 126; in Khmer historiography, 42; location of capital of, 51; royal name of, 41; statues of, 49–50, 58, 58n82, 59fig, 60, 61
Sdech Kân narrative: dissemination of, 39, 61–62, 63; idea of kingship in, 42, 44; idea of leadership in, 174; interpretations of, 45; origin of, 41; performative politics and, 46–47
Sdech Komlong: cement replica of, 60n91
Second Kingdom. See Kingdom of Cambodia (KOC) (1993–)
Shadow over Angkor (Norodom Sihanouk), 77
Sihamoni. See Norodom Sihamoni, King of Cambodia

Sihanouk. See Norodom Sihanouk, King-Father of Cambodia
Sihanoukism: branding as ideology, 110; FUNCINPEC and, 114; as general theory of leadership, 110; idea of, 31, 105, 171; meaning of, 109–10; Ranariddh's representation of, 111, 112; vs. Sihanouk, 110
Sisowath, King of Cambodia, 32, 59n85, 67n7
Sisowath Ayravady, 68, 68n9, 72
Sisowath branch of royal family, 190
Sisowath Kossamak, Queen of Cambodia, 78
Sisowath Pheanuroth, 72
Sisowath Pongneary (Lolotte), 68, 70, 70n17
Sisowath Sirik Matak, 69, 70
Sisowath Sirirath, 68, 69, 70, 71, 99, 104, 110
Sisowath Sovethvong (Lola), 68, 70, 70n17
Sisowath Sylvia, 70n16
Sisowath Thomico: advocacy of ideology of Sihanouk, 108; education of, 101n165; on future of Cambodia, 107, 112; political career of, 68, 100–101, 105–6, 106n187, 106n192, 112, 189; political views of, 69n14, 112; on responsibilities of royal family, 69–70; views of Buddhist socialism, 107
Sisowath Yuthevong, 72, 98, 99
Slater, Dan, 7
Slocomb, Margaret, 26, 30, 128
social opening, 85–92
Sok An, 49n44
Son Chhay, 151
Son Ngoc Thanh, 45n29, 157
Son Sann: as founder of Democratic Party, 133, 154; on idea of democracy, 133; as leader of KPNLF, 134n75; loyalty to Sihanouk, 102, 154, 154n164; political career of, 133n69, 133n73, 154; political views of, 157; split between Sak Sutsakhan and, 154n165
Son Sann Party, 35, 101, 117, 132, 152, 155
Son Soubert, 131, 133–35, 135n79, 135n80, 155n167

Southeast Asia: globalization literature and, 176; indigenization of elections in, 176; moral geography of nations, 21; political legitimization in, 40n2; role of monarchies in, 177; spatial organization of nations in, 21
Souvanna Phouma, 56, 56n71
Soy Sopheap, 193
Srey Sokonthor Bât, King of Cambodia, 41, 53
State of Cambodia (SOC), 5
Strangio, Sebastian, 152
Strauss, Julia, 46
Supreme National Border Council (SNBC), 112n214
Suramarit. *See* Norodom Suramarit, King of Cambodia

T
Ta Di, 58, 60
Tan, Michelle, 28
Tanabe, Shigeharu, 3
Taylor, Robert, 176
Tboung Khmum province, 49–50, 51
Tep Chhieu Kheng, 30, 109
Thach Setha, 152n158
Thailand: absence of ideology in, 29; democratic imaginings and national identity, 120; idea of "nation, religion, king," 76; ideas of kingship, 178; ideas of modernity in, 20; king statues in, 58n79, 60–61; nature of monarchy, 69n13; notion of democracy, 120, 150; role of royalists in, 113, 177–78
Thai neologisms, 32n148
Than Schwe, 40n2
Theravada Buddhism and kingship, 42, 45, 45n29, 75, 179
"The Youth's Will" song, 181
Thomico. *See* Sisowath Thomico
Thompson, Ashley, 42, 60n93, 80, 88
Thongchai Winichakul, 31
Thonn Ouk, 134n75
Tioulong Saumura, 101n165, 140, 141, 148n137, 151, 157
transnational ideologies, 172
Trâsâk Ph'aem, King of Cambodia, 45
Turton, Andrew, 63

U
Uch Serey Yuth, 152n158
Un Kheang, 16, 118
Ung Oeun, 58n82
Union of Youth Federations of Cambodia (UYFC), 187
United Nations Transitional Authority in Cambodia (UNTAC), 5–6

V
Vietnam: ideas of kingship in, 21, 179; invasions of Cambodia, 26, 130–31
Vong Savang, 56n71
voters, 175, 187

W
Way, Lucan, 7, 8n26, 142
Western concepts in Asian political discourse, 31–32

Y
Yim Sokha, 135
Yim Sovann, 135, 152n158
You Hockry, 65, 103n179

CPSIA information can be obtained
at www.ICGtesting.com
Printed in the USA
FSOW04n2142190917
38969FS